A Small Boy Smiling

A remarkable journey of healing from the trauma of child sexual abuse to spiritual awakening

Matt Carey

Copyright © Matt Carey 2018.
(except Soulful Space: Reflections On My Therapy Work With Matt.
Copyright © Sarah Paton Briggs 2018 sarah@thegrovepractice.com)

Published by Matt Carey Books 2018.

Matt Carey has asserted his moral right to be identified as the author of this work in accordance with the Copyright, Designs and Patents Act 1988.

All rights reserved. No part of this book may be reproduced, stored in a retrieval system, or transmitted, in any form or by any means, electronic, mechanical, photocopying, recording or otherwise, without the prior written permission of the copyright owners except for the use of quotations in a book review.

ISBN 978-1-9996033-0-4 (paperback)
ISBN 978-1-9996033-1-1 (e-book)

Disclaimer
The excerpts from the "Characteristics of Sex and Love Addiction" are reprinted with the permission of The Augustine Fellowship, S.L.A.A., Fellowship-Wide Services, Inc. © 1990 All Rights Reserved. Permission to reprint these excerpts does not mean that The Augustine Fellowship, S.L.A.A., Fellowship-Wide Services, Inc. has reviewed or approved the contents of this publication, or that The Augustine Fellowship, S.L.A.A., Fellowship-Wide Services, Inc. necessarily agrees with the views expressed herein. S.L.A.A. is a program of recovery from sex and love addiction only – use of these excerpts in connection with programs and activities which are patterned after S.L.A.A., but which address other problems, or in any other non S.L.A.A. context, does not imply otherwise. Sex and Love Addicts Anonymous is a spiritual program, S.L.A.A. is not a religious program, and use of S.L.A.A. material in the present connection does not imply S.L.A.A.'s affiliation with or endorsement of, any sect, denomination, or specific religious belief, or with any entity.

Disclaimer
In order to maintain my anonymity, in some instances I have changed the names of individuals and places. I may have changed some identifying characteristics and details such as physical properties, occupations and places of residence. The names of AA members and the description of what was said at the AA meetings I attended and described herein have also been altered in order to respect their right to privacy and to protect their anonymity.

Editing by Tom Bartlett, www.facebook.com/bartlettbiographies
Front cover image of the author aged six years, taken by the author's father.

IMPORTANT NOTE TO READERS:

The author of this book describes various spiritual healing techniques and therapeutic treatments which he underwent. The author only describes them so that you may understand what he has personally been through. The author does not dispense medical advice or prescribe the use of any technique as a form of treatment for physical, medical, or mental health problems without the advice of an expert professional physician, either directly or indirectly. The intent of the author is only to offer information of a general nature to help you in your quest for emotional, mental, and spiritual well-being.

In the event you use any of the information in this book for yourself, **THE AUTHOR AND THE PUBLISHER ACCEPTS NO LIABILITY WHATSOEVER** for any consequences if you do decide – of your own volition, at your own risk and contrary to the author's advice – to undergo any similar or dissimilar spiritual healing or therapeutic techniques.

Matt Carey Books
www.mattcareybooks.com

Praise for *A Small Boy Smiling*

A beautifully written, compelling and mesmerising story of triumph over evil and the strength of the human spirit...I couldn't put it down.
Maddie Kitchen

This is a remarkable book from a remarkable man, and is a timely and necessary addition to the #nomore movement from a male perspective. This is a must-read for anyone who is fighting the wounds left from their young lives or who is trying to walk a spiritual path towards healing. I salute his bravery for facing this pain and putting his story into the public domain.
Jennifer Parker, Ph.D.

A spiritual odyssey; from the ashes of despair, hopelessness and crippling shame, rises a truly courageous account of resilience and inner strength as a small boy tries to make sense of it all. A story of great wisdom, embracing forgiveness and compassion, reminding us all of the miracle of being present and conscious.
Mark Campbell

A powerful, compelling and brutally honest book about recovery from both child abuse and alcoholism. It's, at times, undeniably harrowing but it is ultimately hugely uplifting and inspiring. It's both a story of his spiritual journey and a wonderful self-help book for any survivors of abuse and addiction.
Marcus Hoffman

This account powerfully illustrates the challenges survivors' face overcoming the chronic shame and traumatising affects of sustained childhood sexual abuse. And how recovery is hard work, takes a long time and is ultimately worthwhile. A brave account and an inciteful read.
Anonymous

It's hard to read the first part, but how I felt was that I didn't want to 'abandon the child', i.e. stop reading. I felt so profoundly disturbed in places – and yet grateful too, to read an account that I can, dynamics-wise, relate to. I have never read or heard anything like this. A Small Boy Smiling is a story of hope. I'd like to bring my two hands together and tip my head forward to the author of this book, written in the language of the heart.
Anonymous

Matthew's book is brutally honest tale of his experience being targeted by paedophiles as a young child and the life long consequences resulting from this experience. It's not just a description of his abuse - far more powerfully he talks openly and honestly about the tools and techniques he has trialled over the years to face his shame and fear, to ensure he can and does live a fully engaged, open and fulfilling life.
Sarah W

I first met Matt whilst seeking help for alcoholism. His extraordinary story inspired me to realise that my obstacles, too, could be overcome. Matt is a man who vibrates hope and love so strongly that he played a pivotal role in saving my life. His story has to be told so as to inspire others to realise that there is always hope despite suffering extreme troubles and darkness. It is an honour to know Matt and to call him my friend.
Anonymous

A gripping and harrowing story of a very brave, courageous young child. Truly heartfelt story and how a very brave and strong man turned it around. Reading this book gives me the courage to reach out, now I know that we can heal and find peace.... we need to reach out more, it really helps yourself and others. We are all survivors.
Miss Sharon Ashelford

A Small Boy Smiling is a real page turner; a story of triumph over extreme adversity, of sheer determination and an openness that allows the author, as well as the reader, to go on an amazing journey. From a middle class upbringing in a suburban English town, to the city of London, to the crowded, chaotic streets of India, to the peace and inspiration of the Himalayas, and on to bustle of Brazil.... such are the contrasts of this remarkable journey that, from beginning to end, the reader is swept along with the characters, described in such a way that one feels both the depth of the emotional pain and the moments of sheer, unadulterated joy. It is so beautifully written; one can picture every scene as the description is so vivid and colourful that even in the darkest moments the reader lives them along with the author. I found it a greatly uplifting spiritual journey... a superb piece of writing that deserves to be at the top of the Best Seller list.
Pamela Brown

Few of us embark upon a life's journey with extreme, life-changing trauma as Matt has experienced. Very brave - very forthright. Stark and shocking. How else could you describe that type of inhumane behaviour and its challenging effects? Few could ever conceive of the pain he went through writing this astounding book. To have faced all that and come out the other side, still a highly spiritual, loving person is remarkable. There are many delightful tales as Matt travels the globe, meeting the 'teachers' he was destined to see along the way. I sincerely hope it will be made available in all libraries, therapy centres and in Talking Book form to help so many other survivors.
Stephen Peters

Matt's book is very powerful and it is difficult to think that a young boy had to go through such horrible trauma. It made me think of my situation when I was his age, that something similar happened to me. Reading the trauma he suffered has given me strength to know that he got through it and so did I. His story has given me hope.
Andreas

The Salutation of the Dawn

Listen to the Exhortation of the Dawn!
Look to this Day!
For it is Life, the very Life of Life.
In its brief course lie all the
Verities and Realities of your Existence;
The Bliss of Growth,
The Glory of Action,
The Splendor of Beauty;

For Yesterday is but a Dream,
And To-morrow is only a Vision:
But To-day well lived makes
Every Yesterday a Dream of Happiness,
And every To-morrow a Vision of Hope.
Look well therefore to this Day!
Such is the Salutation of the Dawn!

Author unknown [1]

---

[1] From the Sanskrit, "The Salutation of the Dawn", *Masterpieces of Religious Verse*, ed. James Dalton Morrison (Harper & Brothers, 1948), p. 301. Attributed in some sources to Kalidasa, Hindu dramatist and lyric poet of the fifth century, A.D.

CONTENTS

Praise For A Small Boy Smiling iv
The Salutation Of The Dawn vii
Introduction 1
Writing About The Abuse 3

1. The Disgusting Rusty Tin 6
2. The Centre Of Attention 22
3. When The Pupil Is Ready 69
4. An Inside Job 92
5. Finding My Truth 144
6. Treading The Boards 189
7. In Heaven And Earth 196
8. Healing And Meditation 230
9. Love Lost 252
10. The Way To Santiago 283
11. Underlying Triggers 302
12. A Revolution In My Head 317
13. London Calling 353
14. The Last First 382
15. Soulful Space: Reflections On My Therapy Work With Matt,
    by trauma therapist Sarah Paton Briggs 404
16. Trying To Make Sense Of It All 424

Acknowledgments 441
About The Author 443
Appendix 444
Information, Resources And Support 446
Bibliography 453

INTRODUCTION

There were many times when I looked in the mirror and hated what I saw. Looking back at me was the face of a haunted, broken boy, who was full of fear, confusion and a deepening sense of self-hatred, but who didn't know why. The man looking in the mirror tried desperately to understand what the hell was going on, yet he could barely remember anything; there were just flashes of memory, and a deep, visceral feeling of horror buried inside of me, which was crippling his life.

My life has been one of extremes, since suffering the horrific trauma of being regularly sexually abused in public toilets at the age of eight years old, and leading on to teenage alcoholism, 'sexual anorexia' and living with complex post-traumatic stress disorder (CPTSD). And now? I have been blessed with over twenty-five years of recovery from addiction, a successful, fulfilling career in theatre and festival management and, for the most part, a sense of peace and purpose in my life. Far beyond the material success I have achieved, the most important realisation is that I know I am being intuitively guided on a journey of spiritual awakening which is hugely rewarding and profoundly healing. I have become aware of a beautiful presence deep within me, which is a source of immense strength and love.

The psychological and emotional trauma of the abuse has served a much greater purpose than I could ever have imagined when I first reached out for help. It became a powerful catalyst for my recovery and spiritual growth. I wouldn't wish what I went through as a boy on anybody... but the experience of having been abused by different men at different times compelled me to seek recovery and a positive life through spiritual and physical travels, which I might not otherwise have undertaken.

At this point, I feel I should warn readers that I have described the abuse exactly as it happened, in all of its shocking, disgusting detail. To have done otherwise would have been to dilute the impact of my story. One of the reasons I have written this book is to try to help others who may have gone through a similar hell, and to highlight the long-term consequences of child sexual abuse (CSA). I would also like to use my story to call attention to the need for more resources to support survivors of CSA. This book has first and foremost, however, been written for me, as I have needed to;

1. Reclaim my childhood from the sick men who abused, molested and raped me, and in doing so tried to destroy me in body, mind and spirit.
2. Learn to love the amazing, ten-year-old boy who somehow managed to survive – a boy I have for many years of my adulthood despised and rejected as weak and pathetic.
3. Release the blocks within my mind which have crippled my hopes of becoming a loving partner, a good father, and of having a family of my own.

Finally, I am writing my story in the hope that fellow survivors of sexual abuse, of which there are estimated to be well over a million in the UK alone, might find encouragement and strength to get the help they desperately need to heal. I am very grateful to Sarah Paton Briggs, my trauma therapist, who has written a later chapter, *Soulful Space: Reflections On My Therapy Work With Matt*. Sarah brings her considerable expertise and offers a professional perspective to my journey of healing, therapy options, and practical advice to fellow survivors of sexual abuse who may be considering professional therapy.

WRITING ABOUT THE ABUSE

A close friend (a clinical psychologist, CSA survivor, and a recovering alcoholic), who has supported me throughout my recovery suggested I provide a description of the psychological and emotional process I went through to get the memories of the abuse from the mind to the page. She told me that when she read the abuse chapter, she sensed that I had dissociated from the trauma, which is true; I didn't think I'd last five minutes without breaking down. During a traumatic event and throughout the emotional upheaval that often follows, dissociation is one of the mind's most common coping mechanisms in response to feeling a sensation of threat or danger. Dissociation covers a wide variety of experiences, from mild detachment to a complete disconnection from all conscious physical and emotional experiences. It is also a common symptom of Complex PTSD.

Whilst I had spoken about the abuse in therapy for many years, writing everything I could remember about what happened made it feel so much more real, and this horrified me. To be able to get it on paper, I decided I had to deliberately suppress all my emotions, as I describe below. I'm not suggesting this is the best way to do it, but it was the only way I could find to be as brutally honest as I have been, dealing with the day-to-day challenges of living with Complex PTSD.

PTSD is a psychiatric disorder that may develop after exposure to a terrifying event or ordeal in which severe physical harm occurred or was threatened. Traumatic events that may trigger PTSD include sexual and physical assaults, natural or unnatural disasters, accidents, or military combat. The term PTSD was first used by veterans of the Vietnam War, but the problem has existed for a lot longer and has had a variety of names, including shell shock, battle fatigue, combat stress, and post-traumatic stress syndrome (PTSS). One of the symptoms of PTSD is that I often go into shock as the memories come up, and whilst I feel hyper-vigilant and very anxious as soon as I have been triggered, there is delayed reaction to my feeling the intensity of the anger, shame and guilt until later that day.

The challenge was to focus all my attention on the writing whilst doing my best to ignore the emotional trauma that was building up inside of me. As I contemplated making a start, I felt the trauma had been triggered in my mind, and under my skin (the symptoms included physical tension in the groin and lower back, nausea in the stomach, and pain behind my eyes); mentally I knew I was very fragile. I knew this was an inevitable consequence of confronting my painful memories, and that I'd have to accept and work through them as best I could. I feared that if I attempted to write on my own, the shame and rage would attack me, and I wouldn't be able to get very far with the written work. It was also important to me that my new flat felt like a safe place, which hadn't been contaminated by memories of the abuse.

As odd as it may seem to some (but for me to feel more able to suppress the emotions and get everything I could remember on paper), I decided to write down the memories in several cafes across central and north London over a period of six months. I wrote brief notes which gradually became sentences, which were then revised to become paragraphs and a chapter, and which were eventually sent to my editor, Tom Bartlett, for editing. Being in a public place, and having pride and an ego, helped to suppress the negative emotions, so I could 'get the job done'. I followed a schedule of an hour of writing, and then I went to an AA meeting, or for a long walk in Regents Park or across Hampstead Heath, during which time I'd feel the shock, and the shame, and rage come up, and during this I'd practice some helpful concentration techniques to make sure I didn't fully dissociate. Depending how I felt, I'd force myself to do at least three hours of writing about the abuse for two days each week, and then I'd leave it to focus on another chapter.

After some writing sessions, I felt I might lose consciousness. Whilst I didn't have any physical warning (unlike with a panic attack, I didn't have any palpitations, or shortness of breath), I'd suddenly feel very light-headed and my vision would become slightly impaired. If I was out walking, I would immediately find a wall or bench and hold on tight to keep myself bodily conscious until the experience had passed. I avoided travelling on the

Underground when I felt like this, and walking near traffic, just in case my legs did give way. (There were several occasions when the flashbacks to the abuse, and the shame I felt, made me feel suicidal; I didn't trust myself when it felt like this, and so there was another reason to avoid taking the Underground). The sensation was as if I'd had a sudden rush of oxygen to the brain. Perhaps it was that the writing had released a great deal of energy which had been locked into the memories. Later in the evening, the suppressed emotions (the shame, rage, and sometimes the tears) would finally hit me, and I would make sure I was in a safe place, which was preferably at home. I felt so desperately vulnerable at this point, I couldn't handle anyone else seeing me like this.

The whole process of writing the chapter about the abuse was mentally, physically and emotionally exhausting, but it has certainly helped me to release so much of the shame and rage. From start to finish, it took eleven months to write that one chapter.

1

THE DISGUSTING RUSTY TIN

*If you want to see the brave,
look to those who can return love for hatred.
If you want to see the heroic, look to those who can forgive.*[2]
Bhagavad Gita

'Abuse' is a widely-used word these days, and it's a word that covers a range of actions and behaviours, in which one person or a group of people cause pain to another. 'Pain'.... There's another word in frequent use, and applicable to any number of situations. They're only words on a page, and have no power by themselves. I could have come out and said that the words apply only to me, and left it at that, but that would not have been enough.

There came a time when I couldn't keep running away from my past anymore. In my late thirties, a series of events had triggered off my PTSD to the extent that I felt a visceral, primeval rawness within me that I could not bury any longer. Shame had silenced the child for decades, but I could feel the child within me suffocating from years of neglect and self condemnation; I needed to allow him to breathe, to give him the voice he so desperately needed, for him to finally be allowed to tell his story, and to be at peace.

I am now ready to acknowledge and honour the remarkably courageous young boy who was subjected to horrendous sexual, psychological and emotional abuse at the hands of a group of well organised, predatory

---

[2] Swami Prabhavananda and Christopher Isherwood, trans., *Bhagavad Gita – The Song of God* (Signet Books, 2002)

paedophiles, and who has survived to become a decent, kind and compassionate man. The events I describe took place during a period of perhaps 18 months, from the Easter holidays of 1981 to the autumn of 1982, when I was between eight and ten years old.

For most of my life I've struggled to comprehend what had actually happened. I had a sense that this tied in to the fact that, for years I hated looking at photos of myself in the family album; especially any photos which my mother described as of a boy who was handsome and cute. Among several I once detested, there are two in particular which to me are tainted with the abuse because of how I felt when they were taken. In one, I am ten years old and the abuse is about to continue for several more months. I am wearing my school cap and tie, looking at the camera with a real darkness in my eyes; I remember feeling haunted at the time. In the other photo, I am perhaps twelve years old, and standing in the back garden at home, blonde hair and blue eyes, and holding the three cups for athletics I had won at School Sports Day. I had felt a shudder of shame flash through me and a feeling of disgust deep within me when that photo was being taken; I didn't deserve the attention, and was not worthy of any recognition or praise. I remember thinking to myself, 'if they knew the truth about me, if they knew what I was really like, they'd hate me for what I've done'. That was the extent of the self-hatred I experienced as a result of the abuse.

Due to the passage of time, and the barriers I had erected in my mind, the memories of the abuse are, with the exception of those first and last instances, often vague and jumbled, and not necessarily chronological. A few memories involve several seconds of me with two or three men in different public toilets, and I see myself from above looking down on what is happening. Whilst my awareness is 'out of body' I can often vividly 'smell' the rancidness of the toilets and the stench of cheap disinfectant; and 'feel' the cold, slate tiles and concrete floors, the old fashioned rusty cistern, the crispness of the sheets of toilet paper, and the dead leaves collected behind the toilet. But far worse is the physicality of the men; their sweating, their laboured, nervous breathing, and their bulging, staring eyes as they climax in front of me. Then, at other times, I can recall some of the more experienced ones acting with such a sense of menace and control. It was as if they felt that they had a divine right to do what they were doing, and I meant nothing to them now. That reality terrified me more than anything. When I realised they didn't care about me, it meant sooner or later it would stop. You always fear something far worse will happen when it eventually stops.

As I write now, I still feel the dirtiness, fear and tension throughout my body. I see myself from above; what they are doing to me, and what I am told to do to them. It is horrific and shocking to 'watch' but I am switched off, to some degree, both during the abuse and in the recalling of it... and I also know that I have to face these memories to deal with them. I am continually separated from what is happening, and there is a sense in which I am not fully conscious of the experience I am seeing. I am in shock. I know it's me; I can see it's me. The emotional intensity of the memory is delayed. Whilst I feel uncomfortable and nauseous recalling the memory, it is only later that the intensity of my emotions hits me, and I feel very depressed, dirty under the skin, full of rage, distrusting, paranoid, and hyper vigilant to the behaviour and body language of any people, especially men, around me. This could be on an airplane, in a train, at a supermarket: anywhere where I might be in close proximity with other people.

Sometimes I have a memory of being 'split in two', whereby my body below the chest is separated from everything above it. It's as if the physical area of the abuse is not part of me, has nothing to do with me, doesn't belong to me even, and mentally I am somewhere else entirely. The men might have told me this; that my penis was theirs to play with. I can't remember. There were times when the men hardly spoke to me; they just got on with what they wanted to do, with brief, abrupt instructions, and sometimes harsh judgements and threats.

Based on the number of locations I can now remember, thirteen all told that I can recall, and the fact that there were always at least two but usually three men involved each time, I was probably sexually abused, molested or raped at least 30 times. The men worked in rotation; whilst one would abuse me, another would either hold me or stand close by, and a third was a look out, in case we were disturbed... which happened a few times. I have a vivid memory, which is described in more detail later in this chapter, of being gagged by one of the men, when someone came in to use the urinal. I still clearly see the panic and fear in his eyes as he physically restrained and stared at me. I can also 'feel' the physical anxiety in his body which was forced against mine, and his smell, as I write this. The locations were public toilets in local parks, along the sea front, and on the beach of my home town.

Sitting here now in my flat, in a safe, quiet place, my awareness is heightened to the extent I am hyper vigilant and paranoid to sudden noises; and my body tenses at the irrational risk of the front door being kicked in and my being attacked in some way. I know it's irrational, but the mind and body automatically respond regardless; I've come to live with it. As soon as I am triggered, the reaction is immediate, and at its worst crippling. It's one of the symptoms of Complex PTSD.

Back then the parks were usually busy with kids, mostly unsupervised, playing football and cricket. There were two attractive parks near to where I grew up, separated by a road. The first park had a cricket pitch, old wooden pavilion, two open shelters, three separate toilets blocks, and plenty of open space. The second park was more organised; there was a traditional bowling green, children's play area, gatehouse, manicured gardens, and two toilet blocks. During the evenings, the toilets were known by everyone, including us children, to be regular pick up points for casual gay sex. Looking back, I think this acted as a cover for the paedophiles, as no one seemed to question why men were hanging around during the afternoon and early evening, when children were playing. Both parks had several gates and plenty of trees around the edges, which created easy access for the paedophiles to get in and out of the toilets quickly if they needed to. It was common for those who drove to park their cars around the corner, and to approach the toilets through trees rather than walk along the path, which was much more exposed.

When one is abused so many times, one gets to know paedophile behaviour. I remember seeing them park up, and walk to the toilets. This contrasts with the innocence of the setting: children playing, people walking dogs, and others sitting on benches watching the world go by. But it was the ideal environment in which a group of predatory paedophiles could operate: they could watch children playing and develop a strategy to groom the ones they thought were more susceptible. I was one of those children. I was a good footballer, and as I loved scoring goals and showing off ... this was their opening.

During one game I went to the toilet and stood in the latrine. As I undid my zip, two men walked in and stood next to me, one on either side, at what I thought was the safe distance of approximately two feet away each side of me. They started to tell me what a talented footballer I was, and how they knew I was so good that I would be a professional one day. One of the men was tall (although everyone seems tall to an eight year old child), in his early 50s, had white hair, gold rimmed glasses with dark shades so his eyes could not be seen, and was smartly dressed. It became obvious during the next few weeks that he was the organiser of the group. He gave all the instructions, he issued the rules, and he always stood physically very close to me at all times. He had an imposing, threatening, commanding presence. The other man was shorter, and a lot younger. He was probably in his late 20s, and was casually dressed. He looked at me smiling all the time, which really unnerved me. Like most children of that time, I had been brought up to be polite, and to respect my elders, and although I felt uncomfortable, I shyly replied 'Thank you' to the compliment about my footballing skills. Then the taller man turned and moved closer to me and told me that I obviously enjoyed showing off in front of them. I was shocked, and said nervously,

'I am just trying to play well for my team.'

'You are a very talented young boy, aren't you? The goal you scored last week was one of the best I've seen in a very long time. Well done,' the taller one said, with a smile on his face as he looked down at me. He then told me they had seen me playing before a few times, and they had noticed how much harder I would suddenly play when they were watching. He said he had noticed I would often look over at him, and when I scored I would always celebrate and wave at him. He then told me he felt really pleased that I liked him so much in that way. The younger man interjected, moved slightly closer, and said he noticed I had looked at his penis when he stood next to me in the toilet. He said to me,

'That's okay, I know why you wanted a quick look. It looks really nice doesn't it? I'm really happy you like me so much.'

'No, I didn't, I didn't look at....', I was really shocked and scared by what he had said. 'I don't understand, please leave me alone. I just want to play football with my friends'.

The attitude of the taller man then changed very suddenly, and he told me how upset and angry he was that I had been teasing him and his friend, that I had been dishonest, which he told me was wrong. He said he had often finished work early to come and watch me play football, and that I had made him feel very special; I had looked over to him many times and smiled, but now I was saying I didn't like him at all. With both men now standing very close to me, the taller one looked down at me accusingly, and said angrily:

'You are a liar. How dare you lie to me? You have been teasing me, it is wrong to tease people.' He then told me I was a wicked boy to behave in this way. I said,

'I am really sorry, I didn't mean to do anything wrong. I'm really sorry, I really didn't know.' He ignored what I had said, and continued to pile on the pressure.

'What is your name?' he demanded.

'Matthew', I replied very meekly and nervously.

'What would your parents think of you, Matthew? That you are such a liar, that you are dishonest, that you enjoy hurting people's feelings?' He stared at me for a few moments, me looking up at him with dismay and confusion, and whispered,

'Did they bring you up to be a liar?'

'No', I said miserably, 'No, they didn't. I'm so sorry. Please can I go now?'.

Then I broke down in tears. The two men continued to stand close on either side of me, as I looked from one to the other,

'What would your father say if we told him?' interjected the younger man.

'He would be angry with me, please don't tell him. I won't do it again, I promise.' I pleaded.

Then the taller man, who I was later to learn was the main paedophile, suddenly bent over in agony holding his groin in one hand and leaning on the wall, above the urinal, with the other hand. I felt shocked and really scared. I looked back at the younger man on my right, who had moved in closer to me, as he pretended to be concerned for his friend.

'You must help him; he's in a lot of pain.'

'I don't know what to do,' I cried.

He said urgently, 'You must rub him where it hurts, so the pain goes away.'

He looked down at me with a very stern look of disapproval on his face. 'Matthew, you've hurt him so much, it's made him feel very ill.'

I remember pausing, in shock, bewildered and terrified as to what to do, but I desperately wanted to get out of there and so I closed my eyes, reached over, and started to rub the man. I stopped after two gentle rubs, and looked up the the younger man, but he demanded I do it more times and much harder. I started again... I couldn't look at what I was doing, I instinctively looked away, with tears in my eyes. The taller man insisted I just rub harder and faster. I remember him groaning loudly as he came in my hand. I felt sick in my stomach, scared and confused as he became more excited. I remember him sweating and staring at me. My whole body was overwhelmed with tension, with gut-wrenching fear.

The younger man's voice cut in from behind me, telling me I had done very well to help his friend, but he felt I really didn't understand how serious the situation was. The taller man, as he composed himself, went on to talk about my teasing people, and hurting their feelings, and how I had really hurt him; they would have to talk between themselves as to what to do about me. I was choked up with fear and anxiety, but blurted out, 'Please don't tell my father I've been dishonest. He'll be really angry with me.'

The two men then moved slightly away from the urinals, and spoke quietly together for a few moments, looking back at me – I had turned around to face them - with a look of disapproval in their faces. I stood next to the urinal I had just used, zipped up but feeling anxious...waiting for them to decide what they would do with me. Finally, the taller one said to me very seriously,

'My friend has agreed to take me home, just in case I have another painful attack.' I remember him pausing. 'We won't say anything for now, as long as you do not say anything to anyone else as well.' I felt a huge sense of relief.

He continued, 'If you tell anyone what has happened here, we will have to tell your father what you've been doing. Which school do you go to?' I told them.

'I used to know the Headmaster there a few years ago. What is his name?' I told them, and he nodded, and now I was scared I would get into trouble with the school as well.

'And I thought it was a good school. The Headmaster wouldn't be pleased that one of his pupils was caught lying, would he?'

'No, he wouldn't', I answered meekly.

'Well, if you are now a good boy, Matthew, we will not tell anyone what

The Disgusting Rusty Tin

you have done.'

'No, I won't tell anyone, either. I promise.'

I can't recall what was said next, but some arrangement was made, as I remember a few days later waiting for them to arrive, standing fifty yards from another toilet. Fear gripped me as I scanned the park, expecting at any moment to see them. I half hoped they would not come, but then I felt really frightened I would be in even more trouble if they had changed their minds and told on me.

After the first time I was abused, I felt something had broken inside of me; I seemed to be on auto pilot, in shock. I remember sobbing on my own in the cubicle after the men had left, trying to understand what had just happened, and what I should do about it. I was nervous to leave the leave the toilet, and terrified to stay there in case they came back. I decided to pretend I was okay, and hoped I'd never, ever see them again. I went back to the game of football and a few of the boys asked me where I had been for so long. I lied to them, saying I had had to go home for something. I could see one of the men staring at me 100 yards or so away, on the other side of the park. I felt torn between being really scared and confused about what they had told me I had done wrong, and therefore wanting to make things right with them, so they would leave me alone. But then another part of me wanted to run away from them, and tell Mum and Dad what had happened, as I hated being anywhere near them. But I was too frightened to tell my parents what had happened; what if the men were correct? What if I really had done something dreadful? I daren't tell my parents (or anyone else) what had happened, in case I got into even more trouble.

I felt repulsed and terrified by their attitude, their smell and what they were forcing me to do, but felt completely trapped. I remember desperately hoping this would be it; when we met again they would leave me alone. In my eight-year-old mind, being accused of being dishonest, and being called a liar by adults, was really frightening. As children we are brought up to be polite and to show respect. Both Mum and Dad had told me not to talk to strangers, but the grooming had happened so quickly that I had been overwhelmed by everything. I couldn't 'compute' what was going on; I remember feeling shock, fear, bewilderment, and confusion… but I was too scared to tell anyone; I already felt I was at fault, that I was responsible in some way for what was happening.

Looking back, I now realise the paedophiles had convinced me that I had unlocked a Pandora's Box of actions for which I had to pay the price. This sense of sole responsibility was made very clear to me, very early on. The paedophiles had me cornered; by making me feel I was responsible, complicit in the abuse, I thought I had nowhere to run; I was on my own, so my mind created an escape route by dissociating from the abuse.

There comes a point in any traumatic situation when a person's immediate instinct is solely to survive, almost as if a switch has been clicked, and there is a feeling of resignation to the circumstances of the situation. In a sense, the switch temporarily normalises the horror of what is going on. I couldn't see any way out, so I shut down: mentally, emotionally... Besides, I was terrified to try and stop what was happening; the consequences could be far worse. There was a protocol to the abuse, which was set up very quickly by the taller man, and he and the other abusers made sure I adhered to it:

1. I was never, ever to talk with them unless they spoke to me first. This rule was for anywhere - in the park, on the seafront and in the street if I saw any of them.
2. I must always do exactly what they told me to do, without any complaining.
3. I had to wait at a distance outside the toilet before they arrived, and after they entered, to count slowly to 30 before I walked into the toilet.
4. If anyone ever noticed anything and asked how I knew them I was to say one of them was my uncle, and to tell them straight away.
5. I was never, ever to tell anyone about our special friendship. Anyone outside of the group would not understand, and might think something wrong was going on. At some point I was told that if anyone did find out, I could get in serious trouble with the police.

There was always a threat in everything they said, followed sometimes by praise or compliments.

'You were very bad when you lied to us the way you did. You may be a good boy underneath, though.'

'Yes, I am', I answered quickly, hoping this might be the opening to it all finally finishing.

'We shall see if you really are a good boy', one of them would say, and then I would be subsequently molested by each one in turn.

Thereafter the abuse became a regular occurrence, and each time the switch flicked in my mind, which was the only way to survive it. I remember blanking out what they were doing; what they forced me to do. I have memories of a sense of being split in two; as if what was going on in my genital area was nothing to do with me, and as it was happening I would focus on a mark on the wall, or look up into the sky at the clouds (there was no roof above the latrine), and try my best to pretend I was somewhere else.

There were times when I would be obedient to kiss and suck (as best I could) and rub their penises, but when any of them came on my face I would feel really sick and spit in the toilet. (Even today, over thirty years later, I automatically spit as soon as I lift the toilet seat.) For many years into my adulthood I couldn't stand being kissed on the lips by anyone, as I feared I might suffocate. Another time, I recall being inside a toilet cubicle. It was early one Saturday morning and I had told Mum I was going on my bike to see a friend around the corner. Instead, I was soon in the park, waiting for the men to arrive. I was still living under the threat that my father and / or the police would be told of my behaviour, if I didn't obey the abusers.

The memory has been with me all my life, one of the few which I never managed to bury that deeply. There are two men and me (there were almost always three men, and new men would join every now and then). We are in a cubicle, and I am kneeling down with my back to the cubicle door kissing and licking one of their penises... when someone comes in to use the latrine. The second man (who is standing behind me) suddenly grabs me by the shoulder; he gags me with his hand, and stares down at me. I remember feeling his fear, his horrible smell so close to me, and I want to go home to Mum. I hope the person using the latrine might know something is going on, but at the same time I am really scared that maybe everything that has happened is really all my fault after all - so I do nothing, I do not struggle or try and shout out.

When the person leaves, the two men sigh with relief, and tell me what a good boy I am. I'm told: 'Some people just wouldn't understand how special you are to us'. I feel relief that I had done the right thing, but the sense of shock, fear and confusion remains. Most of the memories I have are of me looking down at myself being abused. It's like watching a grainy, horrible film of a child porno, with myself as the main performer.

Another time, I am cycling along the sea front to another toilet. It is early evening, and I know I must be home by 7pm at the latest. I am sitting on a bench about forty yards from the toilet, pretending to 'mend' the chain on my bike. I see one of the men nod at me, and he walks very quickly into the toilet. I count to 30 and follow him in. I can remember my penis being played with; these are memories of the men hardly speaking to me; they just get on with exactly what they want to do. Whether this is because I am so disconnected from the abuse taking place I am not sure, but at times they are so silent and predatory I think of them in the same way as I think of a snake - silent, soulless, and with no empathy.

I recall another time being a Saturday morning about 0900, when I and a friend were both in the same toilet together on the seafront with two men, whilst a third man was on lookout. They had previously encouraged me to bring a friend with me, hinting they might allow me to go if I did. Whilst I cannot remember speaking to my friend about being involved, I have always assumed I must have done. This has been my greatest shame for many, many years; the possibility that I may have, out of desperation to escape, caused enormous pain in his life. There is a chance, of course, that his involvement was nothing to do with me, but the shame it might have been caused by me haunted me for many years.

Over the following months they kept increasing the pressure, saying I was not good enough; that I needed to practice more with my friend at home in secret. Other times I was told how fortunate I was that they cared so much about me; that we had a special love. Much of this would be said as they molested me, as their means of 'making love'. My memory of this is 'out of body' in the sense that as I recall it now I can see myself from above (these memories are 'seen' sometimes from perhaps ten foot above, looking down, and other times is much closer to what is happening).

They also told me there were other men who wanted to meet me, but that these men didn't know how to treat children properly, and that I wouldn't need to meet the other men as long as I was a good boy, and did what I was told. I have a memory of being told at some point that children were sold if they didn't do what they were told. My recall of this is of an 'aside' comment between two of the men, which wasn't said to me directly but that I was meant to hear as a warning. This really scared me, and I can see now how it was part of their frequent manipulation and coercion to ensure my cooperation and my silence.

I have another vague memory, which I sense was towards the end of the period of abuse, of an upstairs bedroom with old fashioned wrought iron single bed. I am lying on the bed being 'directed', with three men and a woman standing around me. The woman is aggressive and distraught; I think she had been bullied in some way to offer her flat? There is a camera being held by one of the men. This memory is very fleeting, and fragmented, so I am not sure whether the camera is for a film or still photography. There is another memory of them inserting something into my anus. I remember them telling me to treat it like a game or a meal. A three course meal to them; abusing my penis, my anus and then me playing with them. They use comparisons - that some children don't like vegetables, but they must eat them as it is good for them.

Back to the present: it took me twelve years in recovery to forgive the men who abused me, but another six years to forgive myself, such were my feelings of shame and responsibility for what had happened to me. I kept telling myself for years: 'if I really didn't want it to happen, I could have walked away.' Paedophiles understand these reactions, and do everything they can to condemn their victims to silence. My abusers also told me at some point there was nothing stopping me walking away, but the underlying threat of exposing me was there - telling my father, my school and the police. The confusion was that whilst I hated them touching me and hated what they coerced me to do, I did sometimes feel the physical pleasure of my penis being tickled, which they told me meant I was the same as them. I had developed a relationship of sorts with the more regular men who were kinder to me and dreaded the ones who were more aggressive and predatory.

I kept asking myself: if I really hate this, why do I sometimes feel some physical pleasure at the same time?

The men were typically middle-aged, though some were in their late fifties and sixties, and they told me they had travelled a long way to meet me. They would offer praise and encouragement, but it was almost always couched in the terms like 'you are getting better, but it's taking a long time', and 'when you are good enough it will finish.' You feel so isolated and lonely; the only way to survive is for the mind to switch off during the abuse. You go on auto pilot and then carry on afterwards as if nothing had happened. The paedophiles convince you it is all entirely your fault, that it is only because of your behaviour that a Pandora's Box has opened, and that you have to bear the full consequences.

I became, albeit as a means of survival, an active participant; I became desperate to please them so the abuse would finally finish, and this is why I felt, for so many years, as if I behaved as a child prostitute. This belief was the source of my deepest shame, one which I would taunt myself with verbally and physically during my teenage years and in my early twenties, whenever the PTSD was triggered. In my mental agony, I would quite often stare at myself in the mirror, call myself every name under the sun, and goad myself as I punched myself in the face.

There were a few times when I pleaded with them to let me go, to please leave me alone, but their only response was:

1. I had to try harder to please them. I had to do certain things first before I had completed my part of the 'agreement'.
2. I didn't understand how serious my behaviour had been. I had broken the law and would be in serious trouble with the police if they found out.
3. I had to meet a friend of theirs, a very important man, who had heard all about me. I was told that he knew I was very special which is why he wanted to meet me.

The memory of the last time they abused me has haunted me in flashbacks from the PTSD for most of my life. Whenever the PTSD was triggered off, at least until the last five years, I would be overwhelmed with feelings of horror, panic and a sense of the abyss.

In that final episode of abuse, I am looking down on myself and I am being threatened by one man in particular who is standing over me, his face right next to mine. Another man stands close by, while a third (an older man, perhaps in his sixties) is by the entrance on lookout.

The man closest to me is a short man, with brown or dark ginger hair and a beard. He is not smartly dressed; he looks rough and unkempt, as if he worked in a factory or a workshop and had come straight from work. The bearded man is the main perpetrator and the sickest of all the men who abused me. I sensed he had forced his way in to the group, as it was clear a few of the other men didn't want him involved, judging from their reactions when he was first mentioned in the weeks before he arrived. There are levels of 'moral behaviour' even in paedophile groups, it seems. He appeared to get a much greater kick out of the power he had over me, rather than the actual sexual contact. He was the one who verbally manipulated and physically threatened me the most, and on this final occasion, he leant down and said to me:

"We know who your father is, we know where you live. If you tell anyone what has happened, we will find you and we will kill you."

He then pulled a pair of scissors out of his pocket, grabbed my penis and moved as if to cut it. I pleaded with him, saying I would never ever tell anyone. I pleaded with him not to hurt me anymore, and that I was so sorry for everything I had done.

'Please don't... please leave me alone' I sob.

The other man, close by, was shocked by what the bearded man had said, and the threat of the scissors, and told him he had gone far too far, then ran out of the toilets quickly. The lookout came in, saw what was happening, and said to the main paedophile,

'That's too much', and then said in a panicky voice to me, 'I am really sorry, it wasn't supposed to happen like this.'

He made no attempt to physically confront the paedophile who was threatening me. His protest was ignored; the other paedophile didn't even acknowledge his presence. The aggressive paedophile stayed leaning down so our faces were quite close to each other. He was breathing heavily, holding scissors between us, and continued staring at me.

I couldn't speak. I was completely in shock, terrified to say anything. Inside me I can remember silently and desperately pleading with the older man to help me get out of this situation, but he just stood there with a panic-stricken look on his face. He kept looking at the door, then looking back at me, then looking at the back of the other paedophile. He then blurted out something about having grandchildren and got very emotional, asking me to forgive him, and then ran out. He left me alone with the paedophile standing in front of me, staring at me, holding the scissors. He put them in his pocket, and repeated 'Don't forget what I said', and then he left.

I felt in shock, totally disconnected from the world around me. I remember wandering around for what seemed like ages; talking to myself, looking back over my shoulder to make sure I was not being followed, eyeing cars as they passed me; paranoid 'they' were in the cars, and crossing the road to avoid anyone coming towards me. I recall being next to a very high wall, with the sun burning down on me, and saying to myself, 'I will never, ever, ever, let anyone hurt me again.'

An impenetrable psychological barrier within automatically went up, and I buried the abuse as deeply within me as possible. It must be as if it had never happened. No one must ever know what had happened to me. I made a pact with myself that I would take this dirty, disgusting secret to the grave. For the last twenty years, this is the wall around myself I've been striving to knock down in order to release the pain. Such were the paedophiles' mind games and intimidation, I really thought it was all my fault, and I hated myself for what I had done. The specific memory of the death threat and the scissors have been the main flashback I have re-lived like groundhog day whenever the PTSD is triggered off. These flashbacks stopped after my emotional rock bottom five years ago, over twenty-eight years after the event took place, when I released so much rage and shame and finally, after all these years, managed to cry.

When I was about twelve years old, a couple of years after the abuse had finished, I was sitting on a bench on my own in the local park waiting for a few friends for a game of cricket, about 100 yards from one of the toilets. I never went in them anymore; if I needed the toilet I ran home, which was just around the corner. Whilst the memories had been suppressed, locked in what felt like a dirty, rusty old box buried deep within me, I felt scared to be sitting on my own and hoped my friends would arrive soon. A man walked over and sat down next to me, saying 'Hello, I often see you playing cricket in the park'. I felt sick as he spoke, scared of what this would lead to. He told me he used to play cricket for the local county. I stopped him in his tracks, and asked him:

'Are you one of the men who abused me?'

He suddenly looked shocked, and at a loss as to what to say. He stood up very quickly, looked at me with panic in his eyes, and said,

'Oh God, you can't say that?'. No I wasn't, I'm so sorry, whatever happened to you, but it wasn't me.' He ran off.

As I watched him leave the park, I remember feeling angry, confused and full of shame. I suddenly felt the men were close by again, and my body felt very tense, and I was frightened. His approach could either have been the textbook grooming, from my experience, or the friendly, innocent approach of an adult. Looking back I don't think he was one of the men, but it dawned on me in therapy one day;

- how many different men were involved during that 18 month period?
- what if he had said 'yes'?
- what did I want to ask him?

I had felt so trapped by their coercion and the sense of complicity, I had no one to talk to. There was a bizarre, fucked up sense of being abandoned by them, and I seemed to have some emotional connection to the men who had abused me. I wasn't sitting in the park wanting to see them, but I was so confused, and I had so many questions, perhaps at some level I thought they were the only ones I could speak to about it, to help me to understand what the hell had happened.

Some years later when I was in my twenties I recognised the same man on the sea front with, I presume, his wife. They looked happy and relaxed, and I felt really guilty and upset. I felt I needed to apologise to him and had an opportunity a few weeks later, when I saw him alone on the seafront...but I couldn't do it.

It was the third time I'd seen this man, and although I had at first had a vague sense of something not quite right about him – despite his shocked response to my question the first time, and the loving, relaxed appearance he projected with a woman the second time – my memories of the abusers' appearance and mannerisms had by then faded to near nothingness. I had nothing to pin on him... but plenty to pin on myself: guilt, shame, complicity, silence... yet nobody, at that time, with whom to talk with about it, and nobody to punish for what had happened... but myself.

So began a long, dreadful descent into self-harm and alcoholism; a lost adolescence from which I was lucky indeed to emerge alive.

2

THE CENTRE OF ATTENTION

Early Childhood, Teenage Years and Alcoholism

~~~~~~~~~~~~~~~~~

*For in every adult there dwells the child that was,
and in every child there lies the adult that will be.*[3]
John Connolly, The Book of Lost Things

Throughout my adult life I blocked out most of my childhood memories, including all the good ones I can now remember that happened before the abuse took place, and much of my teenage years as well. Other than a few vague, fleeting memories I could not remember anything which happened to me before I was twelve years old. I would look through the family album and see myself on holiday or at a family reunion, but have no conscious knowledge of being there or of what happened. The abuse poisoned everything, and affected me far beyond the actual experiences of the abuse itself. Until I was 43 years old, the PTSD effectively served as a powerful anaesthetic in the sense that I had so few memories of anything before the abuse took place. Such was the long-term, crippling effect of the abuse on my memory, it sometimes felt as if the abuse was ALL that had ever happened to me before the age of ten. It was only when I was ready to receive the help I needed, (when I stopped drinking at the age of twenty,

---

[3] John Connolly, *The Book of Lost Things* (Simon & Schuster, 2011)

joined Alcoholics Anonymous, and started trauma therapy), that my view of my childhood started to change.

I am so relieved that during the last eighteen months, and specifically since the most painful memories of the abuse have finally come to the surface, I have remembered a lot more of my earlier, and much happier, childhood. Consequently, I am now able to put the trauma of the abuse into a healthier perspective. I now feel a much greater sense of who I am.

The following few memories are those that first came back to me, and which have helped me to place the abuse in the context of what would, otherwise, have been a very happy childhood. I can now remember lying in my cot in an upstairs bedroom, with the window on my left and the light streaming through the green curtains. It is dusk, and I am reaching up, trying to pull the cord of my 'music machine'. (I was maybe only eight months old). I have another memory of hearing footsteps quietly coming up the stairs, and feeling the rush of bliss when Mum comes gently into the room, and looks down and smiles at me. The thrill is there as she picks me up and cuddles me. Another time, the whole family is present; Mum and Dad, with my older brother and sister, who are looking through the bars of the cot and tickling me. I love the attention. They are smiling at me, and turning to ask Mum questions about me. Flash forward to five years old and I am using Dad as a climbing frame as he sits in his chair in the lounge. I can remember feeling how soft his ear lobes are and how nice he smells. Another memory is when I am five years old and I run into my sister's bedroom and snuggle underneath the bedsheets for a lovely cuddle with her. Then there's the time after Dad leaves for the office on his bike, and I am watching him tuck his trousers into the bike clips, his satchel on the rack above the rear wheel, and ride off. Mum then clears up after breakfast, and we are blowing bubbles in the kitchen sink which I find hilarious.

My memory jumps forward to my first school and I am perhaps six or seven years old. I'm in the kitchen with a few friends and Mrs Barnaby, my favourite teacher, and as I open a pot of yoghurt it explodes onto the ceiling and everyone laughs. I remember loving the energy of laughter, and whilst I am a shy little boy I feel safe and I am happy. A little later I am on stage in a school concert, wearing a Red Indian costume Mum had bought from the best shop in town. (I loved to escape here with her and explore all the shelves of toys. Built on two floors, it was packed full of toys, games, puppets and fancy dress costumes. This was my favourite place to visit in the whole world!) The concert finishes and it is my turn to take a bow; I can remember loving the applause and wanting it to go on and on. I asked Mum years later if I was any good, and after a well-considered and polite pause she said 'well.....you looked bored most of the time, but you came alive when you took your curtain call'.

 I'd completely forgotten what kids TV shows I liked, but can now remember how much I enjoyed watching *The Muppets* (Animal on the drums, and Gonzo, were my favourites), *Scooby Doo, Hong Kong Fuey*, and *Rhubarb and Custard*. Even though my brother, sister and I preferred *Tiswas*, our Saturday morning treat was to watch *Noel Edmond's Swapshop*. (Unfortunately *Tiswas*, with Chris Tarrant, Bob Carolgees and Spit the Dog, was considered far too rebellious and anarchic by Mum and Dad, so we were not allowed to watch it!) I can now remember how much I enjoyed and embraced life as a really small boy, and this has brought me so much closer to my family and childhood friends. I've always felt something of a divide between us due to the shame, which is why I withheld so much from them what I felt about the abuse. I knew I was loved, but because of the shame of being sexually abused I didn't feel I deserved to be loved.

 Shame is the key factor. The shame and responsibility I felt for what had happened created a dirty, rusty seal on the Pandora's Box in which the memories were locked away. I then buried that box in the depths of a metaphorical slimy bog somewhere in my mind. As an abused child, that's what I wanted to happen; I had to shut down completely so that I'd never, ever have to experience the pain again. The abuse had destructively affected so many areas of my life, but now I know it was not the only thing that had happened to me. I needed to accept everything I could remember about the abuse, and let go of the feelings of degradation I'd been carrying, so I could start the process of remembering the goodness I had as a child – living with shame, it felt as if I didn't deserve to know I enjoyed my childhood before the abuse took place. Everything I experienced after the abuse was tainted; I had enjoyable times for sure, but I was not always fully present. Part of me was withheld, and suppressed.

 I think the word 'acceptance' is often misunderstood in this context. For me, acceptance means acknowledging that what happened did actually happen; that I can remember the abuse and no longer live in denial of those painful memories. It is not about forgiveness; not at this stage anyway. It has taken me many years to come to a place of forgiveness, which is another word that I think is typically misunderstood. I have forgiven the paedophiles who abused me, so I can heal; but I don't think it changes their spiritual destiny one iota. Forgiveness sets me free, not them. It has allowed me to start healing, as I no longer focus my anger and rage on them; I no longer seek or live out some fantasy of hunting them down and executing them, as I had for many years.

I came to realise that so long as I focussed the rage onto them, it would continue to destroy me. It was wasted energy; it had no effect on them whatsoever, and I remained locked in the pain. It helped me to recognise I was still allowing them to hurt me, but it didn't help to ignore the needs of the hurt boy whose voice desperately needed to be heard.

There are several stages to healing. I had to come to terms with the symptoms of shock whenever the PTSD was triggered; I still go into shock, but over the years I have slowly become better able to talk through the memories with others, which has helped the adult in me recognise the mind games and manipulation that had created so much of the toxic shame which crippled me. There is more of a 'distance' in the memories of the abuse now. The PTSD was first triggered when I was in my early teens, and I was locked into the trauma and had very little awareness of anything else in my life until each one episode had passed. Over the years I've gradually become more able to be a witness to the trauma; I can still relive the physical and emotional symptoms, but mentally I am aware that I am a 45-year-old adult remembering myself as a child being abused, rather than my awareness being only of the abuse.

Seeing the memories in this way has helped me to cognitively recognise that I was not responsible for the abuse at any stage of the experience. I had to survive, and did whatever I needed to. Furthermore, I could forgive myself intellectually but it took many years to forgive myself emotionally for the self hatred and self-condemnation I felt as a result of the abuse. Only when this gradual process of self-forgiveness took place, was I then more able to talk through what had actually happened in greater detail; the shame lifted, and I found that I didn't hate myself for what I remembered. It was at this stage that I felt such enormous compassion and admiration for the eight year old boy who was so badly damaged, yet survived. He is the one who needs my attention, not the abusers.

With this compassion and love came an all-encompassing healing. I was now able to remember so much more of the abuse, which enabled me to heal at a profound level. The challenge of living with Complex PTSD is that when I am triggered (which is to this day an immediate instinctive response), I do feel immense rage, anger and fear, and this sometimes projects on to men who remind me, through their attitudes and behaviours, of the men who abused me.

It is as if there is a part of the memories over which I have no conscious control. The six most important things I've needed to do in order to heal is to;

- Accept that what happened actually happened, in the context of not denying any of the painful memories or running away from them.
- 'Forgive' the paedophiles so I can focus all my energy to healing the eight year old boy.
- Let go of the shame and sense of being responsible for what happened to me.
- Allow the abused eight year old child within me to have a voice, and to be heard.
- Reclaim the happy memories of my childhood and create a context for the abuse.
- Allow those who love me to hear my story so that I can feel their love, and heal more deeply.

On several occasions throughout my adult life, I have needed the expertise of experienced psychologists or psychotherapists who specialise in PTSD and sexual abuse to help me identify, and to support me through, the stages listed above. I have placed 'experienced' in italics, because it is vital that a professional at the first point of contact knows what to say, and how to say it. As a survivor, I have been so sensitive to how someone speaks to me, and have interpreted a potential counsellor's tiredness, or a weariness in their voice (which is understandable, after a long day with clients) as rejection, or as someone passing judgement on me. Such a response from a professional is enough for a survivor to shut down for many months before reaching out for help again, if ever.

Having found an experienced psychotherapist in my early 40s, in Sarah

Paton Briggs, and developed a trusting relationship with her, I then joined the Survivors of Sexual Abuse Anonymous (SoSAA) programme. At SoSAA, I have found the identification with other survivors has given me the strength to talk more openly about the abuse and its consequences in my life.

My parents have only known, in vague terms, that I was sexually abused as a child. I've only spoken with them about it perhaps a dozen times during the last thirty-five years since it took place. I'd never told them what happened, or how often, or the depth of its impact on me until twelve months ago. My brother and sister have also known very little about the details of the abuse. These were the conversations I told myself I'd never have; these were the issues I'd decided to take to the grave with me. For years I could not acknowledge the abuse had actually happened to me, let alone to those who I know love me. I also knew they would feel a great deal of emotional pain when they learnt the truth of what actually had happened, and I felt I needed to be strong enough to come to terms with my pain before I told my story, and felt their pain. (My healing with the SoSAA programme is described in detail in the *London Calling* chapter).

It's been the most important part of my healing process to allow myself to redefine my childhood away from the filter of the abuse; and in doing so I've started to remember how I felt before the abuse took place, which has been crucial to my overall healing. My approach to healing, and indeed to subsequently writing this book, has been to talk through my early years with family and closest friends. I have sat down with Mum and Dad and looked through the family photo album, which has helped me to piece together the childhood memories. There have been conversations with my brother and sister as I've tried to redefine my childhood years in light of their memories.

Mum recently told me she had remembered an incident, which I can now also recall when I was about nine years old, which had always puzzled her and which, at that time, I refused to talk about. Recalling this particular memory was a significant event in my healing, as it showed that I had found the courage to stand up to the paedophiles and to try and stop the abuse. As the memory came to the surface, I felt such a strong, loving connection to my younger self, and could for the first time really acknowledge how incredibly brave and resilient he had been to survive. One morning after breakfast, I was out riding my bike around the neighbourhood. Then...

A Small Boy Smiling

something happened... Returning home, I rushed down the driveway and threw my bike against the house, at the wall by the dining room window. Then I ran into the house, feeling anxious.... Unhappy. Mum was in the garden and came in quickly after me, showing concern for my behaviour.

"What's wrong, Matt? What's happened? What's upsetting you so much?" she asked me, as she held me close and hugged me. I was distraught, frightened and confused, and I pushed her away.

I gabbled as I spoke,

"Someone from the police will come here and tell you that I stole some milk from a milk float around the corner. But I didn't. I didn't steal anything. It isn't true. They are lying." With that, I ran upstairs crying, sprinted into my bedroom and dove onto the bed, sobbing. Mum followed me into my room, and sat beside me on the bed trying to coax out of me what had happened.

"I believe you, my love. I know you wouldn't steal anything. You're a good boy. I know you. I know you wouldn't do anything like that. What happened? Who's upset you so much? Please tell me, so I can help you."

"I can't tell you. It's nothing.... it's nothing. Just some boys picking on me," I replied, lying to cover up the dreadful truth of what was really going on.

The front doorbell rang; Mum kissed me on the forehead and said to me, "We really do love you, you know that, don't you? You can tell me anything. I'm always here for you." She kissed me again on the forehead, looked at me, and then went downstairs to answer the door. I listened, feeling really panicked, from the landing upstairs as Mum spoke with a policeman.

"We've had a report that a boy, matching I've been told the description of your son, was seen stealing two pints of milk from the milk float in Althorpe Road approximately twenty minutes ago. He was seen on his bike, returning to this address a short time ago."

Mum replied, "My son would never steal any milk. He's a good boy. He would never do such a thing."

"How do you know, Madam? We have a description of the boy. Aged about nine years old, blonde hair, wearing blue tracksuit bottoms, and a red top."

"I know my son. He wouldn't steal anything. You'll have to take my word for that."

The policeman seemed to realise he wasn't getting past Mum, and he left. Mum came back up the stairs, and encouraged me to tell her what had actually happened, but I wouldn't tell her. I was too scared about what the men would do when they saw me again. I remember thinking whether I ought to run away; even writing this memory down after thirty years brings up feelings of immense fear and loneliness, as I recall so vividly how I felt as a traumatised nine-year-old boy.

Nevertheless, despite my emotional reaction to this memory, speaking with Mum about it all these years later has triggered a very important memory which has brought about a seismic change in my attitude to the young boy who experienced the abuse. I can now remember standing up to the men, and telling them on a number of occasions to leave me alone. I can remember telling them that I didn't want this to go on any longer, and that I hated what they were doing. I would tell the police what they were really like. They mocked and laughed at me, and then threatened to tell the police they had seen me stealing some milk,

"There's no way for you to walk away. The police won't believe you. We have very good friends in the police, who know all about you and what you have done. They will not believe the lies of a child."

I now remember managing to get away from them, and running outside to my bike, and riding off as quickly as possible. I have a vague memory of looking back when I was 100 yards away and seeing one of them talking to a milkman in the street behind the toilet we had been in, and pointing at me. It was shortly after this that the policeman rang the doorbell and spoke to Mum.

I stayed away from the park for a few weeks, scared I would see them again. Perhaps a month later, one of the men saw me walking home after school, and walked alongside me. He told me it was very sad that things had got out of hand, and that he expected to see me on Saturday morning at nine o'clock... He looked down at me with a frown, in a disapproving manner and putting particular stress on the word 'expected'. I felt scared of what would happen if I didn't do as he had told me.

A week or so later, the abuse started up again.

Recalling these memories has been a hugely important and a rewarding process as I have now placed the abuse into a different, healthier, perspective. Without in any sense minimising its effect upon me, this process has helped me to recognise that I am much more than the pathetic, disgusting, shameful boy I thought I was. Two things have come about to help me change. Firstly, I can now see that I was not responsible at all for the abuse that happened, and secondly, the memories I have since recalled confirm that the child I was has become the man I am. I am a decent, caring, honest, kind man.

I can now look back with a degree of affection to my prep school days (when the abuse took place) and have some fond memories of those times, without the shadow of the abuse kicking in (a few of which I have recalled below.) Had I attempted to have written about my childhood three years ago, there would have been a very different outcome. This book would not have been written, because at that time, it still felt as if the abuse cancelled everything else out and that, before the age of ten years old, nothing else had really happened.

I grew up in a typical English, middle-class family, the youngest of three children, in a Victorian seaside town in the south of England. Our family home was a large detached house, with a front garden and spacious back garden, and a long drive which was ideal for my brother and I to use as a makeshift cricket pitch. We lived in a quiet residential road in a friendly neighbourhood, and within easy walking distance of the town's parks and the beach, to which I would escape to meet up with friends, climb the trees, and play cricket and football. It was not unusual for the house to be full of energy and excitement as two brothers and a sister had their friends round to play. As kids, the house and garden were also ideal for 'Sardines', which we often played when we were really young. (Sardines is like Hide-and-Seek, but in reverse. One person hides, and everyone else looks for them. When someone finds the hidden person, they quietly join them in hiding — after a while, the group begins to look like sardines, huddled together in a small space. The last person to find the group becomes the next hider).

My older sister and I played tennis in the back garden, with a makeshift net tied up between the large lilac tree and a drain pipe. The back garden was also home to my rather short-tempered pet rabbit, Smudge, and the tennis net served as Smudge's barrier to the wider world. She exacted her revenge for this enforced captivity with her almost weekly 'Houdiniesque' escapes from the garden and into the driveway. She'd watch us from a distance as the whole family would stand around, flummoxed as to how she'd got out yet again.

Playing cricket on the drive was a much more serious affair, as my older brother and I were very competitive, and the two of us would fantasise that we were scoring the winning runs for England against Australia for the Ashes at Lord's. We'd outline the stumps with chalk on the wooden garage door, and being the late 70s and early 80s, we'd do our best impersonations of England's stars - Ian Botham, Bob Willis, and David Gower.

Family holidays were usually in North Wales (where my maternal grandmother and extended family lived, and where both Mum and Dad grew up) or else we drove to Weymouth and boarded a ferry to France. Mum spoke fluent French so she was our interpreter, and I can remember as we sailed across the English Channel pretending to be a spy. I felt very important to be going on another secret, daring mission on behalf of Queen, although it irked me I couldn't really tell anyone about it, of course.

It became a running family joke how Dad would go into meticulous detail packing the car to make sure everything got in; there would be several attempts as he became increasingly frustrated as one of us children would be watching him from the dining room window, and giving a running commentary to Mum, who would be emptying the fridge in the kitchen. There was always one bag or box too many to squeeze in, so he'd start the whole packing process again.

'He's taking it all out again, Mum! What's in the green bag, is that important? Mum, Dad's put the green bag next to the bin.'

When we finally left at the allotted time, Dad would produce a detailed, fully annotated schedule for the journey. His time in National Service, in Singapore in the 1950s, had obviously never left him; travelling on holiday was like a military operation. He listed distances between towns, estimated travel times, whether it was an A or B road, or motorway, known roadworks, motorway junctions, and the locations of Little Chef restaurants. There would be a column on the far right where he had his notes, which was actually a list of National Trust houses en route, which we'd visit should we be ahead of schedule. As if by magic, we almost always were ahead of schedule and so found time to visit them!

One of Dad's oldest friends from his university days in London would sometimes surprise us by turning up out of the blue wherever we were on holiday, and I always looked forward to seeing whether George would suddenly appear (as he so often did) which we, as young children, felt was so wonderfully rebellious and exciting!

After the abuse and during my teenage years, excepting my father and brother, George was the only man I implicitly trusted. His influence on me, even years after his passing, continues to guide me. It's so important to have these people in one's life; sadly I never told him how much I valued his integrity, decency and generosity.

My lifelong love of theatre and acting started at my small independent primary school when I was six years old. My drama teacher, Doreen, was a kind, enthusiastic lady, who had a passion for variety entertainment, and she passed this onto me. She and her husband, Bill, became close family friends, and even during my adult life they often came to watch me perform on stage, until she passed away a few years ago. I loved being the centre of attention, despite a natural shyness; I can now remember that I was a polite, imaginative and energetic little boy who loved life. I would go to Doreen's house every Saturday morning for drama workshops, and as the group grew more popular she hired a hall near the sea front, and twenty of us would rehearse and perform songs, comedy monologues, dances and old variety sketches to an invited audience of family and friends throughout the year. I fell in love with the performing arts and dreamt of becoming an actor when I was older. Doreen, this wonderful lady, also influenced my love for the music hall and variety theatre; something I have been fascinated with, and supported, throughout my life.

When I was eight I started at a very traditional English prep school; a large, three-storey Victorian detached house, set in extensive grounds near the sea front, and less than fifteen minutes walk from home. I remember how scared I felt during my interview, before I was offered a place at the school. I had to read aloud a few paragraphs of a classic, probably Dickens, to a stern looking teacher, and was very intimidated by the occasion. I felt I had to suddenly be a grown up, and I didn't want to yet. The school uniform included a red cap for the boys and a red beret for the girls, which inspired the nearby schools to shout 'cherry heads' at us in the street. That was tantamount to a declaration of war, and the annual derby football matches between the schools was keenly awaited, for our honour to be restored.

The Centre of Attention

The huge horse chestnut tree outside the Form Four window inspired the Annual Conker Competition each autumn, which could be quite a painful affair for our knuckles. 'It's all about the technique,' I was told, in confidential tones, by one of the older, spotty-faced 'professionals' in the year above me. Some boys were, perhaps, too obsessed about winning, and rumours went round the school that a few of them had even scaled the school hedge one weekend and stolen the best conkers to switch and use on competition day. Another rumour was that the eventual winner would be touted for international honours.

The annual PE competition was held on the huge back lawn, and we were encouraged to take it very seriously by the teachers. We had regular practices leading up to the big day, and a few of our eagle-eyed classmates were nominated to keep their eyes peeled on the classroom windows for any spies from other years who might dare to steal ideas from our extravagant display. Dressed all in white, each class lined up in front of a panel of judges (this was *The X Factor*, early 80s prep-school-style), and was forced to perform a variety of star jumps, squat thrusts, marching on the spot, and other twists and turns, during a ten minute routine. We were judged on our timing, creativity, individual coordination, and overall uniformity, with points deducted for any mistakes. Long wooden benches were placed on the gravel path alongside the lawn for our somewhat bemused parents to watch from; the whole spectacle took on a minor version of a very poorly orchestrated North Korean military display.

The Fathers v Sons cricket annual match was an opportunity, weather permitting, for a group of typically overweight forty year olds to reel back the years and injure themselves as they seized a rare chance to prove, to their children, that their stories of exaggerated childhood sporting excellence really were true after all. (I hope I remember this, come the time I have children!). Whilst all the events in the school calendar were important, the Sports Day was by far the most eagerly awaited. It was so quintessentially English. We had the usual athletic races, the cricket ball throwing competition, and the long jump. However, most of the parents seemed more interested in taking part in the tug of war, the fathers' 100 yard dash, and the assault course. There were potato sacks to hop in as fast as possible for ten yards, old roadside cones to dribble a football around, and a large cargo net to crawl under, before a final sprint to the finish line.

School lunches were a fairly tasteless two-course affair cooked by a rather decrepit old dear who we could often see through the kitchen window, with a lit cigarette and an inch of fag ash precariously holding on, as she hunched over the cooker stirring our food. Lunch was typically a slice of spam, mashed potato, some beetroot, and very thick, lumpy gravy. Dessert was either apple crumble or chocolate mousse, (which we called moggy's mess, as to our young minds it unfortunately looked like cat faeces).

The teachers were wonderful, if not eccentric, characters who could have been taken from the set of an old Ealing comedy film from the 1950s. The Geography Master lived, so it seemed to me, in his den at the back of the school. He had served in the British army during World War Two, and he often showed us fantastic slides from his postwar travels in Burma and the Himalayas. (These inspired me to travel extensively throughout North India when I was older.) He was a kind man, and passionate about sport. He often let his passion get the better of him when the boys from the local comprehensive school used to maraud across our cricket pitch on their way home; he would chase after them, throwing the stumps! We would cheer him for that, and then have to watch our backs over the weekend in case any of them recognised us in the town centre or on the beach. I eventually rose to the lofty heights of Head Boy and Captain of the 1st XI.

Discipline was strictly enforced by the Headmaster, who employed a fairly liberal application of the cane from time to time, but it was the formidable battleaxe of a French teacher, Mrs Hillman, who terrified everyone, including most of the parents. I remember a school friend was talking to his father outside the school gate, and said, 'Mrs Hillman wants to see you, Dad'. The father, all six foot three of him, looked visibly shocked and, all of a sudden, thirty years younger: 'What do you mean, she wants to see me? I haven't done anything!'.

Mrs Hillman was in her early sixties, with a bright, white crew cut hairstyle. She was rather rotund in shape and devilishly quick across twenty yards. I've no idea if she ever played rugby, but if she did, she would have been a fearsome prop forward for sure. For all this, she was a brilliant teacher. My standard of French, at eleven years of age, was O-level. I and many others in my class regularly passed old exam papers. Each quarter, our disciplinary record would be reviewed by the Headmaster. It was based on a system of conduct plusses and minuses, and God help anyone who had more than three conduct minuses per quarter. One boy somehow managed to get thirty-six conduct minuses, and the rumour went round the school like wildfire one morning;

'They're going to take him to the bottom of the garden at lunchtime today, and shoot him. Yes, it's true. We won't be seeing him again.' It seemed a fait accompli, and when he miraculously appeared for French in the afternoon, a genuine sense of shock went around the school that he had somehow been reprieved. 'Maybe the Pope got involved to save him this time?' was the next rumour to buzz along the corridors. If this were true, he was very fortunate indeed, as we weren't even a Catholic school.

To put this period of my life in writing has helped me to feel more 'whole', in the sense that such an important period of my life did exist, I can remember it, and I had some really good times. Previously, before I came to terms with the PTSD and the most painful memories of the abuse came up, there was a nothingness. If I bumped into a prep school friend, I felt no affinity whatsoever; it was as if I hadn't been there. I can now look back with fondness at the school's quirkiness. These memories have helped me connect to the child within me, and to feel a greater sense of who I am.

During my school years, my parents actively encouraged my love for the stage, and I had singing and acting lessons outside of school. I competed successfully in several Junior Arts Festivals, which helped develop my confidence even more. Acting had become my favourite hobby, and I was performing in full-length plays and cabarets on a regular basis, both at my prep school and in Doreen's drama group in venues around the town. As shy as I felt off stage, I felt alive on stage, and was told by various teachers and parents (mine and friends') that I had a natural talent for acting. I loved to play different roles, and I felt that it gave me a sense of identity. I was known for being a good actor, and could lose myself in the characters I played.

Just as I was reveling in the positive activities of my school years, something negative apart from the abuse (and also starting with 'a': alcohol) entered my life for the first time. As far as I can recall it was during the second year of prep school that I had my first drink of alcohol, the same year the abuse started. It was a glass of Liebfraumilch white wine at a family party at home when I was eight years old. There was a carton of wine in the hallway next to the piano, and I waited for the coast to be clear before I furtively grabbed a glass and poured the wine.

I quickly went to the downstairs toilet nearby, locked the door, pushed the stool in front of the sink, stood on it and watched myself in the mirror gulp the wine down as fast as I could. I remember feeling really sick; I hated the taste but the effect throughout my body was sensational. It felt like a chemical reaction was surging through me, and I felt ALIVE in a way that I never had before. Despite feeling really nauseous I did exactly the same thing a few minutes later. After that first rush of a whole glass of wine, I unlocked the door, opened it, waited for the coast to be clear again and grabbed another glass of wine. I scuttled back to the bathroom, stood on the stool and once again watched myself gulp the wine down as quickly as I could. I wanted more; whilst I hated the taste, I adored the explosive effect throughout every cell of my body; like a firework display inside - I wanted to feel that sense of power again and again.

Thereafter alcohol always fascinated me. I didn't drink often when I was young; my family were very ordinary social drinkers - in fact, alcohol was rarely drunk at home apart from my father having a glass of Ruddles Bitter or cider sometimes on a Saturday lunchtime. My maternal grandfather became an alcoholic in his later life and whilst I only met him perhaps eight times before he died, I thought the world of him. He had always been drinking whenever we visited and I found his behaviour, and his attitude to life, so attractive. I didn't understand why we arrived as early as possible when we visited him during these years but it dawned on me when I got sober: it was to try and see him before he was drunk. One visit, we arrived in time for lunch and he had already drunk a few glasses of whisky and was playfully drunk. My father and brother looked really embarrassed, but I loved it; I wanted to be like him; he seemed so happy, and witty. Somewhere in my mind, I knew this was how to live life. There's a photograph of me in the family photo album at a family reunion, aged eight years, holding a bottle of wine to my mouth at the dinner table – whether I drank any or not I do not recall, but I do remember feeling important and big to have alcohol around me.

It was also in the second year of my prep school that the abuse started, and there is a photograph of me wearing my school cap, jumper and tie looking directly at the camera, with, as I've said before, such a haunted look in my eyes. I don't think anyone else noticed, but to this day I remember full well how I felt when it was taken. I only have two other clear memories of this specific time insofar as the abuse and school are concerned. After PE classes, the boys and girls would change in different rooms, and I'd wait until the girls came in and then flash my penis at them. Looking back, I think this behaviour was some kind of non-verbal cry for help. (I wonder how a child psychologist would approach this now?) My other memory is of being at home, and whenever I was disciplined by my father and sent into the hall as punishment, I would become hysterical. This was when Peter Sutcliffe, the Yorkshire Ripper, was on the run, and for some reason, I feared he might be hiding in the front porch.... so every time I was sent into the hall, I was terrified he would attack me. Mum would come out and console me, but I never told her or anyone else what was going on in my mind. The fear felt very real to me.

I presume I had made the mental association between the men abusing me, and what I had heard on the BBC about the Ripper attacking his victims under the cover of darkness, and linked the two in my mind. I have no memory of the paedophiles mentioning him to me, but they might well have done as another means of threatening and silencing me. When you've been abused, you know that anything is possible, and consequently the mind creates many nightmare scenarios.

There were obvious signs from my young age that something was wrong. Whenever I was bullied at my preparatory school and public school, I always reacted the same way; I would completely freeze, I would never defend myself. I would stand and take it, not because I was a 'hard man' but because I was crippled by the fear of what would happen if I challenged the bully. Something inside me, no doubt from the abuse, was convinced that if I fought back or resisted in any way, it would get much, much worse. Sometimes the bully at school would grab my throat and start to squeeze until someone intervened, and even then I could not override the shock I would feel which had prevented me from reacting. So I'd take it, often quite literally on the chin, and I'd fantasise how I would destroy the bully later. The rage I felt inside terrified me.

During the early 1980s, when I wasn't at school I would often be at singing lessons with a professional teacher, rehearsing for either the next Junior Arts competitions in Speech and Drama, or another play, or in the nets at my local cricket club, with whom I played during the summer. Life was really busy, and until I was older enough to look after myself, Mum would chauffeur me to and fro, and of course pay the fees for the classes. In the spring of 1983, when I was eleven years old, I joined the youth section of an amateur dramatics society which performed twice a year at the main professional theatre in the town. I suddenly felt I was an adult, rehearsing in a professional environment and then performing in a 700 seat theatre! During the next few years I had various roles in cabarets and sketch shows, and plays including *The Wizard of Oz, Cinderella, Toad of Toad Hall,* and the lead roles of Robin Hood in *Robin Hood*, Prince Charming in *Cinderella*, Christopher Rattenbury in Terrence Rattigan's *Cause Célèbre*, and John Darling in J M Barrie's *Peter Pan*.

During the first six months of 1985, the rehearsal period for *Peter Pan*, I felt a real sense of freedom, and an enthusiasm for the future. The memories of the abuse were buried so deep I was rarely conscious of them; at least there were no visual memories; furthermore, the bully at prep school had moved to another school. There were rarely any triggers to what I would later learn was PTSD. One of these would be sexual attraction, but as I had yet to reach puberty, this still lay in the future. It was later the same year, as I describe in more detail shortly, that I reached puberty, and suddenly became aware of that I was sexually attracted to girls. The sexual energy I felt triggered off the trauma from the abuse, and I felt a sense of horror and shame at the idea of physical intimacy.

I felt very shy around female attention even before I hit puberty; I found it unsettling, so whenever anyone flirted with me I acted as if I was not aware of it or that I was not interested. I learnt to lie to myself and others about my feelings, to protect myself from being hurt. And long as I could lose myself in the characters I played on stage, for the time being, I was happy.

I was so excited to be cast as John in *Peter Pan*. I was twelve years old, and had a lead role in a huge production with a cast of over sixty, and I would learn to 'fly' over the audience! The 'flying' involved an elaborate system of wires which ran on tracks through the grid above the stage, and a team of four men (who looked liked bell ringers) in the wings who were responsible for attaching the wires to a harness worn by each of the 'flying' actors. If the wires got twisted, there was a problem, and if a wire somehow 'escaped' from a harness there was a serious problem. Both happened, but never the latter whilst the actor was in the air, thankfully. The harness was a simple, leather contraption which was very uncomfortable and so I stuffed socks around my genitals to protect them. The actor's end of the wire was attached to the harness using a thin metal rod and an elastic band.

This production was so important to my sense of purpose in life. It brought about a deep realisation that the theatre was where I belonged, and the energy backstage and on stage I found incredibly healing and life-affirming. I could relate to that well-worn phrase:,'the smell of the greasepaint, the roar of the crowd.' It has only been very recently that I can remember in detail how excited I felt signing in at the stage door; having my makeup applied in the basement; getting into costume; feeling the buzz of excitement from the audience as they settled into their seats; the orchestra warming up (well, the piano and drums); and then being called to the wings. I can even remember my opening line,

'Coming mother, we're playing at being you and father. A little less noise there.'

I loved the attention I received for my acting; I loved being acknowledged. I felt alive.

It was also the first time I smoked cannabis. Unlike today, smoking cigarettes was then allowed in the dressing rooms. I was hanging around the pirates' dressing room when they received their cue over the backstage tannoy to go to the wings. One of the pirates had been smoking what I thought was a cigarette, and as he left the dressing room, he was adamant I was not to light it up. He had left it next to the sink (presumably to flush it away if anyone had questioned the smell). I couldn't resist the temptation, and as soon as he left the room I lit it, and had the most amazing buzz as I inhaled my first ever joint.

In the 'home under the ground' scene ten minutes later (during which Captain Hook attempts to poison Peter, but is saved when Tinkerbell drinks it instead), I had an uncontrollable giggle fit for several minutes on stage (I recall my fellow actors looking at me somewhat bewildered), and soon after, in my dressing room, my first attack of the munchies. I stuffed as much chocolate down my throat as possible, as a few of the pirates walked past my dressing room looking rather alarmed. Regardless of the cannabis, that wonderful production of *Peter Pan* was, without question, the most enjoyable time of my teenage years, and a turning point in my life; I knew then that I wanted to work in the professional theatre when I was older.

Other than gulping the two glasses of Liebfraumilch in the bathroom when I was eight years old, alcohol did not play any role in my life at that time. The only incident I can recall was at my parents' 25th wedding anniversary in 1984 when I was 12 years old. I nominated myself to look after the bar and would take the empties outside as often as I could, and would drink whatever I had spirited away behind the hall without anyone knowing. The buzz came back; I adored the feeling that rushed throughout my body. The effects of both the alcohol and the cannabis would be sought after and repeated on a regular basis as I struggled to deal with life.

It was during the latter half of 1985 that I felt a shift within me take place. I was on holiday with a friend and his family at Trewan Hall, a campsite in Cornwall, and I had my first crush. I saw a really pretty blonde girl, appearing to be slightly older than me, playing with a kite on a large lawn near to the main house, but was too shy to say anything or to join in. I admired her from the path, and immediately placed her on a pedestal and in the category of 'out of my league'; a pattern which I have unfortunately followed most of my life whenever I've been attracted to someone. I think I hit puberty at this time, as I felt such a change take place within me. I had an innocence during *Peter Pan*; I knew I was still a child, but now a few months later, I felt I was an adult, and that terrified me.

I started to feel very unsafe for no apparent reason. On the surface everything looked and felt fine; I could flick a switch in my mind and 'act' so no one knew what was going on beneath. I was quite popular with my fellow pupils, and the teachers. But I had begun to feel threatened by the physical presence of certain men, scared of being attacked, even at times with men I knew and had no reason to question or distrust; I would feel dirty, have an overwhelming feeling that something dreadful would be about to happen, and be full of shame and panic if a girl smiled at me; and I began to withdraw within myself and feel so confused as to who the hell I was. Fears of being restricted or restrained stayed with me for many years into my adulthood; I had to feel in control to the extent that even as an adult I would force myself to stay awake on public transport so no one could take advantage of me in any way. Similarly I would avoid using a urinal in a public toilet, and would only use a cubicle; I would sit feeling very anxious with my arm extended in front of me in fear that the door might be forced open. My rucksack with school books would be placed against the door if I had it with me.

There were some other obvious changes taking place. When I had a bath, I felt a disgust with my naked body and hated looking at or touching my penis. There's a photograph in the family album of me holding three cups I had won for athletics at my prep school sports day about the same time, and I remember feeling shame all through me as Mum and Dad told me how proud they were of me. When Mum said that I looked so handsome, internally I recoiled with disgust: I felt I did not deserve any compliments.

I also started to stare at and taunt myself in the bathroom mirror. I would look and demand of myself,

'What is wrong with you? What the hell is happening to you?'

I now started to question whether I could really trust the people I once assumed were 'safe' to be around. I looked for ulterior motives in their actions; I needed to know I was 'safe', a word which kept coming into my mind in most situations. I looked for evidence of duplicity in behaviour. I'd analyse how men spoke and what they did during rehearsal or church. I was convinced that most men probably had a sick, ulterior motive in any given situation.

In 1987, I left my prep school for a larger, independent all-boys school an hour's journey from home. Set on the top of a hill, with thirty foot high walls and a gatehouse (which opened the way to eighty or so steep, stone steps leading to the main building, and then a huge, blue main door), it reminded me of Colditz Castle. I don't remember any barbed wire or Alsatians, but nonetheless it was imposing, to say the least, for a new boy. Whilst I was lazy academically, there was plenty of success away from the classroom. I was a regular member of the 1st XV in rugby, using my pace to score many tries. I was House Captain, Captain of the 1st XI in cricket, and an excellent track athlete, each year winning the 100m, 200m, 400m and 800m. In my final year, I won the Drama Award for my performance of Baker in Tom Stoppard's *Dogg's Hamlet and Cahoot's Macbeth*.

The reason I list all these achievements is because I was obsessed with winning; I had to win, and yet as soon as I had won, there was no pleasure or any sense of satisfaction inside me. I could easily fake the external reactions, and pretend to be happy, but I felt I didn't deserve any compliments or acknowledgement. The shame crippled any notion of being worthy of any success whatsoever, of being worthy of anything positive in my life. The voices in my head were savage and unforgiving. The more successful I was at something, the more self-hatred and self-harming (such as punching myself in the face, and sometimes head butting my bedroom wall) took place. The recurring thought in my mind was, 'If you really knew everything about me...' I felt I didn't deserve to feel good about myself, I didn't deserve to have success.

Looking back, the psychological consequences of the abuse was becoming more real to me by the age of sixteen. As friends started dating and having girlfriends, I could no longer pretend I was shy or not interested. The peer pressure was such that oblivion was my only option. To kill the flashbacks which were happening on a more regular basis, I had to destroy the emotional and mental pain. Every time I played rugby the PTSD was triggered, and I would psyche myself up and at some level of my consciousness I would imagine the opposition player was a paedophile; it wasn't a clear, conscious thought but I would feel such rage towards him, I would tackle him as hard as possible to try to maim him. I wouldn't break the rules, but it meant running at him at full pelt to tackle and really hurt him, and that's what I would do.

In some ways I felt relieved there were no girls at the school as it was easier to maintain the image I was projecting of being a relaxed, 'Jack the Lad' type. The downside was that I started to place girls on a higher pedestal the older I became. The more I was attracted to them, the uglier and smellier I felt inside myself, which would trigger the mirror-taunting as soon as I got home. I felt completely inadequate, emotionally and sexually, and out of my depth around girls I was attracted to. When anyone noticed my interest, and encouraged me to ask one of them out for a date, I would lie and invent an imaginary girlfriend who lived further away, to keep any girls or any more questions at a distance from me. I'm not suggesting I had a queue of would-be girlfriends, but as soon as I had a whiff of any possible interest I closed down immediately. Sometimes the trigger was so sudden, it shocked me and who ever I was with. On the coach home after school one day, I was talking to a girl (who I liked as a friend) and she told me of a mutual friend who really fancied me, and I felt sick to the stomach, my lower back tensed up, and I instinctively shut down emotionally. I projected in my mind's eye that I would be attacked and humiliated if the girl and I

The Centre of Attention

ever met up. I felt so physically and mentally threatened hearing this girl was attracted to me, the 'fight or flight' response immediately kicked in, and I remained hyper-vigilant for several days. I later avoided both girls whenever I saw them in the town centre.

My friend on the coach sensed my sudden change in behaviour; she described it some years later as a cold, panicky energy coming from me:

'You suddenly looked like a very scared rabbit in the headlights, Matt.'

At the time, I felt such shame and confusion about this, and as alcohol changed the way I felt in helping me block out this reaction, replacing it with a feeling of euphoria, I drank more and more whenever I could. It was the obvious solution, it seemed. By my mid-teens alcohol was a point of obsession to me. I would watch a British comedy-drama TV programme, *Auf Wiedersehen Pet*, which followed the lives of seven construction workers on building sites abroad, and it often revolved around them drinking alcohol in bars. I really wished I was with them drinking, and couldn't wait to be old enough to drink properly.

One occasion was a warning of the chaos to come. I was drinking from a bottle of Cointreau, which was 40% alcohol proof, with a friend in the bandstand of a town centre park, and we both became intoxicated very quickly. We made our way to a multi storey car park where we decided it would be a good idea to have a competition to see who could throw the four foot long fluorescent lights, which illuminated the garage, the furthest. The car park overlooked a busy walkway connecting to the bustling High Street nearby, and we took turns to see whether we could throw the tubes like javelins over the pedestrians to the roof of a shop on the other side. We then staggered to the car park toilet and were urinating in the latrine when a large, smartly dressed businessman came in. My friend, Jonathan, who was taller than me, had managed to cut himself on one of the lights, and had blood all over his right hand. In his drunken state he stumbled on the step of the latrine as he was urinating, and to try and steady himself, he grabbed hold of the businessman standing next to him, getting blood all over his shirt. The businessman was understandably furious. He pushed my friend away and pulled up his trouser zip. He then looked at me falling about and laughing at the other end of the latrine. He walked over to me and started punching me; I was so drunk, I didn't try to defend myself and it only stopped when Jonathan intervened. The businessman then grabbed his briefcase and stormed out, swearing at us.

The shock that occurs to me, as I write this, is that this particular public toilet was one of very few located near to the sea front that I hadn't been sexually abused in when I was a child. After I'd recovered from the effects of the alcohol, it never, ever occurred to me that, in my drunken state in the car park, I might I have injured or blinded someone, and I thank God that no one had been hurt. The memory of this behaviour came to me when I was fifteen years sober, and I was horrified to recall it. I never drank Cointreau again, but strangely whenever I was hung-over thereafter I could always taste Cointreau in my mouth.

My love of acting also created opportunities to drink more often. By the time I was sixteen years old, and looking older due to my receding hairline, evening rehearsals were eagerly anticipated as I could get served in the pubs nearby without any questions about my age. I was rehearsing for the musical *Godspell* at the local theatre, and one evening had a lift home with a fellow cast member. She told me she was really worried about her eldest son, Robert, who was drinking too much. Whilst most people would have felt empathy for her situation, I recognised a fellow drinker and called him the following day and suggested we meet for a drink. We got on like a house on fire, and soon were regular and very heavy drinking partners. If Robert won on the horses (which became a rare occurrence the more we drank together, as his skill at betting deteriorated due to his drinking) or otherwise had the money he would leave his calling card – an empty can of Special Brew – by the front gate of my house for me to see when I arrived home from school, and I would make up a story for Mum and join him in town for another drinking session.

Mum would often stay up late and wait for me to come in to make sure I was okay. Knowing this, and wanting to hide my drinking as much as possible, I would slap myself around the face quite hard as I walked down the road, and as soon as I was inside the house, I'd splash water over my face to sober up as much as possible. The plan was to quickly pop my head around the lounge door and say a quick 'Hi, I'm home. I'm tired, so going straight to bed'. It sometimes worked, but other times Mum would be suspicious and would ask me where I'd been, and what I'd been doing. I became quite adept at lying to her, particularly about how much I'd had to drink to keep her off my back. Mum and Dad did confront me on a number

The Centre of Attention

of occasions, but such was my deceit they had no idea how heavy my drinking had become. I managed to hide it from them, mostly.

Whenever I picked up a drink I got drunk, and I absolutely loved it. It would block out my paralysing thoughts of self-hatred and suppress my fears and I would, for a short while, kid myself that I was a witty, confident, and a 'life and soul of the party' type. I wanted to be noticed this way as well; I wanted the reputation of being a charming, roguish character, and alcohol did an amazing job of making me feel like this. It was a sham, of course, but I held onto this as long as I could. There was an advert on TV when I was a teenager for Skol lager - it was not particularly original or creative, as it simply had a chorus of 'Skol, Skol, Skol etc...' This became my psyching up mantra as I walked into town, desperate to get drunk, as a teenager. The goal was to get the buzz I always got, and to feel alive again. Inside I felt intimidated, I lacked confidence and felt I needed to pretend to be confident, and booze helped me do this. I soon started drinking with other problem drinkers in the bars if I could; they would not question how much I wanted to drink, although within time some would;

'People say you are a nice guy, Matt, but you drink far too much. You are always drunk.'

I took this as a compliment, a badge of honour. I felt I'd arrived, I'd achieved something. I had a bizarre romantic notion that being drunk was the answer to life. I had always thought drunks were the salt of the earth. In my warped mind they somehow had wisdom about them, and they had learnt how to live through the University of Life. When I drank, the chemical effect on me felt like rocket fuel; it felt like the missing part of my DNA, and I could not understand anyone who drank halves or, God forbid, soft drinks. These social drinkers ought to be banned from bars, it seemed to me... there was something wrong with them! When I was seventeen years old, I was invited to a New Year's Eve party held at the home of one of the theatre's backstage crew. At the party I was, of course, drunk and took exception to one of the guests who was nursing a soft drink. I insisted that he join me for a proper drink, and when he continued to politely refuse, I became more irritated. I am grateful now that our host intervened before I became too rude, as the guest happened to be former Lightweight World Boxing Champion Barry McGuigan. He was a true gentleman, thankfully.

As my drinking became heavier, I developed a difficulty in urinating without considerable pain, both physical, and psychological. I needed to have a bursting bladder in order to force the urine through my penis; anything less and I could not urinate at all. I felt so ashamed and humiliated and eventually told Mum who, through my GP, arranged for flow tests at the local hospital. This involved drinking until my bladder was full, and then urinating into a tube. The time it took to pass the urine was then evaluated as to whether the flow was regarded as normal. The tests always came back as normal, and I could only assume the flow tests tested just the flow from the moment of release rather than from the first intention to urinate. I underwent an MRI and was encouraged to have an operation on the urethra in my penis, which had a slight stricture in it. This whole process triggered off immense shame within me, especially as it seemed there was something wrong with my penis. That it was 'broken' in some way. I had the operation, and was prescribed antibiotics to help deal with the risk of infection, along with painkillers to handle the rawness of the urethra, which had had a rod inserted in it. I was warned to not drink under any circumstances, but on a night out a few days later, after a few drinks I started projectile vomiting with such violence I was really scared whether about whether or not I would survive.

A few years later I learned my lesson. This was when I had food poisoning at university. I remembered what the reaction of antibiotics and alcohol could be, and decided to ditch the former and continue with the latter. The consequences, needless to say, were horrendous. I had agonising pain in my abdomen, I lost control of my anal muscles (I literally shit myself several times every day until the poison was out of my system), and I projectile vomited so often and so aggressively there was blood.

Three months after the operation on the urethra in my penis, I was a member of the school 1st XV that visited Germany for a rugby competition. We were joined by school teams from eight other countries from around the world. On the ferry across the channel, the bar opened thirty minutes after leaving port, and closed thirty minutes before docking, and I drank solidly throughout the crossing, then awoke on a packed landing to find fellow travellers walking over me to get to the lifts. Two nights later, a reception was held at a posh city centre hotel with civic dignitaries and there were free drinks. After a three course meal and plenty of free booze, I was suitably fortified and decided to organise a bar crawl with a hundred drunken teenage rugby players in the city centre. Needless to say, the sight of so many of us marauding through the streets created tension and alarm, and the bars were advised to close by the police as a result of our raucous behaviour. We didn't actually do any harm; no damage to property was done. Our most violent act was probably our dreadful singing.

Drinking was now obsessive, and accelerated greatly when I was attracted to girls. Any sexual attraction would trigger horrible, irrational fears of being ridiculed and humiliated by the girls I fancied, or of being attacked by their brothers and fathers, or by complete strangers. The feelings were overwhelming; whilst I was not conscious of visual memories from the abuse, the feelings of desperation and utter despair were with me most days. I craved the attention of women and would force myself to flirt as best I could. But when I got the attention it filled me with horror as I tried to handle the emotional flashbacks and overpowering feelings of panic and a fear of the abyss opening up.

Friends would be dating and would sometimes invite me on a double date and I would find any excuse not to go, which in turn would make me feel more self-loathing. I started flirting with one girl called Sam who went to a school near to mine, and who lived quite near me. We caught a different coach each day from the same stop on the sea front, and would catch each other's eye from time to time at the bus stop as we waited for the coaches to arrive. After a while it dawned on me that Sam liked me. I was paralysed with terror as usual, and convinced myself that I didn't find her attractive. I imagined scenarios in which she was controlling and horrible towards me to convince myself that underneath her friendliness, she was actually a bit crazy, and would only hurt me... But then I became consumed with feelings that if I ignored Sam completely, she would be really angry with me, and tell her friends I liked her and was playing games, and that this would lead to me being attacked. I never told anyone I was thinking this, as I was too scared to let anyone into my inner world. If I saw Sam in town I would completely avoid her unless I had been drinking. After a few drinks, I would feel slightly more confident (my fears did not feel quite as overwhelming when I was drunk), but I was still too intimidated to say anything to her. There was no such thing as Dutch courage; alcohol never gave me the confidence to chat women up. Then a friend, Ian, told me Sam really liked me, but that she wondered why I never talked to her.

To try and overcome my feelings of fear and shame, I had to psyche myself up to speak to her. I managed to do this a few days later, and we agreed to meet for a drink in a local bar. I arrived early, two hours early, and began drinking as I was terrified what might happen when Sam got to know me a little… and then she arrived. It was so humiliating. I was sitting at a table with a friend who did not know that Sam and I had arranged to meet up. Sam, and her friend, came over and sat down opposite us, and for what felt like the longest hour of my life I sat there too terrified to even acknowledge her. I couldn't look at her, and I was literally crippled with horrendous fear of… I couldn't tell you then what I actually was scared of, but it was a dread of the unknown. So I completely ignored her for the hour she was sitting there. Every now and then she would look at me, albeit briefly, and I presumed she was expecting me to say something. But I was in a state of shock. I didn't realise it at the time; I just kept taunting myself, 'what the fuck is wrong with you? You are pathetic. You are a horrible, dirty c*nt…They'll get you for this… they'll find you and get you.' After an hour she and her friend stood up and walked out.

I felt relief but hated myself for being such a coward. Later that night, when I got home, I started punching myself in the face as hard as I could. I stared at myself in the mirror, and taunted myself again verbally,

'You fucking cowardly c*nt. You are pathetic and vile. You are nothing, nothing. C*nt, c*nt, c*nt…'

In following days, I tried to avoid her as much as possible, as well as anyone we knew in common, which was probably thirty people. I was traumatised by the experience, or maybe it was that I was traumatised by the thoughts and emotions that had been triggered off. I dreaded it when I found any girl attractive, and would try to suppress the emotions. I seriously considered finding a pill which would kill the sexual energy. The trauma from the abuse that had been triggered off was too painful to live with; the overwhelming sense of being consumed, of being attacked, of being destroyed was so real to me I drank more aggressively than ever before.

A few months after I had been too scared to talk on the date with Sam, I saw a beautiful blonde girl walk into a bar one evening, and I was head over heels 'in love'. Whenever I saw her, I noticed that she received a huge amount of attention, judging by the heads that turned when she walked into a café or a bar. A number of my friends acknowledged that they found her very attractive as well. I said nothing but admired her from afar. But when you are a drunk, being subtle is impossible and soon she became aware of my looking over shyly at her. She would occasionally flirt around me, and the more this happened the more I was convinced she was taking the piss out of me because, in truth, I could not believe that such a beautiful woman could possibly find me attractive. I started writing down the occasions (at least those I could remember) when she looked over at me and smiled. I treated this as possible evidence that she either really did like me, or that she was flirting with me which would end up with me being attacked.

Whilst I became convinced she was 'playing' me, I still fell for her and would do anything to be with her. One night, whilst very drunk and stoned, I wrote her a love poem and bribed a friend with a few drinks and a joint to deliver it in the early hours of the following morning. At the same time a drinking partner had started to attract unwanted attention from a number of guys who would hang around with her. There were physical threats to both of us, which led to a fight at a house party one night. The two of us were outnumbered and, being rather worse for wear, I said rather stupidly:

'If you've got a problem with me, let's sort it out'... which inevitably led to me being punched in the face, and an old-fashioned free-for-all brawl started.

My friend and I both came off quite lightly, but the emotional memories of the abuse, specifically of being surrounded by men who were physically threatening me, had triggered the PTSD and I wanted revenge. Whilst my friend thought it best to chill out I felt such venomous rage I wanted to pay for some guys to hunt them down and put them in intensive care. I would then go in and rip the tubes out. This sick thinking scared me, and was completely out of character; I was, after all, terrified of violence and avoided it at all costs but here I was dreaming up a vile plan to seriously hurt some guys who, like me, got into a fight when they were drunk. I was getting a kick out of the fantasy of seriously hurting them. After a few weeks, this thinking gradually subsided, but my desire to exact such revenge continued to really scare me; I knew there was something seriously wrong.

Throughout my twenties, this desire for revenge towards the men who had abused me would surface only and whenever the PTSD was triggered. I would then fantasise about hunting them down and killing them. The fantasy was the same each time. I would find them one by one; use a baseball bat to put them in intensive care; and then go in at night and rip the tubes out so they'd have an agonising death. It gave me a momentary sense of power over the flashbacks I was getting. I always recognised this was my suppressed rage, but it was so difficult to let it go. When I first had Cognitive Behaviour Therapy (CBT) when I was twenty years old and recounted these fantasies to a Clinical Psychologist at the local hospital, he made the position very clear:

'You need to know how ill you really are, Matthew. You are a danger to yourself, no question, but are also a potential danger to other people. If I had known you when you were drinking, I would have sectioned you, without question. If you drink again, I will section you indefinitely.'

It would be many years before I was able to let go of these fantasises, and to finally 'forgive' the men who abused me. I learnt in AA that this rage was destroying my peace and health; it didn't have any affect on them at all, so I prayed for years for the willingness and strength to let go of this rage and to be able to heal at a much deeper level. It was in 2006, (when I was thirty-four years old) and during a guided meditation at a healing centre in Brazil, that I sensed that the time had come; that I was finally ready to let go. Forgiving the paedophiles was incredibly difficult; I had wanted them to feel the pain and trauma I had been carrying all these years. I felt it was my right to have revenge; the resentment towards them, and the fantasy to torture them had felt so empowering; the exact opposite to what I felt as a child when they were abusing me. Yet I came to realise that I was hurting myself by refusing to come to a place of acceptance, and forgiveness.

I realised, too, that I am not an aggressive, vengeful person; any attempt to fulfil this fantasy would have been contrary to my true nature. It helped me hugely to realise that forgiveness does not release the men from their karmic responsibility; it simply releases my emotional connection to them and allows me to heal. It was a conscious decision, and as far as my ongoing spiritual journey is concerned, only the decision to remain sober on a daily basis has been more important. I had to be sober to forgive them, no question. I describe the experience of forgiveness in more detail in the *In Heaven and Earth* chapter, and it was a life-changing moment. Once the decision had been taken, I felt a dark energy leave my body through my shoulders; the desire to hunt them down, hurt them and to then kill them has never since come back.

The Centre of Attention

It was 1989; I was seventeen years old, living at home with my parents and escaping more and more into a world of fantasy. I had started reading David Niven's *The Moon's a Balloon*, which relates the most wonderful stories of Niven and Errol Flynn's outrageous adventures during the Golden Years of Hollywood. Inspired by these stories, I cooked up a bizarre plan to steal a sheep and place it in the Headmaster's office at school, as a means of achieving some form of attention and notoriety. Robert, my regular drinking partner, and I took this plot very seriously, and after a detailed reccy of possible targets we bought black face paint, gloves, balaclavas, and enough booze to do the job... or so we thought. After a few drinks in a local bar to get us in the mood we drove twenty miles to just outside the city and parked the car by a gate in a wooded area, and walked into the field. Then we discovered that the reality of chasing and capturing a sheep was much more difficult than we ever imagined. They were fast and elusive buggers, and with the school Sports Day only three days away, I became worried that if I couldn't catch a 'docile' sheep, how the hell was I to win the 100, 200, 400 and 800 metre races I had won in recent years!

After forty-five minutes of diving in the mud we finally gave up, and drove into the city centre where Robert dropped me off near the school, before driving home. The school had a mixture of boarders and day boys, and the staff had been oblivious to the fact that the boarders had, for years, snuck out at night to go clubbing, before creeping back in again during the early hours unnoticed. I'd been told of a specific location, behind the art school, where I could climb over the wall and slip into the boarding wing without needing to open any doors or gates. In the morning, however, I was still rather inebriated to the extent I had not washed from the night before, and during the first period, the shocked Geography Master ordered me to clean myself up in the showers. When I returned to the school for an Open Day some ten years later, one of the teachers asked me about the sheep escapade, to which I reluctantly and with much embarrassment admitted that the failed attempt was indeed true.

I was already starting to crack up; I knew I was living a lie and I lived as much as possible in a fantasy world where I momentarily felt safer, but my the fears were not being drowned by the alcohol despite my regular binging. Getting to oblivion as quickly as possible had been the only answer. Increasingly, though, the self-hatred within me developed and I felt such intense rage for my perceived failings, I would often punch myself in the face (usually on the forehead) and head butt walls. No one saw this happening. After most drinking sessions I would go home, and stare and shout at myself in the mirror. Rather like the character Travis Bickle, played by Robert De Niro in Martin Scorsese's 1976 film, *Taxi Driver*, I would taunt myself verbally in the mirror;

'What the fuck are you looking at you c*nt? Fuck Off, Fuck Off...'

I couldn't stand the sight of myself; I hated seeing myself in a mirror or as a reflection in a shop window. I had tried to masturbate but couldn't do it; I couldn't get an erection. I hated looking at and holding my penis even when urinating. I hated anyone touching me; I especially panicked when a woman kissed me, as I felt so dirty that I thought I might contaminate her in some way. When I felt sexually interested, I would experience a dirty tension in my groin. I was continuing to blockade myself into urinal cubicles, fearing someone would push in and attack me. I felt such a sense of disgust with my body, and my thoughts were savage in their judgement and condemnation of everything I did. On the very rare occasions I was kissed on the lips, I would have a sudden fear I would suffocate. In fact, I often wondered what the hell was wrong with women who found me attractive; I found it hard to believe they did, and if they persisted with smiling at me I now considered this to be aggressive.

I had lost any real sense of identity, of who the hell I was; like most teenagers I wanted to fit in, to be liked, to find my way through the myriad of hormonal and social challenges... but I was fighting my inner demons, and these were now being triggered on a daily basis. The memories of the abuse had been buried so deeply that when triggered the intense panic created shock in my mind, and I would feel physically sick to my stomach that something terrible would happen. Without the visual memories being in my conscious mind, the mental agony and physical tension drove me further insane.

I loved being drunk, I hated being sober. Getting drunk was the only way to drown the feelings and thoughts, and I would do anything to get hold of enough alcohol to reach the oblivion I now craved. On Christmas Day 1990, when I was eighteen years old, I remember staring for a minute at a ¾ full bottle of methylated spirit in my parents' utility room, and the thought came to me; 'if I drink this I probably have a drink problem'. I was scared that I was even thinking of drinking meths, but it was a credible option. I didn't drink it, but it showed how desperate I had become to get alcohol into my system.

Despite the drinking, I had somehow gained a B, D and E in my A Levels, which was a huge surprise to me considering how little attention I paid in lessons and my distinct lack of revision. My tutor had told me that, if I actually decided to work hard and revise, I might get two B's and a C, but he knew I wouldn't bother, and so did I. Whilst the results did not matter to me, I was desperate to get away from home, to reinvent myself somewhere else, so finding a course was imperative. This important decision was delegated to my brother, who was seriously ill and bedridden with glandular fever. I told him that his goal was to get me onto a drama course anywhere. My goal was to go to the pub and get drunk. I received offers from a handful of universities and decided on Lincoln, where I would study English, Drama and Psychology. A few months later, I moved into a shared house near the city centre, where there were four bars on my street within one hundred metres (and many others nearby I noticed), and I was fifteen minutes away from the campus. I was determined this would be a new start.

My first night in my new home was a forerunner of what was to come. I left home at 7pm to visit a few bars and made a mental note as I walked of the route I was taking – two right turns, walk two hundred metres and then one left just needed to be reversed and I would be home. After the usual skinful, as I walked out of the bar I forgot to reverse my route and ended up wandering on a vast industrial estate on the edge of the town for the next six hours. There were no taxis in sight and no mobile phones in those days, and after a while I was sober again, which was hell as I had the delirium tremens (DTs), and started to experience horrendous withdrawals as my body demanded more alcohol. College life became a daily alcohol-fuelled misadventure; and within a short time my reputation for being drunk had become widely noticed by my peers. Drinking with the rugby team soon gained me the nickname Terry Fuckwit (from *Viz* magazine); a character who, as the name suggests, was always a drunken slob, with a fag hanging out of his mouth – it was an accurate description! I was quite proud of the reputation, unfortunately (which led me to maintain it). I would regularly miss tutorials, prompting my tutor to tell me when I turned up for the first time:

'Well Matthew, we eventually meet, at last!' I apologised for being late, saying I had a few problems with the landlord, to which she replied without missing a beat, 'Which pub?'

A few weeks later, I was cast in the Alan Ayckbourn play *Just Between Ourselves*, but was so drunk I forgot to turn up for the technical rehearsal. This was nothing, though, compared to the time when I woke up with severe palpitations and the delirium tremens, during which I had an horrific hallucination and saw Hitler, Mussolini and Stalin standing around my bed, looking down and staring at me. My physical health became even more desperate when I drunkenly tried cooking mouldy bacon, and of course became very ill with food poisoning.

Even during the agony I felt in my lower abdomen I still continued to drink, but on several occasions during three hellish days my anal muscles were not working. I was quite literally shitting myself as I walked to get my next alcoholic drink. I went to my GP who questioned me about my drinking. I lied, needless to say, but he didn't believe me, and told me not to drink anything with the antibiotics he was prescribing. The prescription was binned as soon as I left the surgery. I knew there was no way I could not drink, even with the acute pain I had. Shortly afterwards, I remember sitting in a pub toilet cubicle with four pints of Stella lager at my feet, trying to work out how the hell I was going to get pissed. The alcohol was simply pouring through me. I thought; if I had a syringe, I could inject the alcohol directly into my bloodstream but there was no syringe so I sat there with a mouth full of alcohol wondering whether it might soak through into my veins somehow! I was crazy, but getting drunk was more important to me than anything else, including recovering from food poisoning.

I moved out of my original digs and into a shared house with five other students on the other side of the city centre; one of whom was Helen, who became my regular drinking and pot smoking partner. Sixty cigarettes and several joints on top of the alcohol binges was a daily routine by now. Helen was into the Occult in a big way; her fascination was Tarot Cards, ley lines and Spiritualism, which I vocally dismissed as ridiculous. One time we were on a pub crawl, during the 1991 Rugby World Cup, and at the end of a daylong drinking session we ended up in a dive of a bar for last orders. We settled at a table, and Helen pulled out a deck of Tarot Cards and insisted I give her a reading.

'No I won't. It's a load of rubbish. I don't believe in it at all. Do you want another drink?'

'No', she replied mischievously, 'I want you to give me a reading'.

Helen went on and on, so I finally gave in and decided I would make it all up and then carry on drinking. We pushed the empty glasses out of the way, and I started to lay the cards out, but Helen then grabbed them, telling me,

'You're not doing it properly. I'll lay them out and then you give me a reading.'

'Alright,' I replied. 'You're the boss, you get on with it, and then I'll waffle for a minute, and then we'll carry on drinking.'

Helen lay the cards out, and I looked at them for ten seconds perhaps, thinking to myself 'What the hell am I going to say?' I didn't understand what the elaborate designs on them symbolised, and the names at the bottom of the cards such as The Fool, The Magician, The Hanged Man, and words such as justice, strength, and death were off-putting, to say the least. I'd never had a Tarot reading before, but my ignorance of how it worked was clearly irrelevant, as when I looked at the cards over the course of the next minute or so my consciousness started to change, and I began to very quickly sober up. It was as if a channel of communication had opened up in my consciousness and I was able to access detailed information about Helen's childhood. I 'saw' a film on a screen in my mind which was not from my life, but I knew it was authentic; I knew this was not my imagination. Coming after several hours of drinking, this sudden change of events shocked me, and I knew something bizarre was going on. I sensed information coming from, or through, the cards about Helen's childhood, which I had known nothing about. I 'saw' a long hill, and a row of houses, and I 'heard' the word 'Exeter'. The vision focussed on one house in particular; I saw the front door, and as the vision continued I saw the wallpaper on the stairs, the bathroom at the top, I saw a bedroom, and I heard two voices; an older man and a young girl. I intuitively knew this was Helen and her uncle and that he was or had been sexually abusing her, although I did not 'see' the abuse.

The impact of this knowledge was both emotionally upsetting to me, and shocking in its detail. It was, after all, the first time I had ever 'received' a clairvoyant message from the spirit world, and I worried how the hell I should communicate this vision to Helen. I sensed that however I described the vision, she would know and be understandably really upset. Her expected reaction, concerning such a painful experience, frightened me.

She could tell from my face something had 'come through'; 'What is it? What can you see? I know you've seen something.'

I slowly started to explain what I had 'seen'. As much as I could, I wanted to try and prepare her for what I was about to say..

'Umm. Right. Well.... I can see a house....it's at the top of a hill, and..... I've been told it's in Exeter.'

She immediately reacted, 'Oh my God, you know....... You know what happened.' Then she broke down in tears. I touched her hand to comfort her, and felt moved by her obvious distress. I continued, and spoke with as much compassion as I could,

'It's alright.... I haven't been shown anything, but yes, I know... I know what happened.'

She asked me, through her shock and tears,

'What have you been shown?'

'I've been shown a front door, with a wooden bottom and two glass stained glass windows above it, either side of a wooden centre piece. The stairs are immediately in front of you as you go in. The wallpaper has dark orange patterns, the carpet is dark red. At the top of the stairs is the toilet, and next to this is one of the bedrooms'. She nodded through her tears, and her voice broke when she then asked,

'Did you see inside the bedroom?'

'Yes, at first I heard voices, I heard a conversation but was not shown what happened in there. But I do know. Then I saw the double bed which is in front on entering the room. It has an old fashioned purple quilt on it, and a dark wooden headboard. There is a man and a young girl in there. She's about six or seven years old, with long blonde hair.'

She kept her head down, and motioned to me to stop. She slowly spoke, through her tears,

'The man you heard and saw was my uncle.. He abused me many times in that bedroom. I was six when it started. It went on for three years. I shiver whenever I think of him. It's so fucking awful to think about. I can remember his horrible breath, and what he did to me. I felt so disgusting. I've never told anyone about it. I was so scared no one would believe me.'

She broke down and sobbed as she spoke. I tried to support her, but she initially pushed me away. After nine hours of continuous drinking, we were both now completely sober, and in shock at what had just happened. As we left the bar, she accepted my hug and we walked home in silence. We never spoke about it again. In truth, the experience scared me. It was so powerful and so accurate; it had sobered me up.

Curiously, several years later my first spiritual experience of this nature in recovery was very similar, although Tarot cards were not involved. To place this in context, during my early twenties, I had started to feel surges of energy within and around me. I would be in the supermarket or at work in the theatre and would sometimes sense emotional or physical pain or suffering in someone near me. There was often no visual evidence for this, but I would physically feel pain. Out of fear of being laughed at, I initially rejected these experiences as an overactive imagination.

However, a few months after the surges of energy started, I was attending a theatre employee's wedding reception at a local hotel, and felt an instant and powerful attraction to a blonde lady as she entered the foyer. It was as if I had known her all our lives and I had no hesitation in starting to talk with her.

'Hi, how are you? It's great to see you after all this time.'

'Yes, it's so good to see you as well.' She replied, with a hug and a kiss of the cheek. I shook hands with her boyfriend. It was then I realised I couldn't work out how we knew each other. So I was forced to ask, after an embarrassing pause,

'I know this is slightly bizarre, but I know we know each other, but I can't remember how?'

She replied, 'I feel exactly the same. I definitely know you, but where from?' She introduced herself, and her boyfriend: 'It's Gemma', she said, pointing at herself, 'and this is my boyfriend, Richard,'

'And I'm Matt. But, I still don't know how we know each other...' I replied, confused by our shared amnesia.

The reception area became very crowded as more guests arrived, and it was difficult to hear each other, so we walked through to the main room where it was easier to talk. We then went back through school, amateur dramatics, professional theatre, the neighbourhood we lived in, mutual friends, the wedding couple... yet we still couldn't find any connection at all.

Gemma then said to me,

'We were obviously meant to meet and talk, though, because the connection was so immediate when we saw each other.' Richard nodded in agreement. He was thankfully very open about the spiritual dimension. It was also apparent to me, by observing the loving looks between them, and their gentleness in each other's company, that they both cared very much about each other. Gemma then asked me,

'Do you know why? Do you know why we were meant to talk tonight?'

When I had first seen her a few moments earlier, I felt a huge amount of energy flow through me towards her, and I clearly 'heard' in my mind the word 'ovaries', which shocked and embarrassed me. I described the feeling of energy to the couple, but withheld the word 'ovaries' until later. They both confirmed that they too had felt the energy, and we agreed we needed to talk privately to understand what was going on, so we found a table away from the rest of the guests. We talked about spiritual healing, and she told me she needed the healing as she had been going through a very traumatic time for well over a year.

Gemma then asked whether I knew why the healing had come through for her that evening. This was still new to me (the notion of healing), so I took a deep breath and nervously said,

'When I saw you both, I immediately felt the energy and then 'heard' a very specific word; the word was ovaries'.

She gasped and looked at Richard, and then told me she had been raped eighteen months earlier. Also, they were trying to have a baby, and were having great difficulty. From that point the evening became a very powerful and emotional experience for all three of us as we talked in considerable depth about the psychological, emotional and physical consequences of abuse. Our honesty created a feeling of safety and trust between us, and the three of us commented on the loving presence among us, which we felt was profoundly healing us in body, mind and spirit.

Gemma said, 'I feel so connected at the moment. It's strange, but I know, despite all the challenges that are going to happen, that everything will be okay,' She looked intensely at her partner, Richard, and with tears in her eyes. I nodded in agreement, and replied, 'I feel inspired by this presence; it's so real and healing. I feel a peacefulness within me, which I've never really felt. I know it'll be tough, really tough at times, but something is telling me that everything will be okay. Despite the pain, and all the crap that goes with the abuse, it will be okay. No question.'

We agreed that it was also remarkable that no one, during the three hours we were talking, had come over and joined us. This was bizarre, as when we counted the number of guests we realised that, between us, we knew perhaps fifty people at the reception. Whilst there were understandably many tears that evening, I also felt huge strength from them both, and a determination to work through their challenges.

I briefly saw Gemma a few years later, in the town centre. We recognised each other immediately. She was with someone I took to be her mother. I smiled and nodded at her and mouthed 'how are you?' and she beamed back at me so beautifully, I was moved to tears.

Back at university, I quickly suppressed any notion of the spiritual world and anything to do with healing. It was complete nonsense to me. Despite the drinking, I did manage to prove myself as a competent actor and was encouraged to direct a play called *Singer* by Peter Flannery, a challenging three-act play tracing the lives of four people who meet at Auschwitz, and how their experiences would influence them for the remainder of their lives. Its themes are remarkably similar to my own – bullying, physical and psychological abuse, sadism, subservience, and fantasy. I immersed myself in the production, eventually playing one of the leading roles when one of the actors had to drop out, and for the first time in ages I worked really hard to create something very special. It proved to be quite an epic undertaking, and one I really enjoyed whilst at the same time managing to have some control over my alcohol intake, although I was still a daily drinker. I handed over the directing to Carl, who has since become one of my most trusted of friends. He ensured we kept on schedule, and with a really strong cast and production team under his leadership, the play was very well received and fuelled my dreams of becoming a professional actor. Come the end of the academic year, though, my lack of commitment to the English and Psychology modules of the course (and my daily drunkenness) meant I had to re-sit some of the exams, which I subsequently failed. The university wrote to me advising me of this outcome, and with the decision to remove me from the course.

Returning to my hometown was tough for my parents as well as myself, but I was oblivious to the pain they were suffering as a result of my drinking and behaviour. I knew the road was getting increasingly narrow and there was a horrible sense of impending doom every time I picked up a drink, as if the ground was giving way beneath me and my physical and mental health continued to deteriorate. In reality, I was heading for rock bottom... it took a further eighteen months, but then my life was to take on a whole new meaning.

I could not let anyone know the real reason why I had left University after one year, so I simply said I wanted to get a practical understanding of theatre rather than studying the theory for three long years. I doubt many believed this, though! My body was by now reacting to the constant alcohol abuse and I developed chronic back pain at the base of my spinal cord. It was always worst first thing in the morning, and felt like a knife was touching the nerves. At one appointment with my GP, to discuss my back problem, he suggested I attend the local alcohol and drug advisory service, which shocked me. Whilst I knew I drank too much, I was still too scared to actually do anything about it. The various medical and psychological problems I was experiencing were rationalised in my mind as purely coincidental.

Nevertheless I met with an alcohol worker who asked me various questions about my lifestyle, how often I drank, whether I had ever stolen alcohol, and how many units I consumed each week. My mind raced, and a quick glance at the chart on the wall stated 37 units was the maximum, so I lied and told the counsellor it was probably 25 units, maybe less, so well within the recommended limits – as if the limit was a target rather than a warning. When she told me that 25 units per week was still too much, the reality of my drinking started to dawn on me - I thought she had meant per day! This really scared me; my probable intake was more like 150+ units per week, often a lot more, and this level had been going on for a long time by then. Gradually, the denial of my alcoholism was being challenged. However, it would be a further five months before I would actually stop drinking. My GP also sent me for various blood tests and an MRI scan for the back problem. A few weeks later the results came back and I was told I might need an operation, as the nerve endings at the base of my spinal cord had shrivelled up due to the volume of toxins that had been poisoning my system, and the lack of nutrients and vitamins due to my dreadful diet. Any operation, I was warned, would be risky, with a 50 / 50 risk of further damage being done.

I was told a healthy diet, complete abstention from alcohol and drugs, and taking daily Vitamin B Thiamine and several other nutrients and multi vitamins would help recovery. My GP laid it on the line; he told me in no uncertain terms that I had a serious alcohol problem, and that I was about the youngest alcoholic he had ever met. He strongly recommended I also see a psychologist who he had worked with for many years, and who he felt could help me...if I was willing to receive help. As I left the GP's clinic, trying to digest all this, the duty nurse called me back into her office to give me my recent blood test results, which showed my liver was having difficulty getting rid of dead blood cells and which, she told me, was the very earliest stage of cirrhosis. These results shocked me; it seemed ridiculous that a twenty year old could have a damaged liver, let alone be an alcoholic. I wondered whether she had lied to me for some reason. Yet, there had been fleeting moments during the last few months of 'the veil being lifted' and I could see the truth of my desperate position...and these thoughts really terrified me.

All-day daily drinking sessions had become the norm, and drinking with Robert accelerated the physical addiction to alcohol for both of us. Robert had been drinking alcoholically for many years, and when we drank together he would often get terrible shakes in the pub. To deal with this I would take his shaking arm, fold it and hold it steady for a few minutes, which seemed to do the trick. We would sometimes admit to each other that we both had drinking problems, but it was still 'working' for us so there was never any notion of cutting down or stopping.

I was drinking one early evening in *The Red Lion*, a popular pub in the town centre. Near to the toilets was a long corridor, where the barrels of beer were often kept. As I sat on the barrels drinking a pint of export lager, I noticed a credit card had dropped between the barrels.... I quickly grabbed it. At this stage of my alcoholism, looking back I now regret that any sense of morality had long gone, and ten minutes later, my drinking friend Robert and I were in a local off license buying £80 worth of booze. I forged the signature and off we went to the car, and down to the beach to drink. On the way, Robert told me to get rid of the credit card, and I carefully threw it onto the roof of a single storey seafront building, judging as I did this whether I could get it back later, if I needed it. I must admit that my warped sense of morals was such that my thinking at the time was that we had only spent £80; it could have been so much more, and therefore the credit card owner would be grateful to us that we hadn't spent a lot more money. It was as if we had done him a favour by not getting carried away.

The barman at my regular pub raised the subject of my drinking with me one day. I had started the habit of helping him tidy up and collect the empties in the morning before the pub opened, and if I was skint and desperate I would sometimes finish off the drinks I collected. Whether Tony had noticed me draining a glass I don't know, but he suddenly said to me,

'You know, Matt, there are people with drink problems who are not aware of it. We get a few of them in here. It's very sad to see how the drink got hold of them.'

I agreed with him, and then suddenly thought of a fellow drinker, Ian, who often drank with me, and I said;

'What about Ian, he's always in here every lunchtime. He must have a problem.'

Tony replied, 'He's not the only one, Matt, there are others who get here earlier than Ian.'

It did not occur to me for one second he was referring to me.

'Really?', I replied, but still oblivious to what he was obviously saying about me, 'someone ought to have a word with Ian,' Tony looked at me, with what I can now recognise was an incredulous look on his face. He was clearly taken aback by the strength of my denial. He shook his head in disbelief and then disappeared around the corner.

An hour later, Ian arrived and I decided now was the time, so I said to him. 'Ian, you know that, eh, some people have a drink problem, and aren't really, um... able to acknowledge it – well, Tony (I was a coward, after all!), mentioned that perhaps you might, um...'

Ian was not impressed; he was having none of it.

'Me? You cheeky bastard. What about you? What time did you get here this morning?'

I went on the defensive, thinking he was completely out of order to turn the tables on me.

'Well, a short while ago.'

'Half ten!' shouted Tony from around the corner.

The Centre of Attention

Ian continued. 'You should look at your bloody self before you start accusing other people!', and off he went in a huff. Tony re-appeared with a look of expectation on his face that the truth might have finally dawned on me, but I still couldn't see it.

'Apparently...they call that denial,Tone. He can't face the truth!'

Having had the final word, further defending my own drinking habits, I walked away.

My pay from the holiday work I was doing was, by this stage, nowhere near enough to feed my addiction to alcohol. I began stealing money and running scams with local gamblers at an amusement arcade I worked at. I knew stealing was wrong morally; I had been brought up to know the difference between right and wrong, and I had always respected this... until this stage in my life.

Now I could, in my warped, desperate mind, justify my immoral behaviour through the increasing sense of anger and resentment I felt to my employer. I was scared of getting caught but the obsession to drink, to get to oblivion, to kill the thoughts and feelings that were crippling me, easily overrode the sense of right and wrong I had been brought up with. Whilst the process of stealing the money was particularly difficult in a busy amusement arcade, the overwhelming obsession I had to get oblivion was worth the risk of getting caught. Whilst I watched the alcohol being poured in front of me, I would imagine the police storming into the bar to arrest me, but as long as I could get the drink inside of me, I didn't care. The physical and mental relief I felt when the drink was being poured in front of me twenty minutes later made it all seem worth it. In my alcoholic mind I could justify my behaviour through resentment and bitterness. In my grandiosity and delusion, I remember telling myself, 'They don't pay me enough; they don't respect me!' I felt I was a player; the rush of the steal felt exciting, and I knew I'd get drunk very soon.

My memory, however, was being badly affected by the insane levels of drinking, and blackouts were more and more common. One afternoon, I was sitting in a local bar on the seafront of my hometown, and was watching what I thought was an archive clip of a huge motorbike festival which took place every autumn. I asked a friend when it was taking place that year. He looked at me as if I was mad.'Would you look around you, you daft bugger?' I did, and suddenly noticed the bar had filled up since I had arrived with motorbike fans. I then went outside to see that, on my way to the bar that morning, I had walked for the best part of a mile through one of the largest such events in Europe, with over five hundred motorbikes, and had been in complete blackout. Another time, I was smoking a cigarette and had two centimetres of ash to tap into the ashtray. I had the thought to do this, but my finger would not move. This freaked me out; it seemed my brain had difficulty communicating with my finger. I then remembered what I'd been told about damage to the nerve endings in my spinal cord, and feared this was linked with my inability to move my finger. This thought terrified me so I immediately ordered a few more drinks. Another time, there was a group of friends enjoying themselves and laughing, and in my paranoid, drunken state, I was convinced they were laughing at me. Feeling humiliated, I nearly threw the glass ashtray at them. All of this thinking really scared me, but I didn't think to stop drinking, though.

During this time, I found a job on a film as an assistant to the Location Manager for two months, working in various locations throughout southern England. I hoped this mini change of scene from my hometown would change how I felt about life, and for a few days it seemed to be working. But the physical addiction and mental obsession with alcohol was unrelenting, and very soon I was drinking throughout each day during filming, wasting the majority of the wages (which was about £300 a week) on alcohol and cannabis, and returning home each weekend with, typically, £40 to last the long weekend.

I received a telephone call from one of the crew one Sunday morning asking me to get to a stately home in Gloucestershire as soon as possible that day. He told me to arrive sober. I was so screwed up by this stage, and knowing he needed me to be sober and knowing I couldn't do this, I got off the train at every station along the route to drink (I preferred bars to drinking on my own, as much as possible), and eventually arrived very drunk at my destination. I was collected at the station by the Location Manager and they decided to take me to the nearby Working Men's Club to try and sober me up before I started work. I was now at the stage where I often drank myself drunk, sober, drunk, sober each day.

Whilst the work was exciting, and the money was good, the alcohol was always readily available. I knew the writing was on the wall, and when we arrived at the castle for filming one day, the Location Manager called me in, and told me he had to let me go. I remember literally begging him (in classic style, on my knees) to keep me on – in the main because the money was so good, and I didn't know from where I could replace the money to drink if I went home. He stood his ground as he needed to, of course, but had the good grace to tell me that I had a serious drink problem, and that I needed to get help. I knew he was sincere, and I am now grateful to him for being so honest with me.

Soon afterwards, I was walking along the High Street in my hometown on a Saturday morning. I'd already had a few too many drinks on and had unfortunately pissed myself. I remember in my utter insanity looking at the people going about their normal business, thinking to myself: 'these boring bastards; they haven't got a clue how to live'. I was judging people doing their shopping, couples walking and holding hands, a father pushing a pram, and in all truth, underneath it all, I felt I existed in a parallel universe to them. I didn't have a clue how to have an intimate, loving relationship, or how to have children. I envied them so much, and deep down I desperately wanted what they had, yet I viewed them with derision what I saw of their boring lives. Whereas the alcohol had originally made me feel whole and often superior to other people, when I drank now I felt broken and very confused. I desperately wanted but simultaneously feared what these people seemed to have, in equal measure.

Later that day, after I had fallen asleep on a bench in the small park which overlooked the High Street, I woke up feeling very put out that people around me were doing very normal things like having a picnic or reading a book, and I felt as if they had invaded my front room without my permission. Looking back now, this sense of grandiosity and entitlement was ridiculous, but that was my reality at the time. My mental breakdown became more obvious to me over time; my mind raced at 300 miles per hour; fear and paranoia controlled me. I could not trust anyone; I distrusted their motives, and the old feelings that used to be triggered off every now and then were now with me more and more of the time.

My mind was savage and increasingly hostile to myself and others. Anyone kind to me was regarded as a threat, and I worried when the proverbial knife would stab into my back. Anyone being unpleasant or hostile was at least being honest, I rationalised in my insane mind. I told this to a psychologist in early recovery who asked me how I would describe my thinking; I replied, 'being streetwise', to which he said 'perhaps you might consider the word paranoid'. In hindsight, I can agree with that view now.

In an empty bar one night, I was so paranoid that I thought to myself that if I went to the toilet the bar might suddenly fill up and I would not be able to get a drink quickly enough when I came back, and might go into alcoholic withdrawal, (even though I still questioned whether I really had a drinking problem!). I reasoned it was therefore best to buy three drinks and keep them safely behind the bar – and take another two with me just in case I needed them whilst fighting my way back to the bar after the toilet. I even considered urinating in the large plant pot which was tucked away in the corner of the bar, instead of using the toilet, just to be absolutely sure I could get to the bar again. Thankfully, I had enough sense to decide against this drastic course of action. I stood in the bar nursing a drink after returning from the loo, feeling lonely and fearful, when a friend came in and put his arm around me, with one hand on my shoulder. I knew him well, I had actually trusted him in the past, but was still paranoid he might molest me with his other hand.

Later, in the street, I slipped into further paranoia and would sometimes argue with myself; I would hear voices telling me to jump in front of cars. I was terrified cars would come onto the pavement to run me down, so I would walk near to the wall so I could jump over if I needed to. If I was going to die, it would be on my own terms.

All enjoyment from the alcohol had long gone; it never ever came back. This realisation – that the alcohol didn't 'work' anymore - terrified me. Alcohol had been the answer to so many of my problems, it felt like the missing part of my DNA. It had worked as a rocket fuel for me, and now it had turned on me and I was suicidal. The insanity is that I carried on drinking, even though I hated the taste of alcohol, and I hated the consequences of alcoholism, namely the devastating impact it had on me mentally, emotionally, and physically. I would go out with £100 and be obsessed about what I would do when the money had run out, which it invariably would. It was almost impossible to get to oblivion anymore, and consequently I hated every moment, but it had me in its grip completely. Alcohol was the most important thing in my life; I obsessed about it all day, every day. I changed what I drank, where I drank and how I drank to try and get that oblivion back, but nothing worked.

The Centre of Attention

My bedroom habits in the grips of desperation drinking were often disgusting, as I've described in earlier scenes. I would regularly wet the bed, and when the fears were really on me I would often shit in the sink when I was too scared to leave the room and walk to the toilet. The morning drink became more regular; the 'hair of the dog' could take the edge off the shakes, usually, and get me out of the door. But I couldn't look people in the eye; I felt such shame and confusion most mornings. I had regular blackouts whereby I could not remember what had happened the night before. Sometimes I would have fleeting memories of an incident or argument somewhere, and I would try to remember where I had been, and where I needed to avoid.

Living in a small seaside town offered very few places to drink, so I couldn't hide for long if someone was after me for something I had said or done whilst drunk. I was always looking over my shoulder, full of fear and shame. Shortly afterwards, in my desperation one early morning with the shakes, I started drinking Old Spice aftershave, which was disgusting and it burnt my mouth and throat as it went down. I knew this was crazy. The aftershave used to come in white bottles with a gold rim and when used conventionally, drops would fall into the palm of your hand, but for the alcoholic in the grip of the shakes this felt like torture, so I tried in my desperation to rip the gold rim off with my teeth and drink it. As it went down my throat it tasted utterly disgusting, and I felt like it was burning me. The vile taste stayed at the back of my throat for days.

I also started getting the delirium tremens (DTs) most nights, imagining snakes at the bottom of the bed coming up and attacking me, which brought on horrendous palpitations. I also imagined disfigured faces coming out of the walls and ceiling at me. It never occurred to me to actually stop drinking. I didn't ever consider the amount of alcohol I was drinking was creating the shakes, the shits and the DTs. The self-harming became worse during the DTs; in my insanity I would head butt the bedroom walls on occasion to try to knock myself out. My worst night with the horrors brought about what would become my rock bottom – I had such shame about this it took me until I was seven years sober in AA to share that when the alcohol, and the drugs, didn't work... when I couldn't get to oblivion, when I couldn't drown the memories of the abuse, I would take a cricket bat and smack it around my head a few times.

I had reached the bottom of the abyss. It was 28th February 1993. My last drink was a pint of cider which I couldn't keep down. My stomach was rejecting it, and I desperately kept trying to get it down me. I hated the taste, I hated the effect, and I knew it was killing me, but it was the most important thing in my life to get that drink into my system. I walked out of the bar with a mind and body savaged by alcoholism, thinking my life was over. I looked at the town hall clock; it was 9.30pm and I thought to myself:

'There must be something else; this cannot be my life. There must be something more than this'.

Little did I realise at the time, but that was my moment of surrender. I knew I was beaten. I knew I was broken. I desperately needed help for something, but I didn't know what.

Through the 12 Step programme and fellowship of Alcoholics Anonymous, and the guidance of several gifted professionals, I have not had an alcoholic drink since March 1st 1993.

3

WHEN THE PUPIL IS READY

Our deepest fear is not that we are inadequate.
Our deepest fear is that we are powerful beyond measure.
It is our Light, not our Darkness, that most frightens us.[4]
Marianne Williamson

Soon after returning to my hometown in the summer of 1992, after my one drunken year at university, my GP referred me in the first instance to Dr. Ron Hutchinson, and shortly afterwards, to the mental health team at the local hospital, and to the Alcohol and Drug Advisory clinic. I think he knew I needed all the help I could get! Soon after my GP visit, at the local hospital I was diagnosed with post-traumatic stress disorder (PTSD) from the sexual abuse, and recommended to have several weeks of Cognitive Behavioural Therapy (CBT), and an appointment with the clinical psychiatrist to assess whether I needed anti-depressants.

Dr. Ron Hutchinson was a remarkable man; a retired clinical psychologist with a passion for holistic therapy. He was also a deeply spiritual being, and once I grew to trust him, I found him to be truly inspirational. He was in his mid-sixties when I first met him, and was probably a much taller man in his youth; despite being athletic for his age, he walked with a slight stoop. He had thinning black hair (which I always

---

[4] This inspiring quote by Marianne Williamson is from her book, *A Return To Love: Reflections on the Principles of A Course in Miracles* (Harper Collins, 1992). From Chapter 7, Section 3, p. 190-191.

suspected he dyed), and was gentle and calm by nature. Looking back now, after a period of twenty years, he was one of the wisest, most learned men I have ever met. His wife Esther was slightly older than Ron; petite and pretty, she also had a background in holistic therapy, and was always kind, supportive and encouraging to me. Whilst Ron took the lead in the psychotherapy, they were very much an equal partnership. I found Esther's quiet, calming guidance between therapy sessions was often as important to me as the sessions themselves. These two professionals and partners in life worked hand in hand, with Esther offering a very soothing and safe presence, over a cup of tea in their kitchen, whenever I felt overwhelmed with the memories of the abuse.

Mum had also been to see Ron, when she was at her lowest point of her life; her mother had died a few months earlier and the progressive nature of my alcoholism had created a huge amount of worry and stress for both my parents; but particularly for Mum, who lost sleep at night worrying about me, as she had witnessed so much of my mental breakdown. Such was my self obsession, at that time of my life, that I regarded her distress as getting in the way of my life; it was an inconvenience, as nothing was more important to me than the next drink, so Mum's mental health was regarded for the most part as being a pain in the arse. I was not able to empathise with her pain, nor see I had created so much of it through my behaviour, because I was shut down mentally and emotionally to the reality around me.

There were brief moments when I was fleetingly aware of how ill I was, and momentarily considered how this affected others around me, but these thoughts were too overwhelming to consider; then the feelings of shame and fear, the vague, fragmented memories of the night before would come flooding back, and the physical cravings and mental obsession to drink would overwhelm me... and out of desperation to drown the truth, I would start drinking again. It always started with a horrible feeling of dread, a sense that something had happened the night before, and then a sudden flash of memory. On more than one occasion, I remembered a man's face right in front of mine arguing with me about something, but I couldn't hear what he was saying. I must have been so drunk that I was in and out of blackout, and had said or done something to upset him. The morning after the night before, however, the fear was crippling as I tried to piece together what had happened.

'Who the hell was that? What had I done to upset him? What if it's so bad he and his friends are looking for me?' I felt sick to my stomach with fear, and had images in my mind of being found, dragged into the street, and attacked by a group of physically strong, ruthless men.

I'd often wrack my mind in desperation for more clues as to what had happened. I remember staring around me at people walking past on the street, scared I'd be recognised for having done something....something I felt sure had been humiliating. This was the worst of all feelings; being so paranoid that I'd convinced myself I'd done something really dreadful, but having no memory and therefore no knowledge of how to try and protect myself.

'.....if only I could damn well remember where the hell I was. Who was that?'

These scenarios had become commonplace, and I would be hyper-vigilant and avoid certain areas of town where my last clear memory had reminded me I'd been. The crazy reality was that I lived in a small town, so if I had offended someone enough for them to be looking for me, there were only a handful of bars I'd be hiding in, and getting drunk. It was also possible, of course, that nothing had happened at all.

Starting in September 1992, I went to see Ron for a half day session on a weekly basis for six months initially, and on each occasion I was invariably still hung over from the night before. I remember psyching myself up before I boarded the bus for the 45 minute journey to his home. I'd be so paranoid that someone might suddenly attack me, convinced that everyone was staring at me, but terrified to look them in the eye (if I did, I thought they could see into my soul and see how fucked up I was), and I would feel a panic attack coming on. During the first few weeks visiting Ron, I had a number of panic attacks and would have to get off the bus early, as the enclosed space made me feel even worse. My breathing would become very fast and short, so I would hyper-ventilate. My neck would get stiff, my lower back would feel tense, and I feared my heart was going to explode through my chest as the stress levels climbed higher. If I had a panic attack in the street, I was convinced my legs might give way beneath me, and would grab a nearby wall for support. My mind always made it so much worse; it would project scenarios in which I was being humiliated in front of a crowd of people in a public place somewhere. On one occasion, I remember hiding in a park (not, I hasten to add, a park where I had been abused), and staying there for an hour or so before I was able to get home. I would feel so ashamed of myself at times like these. (Thankfully, since the beginning of February 1994, I've only had a few such panic attacks.)

To help me with the anxiety and the panic attacks, I was sent to a clinical psychiatrist who, without even looking at me in the face, scribbled a prescription for anti-depressants. When I walked out of the consulting room I felt resentful towards him and refused to take them. I respect the fact that anti-depressants are sometimes necessary, indeed essential in critical cases, but I'd never taken them in my life. I saw them as a substitute to alcohol, and somewhere inside of me I knew they wouldn't be a solution to my issues.

Over the course of the next few months, both Ron and the clinical psychologist at a local hospital (where I had weekly CBT sessions for several months, from April 1993) taught me coping strategies and concentration techniques to help me handle the panic attacks when I felt them coming on (techniques which I describe later in this chapter.) Whilst Ron was at times very kind and gentle with me, he also took no prisoners, and as much as I resented him for that, it was exactly what I needed. Whenever I arrived hungover, which was every time until I stopped drinking altogether at the end of February 1993, he would sit opposite and pointedly ask me;

'Why are you poisoning yourself?'

It was a question he expected me a reply to, and so he would then wait for me to answer. I was so full of shame and of being judged that I would say nothing for at least two minutes, although it felt like an eternity. He would then repeat the question after intervals of a minute or so until I answered him.

'I don't know, I can't help it. I have to have it. Nothing else matters to me. I need to drink, that's all. Without it, I'd....The cravings are too overwhelming....'

After a long pause, I added, 'It's like every cell in my body is demanding it; and I can't think about anything else.'

He would then teach me about the physiological effect of alcohol on the body and mind of alcoholics; he explained to me why I had such powerful cravings for alcohol, and how this affected the mind to the extent that the mental obsession developed such power over the alcoholic. He helped me to understand how my mind worked, and why I thought and felt the way I did about my life. Slowly but surely, over a period of several sessions, he penetrated through the walls of fear and distrust I had built up around me for protection; in doing so he offered a glimmer of hope that I could get better. On some occasions I would freeze and refuse to look at him. I was locked into the memories of the abuse, which would cripple me with shame, but his patience, the gentle tone of his voice and his relaxed body language were just right to help me challenge the savage voices in my head. When the PTSD had been triggered they seemed more real to me at times than he was. The counselling for the actual trauma itself happened more regularly once the trust between us had developed, which took a few weeks.

The first memory of the abuse that I described to Ron is, even to this day, vividly clear to me. So clear, it's as if it happened yesterday. It came to me after Ron had asked some questions about dating, intimacy and relationships, to which I replied,

'I've never had a girlfriend. I've liked different girls but I'm terrified to let anyone get close to me... I'm scared of getting hurt.'

Ron then asked me to describe the times in my life that I could remember feeling hurt by someone. After telling him a few stories of being bullied at prep school, and the fight at the house party when I was drunk, I suddenly went completely blank. It was a strange experience, which is difficult to describe. I saw nothing in my mind's eye. It was as if I had hit a thick, impregnable mental wall. I was in a state of shock. After a couple of minutes of feeling a profound sense of numbness, I became aware of physical tension throughout my body and with this uncomfortable sensation came a few sudden flashes and I saw myself, as a very young boy, standing in a latrine of a public toilet next to two men. I had a sense of loss and bewilderment as my mind started to reveal a deep-seated memory I'd buried since I was eight or nine years old. This was the first memory of the abuse I can recall describing to Ron; previously I'd only had very brief flashbacks. Over the course of the next forty-five minutes (it may have been much longer, I had no sense of time during the therapy sessions), the fragments began to be pieced together, and eventually, the entire memory came back to me as I have described below.

It was a busy summer's day, a Sunday just before lunchtime. The weather outside was warm and pleasant. I'd cycled straight from church up the sea front, which was heaving with holidaymakers, to the park in the town centre. I was on auto-pilot as I left my bike leant up against the iron railings nearby, and walked nervously into the gents toilet to wait. I was not fully present, I was just going through the motions. I had to be home by 1pm at the latest for a traditional roast dinner with my family, so I knew I didn't have long. I remembered walking in and seeing a long, old fashioned latrine, and I then stood in the middle as two men whom I had not met before walked in and stood either side of me, a few feet away. After a few seconds, one of them nervously looked down at me, and quietly asked, 'Are you Matthew?'

'Yes', I anxiously replied.

A third man walked in, someone I recognised from previous experiences of abuse. He nodded to us and stayed by the exit, as the look out. I walked with the two men into the middle toilet cubicle, and they took turns abusing me. I performed oral sex on each of them. I felt shock and disgust, as I described the memory to Dr. Ron, asking myself, 'How do these men, whom I have never met before, know my name?' I stared ahead, in that dank and smelly cubicle, bewildered. Ron waited patiently, and then gently said to me;

'What is it? What do you see?' I could not answer. I stared at the wall behind him feeling distraught and full of shame, and fear. I was in shock as I started to have very brief flashes of another incident, at a different location. The flashes were so brief though. I saw myself kneeling between two men in a toilet cubicle, and then....nothing at all. My mind went blank, and I was consumed with shame and guilt. I felt so dirty under my skin, it was as if I reeked of some contagious, horrible disease. I always reacted the same way, whenever a new memory of the abuse came back. I would shut down immediately and not speak. I would go within myself so deep I became much less aware of Ron and the room, and would relive the abuse. Whenever I had dissociated (and was unable to communicate for a considerable length of time), Ron would take me into a larger room and he taught me four simple communication techniques. As basic as they were, they were effective and I would use them at home to help me connect to the physical world rather than to the flashbacks I was increasingly experiencing.

In the first exercise Ron would sit opposite me, our faces about a foot apart, and he would ask; 'Please take my hand, thank you'.

At the beginning of the therapy, it would take me at least ten minutes to respond. I was held back by a paralysing fear which came from 'what happens after this?' - the idea of touching a man would trigger the times I had been raped as a child. I hated to be physically touched (or to touch another man), or for my personal space to be invaded by a man. In straightforward terms, a paedophile had told me to do something which led to me being abused, so each time Ron asked me to do anything, however transparent, I would immediately have flashbacks to specific times I was abused and relive the feelings of terror. I needed to process the thoughts and feelings and come into the present moment as much as possible, before being able to make a decision and to follow his instructions.

After perhaps twenty minutes I would respond more easily to his questions, and then we would begin a second communication exercise. We would stand in opposite corners of the room from each other, and he would ask; 'Please walk over to me, thank you'.

The question often triggered memories of the abuse, and Ron would patiently repeat it, after an interval of thirty seconds or so, until I complied, and the exercise would continue until I was able to be more present in the room, and therefore less affected by the flashbacks to the abuse. The third exercise was more tactile, encouraging me to have a greater awareness of my physicality and that of the world around me. Ron would stand next to me, perhaps two foot away so I did not feel my personal space being challenged, which might trigger me again, and ask; 'Please look at the door / window / picture, thank you.'

When I did this, he would then ask me to 'Walk over to the door, thank you. Touch the door handle, feel the hardness and coolness of the metal on your hands.' Touching the various objects would bring me more into the present moment, and from here we would be able to talk through what was going on for me. This particular technique really helped me whenever I felt a panic attack coming on.

The fourth exercise was equally as helpful. We would sit opposite each other, our chairs six inches apart, and with our eyes open, we would each hold a gentle gaze at each other. We were not allowed to move at all; no involuntary flinching, no nervous twitches, no fidgeting, and no scratching which, in the early weeks, proved impossible to do as I had so much nervous energy running through my body. I was hyper-vigilant all of the time, as sitting so close to someone else and looking at them felt very intimidating even though I considered Ron to be 'safe'. There were many times when his face would change into other faces of people (some I knew, some I did not recognise), or contort into hideous ones and I would have to re-focus my eyes to be able to see his face again. He encouraged me to use simple breathing exercises to feel more physically relaxed, and to try and not pay any attention to what my thoughts were telling me. We would talk through these later.

'What if I'm wrong about this man? What if he is leading me on, and then it starts all over again? How do I know for sure that I'm safe here? Am I being a fucking mug again?'

As these thoughts and emotions overwhelmed me as they often did, I would 'see' myself being attacked by different men, physically restrained, raped; and I immediately shut down. To bring me back into the present, Ron and I would start the communication exercises again, in the order I have described. The exercises usually lasted ten minutes, but would be much longer if I had disassociated, until Ron felt I was more relaxed and present.

The four exercises taught me to be able to handle the physicality of someone being quite close to me, and to develop a greater level of control over my instinctive reactions. It helped me to realise that whilst I might feel an overwhelming urge to run away when I was triggered, I could be present enough to evaluate the situation and come to a calmer, more balanced decision. Gradually, over an hour or so using a combination of these exercises, our communication would improve, and I felt more able to talk about the abuse in more detail.

When Ron thought I was feeling sorry for myself, which was a normal state of affairs at that time as I was blaming everyone else for my predicament (I struggled to take responsibility for myself at that stage), he would say;

'Matt, you must stop blaming everyone else. Sooner or later, you really must grow up'.

I wanted to punch him; in my mind's eye I would see myself diving over the desk and strangling him, when he challenged me in this way, but in retrospect I actually needed the tough love. I needed someone to help me see that I had to change the inner narrative of self-hatred that I had been holding onto for so long. I never felt he was judging me when he said this; he said it as a statement of fact; as an instruction, and I sensed he genuinely had my best interests at heart. I had felt a victim for so many years, for obvious reasons perhaps, but in order to heal I had to have a quantum change of attitude, and Ron and AA enabled me to bring this about. He had such a wisdom about him, which I found intimidating at times. In truth, I was somewhat in awe of him, and this sometimes scared me.

Another form of therapy Ron encouraged me to work with involved the use of clay, and small items such as a rubber, a coin or a chess piece, to bring physicality to the memories I was struggling with. As many of the memories were 'out of body', it helped to 're-create' them from a similar viewpoint, i.e. looking down on the table as I moulded the clay was the same as my memory of looking down on the men as they abused me. The dexterous nature of working with clay somehow helped release the emotions locked within the memories; as I used the clay to mould the body of an abuser I felt the anger, fear and shame in my mind and body move to my hands and fingers, which was then directed at 'him' rather than myself. I found there's a psychological link with childhood when working with clay, as it brings up fleeting memories including, for me, playing with bubbles with Mum at the kitchen sink when I was very small after breakfast one morning. This really upset me as I had, at that time, very few memories of childhood other than the abuse. The upset and sadness came from the realisation of how much the abuse had stolen from my childhood, and how little I could remember of my earlier years, before the abuse took place.

This creative process made the whole horrific scenario more real to me. Over several weeks of using the clay to recreate several incidents of the abuse, I started to recognise the flow of emotions between myself and the paedophiles. Beforehand, all emotions were thrown together into 'shock' or 'numbness' whereby I could not identify how I felt until I could extract each emotion in turn, and talk through what had happened and how I felt.

The combination of therapies that Ron introduced me to helped me to, at least, intellectually recognise that I was not responsible for the abuse. That I was not to blame for what had happened to me. The emotional healing beyond this took many, many more years.

As our relationship developed over the weeks and months so did the trust between us and I very much felt a truth in the saying 'when the pupil is ready, the Master will arrive'. Ron taught me I had to understand myself before I could understand others. He helped me realise that my wholly negative view of life was because the filter through which I viewed the world had been damaged by the trauma I had experienced, and that this could only be healed through re-living and releasing the energy within the memory. This process of healing was an emotional as well as a physical experience.

First and foremost, he taught me how to communicate with myself; how to identify what I was feeling, and how to deal with my thinking. I had shut down so much emotionally that I had lost all sense of who I was; my emotional awareness did not stretch beyond fear, anger, and self-pity. I had to challenge the internal voices which would often tell me to;

'Go on, just do it. Jump in front of the car, go for it, you fucking coward.'

During this stage of therapy, I often had intrusive thoughts of being deliberately run over, or I'd imagine what it would feel like to be crushed by a train. Sometimes I'd wonder what the sensation would feel like if I were to jump off a bridge. Would there be a momentary feeling of freedom? How conscious would I be of the impact when I hit the ground? To counter these intrusive and frightening thoughts, Ron encouraged me to visualise a large on / off dial switch; I chose the one on the old-fashioned wireless Dad had, which when I turned it to the far left would turn the volume down, until the radio 'clicked' off. I also learned that a good way to counter the voices was to tell them to simply 'Fuck Off'.

The sessions were expensive, £200 each time, and after awhile I felt too proud to ask my father for another cheque (despite my parents' offer of on-going support), and so told Ron I could not afford to attend any longer. Ron's immediate reply was to ask me to bring a pint of milk or some eggs the following week! This validation of his support really boosted my healing - Ron's belief in me helped me to believe more in myself. I went to Ron twice a week for a whole day for over eighteen months; each session was based on what the immediate issue was at that time. As he provided solutions to my immediate problems, my faith and trust in him, and myself, increased.

With a foundation of trust established, we started specific counselling for the childhood rape and abuse. Ron introduced me to a device which could register the level of energy or emotional charge in the memories I was describing, through a wire attached to two aluminium cans which I held in each hand throughout each session. By talking through each memory, deliberation, and rehearsing (what I would say, how I would say it, how I would stand, reminding myself to have gentle eye contact), I psyched myself up and walked up to the huge red stage door. The doorkeeper opened it, and I spoke so quickly I was amazed he understood;

'Umm. Hi, I am sorry to bother you, I was wondering whether there were any jobs going, umm, backstage jobs that is? Please?'

He looked down at me from the raised step he was standing on, and politely replied, 'Sorry, no, we haven't anything at the moment.'

I replied with a massive smile of relief: 'Thank you!'. He looked rather bemused by my reaction, but for me the idea of a 'yes' was far, far worse than a 'no'!

Working through the memories of the sexual abuse with Ron, in at least as much detail as I was able to remember at that time, had started a very long journey of healing. In truth, I am still on that journey, such is the long-term impact of trauma of this kind. On a day-to-day practical level, the CBT with the clinical psychologist at the local hospital helped me to mentally challenge my negative thinking when I was triggered; this did not stop the triggers, but offered an alternative to the intrusive thoughts I was having. After a couple of sessions he said to me,

'Matt, you are probably the most negative person I have ever met.' To which I replied in the affirmative,

'Yes'. He then said, with a gentle smile, 'that's about the only positive thing you've ever said.'

I've seen the humour in this for many years now, although I didn't at the time. It always gets a good laugh when I share it at an AA meeting!

CBT offered immediate and practical ways to improve my state of mind, and help me to cope with my day-to-day problems. However, it didn't deal with the underlying trauma. The clinical psychologist gave me a form with five columns which I had to fill in each time I experienced anything that had particularly upset me. I was to briefly describe the event, put a % to how upsetting it was (0 = not at all, 100 = terrified), what my thoughts were at the time, and then consider what a more positive mental reaction might be.

During the weekly sessions, we would discuss the form and talk about how I could replace these thoughts with less distressing and healthier thoughts. I remember on one occasion seeing a man wearing an old yellow jacket and NHS issue glasses, sitting on a bus that had momentarily stopped at the bus stop; he looked at me, paused, and then looked away. The PTSD was immediately triggered off; my physical reaction was one of panic that I might be attacked; my body tensed up, I was paranoid, and I immediately scanned the people around me for threats. I felt very confused and distressed. All this happened in a split second. The CBT helped me to process the incident by challenging the assumption that the man on the bus might attack me, and that I couldn't deal with it if he did. I wrote on the form;

- He looked much older than me and I am physically stronger
- It is daylight and there are plenty of people around, so being attacked is very unlikely
- I do not know the man, so ought not to automatically presume he is violent
- He may have thought he knew me and then realised he did not, so looked away
- Perhaps he was day-dreaming, and had not even noticed me

On another occasion I was threatened by one of the teenagers I had had a fight with at a house party a few years earlier. A week or so after the fight had taken place I walked past him in the High Street. He was standing outside a bar with a group of male and female friends. As soon as he saw me, he lurched towards me in a threatening manner saying, 'You're going down tonight.'

The PTSD was triggered off immediately, and I felt a toxic combination of gut-wrenching fear, shame and immense rage. The fear and rage was directed at him, but I saw in my mind's eye images of myself being physically restrained and beaten up in the middle of the street by three or four men, whilst he and his friends are standing around me laughing. There was also a terror of what I wanted to do to him in revenge. I saw images of me torturing him which horrified me. They were so far removed from my true self but I couldn't get them out of my head. I feared for my sanity, but felt too scared to tell anyone in case I was immediately sectioned in a mental health unit.

The shame was at my sense of being so powerless, of not being able to protect myself either verbally (with a calm, witty response to impress the girls standing near him) or physically by beating the shit out of him with a baseball bat. There were sudden flashbacks to the abuse, and I remembered being surrounded by different men who were playing with me sexually. I felt dirty, disgusted and full of shame that the girls seeing me in the street must know that I was a pathetic, asexual runt. That was how I often saw myself during my teens and early twenties. I could feel an explosion of energy building up within me; rage at the paedophiles, rage at the teenager, and rage at myself. I had to escape, to get away from this situation. Whilst the teenager didn't follow me, that I recall, I kept walking away whilst I feared my legs might give way beneath me, and I'd collapse on the pavement struggling to breathe. With the flashbacks I was immediately back there in the toilets again, and I shut down mentally and emotionally (I went numb) and needed to escape to a safe place.

Looking back, I can see how the flight response of the PTSD has perhaps saved me from acting out violently many times. Although I absolutely abhor any violence, there's such a fine line when one is triggered, as there is such a visceral, primeval response to the perceived threat. I had to find a place of safety, from everyone, so I disappeared to the beach for perhaps an hour until I could muster enough energy to 'flick the switch, put on the face' and make out everything was okay.

In these moments, I tried to remind myself what Ron and AA had taught me about being present, and the importance of talking with friends who understood what I was going through, so after a while I'd find a telephone and call Peter or Jennie for support. In my minds eye I continued to replay tapes of myself bludgeoning that teenager to death with a baseball bat; in those moments he was, for me, the face of the men who had abused me. The intensity of my reaction to his comment stayed with me that weekend and for most of the following week as I remained hyper-vigilant to the behaviour of men around me, and distrustful of their motives.

I wrote down my reaction on the CBT forms when I got home. The clinical psychologist was aware of the self harming I had done in the past (when I would taunt myself in the mirror, and punch myself in the face), and he asked me about my response to the fight. I told him that I had wanted to pay some lads to do them over, and put them in hospital. I would then go in and rip the tubes out. This was the occasion (as described in the previous chapter), when the clinical psychologist said to me,

'You need to know how ill you really are, Matthew. You are a danger to yourself, no question, but are also a potential danger to other people. If I knew you when you were drinking, I would have sectioned you, without question. If you drink again, I will section you indefinitely'.

He was correct. I knew I was not well mentally, but I didn't really understand how ill I was at that time. The fight at the house party had brought up all my suppressed rage; the boys I had the fight with became the men who had abused me. I was transferring all my rage. What upset me also was that I hated any violence. I knew it was wrong to attack people, but the energy within the memories was so overpowering whenever I was triggered, it was exhausting to deal with it. This was especially challenging as I had so much suppressed hatred and rage buried inside.

The mental process, as laid out in the forms, in most cases would often be enough to take the edge off the immediate 'fight or flight' response I used to have. It was a process I found myself adopting to deal with many of my immediate, first thoughts about people and situations for the initial years of my recovery. My greatest realisation with CBT was that even though I might feel a tremendous amount of negativity within me, it didn't follow that anything dreadful would actually happen. Over the months of working with the clinical psychologist we would look back at the original forms I had filled in, and once he asked me;

'There are so many times you describe with absolute certainty that something dreadful was about to happen; that someone would attack you, either verbally or physically. The 'impending doom' scenarios. I would like to ask you how many times anything like this ever happened?'

After a long pause I replied, 'Well, nothing has.....yet.'

As I started to recognise the triggers to the PTSD, I became more able to challenge my instinctive mental and physical reactions, and replace them with a more healthy, moderate response. I learnt I didn't have to follow through with my immediate thoughts and feelings.

Time has been a great healer in this respect; the reactions to the triggers are rarely as savage, nor as often, nor as overwhelming as they used to be. With over twenty-five years of living and dealing with PTSD, I now understand why I react to certain events; I can often anticipate when a situation might trigger the symptoms of the PTSD, and I then remove myself. Whilst the list is comprehensive, over the years I have found the intensity of my reaction has thankfully diminished unless I have a combination of triggers at the same time. The exception to this is any scenario which shocks me, such as sudden aggression, being near to a man with suppressed anger or what I perceive to be predatory behaviour, or men I perceive to be deceitful or lying.

Thankfully, the flashbacks are no longer so aggressive and savage. Instead of re-living the abuse (of feeling it is happening in the present) as I did for many years, during the last five years I have become more conscious of the memories being played on a screen in my mind, which has helped to lessen their impact on me. I know I am a witness to it rather than being in it again and again. There is a sense of distance from the events when I now recall them. There is a caveat here, however: although it is rarer these days, if I am triggered by a combination of specific triggers at the same time, the symptoms can often feel overwhelming. I have listed the triggers that I have experienced over the years in three categories: physical, emotional, and psychological.

Physical triggers

- Being sexually attracted to a woman: There has been a profound healing since my mid thirties, but during my teens and for much of my twenties and early thirties, I felt a sense of an abyss within me which was triggered by sexual attraction. The abyss felt like being trapped in a timeless void; of being entirely isolated, without any possibility of rescue or escape. The fear was always much worse if the attraction was mutual. I associated sex and intimacy with humiliation and the threat of death; my psychological and emotional reaction to sexual attraction was to shut down and block out all notion of any involvement. It felt like a heavy, ancient castle gate suddenly dropping down to protect me from an attack, and I'd retreat to a place of numbness. The challenges of dating and complex PTSD are described in the *Love Lost* chapter later in the book. I felt intimidated whenever there was any sexual attraction; and besides, during my teens and my twenties, I couldn't believe anyone would find me physically attractive.
- Alpha males: Men who I perceived to be domineering or grandiose in their attitude, and who might have aggressive tendencies. Men who have

an arrogant swagger
- Sudden changes in physical behaviour by a man
- A certain predatory look in a man's eyes
- A man unexpectedly touching me (i.e. on a crowded bus), especially a more physically powerful man
- Hearing a man's breathing or his natural bodily smell when physically close (i.e. in a lift)
- Certain smells, such as cheap disinfectant
- Being physically ill, and having to go to the toilet: The last place I want to be when I am physically sick is in a toilet. It took me until I was in my early thirties to feel comfortable enough to use a latrine in a public toilet. There were still many times when I was too tense to urinate though, and would retreat to a cubicle where I felt more at ease.

Emotional triggers
- Aggression (to me or anyone else)
- Suppressed anger (especially by men)

Psychological triggers
- Men talking to children 'inappropriately', (specifically leaning down and with their two faces very close to watch other) or children crying / distressed
- Deviousness / lying
- Playing mind games, i.e. a scenario whereby what I thought was 'real' has been otherwise described very differently by a man for his own agenda
- Men not 'present', being preoccupied
- My being unprepared for a situation when I am with people I do not know that well

I have found the severity and regularity of the symptoms have, overall, diminished over the last two decades. However, during the last five years, a combination of key triggers has brought up more detail in specific memories; ones which I had previously blocked. These events, the process of recalling these memories, and the healing I have since experienced, are described in the *London Calling* chapter.

Symptoms of post-traumatic stress disorder (as experienced by the author)
- Visual and emotional flashbacks: The flashbacks have changed during the last five years, since I have been able to release so much of the rage and shame I had been suppressing. I would get a screen in my mind's eye, which would play, whether my eyes were open or closed, the same, specific experience of the last time I was abused, again and again obsessively, like 'groundhog day'. The re-living of the memory would make me feel dirty, ashamed, and overwhelmed with rage, utterly exhausted, and contemplating, in detail, suicide. I would think where I'd buy the rope, how thick and strong it needed to be, how it would feel around my neck as it tightened, which tree would be best in terms of privacy so no one would disturb me etc...
- Hyper-vigilance: I instinctively scan the environment looking for potential threats, and / or an escape route.
- Fast blinking: Often when the memories are triggered, after a while I get a pain behind my eyes, rather like the eyes are stretched when one is in shock.
- Sudden, immense rage and distrust towards men in particular: I become very conscious of my physical proximity to men; how they are moving, whether they are moving closer to me or not.
- Tunnel vision: During my early twenties, I remember on a number of occasions sitting and talking with friends who were perhaps two feet in front of me. As soon as I was triggered (by them or someone else), I started to see them as if they were further and further away from me, as I disassociated from the situation. The 'volume' of their speech became much quieter. Thankfully, I haven't experienced this for many years.
- Stiff neck, tightness in brain stem, painful lower back.
- Tightness in throat, chills throughout the body, nausea in stomach.
- Tension, a feeling of 'dirtiness' in groin, due to being violated.
- Depression and suicidal thinking.
- Sometimes a sudden jerking movement of arms, energy moving quickly through my body.

- Physical, mental and emotional exhaustion.
- Absent-mindedness / forgetfulness / confusion.
- Nightmares: usually of scenarios in which I am trapped (being suddenly paralysed, and not being able to move my legs was a common nightmare) or attacked, either physically or intellectually. In the early years, I had nightmares involving snakes.
- Daytime intrusive thoughts, and mental projections: usually of men breaking into a toilet cubicle when I am using one.

All survivors of sexual abuse will, I feel pretty sure, agree with me that the trauma runs so deep, affecting every area of your life, that you think you'll never be able to let it go. There have been so many times when I've realised yet another layer of the onion needs to be peeled off and dealt with... but through Ron's and Esther's collective expertise, practicing the CBT, regular meditation, and with the continuing support of AA's 12 Step programme and fellowship, I know I have the foundation to deal with anything that happens in my life.

This realisation has been gradual, however, and it has taken time to recognise the building blocks were being put into place by a Higher Power.

Ron would hold open talks for his clients and friends on spiritual topics such as healing, reincarnation, the Law of Karma, and quantum physics. We would often follow this up during the next therapy session, and he would explain how sometimes the issues we have with people, in this life, can be linked to previous lives, and that a more holistic approach can help the healing process. We would talk about spirituality, awareness of consciousness, and how the mind works. On one occasion, after we'd been working together for several months, I said to him;

'I am really paranoid about a guy at work. It's the way he sometimes looks at me.'

Ron replied, 'You have a thought which suggests to you that you are paranoid. However, the fact you are aware of this thought of paranoia shows you are not, actually, paranoid at all. You are uncomfortable around this person, of course, but the truly paranoid person is not aware that he or she is paranoid'.

He paused, and then said, 'Matt, this is hugely important to understand. Who is aware of this thought of paranoia? Who is the witness to this thought, or any thoughts you have?'

I looked at him, trying to follow what he was saying. After a while, I replied, 'I am aware of these thoughts.'

To which he replied, 'Who are you? Who is this silent witness to these thoughts?'

Ron then used the analogy of the cinema screen that many spiritual teachers use when illustrating the point that our true being is the witness, rather than that which is being witnessed.

'As utterly convincing as it seems, your true self is not these thoughts, these feelings, but the background upon which they arise.' He went on to say, 'our true self is not the images on the screen, but the screen itself.'

It was the first time I had realised, at least intellectually; I was not my thoughts, nor my feelings for that matter. They would come and go, but I would latch on to them like glue, and obsess, worry and believe I was these thoughts and feelings. I didn't know what this meant at that time, but something somewhere in my consciousness shifted at this realisation.

This was the tiniest step towards a lifetime's interest in spiritual philosophy and what is known as Advaita Vedanta. I love how the late, modern-day American spiritual master, Dr Wayne W. Dyer, from his bestselling book *Getting In The Gap*, described the gap between the thoughts:

'This is the gap, and it's a space that allows us to build, create, imagine, and manifest all that we're capable of creating with those thoughts. It's a place of ecstatic peace and serenity. I think of the gap as God's house, since God is the omnipresent, invisible force that is in all of creation.'[5]

I knew I had a long way to go before I could even get a glimmer of an understanding and apply this realisation in my life. I had to find a practical structure which would be the foundation to my life. I needed a process which would help me let go of my past, that would show me how to live life on life's terms, and develop self worth, self esteem, and self confidence. Crucially, it had to give me the power to stay sober, and to develop this

---

[5] Dr Wayne W Dyer, *Getting In The Gap*, (2014). Hay House, INC., Carlsbad, CA.

fleeting relationship with a power greater than myself into a more conscious reality.

Perhaps Ron's greatest legacy has been his interest in spirituality and his encouragement that I attend AA and find a power greater than myself, this has sparked off something very deep inside of me. It has become the fascination of my life to explore various religions and spiritual paths to find Truth. Meeting clinical psychologist Dr Ron, and his wife Esther, was therefore a huge turning point in my life. Whilst Alcoholics Anonymous (AA) has been instrumental in getting me sober and has enabled me, through working the 12 Step programme, to stay sober and grow spiritually, I remain indebted to Ron and Esther for so generously offering me their wisdom, guidance, and love at the very beginning of my journey of healing.

Their professional experience and spiritual wisdom were utterly essential for my emotional and spiritual growth in those weeks before I was to join Alcoholics Anonymous. He got me through the doors of the fellowship, and remained, for the first eighteen months of my recovery, my most important teacher. Ron had a mystical air about him which fascinated me; whilst he was a vastly experienced psychologist, he had obviously studied a wide variety of spiritual philosophies, the world's religions, and what was then regarded as alternative therapies such as aromatherapy, hypnotherapy, and regression.

Without their love, professional expertise, and spiritual awareness at a time in my life when I was at my most vulnerable, I might not have ever made it to AA. Such was the state of my mental health at that time of my life that, had I not met Ron and Esther, and subsequently not attended AA, I am in no doubt that sooner or later I would have taken my own life.

Looking back, they were the kind of couple you'd really look forward to having dinner with on a regular basis. It seemed to me they must have led such fascinating and enriching lives, and with their generosity of spirit they would have helped so many people. What a remarkable spiritual legacy to have achieved.

I followed Ron's guidance and at the end of February 1993 I managed to block out my fear and find the courage to attend my first AA meeting. I had resisted going to AA for as long as possible, but I knew in my heart that I didn't have the strength to stay away from alcohol on my own. Despite all the chaos it had brought, alcohol still intrigued and fascinated me. Deep down I knew it would be only a matter of time before I would give it another go, and the consequences of this really scared me.

I was twenty years and three months old when I reluctantly walked, with much fear and many reservations, into my first AA meeting. This seemed to me to be the ultimate humiliation, and my preconceived ideas about AA did nothing to encourage me to go. I was convinced that: it was full of old, broken people who sat around a long table feeling depressed all the time; it was a religious cult of some kind which would demand from me money which I didn't have; I would lose my identity and freedom to a group of people who would want to control my life. How wrong could I be?

Walking into my first meeting is still the most important decision I've ever made in my life. I'm not claiming AA is perfect; it's not. But it's perfect for me. The 12 Step programme of recovery, and the Fellowship of AA, has since become the spiritual foundation to my life.

With over twenty-five years of sobriety, it continues to offer me the opportunity to grow and explore my truth which is so deeply rewarding and healing for my mind, body and soul.

Despite all my initial reservations about AA (none of which are true, by the way), the remarkable fact is this; since my first meeting on the 1st March 1993 I haven't had an alcoholic drink.

4

AN INSIDE JOB

There is only one cause of unhappiness: the false beliefs you have in your head, beliefs so widespread, so commonly held, that it never occurs to you to question them. [6]
Anthony de Mello

As odd as it might sound, I had a relationship with alcohol long before I picked up my first alcoholic drink. From the age of perhaps seven years old I remember being fascinated whenever I saw adults drinking, whether it was in a restaurant where we were eating as a family, or watching a bar scene in a 1950s Hollywood western film on TV starring John Wayne or Gary Cooper. Even at that age, there was an inner conviction that drinking alcohol would feel really good; I would be a man; funny, intelligent, popular, and the life and soul of the party. These were some of the automatic associations I had as a child when I thought of alcohol. It felt as if it would be an intrinsic part of my nature to drink alcohol. By my late teens, it became the most natural thing in the world to sit in a bar all day, usually alone, and drink myself into oblivion. Looking back, I cannot really remember having a 'social' drink, in the sense that I never drank to be social with people; I drank to get drunk, so one was never enough; I always 'needed' more, a need that became more obsessive and desperate the more I drank.

Initially I loved the buzz, the sense of invincibility it gave me which momentarily opened up a fantasy world in which I could be whomever I

---

[6] Anthony de Mello, *The Way to Love: Meditations for Life* (Image, 2012)

wanted to be. I drank for that effect, regardless of the taste. In fact, I very rarely enjoyed the taste of alcohol, which begs the question, especially when the effect became depressing and I felt suicidal, 'why do I drink so much, so often, when I hate the taste and the effect so much?'

After my last alcoholic drink, which was on the 28th February 1993, I remember feeling so overwhelmed with fear and bewildered with that question I demanded of myself an answer to the question, 'what the hell happens now?' I couldn't imagine living, or wanting to live, without alcohol, even though I remember thinking to myself;

'I hate the taste; I hate the effect; I know it's killing me, but it's the most important thing in my life.'

I found the answer to this, and to so many other questions, in Alcoholics Anonymous. I had at first many reservations about attending an AA meeting. I don't know how many social drinkers sit in bars condemning AA, and triumphantly announcing why they really don't need to go to an AA meeting, but I did so on a regular basis! I saw myself as a heavy, social drinker for most of my time drinking. To rephrase a well-known quote from Oscar Wilde: '(I was) lying in the gutter, looking down at the stars.'

'I'm not like them,' I would say judgementally. 'I'm not homeless, I don't drink out of a bottle, sitting on a park bench having pissed myself again,' as I racked my brain trying to remember what the hell had happened the night before. Shortly before I stopped drinking, I asked my brother, in a rare moment of candour,

'Steve, what happens when you drink alcohol?'

He didn't understand my question, which in itself should have told me that my reaction to alcohol and my behaviour around alcohol was not healthy. My brother has always been a normal, social drinker so to him nothing 'happens'; he just enjoys having a drink once in a while. I went on to ask him a few more questions,

'Do you ever get a really strong, overwhelming urge to have another drink? Do you feel like every cell in your body is demanding it; that you've just got to have a drink?'

He said he didn't ever feel any physical craving for alcohol, and he told me it really didn't matter to him when he went out whether he drank alcohol or a soft drink. The idea of not drinking alcohol terrified me; I thought it was impossible to live without alcohol, and thought people who didn't drink were odd, boring and couldn't be trusted! But then I also knew it was not normal or healthy to drink Old Spice after shave and punch myself in the face. I could see that social drinkers, like my brother Steve, did not obsess about alcohol; they did not steal alcohol, nor did they have blackouts and try to desperately remember what happened and then cover up their behaviour to family, friends and sometimes work colleagues by lying. Despite this awareness, I found it so difficult to admit it to myself and to go to the next level and accept that I was an alcoholic. To do so meant, I knew, that I would have to abstain from alcohol forever – and despite the mental and physical consequences of recent times, the thought of swearing off forever terrified me.

My attitude to AA as I walked very nervously to my first meeting was of panic and defiance; I wanted to 'sort a few things out' and then go back to enjoying drinking again. I hid behind a tree in the garden outside the church where the meeting was taking place for several minutes before plucking up the courage to go into my first meeting. I didn't know this at the time but an AA member, Jennie, who has since become one of my greatest friends in recovery, and has hugely influenced my healing, saw me hiding and mentioned this to a male member who was there to meet newcomers. I crouched by the tree, anxious to the hilt and paranoid I might be recognised walking in, and to make it worse (or so it seemed at that time), I noticed a man hovering near the doorway who looked over in my direction, smiled, and started walking towards me. He was dressed casually, in his mid 50s, grey haired, medium height, and of slight build. I was soon to learn his name was Peter, and he was to become my 'guardian angel' during the first few years of my recovery. As he approached he held out his hand and gently asked in a strong Glaswegian accent that I could barely understand;

'Are you Matthew?'

The rush of adrenaline felt overwhelming as was the desire to run, but I knew I was desperate, that I needed help, so I replied 'yes' and he shook my hand, and introduced himself,

'My name is Peter, they call me Peter Rabbit. I'm a recovering alcoholic.'

I racked my brains trying to work out how he knew my name, and then remembered that Tash John, who I'd met at Ron Hutchinson's a few times, said he would let his friends at AA know I might be coming along at some time. He had mentioned the name, Peter, specifically to me a few weeks earlier.

'You are incredibly brave to come to your first meeting, son. You are very welcome. I know how you are feeling; the mind racing three hundred miles an hour; feeling sick in the stomach, the stiff neck... You are not alone anymore. You need never drink again.'

His words really, deeply touched me. I was speechless. I didn't know what to say, no one had ever told me that I needn't ever drink again. It was a massively powerful statement to hear at that time. As we walked into my first meeting, I knew, intuitively, something extraordinary had come into my life. To walk into that AA meeting with Peter was, without doubt, the most important decision I had ever made in my life. That meeting took place on 1st March 1993, over 24 years ago, and Peter was correct: I haven't needed an alcoholic drink since then.

The story of AA is well known to most people. Founded by two alcoholics, Bill W and Dr Bob, in the United States in the 1930s, AA now has more than 117,000 groups in 180 different countries and an estimated worldwide active membership of more than two million. What is not so well known is how the AA 12-step program has inspired and been adopted by over sixty other 12-step based substance abuse, dependency and self-help fellowships, including Narcotics Anonymous (NA), Gamblers Anonymous (GA), Overeaters Anonymous (OA), Sex and Love Addicts Anonymous (SLAA), Co-dependency Anonymous (CODA), and Adult Children of Alcoholics (ACOA), to name only a few. There is also Al-Anon, which offers support for the spouses, family members, and friends of alcoholics. (Wikipedia states there are over 200 self-help organisations that use the 12-step programme! That may be true, although I haven't been able to confirm this). Nevertheless, when one considers the many millions of people who have found recovery as a result of the 12-step programme, it must surely be one of the most remarkable stories of the 20th Century.

There were probably forty people at my first AA meeting, packed tightly into the small, smoky basement room of a local church, over the road from the preparatory school where I had been Head Boy. On the walls were hung, I noticed, slogans printed on A4 card with messages such as;

- One Day At A Time
- Keep It Simple

- This Too Shall Pass
- Together We Can

As crass as these statements seemed to me at the time, they became really helpful when I started to realise how difficult it was, during my first year in particular, to stay away from a drink. Even now, if I am feeling lonely these maxims come in useful to calm my nerves and help me relax. There were also two old, rather faded black and white framed photographs on the coffee table at the front of the room, which showed, Peter told me, the co-founders of AA, Bill W and Dr Bob.

The room started filling up at 7.15pm with more people, and as the room got busy so the smoke got thicker. I was relieved I could smoke; I was on over sixty Marlboro cigarettes a day, and whilst the detox medication took the edge off the physical shakes to some degree, the sweats, muscle pain, and mental withdrawals were horrific. I was chain smoking non-stop to try and relieve some of the stress and tension. The other benefit of being in such a smoky room was that I couldn't see everyone, which suited me as I was paranoid everyone was staring at me. I quickly scanned the faces I could see, dreading I might recognise someone I'd had some altercation with in a local bar, or from school, or from around the town in general. I felt a huge sense of relief; no one looked familiar. It didn't occur to me at that time that, had I known anyone, we were there for the same reasons! I sat down next to a chap who welcomed me and introduced himself as Tony.

'Ninety meetings in ninety days, that's what they told me when I first came to AA, and I'm still here. It's been over fifteen years now, and it's a good life.' He paused, looked at me more closely and said, 'you're young, you've got it all to live for. Just don't pick up the first drink each day, get to a meeting, and you'll be alright.'

He smiled at me; I saw kindness in his eyes, but my 'filter' would not allow me to trust my initial reaction at that time, so I mentally rejected him, deciding he could not be trusted, that he must have some agenda. He suggested I listen to the similarities not the differences when people spoke, and then gave me his telephone number, saying,

'You can call me anytime, if you need a chat. And I mean anytime,' he repeated, with a smile.

His friendliness was genuine, and during the next few months Tony was as good as his word, meeting me regularly for coffee, and he was always encouraging me. He is now over 35 years sober, lives in Manchester, and has since become a very good friend in recovery. Such was my mental state, his kindness did nothing to lessen my nerves. The idea of being in a small space with (mainly) men was a trigger for the PTSD, and in my mind's eye I could see myself suddenly being physically restrained, and the doorway blocked, preventing my escape. I tried my best to block this out; to flick the switch in my mind which Dr Ron Hutchinson had recently taught me.

I also felt it was grossly unfair to be in an AA meeting at the age of 20 years and 3 months; it really felt like the end of the world. It was, of course, a new beginning, I just couldn't see it yet. Although my life improved considerably once I got actively involved with the AA programme, it would take well over a year before I really felt a deep sense of gratitude for having got sober so young. I sat nervously flicking through some AA leaflets Peter had given me, hoping no one would talk to me, and trying my best to focus on what the leaflets said, rather than the inner torment racing through my mind;

- I was too young to be an alcoholic. I knew I had a problem with alcohol but no way was I an alcoholic at the age of twenty. It wasn't fair. There must be some way I could enjoy drinking again.
- Alcoholics drank on park benches and were homeless. I wasn't homeless. I conceded that I had drunk on park benches.
- I'd never lost my job because of drinking. (Untrue, I got fired from a film for drunkenness.)
- I wasn't the same as these people. With a combination of chronic low self-esteem and huge arrogance, I remember thinking that I'd had a public school education so they couldn't teach me anything I didn't already know.
- I decided I just needed to sort out some stuff, and then I would be able drink again and enjoy it.

There was plenty of self-pity and self-centeredness – I decided that no one here could understand how I felt; so I might as well run out of the room as fast as possible and get drunk. But I was too terrified to move an inch; there were too many people between me and the door. I knew I'd have to last the meeting, and then, I consoled myself, I would go and get drunk. Yet,

I knew in my heart that drinking was not the answer. I just didn't know what the alternative was, nor whether it was really worth the effort to 'exist' in life without the fun and excitement of drinking.

Peter introduced me gently to a few other members, and I was struck by how friendly, relaxed and happy they seemed to be. This was not at all what I expected. In my mind, I thought there would be twelve smelly old men in battered suits with string around their waists (and perhaps the odd crazed woman talking to herself in a corner) sitting around a table staring at a bottle of whisky, bemoaning their lives and all secretly desperate to drink - and then most of them would give in and go to the park to drown themselves with stolen White Lightning or Special Brew. It never occurred to me that social drinkers do not conjure up such judgements about meetings of AA when they are getting drunk on their own in a bar. The point was, I couldn't imagine anyone being able to stop drinking and be happy – and anyway, I thought, it didn't matter, because I was not an alcoholic and didn't belong here with these people.

I was given half a cup of tea, which puzzled and annoyed me, until Tony pointed out that most newcomers are so nervous at their first meeting, they sometimes shake and have difficulty holding a full cup. As I tried to drink the half-cup, it dawned on me that he was politely describing me. I was shaking with nerves, as the energy bristled through my muscles, and my limbs were shuddering and jerking involuntarily. As I put the cup to my mouth, I was scared I would suddenly jerk and tea would spill over me, so I put it on the floor, and hid it behind the leg of the chair. I quickly scanned the room again, trying my best to avoid eye contact lest anyone spoke to me. There was a broad spectrum of society; smartly dressed retired men and women, a couple of office workers in suits, some who looked like they had just been to the gym, and a few like me, looking broken and lost.

The meeting then started. The Secretary welcomed everyone and read The Preamble, a brief reading which described what AA was. He then specifically welcomed any newcomers, at which point I felt panic hit me as I anticipated everyone staring at me, and expecting me to say something. Two people nervously introduced themselves, during which Tony, sitting next to me, said,

"You don't need to say anything if you don't want to. You don't need to do anything. Just try and relax as best you can.' I felt a massive sense of relief, kept staring at the floor, and said nothing. The Secretary then introduced the main speaker for the meeting.

The main talk was by a former Royal Naval officer who was in his early 70s. He looked the archetypal retired military man; grey hair, swept back above his head with Brylcreem I am guessing, a pencil thin moustache on his upper lip, and he wore a smart, tweed jacket, and looked more at home at the golf club, the Magistrates bench, or in a scene from a John Mills' Second World War film than at an AA meeting; a few of my harsh judgements about AA and its members started to fall away at my first meeting. He said it had been twenty years since his last drink, and that he felt very grateful to be sober.

He described how he had enjoyed an active social life for many years, and that there had been no serious consequences to his drinking until he was in his mid forties, when he developed physical cravings for alcohol to the extent he started drinking in the morning, to take the edge of the shakes. Within eighteen months, he had developed such a problem that he started lying to his wife about money; he would disappear on drinking sprees and not tell her nor work where he was; he started to have frequent blackouts, and then the delirium tremens. His wife eventually confronted him about his drinking and his dishonesty, which he had considered to be an affront. He flatly denied there was a problem. She gave him an ultimatum which shocked him; she told him he needed help, and gave him AA's details. At the same time, his Commanding Officer had noticed, during the preceding eighteen months, the considerable deterioration in his physical health and mental aptitude. He was told in no uncertain terms that whilst the Royal Navy would support his residential treatment for alcoholism, it was, as far as his on-going employment was concerned, non-negotiable. They could not tolerate his behaviour any longer. Either he accepted their offer of treatment, or he would face a disciplinary. During six months of treatment, he started attending AA meetings, and had stayed sober ever since. What really shocked me about his talk was his honesty and sincerity, particularly when he spoke about his behaviour when he drank.

'When the drink really got hold of me, I became more desperate in my behaviour and much more devious in my thinking. I had been an honest man all my life. I valued honesty and integrity in others, particularly as an Officer in the Royal Navy where your word is your bond, but when the obsession with alcohol hit me, in my early forties, my morals soon went out of the window. I became someone I detested; I was a liar, I had the morals of an alley cat. My wife would beg me to stop drinking, but I couldn't. One morning, I remember the poor woman saying to me, "where has the man I married gone, who the hell are you?".'

He went on to describe how the obsession for alcohol had destroyed his marriage, and almost his second. He had found AA just in time, and the marriage survived. Nevertheless, his alcoholism had brought about bankruptcy, and the initial estrangement of his children. I had never heard anyone speak so openly and honestly before. I could relate to the way he drank so desperately during the last eighteen months, before he got sober, so to see such a respectable, polite gentleman speaking the Queen's English about the horror of his life was truly shocking. He was not what I expected an alcoholic to look like! Despite the obvious pain and losses that he and his family had experienced as a result of his alcoholism, I felt envy, and I resented him for having 'enjoyed' his drinking for so many more years than me. I felt it was so unfair that the drink no longer 'worked' for me.

I have little memory of anything else that was said at the meeting, but I recall half a dozen or so members speaking from the floor. No one stood up when they spoke, which I had expected. I had a vague memory of an episode of the US 80s police series *Cagney and Lacey*, where in a scene based in an AA meeting, and everyone stood up when they spoke! The only other thing I remember, at the end of the meeting, was a reading from the book *Alcoholics Anonymous* (referred to by members as the Big Book, and after which the fellowship is named), called *The Promises*.[7] The sentence that really struck me was, 'we are going to know a new freedom and a new happiness. We will not regret the past, nor wish to shut the door on it. We will comprehend the word serenity, and we will know peace.' These sounded outrageous statements at the time. I remember wishing in my deepest heart that these promises could happen for me, but I seriously

---

[7] *Alcoholics Anonymous* (Alcoholics Anonymous Worldwide Services, INC, 2001). Pages 82-83. Listening to *The Promises* being read aloud at the end of an AA meeting during my early recovery helped me so much. These inspirational words offered a sense of hope and encouragement and still serve as positive affirmations in my daily life.

doubted they would. As soon as the meeting was over, I bolted for the door as quickly as I could, but Peter was there hovering again. I had no choice but to mumble a few words of thanks before I escaped.

Peter had been sober for fifteen years by that time (when my dear friend passed away he was twenty-seven years sober), and I soon learned he was much loved by fellow AA members for giving of his time so freely, and for his kind words of support and encouragement. He was a gentle yet passionate soul who inspired me the more I got to know him. He would often collate a small book of prayers, spiritual poetry, and messages of hope and hand them out to newcomers, like me, and these I have always treasured as a memory of a wonderful man. As I left the meeting, he gently said to me 'Well done. Keep coming back, it really is worth it. The best years of your life are ahead of you. Here's my telephone number; you're welcome to call me anytime. Come to the meeting here tomorrow evening at 7.30pm, I'll be here at 7pm setting up.'

I knew he meant it, I sensed he was telling me the truth, but I seriously doubted I would not drink again. I walked home very confused, a little hopeful, but convinced AA would not work for me because I felt so different.

I didn't have a drink that night; though every cell in my body and mind screamed for alcohol. I hung in there, thinking what Peter, Jennie, and Tony had said to me, and asking myself, 'why would they lie to me, if it really was worth it?' I had to give it another go tomorrow, for I was scared as to what would happen if I drank again; whilst the idea of having a drink terrified me, so did living with my savage mind and the demented voices which were tormenting me with their venom, judgement, and condemnation.

My brother and sister had both left home and now lived in London, so Mum and Dad bore the brunt of the emotional and psychological challenges of my early recovery. They went out of their way to support me as best they could, given the difficult circumstances. I tried to explain what was going on, but they couldn't understand from their personal experience when I described the physical cravings, nor the mental obsession. Mum went into 'Mum mode' and supplied me with countless cups of tea, biscuits, and offers of meals to strengthen me up. However, I couldn't eat anything. In fact, my diet was dreadful at that time, in part because I'd ignored regular meals for well over a year (I was drinking; food got in the way - it soaked up the alcohol, and cost money), and also because I felt so tense that I couldn't keep any substantial food down. I would pick at food, and when I did eat, I preferred light meals such as soup and salads, which I couldn't choke on. I was so tense and scared about getting anything solid stuck in my windpipe; I'm still very self conscious of this even now.

I weighed myself during my first week sober; I was 8 stone, 6 pounds, when the average weight for a male my age and height was just under 12 stone. Mum resolved to feed me up as soon as possible. My parents did everything they could to help my recovery, but it must have been really tough for them, living with me under their roof, at this time. Although my behaviour and huge mood swings improved as the months went by, I was so tense and anxious during the first eighteen months of my recovery, I was exhausting to be around for any length of time. They were incredibly supportive of me. There was no financial pressure, so I knew I had a safe place to live, and I wouldn't go without food; if only I would eat more! They had covered all the costs for the psychological sessions with Dr. Ron Hutchinson, which over time must have exceeded a few thousand pounds (even before he waived his fee and I took milk and eggs). I was too self obsessed to acknowledge their support during this time. It took a good year before it dawned on me how much they must have been through, mentally and emotionally.

Mum's tea and talking into the early hours got me through the night, without any sleep, but crucially without a drink. My mind replayed old tapes of my past on an endless loop. Nonetheless, I went to my second meeting the next day. Once again, everything inside me tried to convince me not to go, so I kept flicking the switch as Ron had shown me, and just put one foot in front of the other until I walked through the door. There is a great saying in AA, 'get the body to the meeting, and the mind will follow'.

Peter was already there putting the chairs out. He greeted me with a huge smile,

'Well done, my friend.' He paused and said quietly, 'I know how scared you must have felt as you came here tonight. You are not alone. We all know the fear, the panic, the madness in the mind telling us, shouting at us, don't go there, don't join those crazy people, you're not like them...'

He spoke my language; it was an incredible feeling to know that there was someone else who understood what I was thinking, and how I was feeling. I replied, 'I just don't know where else to go. Part of me wants to be here, but the other me wants to run, keep running...'

Peter nodded, and said, 'none of us walk in here smiling when we first join AA. We come in here broken, humiliated, and scared. I promise you. Believe me, everyone at the meeting last night, when they first came to AA, knew exactly how you felt, how scared you were.

'We've all been there. So now we help each other; and together we get stronger.'

Then he walked over to the table in the corner of the room which displayed the AA books and leaflets. He found one leaflet called 'Who Me?' and handed it to me, saying, 'Try and answer the questions listed inside about your drinking as honestly as you can, and we'll talk through them after the meeting.' The '20 Questions' had been written to help the newcomer to AA look closely at the physical, mental and emotional consequences of their problem drinking.

The questions asked whether drinking had affected family relationships, employment, physical and mental health, finance, and reputation. A few made for very uncomfortable reading, as they were undeniably about the direct consequences of my drinking:

- Have you ever felt guilt or remorse after drinking?
- Have you turned to lower companions and an inferior environment when drinking?
- Do you want a drink the next morning?
- Do you drink to escape from worries or trouble?
- Have you ever had a complete loss of memory as a result of drinking?
- Has your physician ever treated you for drinking?

Excerpt from the *20 Questions* (Alcoholics Anonymous 12th Step Starter Pack)

It then stated if you answer 'Yes' to three or more, you were probably an alcoholic. I answered 'Yes' to 18, which seemed ridiculously high; so I went through them again, trying my best to get a much lower number. Peter asked me how many I had put 'Yes' to, and I answered '7', which seemed much more reasonable. He replied, with a twinkle in his eyes,

'Was that the second or third time you went through them?'

He and a few other members invited me to have a coffee with them after the meeting, but I lied, saying I had to go and do something (I even used those specific words!); it wasn't quite that I had to go and see a man about a dog, but I'm sure they knew I was too scared to join them. There was no pressure at all though; looking back, they understood the importance of the gentle approach. Nonetheless, despite my fears I went to an AA meeting the next day, and the day after that, and so on, until I had somehow managed a whole week without picking up a drink. This blew me away; I never thought I could go a day without alcohol, let alone a week, but the strength within the meetings, and the support of Peter, Jennie and others was helping me to keep away from a drink each day.

The following weekend, I went to a friend's 21st birthday party in Gloucestershire. There I would meet up with old school friends, many of whom I hadn't seen since we had all left and gone to university. I got a lift to the party with an old drinking friend and felt really shaky on the way. I was scared I would start drinking again as soon as we got there. I could taste it in my mouth, and this developed into powerful cravings. I knew it was inevitable - I was going to drink. My AA friends had warned me it could be a dangerous environment for me; that I might drink... and they encouraged me to put my fledgling sobriety first. One of them told me 'there will come a day when you will be relaxed with people drinking alcohol around you; that's one of the many gifts of recovery. But it's too soon for you at the moment.'

In my arrogance I ignored them, thinking I knew better. I didn't want to lose face with my friends; I wanted desperately to be normal, whatever the hell that was! In my desperation to be a typical twenty year old and fit in, I was still going to nightclubs after my regular AA meetings every Friday and Saturday night with another member, where I would nervously gulp eight pints of Coca Cola, and then sit on the loo all night. I hated every second of being there; I felt so paranoid and different from everyone else, and this was my best impersonation of being normal! If I felt particularly brave (or stupid), I would watch people at the bar who I thought might have a drink problem, and would ask them if they had ever been to an AA meeting, as they probably needed it. It did not go well, and often I would receive a curt, abusive remark in return.

Back in the car the night of the party with my friends, there was a dreadful sense of an inevitable fate hanging over me as we drove through Bristol on our way to the party. I feared I might started hitting myself again, in front of party guests, and then the words of the clinical psychologist came to me: 'if you drink again, I will have no hesitation but to section you indefinitely', which scared me even more. As the car stopped at a traffic light, I looked to my left, and suddenly, as a gap emerged in the crowd walking along the pavement, I recognised Mark. We'd met at a meeting a week earlier, and he had taken me for a coffee afterwards, and had helped me with his words of encouragement. He was drunk, leaning against a wall; he looked in a terrible state. The kind , friendly man I had met the previous week was not there; all I saw was a terribly sick man, lost and bewildered.

The reality of taking a drink at the party hit me hard. I didn't want all that agony back, and in my heart I knew that one drink would trigger everything off again; it always had done after all. When we arrived at the party, I called Peter and told him what had happened. He said it was my Higher Power, a wake-up call to remind me of the painful reality of what happens when we drink again. He told me to pray for Mark, and for myself, and to stay safe. I was to call him every hour until I went to bed. Despite being shaky and feeling overwhelmed at the party, I managed to stay sober. The tragedy is that I have not seen Mark since that moment over twenty-three years ago, to thank him. I've asked after him over the years, but no one knows what happened to him.

Scared by the experience at the party, I resolved to go to a meeting every day the following week. This was a positive move forward for me as until then I had had to force myself to go every day, and such was my mental state I often felt so fearful I might back out at the last minute. I defiantly resisted much of the 12 Step programme; whenever I looked at the scrolls on the walls of the meeting (which listed the 12 Steps), I resented seeing the word 'God' (if there was a God, why had I been abused etc), the phrase 'searching and fearless moral inventory' (I had lied, stolen and compromised my moral integrity, but I didn't want to admit that to anyone), and 'amends' (such was my self-pity I didn't want to acknowledge I owed anyone an apology for my behaviour). Despite this, it was the support and encouragement of the characters in AA that got me back through the door every day. It was such a huge relief to know that I wasn't alone with my crazy thoughts and feelings; that others obviously understood what was going on, and more importantly, had found a way to let go and enjoy life once again. This gave me enormous hope, even if I struggled to trust them!

The challenge I had, in the first few months at least, with some of the old timers (members who often had over ten, twenty and in some cases thirty years of sobriety), was that they were the same age as some of the paedophiles who abused me and this triggered the PTSD. Sitting near them and trying to listen when they spoke at meetings was for me through a filter of hyper-vigilance (I felt physically very anxious and would instinctively scan the room for potential threats, questioning the motives of the men around me), feelings of nausea and, at worst, flashbacks to the abuse. Nonetheless, over the next few months I gradually got to know and eventually befriend a number of old timers who have since had a massive influence on my sobriety. With their gentle encouragement, a shift took place in my attitude to AA. Previously I had hung around with other new members, and we had bemoaned our lives and felt sorry for ourselves. An old timer noticed this and said to me,

'Matt, you need to talk with members who identify with your story, and have worked through these challenges without drinking. They're the ones who can really help you.'

Their message was direct and simple:

- Don't pick up your first drink. Pick up the phone instead
- Go to meetings on a regular basis. If possible go to 90 meetings in 90 days
- Take on a regular commitment (put the chairs out, make the tea, put slogans up)
- Get a sponsor (a trusted member to guide you through the 12 Steps) and a home group (a regular AA meeting or meetings you commit to attending each week)
- Get telephone numbers of sober members and use them

Peter also encouraged me to do what he called trebling up: (1) get to the meeting early, (2) listen and share at every meeting, and (3) stay on afterwards to help tidy up. I met several inspirational old timers during the first years of my recovery, who all played a vital role in helping me stay sober. They were, among several others; Peter Rabbit, Grateful Dave, Flat Cap Bill, Jennie, Pauline, Biker Steve, Penny, Barry Fang, Teacher Mike (my first sponsor), Tony, Tobacco Alan, Mike Mc, and Chris H.

An Inside Job

Grateful Dave was always, always...incredibly grateful. He would bounce into meetings wearing a tracksuit with a huge smile on his face, ask how everyone was, encourage newcomers, and gently offer suggestions where there were problems. He was a force of nature! He was in his early sixties, good looking, genuinely charming and he had an infectious energy. He ran a badminton club every Saturday evening in a local hall, and would encourage members to come along and give it a go. He drove members to meetings across the county; he was a genuinely kind, sincere man who helped many, many people, but he did my head in during the first few months of recovery. I could not understand how an alcoholic could be grateful to be an alcoholic, and be so happy - it just didn't make sense to me. He seemed to be living on a different planet; alcoholics had to be as miserable and as self piteous as I was, surely!

It took me a few years to appreciate the fact that my being a recovering alcoholic had given me the opportunity to meet so many amazing people in AA, and with their love and support, and with the 12 Steps as the foundation to my life, I have found the strength to confront my childhood and to be able to, for the most part, find peace of mind. I've needed the structure of the AA Fellowship in my life in order to come to terms with the abuse. Had I not become an alcoholic, and then to have found recovery, I doubt very much I would have been able to do this. I cannot imagine a life without the love and kindness of my many AA friends.

Whilst Grateful Dave remained an enigma to me for some time, during my first few months it was Chris H who really fascinated me. Chris was a tall man, intelligent and articulate, with a great sense of humour and a hearty laugh. His alcoholism had almost destroyed him before he eventually crawled into AA in his mid-forties. He had stayed sober for eight years in the Manchester area, and then a promotion had brought him and his family to the West Country. Shortly after that, he had had an horrific relapse during which time he met me in the pub. As soon as we started drinking together, our alcoholism deteriorated very quickly. There was no pretence about our drinking. We both knew we each had a problem, but at that stage it was 'working', that is, we could live with the consequences of the morning shakes, blackouts, and depression.

At last orders every night, Chris would buy eight pints of export lager (four for each of us) and would disappear to the toilet. While he was in there, I would down two of his pints as quickly as possible which he was too drunk to notice when he returned. I liked drinking with Chris; he was generous with his money, and he always bought me drinks (in recovery he said he'd effectively taken me 'hostage', but I didn't care; I was onto a good deal, as far as I was concerned). We were the kind of annoying drunks who would mis-quote Shakespeare quite loudly at each other at the bar, and would hog the Quizmaster machine, taking great pride whenever we won the jackpot. The only times I can remember us falling out was when he had the audacity to question my drinking, but this served me well when we got sober, as he could remind me how bad my drinking really had been.

I came into AA a few weeks before him, and when he returned after his relapse, his marriage was on the rocks, he was going bankrupt, and his children were not talking to him. He was so distraught when he spoke in meetings about his situation, I was amazed he had not gone back to the drink again. I would watch him with the same curiosity as you might watch an animal in a zoo as he tried to speak; this physically imposing man, as he broke down in tears, with his body shaking through the alcohol withdrawal; it amazed me that an alcoholic in so much mental and emotional pain was not drinking.

I felt a tremendous compassion for him, after all we had drunk so often together, and here we both were in AA trying to get sober together. The difference between his bravado when we drank together and the man I saw in such a pitiful state helped me to recognise this illness in myself. What also struck me was that I still felt dead inside; apart from having feelings of anger and fear, I had no other emotions as such. I could not cry; I still felt dead inside emotionally. Chris showed me it was alright to cry. In recovery, we became great friends, and he was an immense support to me throughout my life until he tragically died in a car accident some ten years ago. I was devastated for his family (who I knew very well) and for myself when I heard the news. Chris could put problems into perspective very quickly for me. When we'd been sober for over a year, I remember him saying to me when I was having a good moan one day, 'it took me over thirty years (of alcoholic drinking, bankruptcy, marital problems) to finally get here. You got here in less than five. One day you'll see how fortunate you really are.'

In reality, Dave and Chris were my best teachers in the sense that I learnt you could be a sober alcoholic and go through immense pain, and be a sober alcoholic and be happy, and grateful. Both Grateful Dave and Chris H taught me an invaluable lesson – you can be happy or in turmoil and still not drink!

When I managed to get a month without a drink, it seemed like a lifetime. I still had a lurking belief within me that one day I could drink again, and enjoy it like I had at the very beginning. As much as the meetings were helping me, I was not committed to AA, and I tried my best to be as elusive as possible as I felt so scared of letting people get to know me. I would arrive as near to the start time as possible, sit close to the exit door, and escape as soon as it finished. Another AA member, Tim H, and I would vie with each other to try and get the chair nearest the exit at every meeting, so we could both dart out quickly. What began as a serious 'survival' strategy developed, as I became more relaxed after a few months, much more of a game between us.

The reality was, my emotions were like a rollercoaster and would jump from one extreme to another, within a split second, depending on where I was, who I was with, and what I was obsessing about. It helped me to know that I was not alone, there were many other AAs who felt the same way. Such was my fear of rejection in the first few months, I had yet to talk openly in a meeting. On one occasion, I recall sitting outside a circle of members in a meeting when there was a long silence between speakers, which I always hated. I suddenly had this overwhelming urge to open my mouth, but with this urge came a huge fear which played out in my mind's eye;

As soon as I opened my mouth and said my name, I foresaw the whole group turning round and en masse shouting, 'Just FUCK OFF'! For about a minute before I eventually introduced myself, I visualised the mental switch that Ron had told me to use, and then said for the first time;

'My name's Matt.......... and I'm.... an alcoholic.'

Due to my nerves and chronic self consciousness, I remember not being able to say the word 'alcoholic' correctly, I swallowed the middle two syllables so it sounded more like 'alk...lic'. It didn't matter; practically every AA member remembers how they felt at that moment when they first find the courage to speak at a meeting.

'Hi Matt, welcome,' replied the group.

After a panic-stricken few seconds of silence, during which I felt my heart was trying to explode out of my chest, I heard aggressive, savage voices in my mind taunting me after I dared to open my mouth.

'You fucking bastard,' it told me. 'Everyone knows you're a fucking c*nt. C*nt, c*nt, c*nt. Just run; get the fuck out of here before anyone talks to you. Don't you fucking look up; don't you fucking DARE. If you look up , they'll see your eyes and they'll know how fucking sick you are.'

As this mental onslaught started, I managed to say to the group, 'I don't know what else to say...Thank you...'

Much to my relief, the group thanked me for talking, and a few members looked over to me, and smiled, which was encouraging. I can't remember hearing anything else during the rest of the meeting, as the voices inside my mind were louder than any external voices; I've often described it as the savage mind, which I experienced for much of the first year of my recovery. The voices raged at me non-stop for the rest of the night. I couldn't sleep when they attacked me; they were voices of such venom and hatred, it seemed the more I resisted them (or tried ignoring them), the louder and more vicious they became. My AA friends had a very simple, practical solution when I plucked up the courage and described to them what was happening.

'My mind is out to get me', I would say, and and they would laugh. 'Join the gang, Matt,' they told me. 'Tell the voices to 'fuck off' and get on with your day'.

One of them went on to describe how he called his main inner critic 'Chuck who doesn't give a fuck.' Another referred to his negative voices as 'The Committee of Doom', which made me laugh. Over the course of the next eighteen months, from March 1993 through to Summer 1994, my own 'Committee of Doom' started to quieten down the more I spoke about how I felt. It was a simple equation; the more open I became, and the more suppressed energy I therefore released, the less I was aware of them, and soon I was automatically telling them to 'Fuck Off' and getting on with my day, as suggested by my new AA friends!

This healing coincided with Ron's teaching about being a witness to one's thoughts. He helped me to recognise thoughts were only thoughts; of themselves they had no energy unless I fed them with my attention. So long as the PTSD was not triggered, my general state of mind slowly lost much of its savagery and self-condemnation.

Whilst my mind was a challenge, so too were my emotions. In AA we talk of alcoholism as a threefold illness; mental, emotional and spiritual. I struggled to know what I was feeling most of the time; I was a mass of confusion. I recognised fear and anger. A fellow AA member, Tash John, had seen a documentary about laughter therapy and suggested we use the same principle try and shift some of our anger. After the Newcomers group, one Monday evening, we went to the beach, and walked out as far as we possibly could without sinking in the mud. We found 'our spot', and standing ten foot apart, we started screaming 'aaaggh' at each other as loudly and for as long as we possibly could. After five minutes we both became so exhausted that we had to stop. We both felt quite sick, and John had a coughing fit. I asked him if he had shifted any anger. He thought about it, and after a long pause replied,

'No, not really.' I said 'Same here, maybe we should try it again tomorrow?'

As we turned to walk home, we were horrified to see six strangers (presumably concerned at our behaviour) approximately forty metres away who were walking very tentatively in a wide arc directly towards us. They were not overtly threatening us; on the contrary from their body language they looked hesitant and nervous as they approached, but such was our shame and embarrassment, John and I turned to each other, said 'Fuck' and ran off in opposite directions along the beach to escape. I didn't leave the house for three days in case one of the six recognised me!

I was now seven months sober, and still struggling to accept I was an alcoholic. I knew I had a drink problem, but I could not accept I was an alcoholic; yet I had dreams about drinking; sometimes I would wake up and taste it in my mouth (even though I hadn't drunk for several months at this stage), and I was still thinking about alcohol 24/7. I really wanted to believe, though, that one day I could drink again normally, even though I had not drunk without serious consequences for so long. Even after my detox, I would sometimes wake up with the taste of cointreau, an orangey syrup liquor, in my mouth, even though I had not had any since I was a teenager. This scared me as it felt as if every cell in my whole body was desperately craving a drink, and I felt that I would break down and drink, so I reluctantly telephoned an AA member who agreed to meet me in a local café, believing this would help to calm me down.

Peter and Jennie had both been encouraging me to find an AA sponsor, someone who would be my confidante and would take me through the 12 Step programme. They advised me to listen in meetings to men whose drinking I could identify with, whose recoveries I respected, and who I felt I could trust enough to be open with about my life. Essentially, I'd be looking for a mentor I could talk to on a regular basis who would support my fledgling sobriety. Whilst several other members who had joined AA at more or less the same time as me had found a sponsor, I had resisted the whole idea at every turn. To have a sponsor meant I would have to be honest about my past, and I was too ashamed to admit much of what I was holding back, to myself, let alone be honest about it with an older male.

Although an AA sponsor could not counsel me in any professional sense about the sexual abuse, it was inevitable that the abuse would come up, as it affected every area of my life. I was crippled with fear and anger so much of the time in early recovery, and this was as a direct consequence of the PTSD, which had been diagnosed as being a result of the abuse. I had an instinctive, subconscious reaction to most men so I was arrogantly dismissive of many of the male sponsors I could, in theory, approach. I found it far easier to judge and condemn men and find reasons not to trust them; it was a way of creating a protective barrier around myself so I would not be abused and humiliated again. Asking a man for help felt humiliating. I needed to have control; I felt that any slight crack in the barrier could open up even more pain, and I dared not risk that. The mantra I had created for my self-protection, after the last time I was abused - 'I will never ever, ever allow anyone to hurt me again' - was now working against me, and against my hope for recovery.

I much preferred the company of women; so long as I wasn't sexually attracted to them. As soon as there was a hint of sexual chemistry, the PTSD was triggered and I would feel shaky, insecure, and dirty. Sponsors often suggest to new sponsees that they avoid getting into a relationship until they are at least one year sober. I didn't have this problem: whenever a woman I found sexually attractive smiled or said 'hello' to me, I usually had a panic attack! After a few months in AA, I became friendly with Pauline, a lady member of AA who was a few years older than me, and we would spend a few afternoons each week at her flat, which helped me to open up more, and encouraged me to allow people to get closer to me. Pauline was very kind and compassionate with me; I felt safe with her, and with her two daughters, who had known of me during my drinking.

Their friendship helped me to accept my masculinity a bit more. As much as I loathed my body and my personality, at that stage of my recovery, having their friendship and to feel they accepted me for who I was, was very healing for me. It helped me to confront the fact that I'd always felt so different from women of my own generation when growing up. The rites of passage I presumed they had all gone through - the first date, first cuddle and kiss, the first time they'd made love with their partner and had sex etc.. - I had been too terrified to experience, and so I felt very much out of my depth with my peers.

When we spoke about sponsorship, Pauline suggested I listen at the meetings to an old timer called Teacher Mike, and to see whether I felt he was the right sponsor for me. I knew deep down that I had to take a risk, and 'flick the switch' to block out the fears, so I found out who Teacher Mike was, and made sure I attended his regular meetings. I wouldn't go so far as to say I stalked him, but I did make detailed notes at home of what he said at meetings in my attempt to make sure he was trustworthy and 'kosher'! After several weeks of procrastination, I asked him and he agreed to be my sponsor.

Mike was in his late fifties, a retired teacher and a Cambridge graduate. He was a highly intelligent, well read, articulate man, who had a fondness for theatre, cricket, poetry, and liberal politics. We had a lot in common, which encouraged me. I would often join him for coffee in our favourite café, where he would usually be found sitting half way back, finishing the Daily Telegraph crossword. He had grey, curly hair, glasses perched on his forehead, a smart cravat tucked inside with his open necked Marks and Spencer's chequered shirt, braces with his blue corduroy trousers, and his sleeves rolled up as if he meant business.

When I listened to Mike in meetings, I had been attracted by his spiritual approach to life. He would often talk about the Higher Power, not in a religious or ritualistic sense, but as a living presence in his life. After asking him to sponsor me, we arranged to meet the following afternoon to get to know each other a little better. My heart sank at the idea of this. As much as I knew I needed to open up and talk about myself, the idea still terrified me. I was scared I wouldn't be able to deal with the intensity of the emotions, and that Mike might judge me.

I arrived at the agreed time, and after a few minutes of general conversation, he asked me;

'Are you willing to go to any lengths to stay sober?' and I immediately replied 'Yes'.

Unfortunately, that was the first lie I told him.

Whilst I sensed he was a decent, intelligent man, it was too fast. I needed a lot more time to feel safe enough to open up with him. He was a kind, sensitive man, and he soon realised how difficult it was for me to talk about my childhood. There were times we met after I had been to see Dr. Ron Hutchinson and when the session has been really raw, and I was still reacting to it, Mike would say to me,

'You're not here, are you? You're somewhere completely else.' He was correct. During our first few months working together I'd often be lost in my own world, or as he would gently say to me,

'You've shut down again. Where are you, now?'

When I was shut down, more often than not I'd be in flashback; feeling numb and in shock as the memories of the abuse would replay in my mind again and again. These were the times when I experienced tunnel vision, and Mike would look as if he was at the end of a long tunnel and his voice would sound much further away. The clinical psychologist at the hospital had explained to me that this was a way of dissociating when the PTSD was triggered, and it was important to use the concentration techniques to help keep myself conscious. It was nothing personal to Mike, but when this happened, I felt very vulnerable in every sense; physically, mentally and emotionally, and as soon as I felt strong enough I'd take myself off to a safe place, away from everyone else. This was usually the beach, the woods or my bedroom. It depended whether I had to walk near crowds of people, as to where I went.

When we first started to work through the 12 Steps, I could not be completely honest with him. I felt such shame and horror about the abuse that I edited out all the issues I thought he would judge me for; I was scared he would reject me if I told him the truth. There had been times during the first few months of my recovery when I had punched myself in the face when the PTSD was really overwhelming, and I was especially scared to be open about this with Mike, or anyone else for that matter. For a while I didn't want to give an inch, for fear that at some point he'd see me for the disgusting, revolting fraud I often felt I was, underneath.

I had a huge ego coupled with chronic low self-esteem. I also had an intellectual arrogance which I used as best I could to create smoke screens behind which I would hide. I used all my skills as an actor to convince him (and practically everyone else) that I was fine. In addition to this, I was still in denial regarding the extent of my alcoholism, so when Mike asked me to describe the physical and mental problems during the last year of my drinking, I couldn't face talking about the after-shave, the self harming and the hallucinations. My mind would jump to the good times in the early days, and the euphoria of those times, rather than the desperation drinking and destructive behaviour of the last few years. Part of me still longed for those times to return.

'Tell me about your drinking. What was it like at the beginning?'

'I loved it. Although I hated the taste, the effect was fantastic, it was like rocket fuel. It was like the missing part of my DNA. I adored alcohol for how it made me feel. I felt whole,' I replied.

'What happened during the last year of your drinking? You were at university, weren't you? Why did you leave?'

'Well, the drink stopped working. There was no buzz, no feeling of euphoria, I hated it, I hated myself. I hardly went to any lectures. I didn't care about the academic world at all; I only went to uni to get pissed. It was as simple that.'

'What was it like at its worst? What was your rock bottom?'

It was here I couldn't be brutally honest with him. It took a few months to finally open up about my mental health issues. I was so ashamed of the self harming, (the punching myself in the face, the cricket bat, and the verbal taunting in the mirror), the hallucinations, the stealing, and trying to drink with food poisoning. So I omitted these crucial experiences, and replied,

'I was really ill every morning. You know; physically sick, and I had black outs. I had very vague memories of the night before, of something happening, an argument or whatever, something negative, but I couldn't remember who with or where, and then an horrific sense of dread, of shame, and panic.'

When he asked me again to describe in more detail my behaviour when I drank, and the consequences to my health, I automatically omitted these key issues, which I didn't see as being dishonest in any way. What I told him was factually correct, but without all the details: I needed to share the truth, the whole truth and nothing but the truth, if I was to receive the full benefits of this spiritual programme. I had to be brutally honest with Mike about the reality of the drinking, if I was to accept I was an alcoholic.

We have a sentence in the Big Book of Alcoholics Anonymous which is pertinent regarding the need for rigorous honesty if we are to heal, which is, 'half measures availed us nothing'. I have learned in recovery that if I edit out the absolute degradation of my alcoholism, and therefore pretend it wasn't so bad, I am far more likely to return to drinking. The mind has a remarkable way of re-inventing our past if we are not vigilant and rigorously honest with ourselves, and others, throughout our recovery. This is not to beat ourselves up, or to dwell morosely on our drinking, but to remind ourselves where we have come from, to re-focus our efforts to stay sober on a daily basis, and have gratitude for where we are today.

As Mike and I continued talking, I had to admit to him that I was still obsessed with alcohol, and feared there was no way I could stay sober especially if the flashbacks to the abuse continued; I was bound to drink at some point, it seemed to me. I remember meeting up with Mike before a meeting and saying to him,

'I can't stop thinking about a drink, all of the time, it's driving me crazy'. His reply helped me so much.

'You are an alcoholic but you have not accepted it yet. When you accept it, the obsession will probably leave you but at the moment it has a purpose; it is teaching you a lesson – only alcoholics obsess about alcohol.'

His reply floored me. It had never occurred to me that only alcoholics obsess about alcohol, and then go on to deny the reality of their destructive behaviour. We agreed I needed to talk in meetings about the denial much more, and it didn't take long for the penny to drop. At one memorable meeting a week later, I shared my anger and frustration;

'Why am I an alcoholic, why?" to which an old timer, Flat Cap Bill, shouted back "why not?"

I had no answer to that! This was the breakthrough I needed. Flat Cap Bill's reply had opened a door in my mind which helped me to accept that it is what it is. I remember thinking to myself, 'You're an alcoholic. What's the big deal? Just get on with it'.

Flat Cap was a real character. He was in his late 70s when I started attending meetings, and during his twenty-six years of recovery had helped many people get sober. Whenever he spoke at meetings, he focussed on the simplicity of the programme, and the importance of living one day at a time. For Flat Cap, life was about living in this moment only. Nothing else mattered. All we had was now, so make the very most of it. I remember him saying once (and I've often repeated it since), 'There is no good enough reason why any of us should ever pick up another alcoholic drink, but we can find plenty of excuses if we really want to!'

The following week I visited the beautiful Georgian city of Bath for the day, and whilst wandering around I decided to buy a book in WHSmiths. I sat on a bench outside when I suddenly noticed a bar nearby, and the thought hit me;

'I bought a book, I didn't buy a fucking drink!'

My thinking around my drinking had at last started to change. I had a clarity about my past I had not seen so clearly before; I knew there was no way I would have passed that bar and not had a drink before joining AA; it would have been impossible. I went in search of a public telephone, and called a friend in AA to tell them what had happened. Before AA, everything had become about getting a drink. My life's obsession, it seemed, had been to get drunk; if I went out with £100 in my pocket, I'd be thinking about where the hell would I get a drink when the money had run out? It was desperation drinking.

Mike asked me to recount the last twelve months of my drinking and to list key incidents / attitudes which were evidence of my addiction to alcohol. I finally got honest with myself.

1. I stole to fuel my addiction to alcohol, which is contrary to my personal morality, and something I have not done since stopping drinking.
2. I sometimes drank aftershave to try and stop the shakes in the early morning. I was therefore physically addicted to alcohol. Mike hit the nail on the head when he said to me, 'Who in their "right" mind would drink Old Spice after-shave?'
3. I had the delirium tremens most mornings during the last eighteen months of my drinking, and was always obsessed about alcohol. I could not stop thinking about it. Despite having a physical detox, this obsession lasted for the first nine months of my recovery.

4. I often had blackouts; I could not remember, or had very vague, fleeting memories of what had happened the previous day. This filled me with fear and shame.
5. I always drank in excess of the British Medical Association's recommended maximum number of units which in 1993 was 37 units per week for men. My estimated average, at my worst, was more like 160+ units per week. In 2016, the UK Chief Medical Officers' guideline for both men and women is that to keep health risks from alcohol to a low level it is safest not to drink more than 14 units a week on a regular basis. In truth, most alcoholics have no idea how much they drink; you're too drunk to know.
6. I lied to family, friends and work colleagues about my drinking, and caused damage to these relationships.
7. My alcoholism cost me my place at university, and a job on a film.
8. The medical tests during the first few months of recovery showed I had early stage damage to my liver, and to the nerve endings at the base of my spinal cord.
9. The consequences of my drinking has become much worse on all levels – mentally, physically, and emotionally, the more I drank; I could see how this condition, illness, or disease (the label is not important) was progressive.
10. I hated the taste, I hated the effect, I knew it was killing me, and yet <u>it was the most important thing in my life.</u>

These ten factors helped me to recognise that my drinking had indeed gone beyond problem drinking, that I was an alcoholic. With this came an acceptance and an enormous sense of relief, and with it a commitment to stay sober. It suddenly felt like it wasn't the worst thing in the world to be an alcoholic after all, and, with AA, I had found a solution to my problem. Now I had finally accepted I was an alcoholic, I felt so much more part of the fellowship, which in itself felt profoundly healing. I felt, 'I belong here. This is my home.' I listened more intently in meetings, and felt more connected to the other members, where previously I'd felt estranged from them. The honesty I heard was unbelievable; members would talk openly about their childhoods, their relationships, their hopes and expectations, their fears... They could even laugh at themselves, and it shocked me that they could also cry in front of others.

One lady really helped me with her honesty. Bridget was a lovely, gentle soul, who had been sober for over twelve years when she was diagnosed with breast cancer. Whenever she spoke about the cancer she was so open, vulnerable and courageous about her fears for the future. She spoke of how important acceptance and prayer were to her life, which offered such hope and encouragement.

'I have come to terms with my diagnosis. I do feel scared by what might happen, of course, but the programme helps me to live each day as it comes. I do not want to drink. It's never crossed my mind, which is the remarkable thing. You see, I know I'm not alone. The fellowship has been very kind and supportive. It's a huge blessing. We are so fortunate to have this programme. I have friends who tell me they feel very isolated in their lives; when I tell them a little about AA, they sometimes feel rather envious of what we have here. I am very grateful to have AA in my life.'

With her courage, I felt as if other members present, including myself, had permission to go in really deep and talk about their core issues as well. It seemed her strength opened the door for others to follow, which was inspiring to me, and I resolved to open up more about my childhood. Grateful Dave gave me a lift to a meeting I hadn't been to before, outside my hometown, and I decided I would share just a little about the abuse, at the meeting. It was held in an old fashioned church hall, with thick oak beams, and wood paneling on all four walls. As we entered the room was half full, with perhaps fifteen people, and although I felt tense, I appreciated that there was a calm, relaxed atmosphere. I hoped no one else would arrive, as I still felt intimidated by large numbers.

The meeting started, and after ten minutes I was desperate to share, the decision has been made and I couldn't hold it in any longer. I was willing the person already talking to shut the hell up, I resented him for going on for so long about his blasted holiday! When my turn came, I was deliberately vague about the specifics of the abuse.

'My name is Matt....... and I'm an alcoholic.'

'Hi Matt', the group responded in unison.

'My sponsor has told me I need to share more honestly about what's been going on recently, and to talk about the fear and shame I feel.' I paused, drew breath, and tried to block out the thoughts in my mind that were shouting at me and threatening to 'fuck me over' if I carried on.

'It's a long story, and... I'm not going into detail. It's... it's far too soon to do that. I was... I was.. abused when I was a kid, many times by different men... It was fucking horrendous. I get triggered by men quite regularly and get flashbacks which are really difficult to live with. I feel scared to be around people most of the time anyway, but when the flashbacks happen, I want to run away and hide. I... I feel....'

As I spoke I felt the PTSD triggered off. I felt energy moving quickly inside my body. There was a tension and a feeling of dirtiness in my groin, I felt sick to my stomach, and I suddenly had a stiff neck. My lower back was also very painful. The voices in my mind were savage in their judgement and condemnation of me. I was desperate to drink to drown everything out. I felt so small again. I was 'locked' into the memory of the last time I had been abused, which was replaying like a CD on an endless loop in my mind. I ended my share by saying,

'I'm trying to pray for this shame and fear to go. I haven't had a drink for a few months now. I still want to, though. I'm still obsessing about it all the damn time, it's driving me crazy. Umm.... Thank you.'

'Thank you Matt', the group replied en masse. I noticed several members gently smiling at me, with compassion in their eyes, although, at the time, I distrusted their reactions. My mind telling me they would hurt me. An old timer, sitting next to me, who must have noticed my physical and emotional reactions, gently leant over, and said the most empowering, most beautiful few words which really helped me. He simply said,

'I don't think you will ever drink again'.

Perhaps only another alcoholic can really understand how incredible it was to hear those specific words at that moment in my life. There are no other words which could have inspired me as much. He was a guardian angel for me. The next day, I told Mike what the old timer had told me, and what had happened at the meeting, and he told me to pray for the strength to confront the pain of my childhood. He encouraged me to pray each day, and throughout the day, for the strength to stay sober, and specifically for:

❖ Peace of Mind
I still had savage inner voices judging and condemning me

❖ Calmness of Being
I still had regular panic attacks

❖ Sanity of Thought and Action
I was still obsessed with alcohol; I thought about drinking almost all of the time

I started to pray as Mike suggested, although my technique was somewhat different to that of most people. I would sit on the loo telling God, or Higher Power or whatever, how I felt; my fears, my hopes, and I usually ended up by shouting and swearing out of frustration, and often self-pity. Nevertheless, it did help; I did feel a shift taking place, so I continued each night before I went to bed. In truth, I yearned for peace of mind, as I couldn't go on living with the flashbacks and the overwhelming fear. When Mike asked me how my prayer life was; I told him about my toilet habits and he was delighted:

'Excellent, you are developing a relationship with a Higher Power!' he told me.

Mike encouraged me to find a power greater than myself, which could be whatever I chose; he assured me that it didn't have to be a religious deity of any kind. I decided it would be, for now at least, the collective strength and wisdom of my regular AA group, which I could see was much greater than I was on my own. Like many AA newcomers, I recoiled when I saw the word 'God' on the scrolls displaying the 12 Steps; it confirmed in my prejudiced mind that AA must be some kind of religious cult. AA is certainly not a cult. There is no cost to attend AA meetings, and members donate as much or as little as they feel like to the 'pot' at the end of a meeting to help cover the rent and refreshments, but there is no pressure to make a financial contribution. Beyond the focus of staying sober and helping other alcoholics achieve sobriety, and structured guidance through the 12 Steps, to live our lives on more spiritual terms, there are no doctrinal absolutes. Indeed, 'the only requirement for membership is a desire to stop drinking', so even abstinence from alcohol is not a prerequisite to attend AA.

During the late summer and autumn of 1993, I had a series of spiritual experiences which created a psychic shift in my thinking, and were a major turning point in my relationship with AA. One Saturday morning I was feeling very sorry for myself (not an unusual event it must be said). Whilst walking along the street I had, for the first time, a very powerful intuition; an instruction to go into a specific second hand bookshop, which was perhaps 400 metres away. I knew I had to follow this instruction; it was felt with such a strong conviction. As I entered the bookshop I was immediately drawn to the self-help book shelves, where one specific book 'jumped' out at me, so to speak. It was a compilation of spiritual experiences from a variety of authors. I opened the book randomly and my eyes settled on a paragraph which, to my utter amazement, read:

... when later historians look back at the history of western Civilisation, they might well judge America's greatest gift to be the creation of Alcoholics Anonymous.

I had an overwhelming feeling of elation and felt a rush of excitement flow through me. With this came a sudden clarity of mind I cannot remember having experienced before, and I thought to myself, 'But I'm in AA...! I've got to really get on with the Steps, it's time to take this seriously.'

A few weeks later, at the end of September 1993, I had another spiritual experience which completely blew me away. I was having a really tough week, and felt overwhelmed with the PTSD symptoms. I just wanted to go to bed, pull the duvet over me and hide away from the world. One Wednesday evening, at the end of a regular AA meeting, a friend asked me to go to McDonald's for a coffee with him. I didn't feel I had the energy to talk with anyone, so I said,

'No, sorry, I can't. I've got to get home straight away,' which was not true.

A few minutes later, another AA friend also asked me to go for a walk, and this time, (remembering what someone had said in the meeting about the importance of helping others), I gave myself a kick up the backside, and said yes. After ten minutes of walking and talking, we coincidentally ended up outside the same McDonald's. My friend left and went home, and I decided that as I was here, to go inside. The place was deserted with the exception of a cubicle with two AA members and an old man I did not recognise, and the staff standing looking very bored behind the counter. The old man was in his mid to late sixties, with dishevelled, greasy, grey hair, sideburns and a few days' stubble. He wore an old, faded brown corduroy jacket, and had cheap NHS glasses.

An Inside Job

At first sight, he looked like a lost, bewildered soul. I knew how he felt, and sitting as he was next to my AA friends, I presumed he was a member I hadn't yet met. As soon as I sat down next to him, he started telling me his life story; how he had been in and out of prison for over 30 years for crimes he knew he shouldn't have done, and which he knew were wrong. I presumed he must have been a career criminal, and had been convicted for violent offences during some robberies.

'I am ashamed of the things I have done. I have tried to change. It has been very difficult, I started going to church a few months ago. I have asked God for forgiveness, and for the strength to stop these.....these acts.' He used the specific word 'acts' which confused me. Why say 'acts' and not 'crimes'?

I asked him, 'I don't understand, you used the word 'acts'? What do you mean by 'acts'?'

He stared in front of himself, avoiding eye contact.

'I... There were three of us. Two brothers, and me. We would play football with children on a local estate, and then, after we got to know them and they trusted us, we'd invite them back to play cards, at the brothers' house, and have a bit of drink. After cards and a few more drinks, we'd take them upstairs and play with them in the bedrooms. We'd all 'play'. We did whatever we wanted to, and then we'd play cards or another game.....' He paused, and then added, 'There were a lot of them over the years.'

He didn't look at me as he spoke; he stared down into the middle distance. There was no gloating from him, nor any revelling in his sudden confession. He knew what he had done had been wrong. When he finished he paused, and very slowly he turned and half looked at me, to see my reaction. I was in shock, quite literally, as memories of the abuse were triggered off and were playing in my mind. Then, in the brief silence as I looked at him, the rage erupted within me; I felt a deep-seated visceral desire to kill him. I could see myself beating him to death with the cricket bat I had used on myself so many times. The images in my mind's eye were of his face being broken into pieces, and me stamping on him. I was not shocked by my reaction; I felt wholly justified and, in that moment, I saw it as my 'right'.

I could have killed him; there was a huge part of me that wanted to. When the rage was triggered off within me, with him sitting next to me, it was simply a mental flick of a switch as to what happened next. I had the desire and the strength to kill him, but I didn't. I was conscious enough of my own sense of self to experience this rage, without taking revenge. Whilst I would never condone such violence, I judge no one who might have acted out in a similar situation. It is, in all truth, a very fine line. I remember saying to a lady member of AA when I was a few months sober, and whom I had learnt to trust, that,

'As shocking as this will sound, and I promise you I absolutely hate violence, I know I have the rage inside of me to kill someone.'

Sitting next to the paedophile in McDonalds, he must have sensed my rage, and he suddenly started to backtrack on his story.

'I wasn't involved that much... it was the two brothers. They organised everything, they invited them in, got them drunk and did.....they were vicious, they did dreadful things. They were far worse than.... I was..... I was only sometimes there..'

I knew he was lying. He'd suddenly realised what he had admitted to, and did his best to make out he had not been as active as they had been. I was in shock. It all seemed so unreal. The only words I said to him were said very slowly, deliberately, as I tried to take in what had happened,

'You know what you did, you know what you are responsible for.' To which he replied, staring into the middle distance, 'Yes, I know..... I know what I did.'

As I looked at him, when he replied to me, I got the impression he was not enjoying what he 'saw'. I sensed he knew it was wrong. He knew he was responsible for so much pain. I despised him. I absolutely hated this sick, evil man. I tried desperately to remember if he was one of the men who had abused me, but I couldn't. But as I listened to him, something had started to shift deep within me. I had a moment of clarity which momentarily broke through the rage and hatred I was feeling. I sat there, wide-eyed and in what felt like a different state; a more elevated state of consciousness.

I suddenly saw a very sick, lonely, fucked-up, seemingly guilt ridden, pathetic old man, who had turned to God to help him with obsessions that society says are abominable. I saw that I, too, had turned to God for help with obsessions that society says are unacceptable. In that moment I saw that he and I were no different. We were opposite sides of the same coin. I became amazed by the incredible circumstances that had brought this 'meeting' about; how unbelievable it was for an old man to be so open about something society rightly says is despicable, and the fact that he was telling me, someone who had been abused so many times, and had been praying to a God I did not understand and questioned whether was actually real, for the strength to confront the pain of my childhood. During these thoughts, it was as if he wasn't there, (it was as if time had stood still for this awareness to happen) and I was brought back to 'earth' when I suddenly had a very brief, fleeting moment of compassion for him which shocked and angered me; I suppressed this emotion as quickly as I could. I then had a sudden desire to get out of there as quickly as possible.

As I quickly walked home, I cried for the first time in years and felt a cleansing taking place deep within my body where so much of the trauma was trapped. This whole episode brought about a profound change in my consciousness; I started to feel amazingly clear and empowered in a way I had never, ever had before. It was a transcendental spiritual experience; I knew I was not alone, I knew there was a loving presence with me at all times. This was no longer an issue of faith, it was a certainty; a knowledge that God or Higher Power really did exist, and its loving presence was within me.

Memories came flooding back of times in my life when I had inexplicably behaved in certain ways, which I had not understood before. Why I had suddenly run way from a female friend smiling at me on one occasion; another time when, after the abuse, my uncle picked me up in the kitchen, and I went hysterical. Why, at my prep school, during the time the abuse was taking place in the public toilets, I had flashed my penis at the girls as we changed for PE. With each of these, and several other memories, there was a loving, gentle commentary in my mind explaining everything to me. As soon as I arrived home, I grabbed my diary and wrote down everything that had happened, and continued to receive messages of encouragement and healing. I then went into the back garden in an enlightened state of consciousness, crying with joy, staring at the stars in the sky above when I heard a beautiful voice say to me;

'You must forgive and let go'.

'Everything will be okay. EVERYTHING will be okay'.

And I sensed this meant... down to the minutest atom.

Whilst I would not consider myself to be a Christian, that night before bed, I decided to read the *Footprints in the Sand* prayer. I read it every night for several weeks, and each time I cried tears of gratitude for the healing I had received.

"... I noticed that many times along the path of my life, There was only one set of footprints. I also noticed that it happened at the very lowest and saddest times in my life. This really bothered me, and I questioned the Lord about it. "Lord, you said that once I decided to follow you, You would walk with me all the way; But I have noticed that during the most troublesome times in my life, there is only one set of footprints. I don't understand why in times when I needed you the most, you should leave me."

The Lord replied, "My precious, precious child. I love you, and I would never, never leave you during your times of trial and suffering. When you saw only one set of footprints, It was then that I carried you."

Every time I read those lines, I felt a presence draw even closer to me. I felt lifted to a higher consciousness; I experienced an awareness, a deep feeling of peace which I'd never known before, and which remained with me for the next six weeks, at the same intensity. It then started to retreat into the background, but this presence has, in truth, never left me. I felt, and still feel over twenty years later, that a divine synchronicity was at play that evening. To arrange the circumstances by which a survivor of child sexual abuse could sit next to a self professed paedophile, and receive such healing, still affects me. Who would have thought meeting this man would have been the catalyst for such a powerful spiritual awakening? Beyond the spiritual healing I received, there was immense emotional and psychological healing as well. Whenever I had recalled the memories of the abuse, my view of the paedophiles abusing me was of physically and intellectually powerful men, who were dominant, in complete control, and I was at their mercy..

Meeting the paedophile in McDonalds destroyed that view. I no longer saw them as being the anonymous bogeymen, hiding in the shadows, waiting to attack me. I began to see them as they really are; weak, sick, fucked-up, cowardly, and soulless. I recognised they lacked the capacity to genuinely love; any obsession that is ultimately so self-serving and narcissistic is devoid of love and intimacy. It is base, tribal, manipulative and predatory. Before I walked into McDonalds, I was terrified of everything this man symbolised; a few hours later, far from fearing him, I had started to pity the lonely, pathetic creature I had met, and the paedophiles from my childhood he effectively represented. It would take another twelve years before I came to forgive the men who abused me. Meeting and listening to that paedophile had, however, created a shift in my psyche, because I felt I had some power now over the memories of the abuse.

The PTSD did not really affect me that much during those six weeks, at least I do not recall any crises happening. As the spiritual experience receded into the background, I got the sense that I had to now take more responsibility for my recovery. I had been given a 'taster' of a higher consciousness, now I had to get on with the 12 Steps!

I approached the 12 Steps with more sincerity and energy than before, and got more actively involved with meetings - by arriving early to set up, making the tea, and gradually talking more openly about my thoughts and feelings. Mike told me to listen more carefully as well, and as I did I gained greater identification with other members, which created a stronger sense of belonging. I knew I was no longer alone, and that felt so empowering. Many others in AA had walked the path before me; I could learn from them, and that felt inspiring. As I settled into a routine of regular AA meetings, talking with my sponsor, and meeting other members socially, I later told them what had happened in McDonalds, and how it had inspired me to get on with the programme;

'I've been praying for last few weeks for the strength to talk about abuse in my childhood, to be able to be honest about what happened to me, so I can let it go and get on with my life. I had a truly amazing experience in McDonalds of all places; I had a spiritual awakening which has shifted something deep inside of me; I feel I have the energy to get the crap out at last.'

I started to talk about what happened, (not in specific detail as that wouldn't be appropriate in an AA meeting), but more about how I felt; the anger, fear, rage and confusion... and by sharing it I felt a release of suppressed energy, which encouraged me further. As frightening as it was in the early weeks and months of my recovery, having the courage to open up in an AA group in front of fifty people, on a regular basis was healing me. It also helped me to gain a better perspective on my life, as others related to my issues, and shared their experiences which gave me strength to move forward.

The tangible benefits of working through the 12 Steps with a sponsor relied on honesty, and though I was making good progress with Dr Ron, the Cognitive Behavioural Therapy sessions, and with Teacher Mike, many of my memories of the abuse were still 'locked away' in my mind. The PTSD still affected me, the difference was I had a group of friends, including some male friends I had begun to start to trust, who understood and supported me when I was triggered. Some of them also had abuse issues that they were struggling with, so together we could support each other. With this process the barriers slowly started to drop, and I can remember forcing myself to talk more openly at smaller meetings, where I usually knew everyone and where I felt safer.

Sharing more openly was a double-edged sword sometimes. I would often feel some release, but there were times when the PTSD was triggered, I'd feel like I'd been emotionally run over and physically exhausted, as it brought about a massive release of suppressed energy. When the exhaustion passed I often felt much lighter within myself, and I became aware of an inner calmness, at least for a while. I remember a three day period when the anxiety was so high that Larry, by now one of my closest male friends in AA, insisted he stayed with me to make sure I was okay. We would meet in a local café before a meeting, but I was so physically tense I would hyperventilate, and feel another panic attack was imminent. The nervous energy running through my body was such that I just couldn't sit still. I felt anxious, paranoid, and convinced that everyone was staring at me as my limbs would suddenly jerk nervously; my mind was like a CD playing on continuous fast forward all day. I felt I had to keep moving. We walked many, many miles over the course of the three days, and except for calls of nature and calls to his sponsor, Larry got me through it.

Larry and I worked together at the theatre for a few years when I was first Front of House Manager. Larry was on the Technical crew, working backstage. Although no one else at the theatre knew he was a fellow AA, they knew he and I were good friends, and so when I was really stressed during a show (as was often the case during the first few months of learning the job as I went along), he would be sent round to the foyer to calm me down! It is sad that, after many years of close friendship, when Larry moved to the south coast I unfortunately lost his telephone number, and having moved a few times myself, we have not had any contact for almost a decade now.

Back to obsessive walking: for a long time it became the only way of burning off the nervous energy I had within me some days. Teacher Mike told me he often noticed me walking repeatedly around the town centre before we got to know each other. I'd do a 800 metre very fast walk along four streets in a loop over and over again. He said he was often tempted to stop me and ask my where the hell I was going. I had no idea, but wherever I was, it didn't feel safe. My fear had been;

'if I feel this pain, I won't be able to handle it; it will control me, overwhelm me mentally, so I'll go nuts and I'll drink again'. What actually happened was, although I hated feeling the trauma, I learnt over time to channel the anger I felt to help me stay sober. I would say to myself;

'I'm not going to let those sick bastards try and destroy me again.'

The anger worked in my favour to help my recovery, instead of it remaining suppressed and destroying me. (I don't want to give the impression that all the rage, anger and shame left me during this period of my recovery. I had simply made an important beginning at this time; the reality is that the rage, anger and shame has stayed with me throughout my adult life, but has guided me to find and develop a spiritual approach in my life, and to learn how to channel it appropriately).

I reached the stage where I really understood how important it was to be open about my experiences; that the healing could only come about if I was rigorously honest, as we often share in AA. The problem was that I often didn't know how to filter what I said outside of AA circles, before it was too late. I had to learn how the filter my newfound openness. On one occasion, a lady friend stopped me in the street, and asked how I was. Buoyed by my new mantra of sharing more candidly about my thoughts and feelings, I had verbal diarrhoea and told her absolutely everything that was going on in my life. It was a strange experience; I felt out of control in the sense that once I opened my mouth, I couldn't stop talking very, very fast. It was almost like a fast-forward button on a DVD player!

'I had a spiritual awakening a few weeks ago, and since then it's really helped me to be more open about the abuse which happened when I was a kid. I'm being honest about the times I used to punch myself as well, which I've always been too scared to admit. I'm seeing how much anger I've buried deep down inside of me, and so I'm trying to get rid of it by talking and praying and walking. I'm doing a lot of walking at the moment.....' And on and on I went, for several minutes, with what was an emotional dump on the poor girl.

As I was speaking, I suddenly noticed her face had changed from her usual bubbly happiness, and now looked very pale. She made her excuses and suddenly disappeared! I had to learn to judge what was appropriate and when. It was painful at times, as I had no notion of small talk.

During the next six months, Mike and I continued working through the 12 Steps. The AA programme offers a structure with which we look back through our lives in detail and talk through our resentments, the thoughts and feelings behind our behaviours, and learn how to let go of our fears, judgements of others (and ourselves), and to recognise how, so often it had been our own thinking (the filter to our reality) that had created a lot of the chaos we had experienced in our lives. Recognising these underlying issues, and seeking through an ongoing process of honesty and willingness to let go and to therefore grow, the programme enables the seeker to live a more peaceful, productive and enjoyable life. Beyond the initial goal of continued abstinence from alcohol, which in itself seemed to me to be an utterly impossible achievement in the early days and weeks, the programme comprehensively addresses one's physical, mental, emotional and spiritual attitudes to life.

When one has worked through the 12 Steps, one is encouraged to 'carry this message to other alcoholics, and to practice these principles in all our affairs'. It is truly a spiritual programme of action. What has been been so freely given, one is encouraged to help offer to other alcoholics so they too might recover. The oldtimers in AA often used to say; 'to keep it, you've got to give it away'.

It was leading up to my first Christmas in sobriety, and it seemed as if every advert on television was for alcohol. I saw countless images of young people having a great time drinking, and despite accepting I was an alcoholic, I just felt so odd and different from my peers. As Christmas neared, I started a new job as I needed some money. I was an elf in Santa's Grotto in the local shopping centre, which did nothing to help my self-esteem nor my street cred!! I had to wear very tight-fitting green tights, an overly large jacket and a ridiculous red Robin Hood hat. I dreaded being recognised, so I spent most of the time hiding at the back, and chain-smoking far too many cigarettes by the fire escape. I was probably more scared than the screaming kids waiting to meet Father Christmas, and had a number of panic attacks. I had palpitations along the left side of my body, a stiff neck, fast breathing; I was sweaty, and I feared I would collapse. During the week before Christmas week itself, I woke up in the early hours with massive palpitations along the left-hand side of my body; I was terrified I was having a cardiac arrest. There were flashing lights around my eyes, a stiff neck, a thunderous headache, chattering teeth and I was convinced I was dying.

Mum rushed me immediately to Accident and Emergency and I was placed on my own in a room with the lights turned off. Mum described my symptoms to the duty nurse, the emergency doctor, was called and I was told I might have had a brain hemorrhage, or it could be meningitis. Only after I had rested and the symptoms had significantly diminished could they conduct a brain scan and then, if required, a lumbar puncture to see what was happening. I was told I must not move under any circumstances; if I'd had a brain hemorrhage any movement could cause considerable damage, and could be potentially fatal. A nurse sat next to me throughout the night, which was comforting. She looked at me, and said with a look of concern in her eyes,

'You must not move at all. If you've had a brain haemorrhage, the slightest movement could really damage you. So please stay completely still, okay?'

She paused, and then gave me an encouraging smile, saying, 'So even if you have an itch somewhere; within reason, just tell me, I'll handle it.'

Her face broke into a broader smile, and she had a twinkle in her eyes, when she said 'within reason' which I found comforting. I understood how potentially serious my situation was, and I felt really scared. I'd been through so much during the last year, and I didn't want to become a brain-damaged invalid, reliant on other people. This image stayed for a short while in my mind, and I decided I had to challenge this negativity straight away using CBT techniques, or I'd become really withdrawn and depressed.

It helped me to realise there was nothing I could do to change the situation. I had to accept this situation for what it was. I surrendered my predicament entirely into the hands of a power greater than myself. I think this was the first time I genuinely surrendered and accepted that my fate was beyond my intellectual ability to change my situation. With that realisation came a remarkable feeling of peace flowing through my body, which encouraged me. I remembered the message I'd received during my spiritual awakening a few months earlier, and decided to trust it;

'Everything will be okay; <u>everything</u> will be okay.'
I then did my own rather elementary brain test;
What is my full name?
Where do I live?

I recited the Serenity Prayer, and I remembered the words of one of my favourite poems called 'London Airport' my brother had on a poster on his bedroom wall;

Last night in London Airport
I saw a wooden bin
labelled UNWANTED LITERATURE
IS TO BE PLACED HEREIN.
So I wrote a poem
and popped it in.

By Christopher Logue, copyright © Christopher Logue, 1969

I thought: at least my memory is okay, I know who I am. I know where I live, I can remember a poem. I settled as best I could but couldn't sleep. In the morning, the symptoms had settled down enough for me to have a brain scan. I was gently wheeled along a corridor when, despite lying resolutely flat. I could see, to my horror, an AA member named James walking towards me. As soon as he recognised me I panicked, thinking he must think I've had a drink. Without considering the consequences, I automatically sat bolt upright and shouted at him;
'I haven't had a drink. I haven't had a bloody drink'.
The nurses were understandably shocked and alarmed at my sudden movement; worried that I might cause myself further damage to my brain if I'd had a haemorrhage. They pleaded with me,

'You must not move', then saying to my friend, 'He may have had a brain hemorrhage'. James helped calm me down, and walked alongside the bed encouraging me to lay still, to try and relax as I went for the scan.

I had the brain scan, which showed no abnormalities, and then at lunchtime I had a lumbar puncture (it is very unpleasant; fluid is drained from the base of the spinal cord as you lie in the foetal position) which was also clear. The palpitations, stiff neck, nausea and anxiety persisted throughout the day. I was kept in for a week for further observation and after a few days in my own room, the decision was taken to move me onto the geriatric ward. It was the only ward with a bed available. Most nights one of my fellow patients, a gentleman well into his late 80s, would prowl the ward with his stick held as if a rifle looking for jerries (aka Germans). It was not uncommon for curtains and mattresses to be attacked, under cover of darkness, and the nurses would chase after him trying to calm him down.

Family, friends, and AA members came to visit me, but after five days enough was enough, and in spite of the doctor's advice, in my arrogance, I discharged myself. I should have listened; I had a further dozen or so fits over Christmas and New Year, which were eventually put down to the PTSD being triggered. I went to a regular AA meeting in the New Year and in typically obsessive detail recounted the whole story, ending with the sentence:

'I had a brain scan, and there's nothing wrong with my brain', to which whole group spontaneously erupted into laughter, and old friend Flat Cap Bill replying, 'Nothing wrong with your brain!'

I laughed with them at the absurdity of my comment, telling them to 'feck off' as tears rolled down my cheeks. I needed the laugher, their kindness and encouragement. It helped me to laugh at myself.

Christmas 1993 was tough; it felt like I'd survived a battle, which sounds OTT, but the PTSD had been crippling throughout the festive season. After several fits before and during the Christmas week, when I'd felt resentful seeing all the adverts for alcohol everywhere, and sorry for myself that everyone else, so it seemed to me, was getting drunk and having a great time. (That was the version playing out in my head, anyway), I was feeling ready for a change.

I've since learnt from the professionals and in AA that alcohol affects social drinkers differently than it does alcoholics. I'd always assumed that everyone experienced the incredible buzz and feelings of euphoria that I had had at the beginning of my drinking, and this was one of the reasons why I felt so resentful towards them for being able to enjoy drinking without the consequences I'd experienced. It helped me greatly to learn that social drinkers do not experience such a powerful chemical affect as alcoholics have; when this was explained to me I didn't feel I was missing out so much after all. Several new AA members, including myself, knew we needed extra support on Christmas Day itself, so we organised a series of drop-in meetings in a local hall. In the hour or so between meetings, we'd play daft games like Twister, Kerplunk, and some card games. I learnt to never play Twister again with Grateful Dave; I've never met anyone so competitive about winning! Before each game, Dave looked as if he was psyching himself up as he limbered up in the corner. Wearing his tracksuit, he reminded me of Rocky Balboa in *Rocky V*!

At the turn of the year, Teacher Mike encouraged me to find some part-time work and to get involved with some hobbies. I'd been signed off on disability benefit since September 1992 by my GP with 'drink and depression' and I agreed with Mike: I needed to move on. I contacted the local theatre through a mutual friend and in early February 1994, I started work as a Technical Assistant on a casual basis. Little did I know back then, that this was the beginning of a thirteen year working relationship with this theatre, one which came to play such a crucial role in my emotional and psychological healing. After working backstage on and off for eighteen months, I was to be promoted to Front of House Manager; a position I held for the next four years. Then I was promoted again, to the position of Programming and Marketing Manager, which I held for seven years.

Growing up, I loved the energy and creativity of the theatre. I'd performed on the stage of this particular theatre many times as a child, and these plays gave me, without question, the best memories of my childhood. I'd also acted at other venues in amateur plays, and cabarets at local hotels. I'd had a passion for acting from a very young age; I loved everything about it. From the excitement of the first read-through of the play, to the nerve-wracking audition, the creativity of the rehearsals, to the nervous energy of the opening night; I felt at home on the stage. As a child actor I very rarely felt nervous before I went on stage (that came later), and the buzz after the show would keep me awake for hours. As grandiose as it seems, I remember getting home from a drunken after-show party in my late teens and sitting at the end of my bed, re-living the applause, not able to draw the bedroom curtains; to do so would close out the audience! There are shades of Norma Desmond from the Billy Wilder film, *Sunset Boulevard*, here. Played by Gloria Swanson, Desmond is a faded silent film star living in a fantasy world.

I fully immersed myself in every character I played, and tried my best to really know them, to understand their emotions and what made them 'tick', and if I liked them, I would 'be' them for a while. The theatre was a place of dreams for me; I could let my imagination run wild and be whomever I wanted to be. Returning to the theatre as a Technical Assistant, in my early recovery, felt like coming home. It also encouraged me to get back on the boards myself, so I joined an amateur dramatics group nearby, which had its own studio theatre.

The Assistant Technical Manager took me under his wing, and taught me the ropes. It all started with the show contract, and the technical rider. (The show producer sends the rider ahead of a performance, in which is listed in considerable detail what the theatre, and what the production company, are each contractually responsible for. It might include, for instance, the minimum stage dimensions for the show, whether the pit was large enough for the orchestra, the number of bars on the grid above the stage to meet their lighting requirements, and a production schedule. The schedule gives a timeline for the day, and so confirms the arrival time of the visiting company, set up times for the technical equipment, the lighting and sound requirements of the theatre, sound check and rehearsal times, the number of dressing rooms required, refreshments etc).

The accuracy of the advance communication between the producer and theatre is vital to ensure a smooth day setting up for the evening performance, and I found it surprising how many times show producers would change their technical requirements during a long run of shows, and fail to send us the updated rider. It often caused unnecessary challenges during the set up. Our Technical Manager would then delegate key responsibilities to his crew to make sure we had rigged or removed the lights and sound equipment before the production company arrived; as far as the theatre was concerned he was ultimately responsible that we had everything covered to ensure a smooth and, hopefully, an enjoyable day.

A typical day would start at 0830 in the Crew Room backstage for a cup of tea, and when the visiting production crew arrived at perhaps 0900, we'd unload the lorry and start setting up the equipment as per the rider. At 1300 we'd usually disappear for an hour for lunch; I'd usually grab some sandwiches and go to an AA meeting nearby, whilst a few of the crew went to the pub. (This was over twenty years ago; the health and safety laws are much more strictly enforced now, and there's no way that liquid lunches would be tolerated). After lunch, the technical set up would be completed, the initial sound checks finished by 1530, and at 1600 (or thereabouts) the performers would arrive, usually after a long journey from their digs, often midway between their previous theatre and ours. More often than not, the first thing we'd do was to put the kettle on, and brew some tea for them. I soon learned that the offers of decent showers, clean, warm dressing rooms, a round of sandwiches and a cup of tea were a great way to ensure a smooth day all round.

If it was a busy show for the crew (with many technical changes required during the performance), we'd listen out for the visiting Stage Manager to call us onto the side of stage, where he or she would take us through the show cues for moving scenery, curtains, stage furniture and props etc. During the show itself, these cues would be called, over headsets or in person, by the Stage Manager in the 'corner' of the wings from where the whole show would usually be controlled. We'd grab some food at 1800, and wait for the 'half' (a theatre term meaning 35 minutes before the show starts.) At that time we'd have to be back on site, and to report to the Stage Manager in the corner. My favourite time was listening to the audience arriving on the internal speaker system, which operated throughout the entire backstage area. I could hear and feel the energy and excitement building up as the theatre got busier, and it reminded me how much I'd loved acting as a child, and how much I had actually missed it.

After the show, if it was a one-nighter, we'd do the 'get out', and take down all the technical equipment belonging to the visiting company and pack it away on their lorry as quickly and as safely as possible. It was often after midnight by the time we'd have our final cup of tea in the crew room before going home. If we had a really big show the following day, with an early start, we'd sometimes stay on to get the technical equipment in place for the following day. The larger shows such as English Touring Opera, The

Chippendales, Elkie Brooks, and the West End dance shows would often travel with a couple of 'artic' lorries full of sound and lighting equipment, costumes, and catering equipment. They would arrive overnight from another theatre, and we'd have a crew of six or more of us at 0800 to start a very long, knackering day!

There were times I had to use the Cognitive Behavioural Therapy (CBT) techniques I'd learnt and process my instinctive reactions to some of the banter in the crew room which had triggered me. Looking back, it was usually witty, innocuous comments about an attractive woman on the TV which would then prompt one of the crew to ask me (and others present) about who we were dating ('no one' was the honest answer; I still felt too far out of my depth). It was fun, knockabout stuff but it would trigger me nonetheless, and I had to learn to go with the flow of it, and not allow the harsh, critical mental reactions to control my behaviour.

There was the risk and a genuine fear in my mind that I might 'lose it' sometimes, when it felt so raw and there were a combination of triggers (the physicality of the job could be a trigger, especially when our bodies were in close proximity when lifting large cases of equipment), but these guys were decent and without any malice whatsoever...but I had to use all my energy at times to practice what Dr Ron and the CBT had taught me. After a while it got easier, as I settled into the team. I found the easiest, most practical answer was to tell myself,

'Fuck it, Matt; just get on with it...' I learnt to use my anger to help me get on with life.

Yet even with those triggers, overall I loved every minute of it! It gave me a sense of purpose which I so desperately needed at that time in my life. I had some sense of direction, and to be trusted with some responsibility gave me hope and encouragement for my recovery. The main benefit of the job was that it helped me to forget about myself for a while; I'd become so self centred and introspective, I felt a massive relief to be focussing on something positive and creative instead. I worked at the theatre on a casual basis on many shows between February and September 1994, and I had the opportunity to work with stars such as Freddie Starr, Elkie Brooks, Danny La Rue, Max Bygraves, Sir Ken Dodd, Ronnie Corbett, Jethro, and Barbara Dickson. I could feel myself growing in confidence, and started feeling more optimistic for my future.

At the end of October 1994, I was fifteen months sober and briefly working for a week in East Croydon. I decided to visit my brother, Steve, who then was living in Clapham, and working in central London. As my work life had become much busier, over a period of six months I had gradually dropped off my AA meetings. I felt out of sorts, to the point of questioning whether I still needed to go to AA at all. I met Steve at his flat, and at my suggestion we went for a few games of pool in the pub at the end of his road. He asked me whether I was okay to go to a pub, and I assured him I was fine. I think I wanted to test myself; my thinking being, 'if I could not drink here tonight, then I obviously didn't have a problem because an alcoholic would drink, because that's what alcoholics do'. We had a good evening together, but in my mind I had convinced myself that AA was no longer for me; I had my drinking problem licked! I still had some fear about my thinking, and I went through a phase of justifying why it was now safe to drink.

I told myself I'd had so much therapy; that I'd worked so hard to let go of the pain of the abuse, which was the real reason behind my drinking, so it would be different now. I would be able to control it. I told myself that real alcoholics die from alcoholism, they don't ever stop, so the fact I had now stopped for fifteen months meant that I couldn't be an alcoholic. Deep down I knew I was desperately clutching at straws, but the obsession to drink was 'on me' and I heard a voice in my mind make the decision;

'Okay, tomorrow lunchtime, in the hotel bar, you can have one drink as a test. Then see what happens. If it feels okay, then have a few more in the evening. If that goes okay, then make a decision whether or not to carry on.'

There was a part of me that was scared shitless by these loud, intrusive and seductive thoughts. The so-called glamour and adventure of alcohol had suddenly become very attractive, and my mind projected images of me being the life and soul of the party; being popular with women, and successful in business. I suddenly started craving alcohol for the first time in ages. The obsession to drink again was on me; the voice of sanity challenging it was destroyed by the all-consuming desire to drink, and I felt terrified. There were no thoughts of after shave, self harming, stealing, loneliness, panic attacks, paranoia, or being crippled with fear. On my way back to the hotel in East Croydon I needed to get a train from Clapham Junction. I stood on the platform at near midnight with a dozen other people waiting for the train. I felt sick to the stomach, knowing I was mentally screwed up, and I feared what would happen back at the hotel when I started drinking again. I prayed in desperation to the Higher Power to give me the strength to stay sober, and for my head to 'shut the fuck up'.

Suddenly a group of ten drunk, aggressive football fans could be heard further down the platform. They started to walk towards the twelve of us who were standing on the platform waiting for the train to arrive; they were clearly spoiling for a fight judging by their verbal threats. I was immediately triggered by their aggression; I tensed up, and in my mind's eye could see myself being surrounded and attacked by the group. I noticed nervous looks between the others waiting near me. As they came closer, one of the drunks veered over to me and got right in my face.

'Who the fuck do you support then?'
Knowing it didn't really matter what I said, I decided to be honest and said,
'It's more cricket where I come from'.
'Yeah, and where's that?' he threatened, prodding his finger into my chest.
I told him the name of the town.
He looked surprised, staggered slightly backwards, and then said, 'I used to live there'.
'Whereabouts did you used to live?' I asked, sensing something odd was happening.
He leered at me, 'I don't fucking know, somewhere near Tesco.'
It came out of nowhere, and I suddenly asked him, 'Was it Hope House?'
He was shocked, and after a brief pause asked me, 'How the fuck did you know that?' (Hope House was a dry house for recovering alcoholics, one of many at that time in my hometown).

I asked him why he had left the town, and he told me he'd recently started drinking again, and was told to leave the dry house. He had come back to London, and had lost everything. His wife and children had left him, he'd been sacked, and he was living from floor to floor. His tone and manner changed the more he spoke to me about his life. For all the aggression a few minutes earlier, he was clearly a broken man. He sounded more coherent as well. I really felt for him. I told him what was going on for me, and how meeting him had actually really helped me. I said I was desperate for a drink, but was terrified at the same time what could happen if I started again. I described my mental state, and how a drink seemed very attractive to me.

'My head's telling me it'll be different this time, as I've had counselling, and I've talked through a lot of the crap that was getting to me. I keep thinking of the good times, you know, the parties, the times when I felt so alive, when I loved the buzz and the excitement it gave me. I know this didn't last long, and when it turned on me, it had me. I was desperate, out of control. I know this, but I'm scared I'll drink again.'

He pleaded with me, 'Don't for God's sake, I can't stop now. I know it's destroying me, but it's got me. I'm hardly eating anything, I've lost three stone in no time. I'm paranoid, hardly sleeping at all, terrified someone's going to break the door in. My head is screaming at me all the time; I wake up sweating and shaking, desperate for another fucking drink. I've tried to stop, but I can't.'

He looked so lost and frightened as he spoke, a reality I knew all too well. This great hulk of a man suddenly looked like a frightened small child, out of his depth, bewildered and humiliated. He told me how his life had deteriorated so quickly once he'd picked up the drink, and that he felt it would inevitably kill him.

'I can't see a way out of it. It feels like I've had my chance, and I've blown it. I should have worked harder to stay sober. I fucked up, and now I'm terrified about stopping. I get dreadful nightmares every night, I had horrific delirium tremens last time I stopped. I really scared to go through that again.'

I described the hallucinations I had. 'I've had the DTs as well. I had snakes in my bed coming up and attacking me, which was terrifying. Another time, I saw Hitler, Mussolini and Stalin standing around my bed staring at me. That was so real and horrific.'

I then told him how I had prayed for strength a few minutes before he and his friends had come onto the platform, and how blown away I was by meeting him. It felt like some exquisite divine orchestration had taken place for us to meet. I wanted him to connect to the power of this coincidence, and recognise it was as much for his recovery, as it was for mine.

'Us meeting like this is so unbelievable isn't it? It's crazy. I needed a kick up the arse about AA, to get to more meetings, but I was too proud, or stubborn, to call anyone, and here you are to warn me what happens when you drink again. You've helped me so much. You've reminded me of the hell I would go back to. I want to thank you.'

He nodded in agreement, and I could tell he felt the same way about the synchronicity of our sudden meeting. He was clearly very emotional; I could see so much pain in his eyes, and a few tears. I continued, 'You've got sober before, though. You know it works. You know what you need to do. You also know there's a lower hell out there if you carry on drinking. As I'm telling you this stuff, I'm also telling myself what I need to do. We both need to get to meetings. The strength in the meetings will help you stop. I know it's damn hard at times, but it really is worth it. The more I talk about it, the more I know my life is so much better without the fucking stuff.'

He then told me, 'I feel too ashamed to go to a meeting. I don't want to be judged, I feel enough of a fraud and a failure already, without some sanctimonious jerk telling me I am.'

'That's your head talking bullshit. See it for what it is. That isn't going to happen. No one will judge you; and even if someone does, God help them, they've obviously forgotten how fucked up they were, and how difficult it is to stop in the first place. If they've forgotten what hell is like, they're more likely to go back to it. Anyway, who the hell are they to judge? You've got to challenge the crap your head is telling you. You've done it before, you can do it again. No question. You know you're not alone, and your story has value; it can help knock others, like me, out of their complacency.'

He nodded as I spoke, and then replied, 'I know you're right, but my head is screaming at me to tell you to go to hell, and get completely rat-arsed. I know where that takes me, I know I have become someone I loathe and despise. Someone my wife hates for all the damage I've done to her and the family. Someone whose children are frightened of being near me.'

I really felt for him, and said, 'Underneath the pain and fear, the decent, kind husband, and the loving father is there. You just need the strength to deal with the crap, let it go, and get on with your life, sober.' We spoke for another five minutes and encouraged each other to get to an AA meeting the following day, and to talk about what had happened. We both knew that our meeting on the platform, at this specific time in both our lives, was no coincidence. It was too significant; the timing, the mental challenges we both had, and the fact we both had lived in the same town.

His 'friends' staggered over to us and one of them started to verbally threaten me, but my newfound friend was having none of it. He grabbed the guy by the throat, and told him bluntly,

'Back off, you ****, he's a good mate of mine.' His friend looked shocked, and as soon as the grip on his throat was released, he slunk away rather sheepishly, no doubt trying to work out what the hell was going on. The train arrived at the platform; we shook hands and thanked each other. Both of us were clearly emotional, I boarded the train, and as it slowly moved away, a lady sitting opposite me leant forward and asked me,

'Are you okay? You have such a look of surprise on your face. It's as if something amazing has happened.' I replied, 'I'm fine, thanks. Something amazing did just happen.'

I never saw him again, but the living hell he was so obviously in after he'd started drinking again stopped me from picking up a drink that night; he was the mirror to myself as I was when I drank. He showed me the truth; how active alcoholism brings such desperation, fear, loneliness and utter brutality to the alcoholic and, of course, to their families as well. I hope he's sober, that his wife and children are with him, and that they are happy. Meeting him and seeing the truth of active alcoholism removed the obsession and craving I had to drink that night. I returned to my hotel knowing something I could not understand was, once again, looking after me. The obsession to drink has only returned on one other occasion; in Prague when I was on holiday in October 2001.

This time I had been in denial of some emotional pain and had not talked about it to the extent I clearly needed to; consequently I often sat in meetings making out everything was fine, whilst sitting back and judging other members. The obsession returned very suddenly and terrified me; I'd forgotten how powerful these intrusive, aggressive and compelling these thoughts could be. As the mental obsession overwhelmed me, so too did I physically start craving alcohol. Once again, I was saved when I recognised an AA member in the centre of Prague whom I'd seen at AA meeting a few days earlier. I was standing in my hotel lobby feeling very anxious whilst I obsessed about whether or not to have a drink, when the AA member stopped on the pavement outside the entrance to look at his watch. As I looked over I recognised him immediately and ran outside to ask for his help. He readily agreed, and we sat together in the hotel lobby for thirty minutes of honest remembrance of the pain and desperation of my drinking. I recognised I didn't want that hell to return. I spoke about the emotional pain I'd been running away from, and soon after, the obsession left me without my needing to drink.

When the obsession left me at eight months sober... other than those two occasions, in over twenty-fours years I have not wanted to drink at all. On both of these occasions, I had become complacent and arrogant. I only went to a few meetings sporadically, and I was not being emotionally honest with myself and others. Peter Rabbit warned me of this risk when I first got sober; 'eternal vigilance, my friend. Never forget to be eternally vigilant.'

5

FINDING MY TRUTH

You wander restlessly from forest to forest while the Reality is within your own dwelling. The Truth is here! Go where you will – to Benares or to Mathura;until you have found God in your own Soul, the whole world will seem meaningless to you.[8]
Kabir (1440 – 1518)

'There must be something else, this cannot be it' was the thought that came to me immediately after my last alcoholic drink. It was 9.30pm on 28th February 1993, and a turning point in my life. I knew I could no longer go on living this way; I was completely broken, I couldn't pretend anymore, I knew I had to change...but I didn't know how to.

In hindsight, from over twenty-five years of sobriety, this inner yearning was a desperate plea for something to help me. It was the catalyst for a process which began immediately; something started to have an influence in my life, although I was not immediately aware of it at the time; I knew this intangible, unseen force was there because, despite the physical cravings for alcohol (which lasted several weeks after that last drink) and the mental obsession (which lasted several months), I have not had an alcoholic drink since. That something has slowly and gently developed into a relationship with my Higher Self, my Higher Power, or as we sometimes say in AA 'the God of my understanding'. I have since learnt the label or name of this

---

[8] Larry Chang, comp., & ed., *Wisdom for the Soul: Five Millennia of Prescriptions for Spiritual Healing* (Gnosophia Publishers, 2006)

Self/Power/God does not matter in the least. It's what it DOES and how it helps that matters.

I love the fact that AA is genuinely inclusive in that it welcomes people of any religious faith or none; it was vitally important for me to know early on in my recovery that the 12 Step programme is spiritual, not religious. I had too many hang ups about religion; in the first year of sobriety I found it was just enough for me to get to regular AA meetings. They gave me the strength, hope and encouragement to stay sober. AA became my Higher Power; a very simple and practical answer during a time in my life when I was so screwed up about everything else. It still feels liberating that followers of all faiths and none can flourish with a 12 Step programme in their lives. There are atheists, agnostics, born again Christians, Hindus, Muslims, Sikhs, Jews, Buddhists and others in AA, each of whom respects all others' beliefs, and supports all those at meetings to remain sober. With AA at the core of my life, I had a freedom to follow my intuition and explore all manner of faiths, traditions and techniques to find what really would work for me.

My experiences with Dr. Ron Hutchinson had convinced me it had to involve meditation; I knew the problem and the solution lay with how I dealt with the vagaries of the mind, and particularly, how to live with PTSD. In this search I knew I had to find a spiritual base.

The lives of the great spiritual masters have fascinated me throughout my adult life. I've often wondered what it must have been like to have spoken with Jesus, Buddha, or Lao Tzu and to have learnt directly from them, rather than relying on the writings and interpretations of the original teachings by those who came after them. I read everything I could find about modern spiritual healers such as Harry Edwards, Ted Fricker and George Chapman, in an attempt to try and understand more about mankind's relationship with the divine, and our ability to heal ourselves and others. Even as a young child I was fascinated with the idea of the world, the universe, and why we are here. There were times, long before the abuse started, when I would drift off and go very deep into my own inner world, and would ask myself rather profound philosophical questions;

'What if there were no human beings, no animals? What if there was nothing alive on the earth?' And I would imagine a world completely empty of all life forms, and the emptiness inside scared me. The mind would quickly reply, 'yes, but there would be mountains, rivers, trees, plants...' I'd ponder this reply, but the idea of an earth without human beings and animals still horrified me. I would ask myself these questions again and again. Then my thoughts would go ever further and become more extreme. 'What if there was absolutely nothing? What if nothing had ever existed? No human beings, no earth, no universe - nothing?'

The thought of eternal and everlasting nothingness really terrified me. I felt a horrible emptiness inside as that thought penetrated deeper into my mind, and I considered this reality more carefully; 'what if there was absolutely nothing, no life, no existence?' These thoughts of nothingness immediately, but only initially, really horrified me. Oddly enough, there are similarities between these childhood thoughts of nothingness and the sense of loss and emptiness I have felt when the PTSD is triggered, and particularly when I've had visual flashbacks to the abuse. It feels like a void or a vacuum within myself which has no depth. Over the course of a few weeks, as these frightening thoughts of nothingness came to me, I began to realise the flip side. Rather than think and worry about what isn't, I began to develop a much greater sense of the miracle of what is.

The miracle of life, of creation, the earth, the universe and everything in it is so mind-boggling and humbling at the same time, and the recognition of this pushes aside any feeling of nothingness, or hopelessness. It also seems at the same time to be remarkable and tragic that humanity appears to ignore how amazing the miracle of consciousness is. No one spoke about this miracle when I was a boy. But also, back then, it occurred to me in a flash; there must be something else besides the physical universe. I felt there had to be some an underlying consciousness permeating creation...; although I'm sure I didn't use these words at such a young age! More than that, I sensed that even if the physical universe did not exist as I had momentarily imagined, somehow 'I' would, and this 'I' was connected to the wholeness of everything. I suddenly felt an even greater sense of wonder as I considered once again, with a real clarity in my young mind, the miracle of life, the earth, the universe, and that I was an intrinsic part of the whole.

I know I didn't use words such as 'consciousness' or 'creative energy' as this instinctive response formulated in my mind; they were grown up words for a young child, after all; I'm not sure I even 'thought' what I have described above. It seemed an intuitive knowingness which has become real to me; a sacred remembrance almost, that 'I' (the collective 'I', meaning all conscious beings) would live for ever. I felt, momentarily in that childhood state of profound thought, a deep feeling of connectedness to the creative energy of the universe, and to the miracle of consciousness. These spiritual experiences I think are common in very young children, and are important to re-connect with in our adulthood when we are guided, often through pain and desperation, to find some meaning to our lives. 'Be ye as little children to enter the Kingdom of Heaven', Jesus said. I've always assumed he meant the sense of love, wonder and awe little children have for the world and all that lies beyond in our universe.

Dad is a devout Christian and has attended church since he was a child. He has been very active throughout his life in the church's activities in the local community, which is something I've always respected him for. I am grateful to Dad that whilst he encouraged my brother, sister and I to consider a Christian faith, he never tried to indoctrinate any of us. His understated approach gave me a sense of freedom to explore what was my truth, which is an approach I have followed throughout my life. Until we entered our teens, my brother, sister and I would go to church with him.

Sunday School was held in the large hall next to the church, and had the best-polished and shiny-surfaced floor I'd ever seen to slide on, which ensured my regular attendance each week. This was, without question, the most enjoyable thing about Sunday School as far as I was concerned. It was probably the highlight of the week when I was seven years old. We would sometimes have a few minutes whilst the teachers were in the smaller room setting up, and we'd have sliding competitions (with our shoes off of course; scratches on the floor meant trouble!) When the teachers were ready, we'd traipse in to the room next door to learn all about God and how much he and his only son Jesus really loved us. I think I drove the teachers mad with my questions, but I needed to understand more about how Jesus related to my earlier spiritual thoughts of the miracle of life, the creation of the universe, and everything else. I had an active, inquisitive mind, and wanted to know the answers to my questions, such as:

- ❖ 'What happened to all the people who had been born during the thousands of years before Jesus lived? It seemed really unfair if they were nice people, that they didn't go to heaven.'
- ❖ 'What about all the really good people who didn't know Jesus because

they lived a long way away from Galilee, and had never heard of him? Did they go to hell?' (I didn't really know what hell was, but from what the Sunday School teachers had told me, it sounded like a really horrible place.)

- ❖ 'What about the people who had been brought up in another religion? Why were they not be allowed into heaven?' (I thought of a friend who lived around corner from me, who was a Sikh, and the idea he might go to hell really upset me.) ' Why would a loving God do this?' (I don't remember getting answers from the teachers, but these were genuine questions which bugged me. It didn't make any sense to me.)

As a young boy I knew, intuitively, that some amazing power existed which had created the universe and everything in it; I just didn't know how it could possibly relate to me, and whether I could or should be able to communicate with it. What I had been taught in church and Sunday School about Jesus being a beautiful soul, a great teacher whose life was something we could aspire to, I understood and really wanted to follow. I loved all the stories of the miracles; they felt true to me, but something within me resisted, even at that young age, much of the ritual that took place in the church. It was so repetitive and boring, and to me it had no emotion. It also made Jesus seem far too removed; he became remote and inaccessible to me. When I was old enough to join my father in the church itself, my questioning mind had issues with some of the prayers. I took exception to certain sentences when the vicar gave bread and wine to symbolize Christ's body and blood. These symbols just did not ring true for me. Even as a young child of seven or eight years old, I felt they were incorrect and therefore, (much to my father's irritation, he was, of course, standing next to me), when the Vicar asked the congregation to stand and recite aloud these prayers, I would only say very loudly the lines I agreed with, and was silent with the ones I didn't.

For instance, in an authorised confession, which is part of The Distribution of Holy Communion, I could accept I had 'sinned' in 'thought, word and deed' (though I resisted the word sinned even then), but I would deliberately delete the sentence, 'For the sake of your Son Jesus Christ, who died for us'. And then, after The Lord's Prayer was spoken, during the giving

Finding My Truth

of Communion, I would not say the sentence, 'Jesus is the Lamb of God who takes away the sin of the world'. Something within me rejected these core Christian teachings straight away. I don't remember telling anyone, but I just didn't believe they were true.

In my mind, looking back, I thought it seemed ridiculous that if someone had done something really bad, it was then okay if he or she believed in Jesus and said sorry, and repented, then they would go to heaven. If they didn't believe in him, and led an amazingly good life, he or she would go to hell. The crunch, though, was a few lines later when it goes on to say, during The Prayer of Humble Access, 'We are not worthy so much as to gather up the crumbs under your table'. I was expected to believe in an amazing power that created everything, and was then made to feel unworthy in its loving presence. I did not tell anyone about my reservations with the church's teachings. When I was eight years old, my father was keen for me to join the choir. I did, somewhat reluctantly at first, although in fairness I enjoyed the singing, I made some really good friends, and I got some pocket money. (We were paid for each service, and extra for weddings, but I remember thinking to myself during the occasional marriage ceremonies, 'there're not enough people getting married in this town.')

During the Sunday service, I usually read Enid Blyton's *The Famous Five* books during the sermons, much to the displeasure of Miss Turner, an alto singer, who sat in the stall above and behind me. Quite often her large, hairy paw would suddenly appear over my right shoulder and there would be a sudden snatch... and the inept smugglers in the west country, the tales of buried treasure, and outrageous lashings of ginger beer would be replaced with something tedious and obscure, for an eight-year-old, about the Book of Deuteronomy. I remember wondering whether Miss Turner was actually a secret Enid Blyton fan as, whenever I turned around, she looked as bored to tears as I felt during the sermons. Whilst I never heard her snoring, the times I sneaked a look back I noticed that she would have her eyes closed, breathing quite heavily, and would be resting her head against the wooden frame of the church pew. A few friends in the choir dared me, in return for a liquorice sherbet fountain, and I once asked her whether she sometimes had a little sleep. She looked horrified at my impertinence, and looked down at me with a very disapproving look on her face, and said quite haughtily,

'I am not sleeping. I am resting my head, and listening very carefully to what the Vicar is saying.'

Her eyes looked ready to pop out of their sockets as she stressed 'very carefully'. I preferred Mum's view on the spiritual life. Whilst Mum has never gone to church (that I can recall), she's always been a very spiritual person by nature; I learnt from Mum that you don't need to go to church or to have faith in God to be a decent, kind, honest and loving soul.

I think we all have moments in life when we sense a veil being momentarily lifted to reveal a higher consciousness within us. For what might be a nano-second there is very brief 'eureka' moment, and a sacred remembrance of what we already know. When I grasp at this truth, the veil immediately drops, and I get a sense of 'not yet, I have work to do'. I knew intuitively from my early childhood that this consciousness is the key to absolute reality.

It wasn't until I traveled to India in 1996 that my whole world view and sense of self was turned on its head. I didn't realise at the time of my childhood angst that the process I had followed in those childhood experiences (as described on page 123) is called 'Neti-neti', a Sanskrit expression which means "neither this, nor that". This approach has been used in Hinduism, mainly in Jnana yoga and in Advaita Vedanta, for several thousand years to help a spiritual seeker understand the true nature of God (or absolute reality). By practicing Neti-neti over several years and with a structure of regular meditation, I gradually became aware that I am not the body, nor the emotions I feel, nor the thoughts I have – my true identity is this: I am the awareness of them. I am the witness.

As one focuses more on this awareness, and attains a thought-free state, one eventually resides in a state of stillness; this stillness at its highest expression of consciousness is what some label as God, or ultimate reality. In contrast, I had believed for most of my life that my body, my emotions and my thoughts are the real and only me. Advaita Vedanta states our true Self is pure awareness or consciousness, and is the underlying absolute reality of the whole universe. I liked the sound of that, however remote it was to my day-to-day reality when I first came across it during my initial journey to the 'subcontinent' in '96.

Whilst these spiritual interests developed during my twenties and thirties, they did not negate the importance of the counselling I have needed, on and off, throughout my adult life. There is an AA slogan, *First Things First*, which has reminded me keep my feet on the ground, and deal with each issue in the most appropriate manner. Trying to meditate when the PTSD has been triggered and I am full of rage is pointless; I need first to find a safe place, and to release the emotion in a healthy, non-violent way. Using gentle breathing and concentration techniques (as described in the *When the Pupil is ready* chapter) certainly help me.

Meditation and self-enquiry work best when I am already in a state of relative calm, a foundation from which I can more easily 'go within' and focus on the awareness. This overall process has been profoundly healing, and has helped lessen the impact any disturbing thoughts can have on me. A thought passes on the screen of the mind, and by being aware of it and not involving or identifying myself with it, it passes. With practice this method brings about an immense peace, as gradually I become more aware of the seer (the witness) rather than that which is seen. (Self-enquiry is described in more detail later in this chapter). The Brihadaranyaka Upanishad (Chapter 2, 4:12), part of the ancient religious Hindu scriptures known as the Vedas, describes the realisation of the Self so beautifully;

> *The separate self dissolves in the sea of pure consciousness, infinite and immortal. Separateness arises from identifying the Self with the body, which is made up of the elements; when this physical identification dissolves, there can be no more separate self. This is what I want to tell you, beloved.*[9]

The childhood spiritual experiences were long forgotten for many years, until I started meditating in my mid-twenties, when some form of spiritual understanding started to very gradually take shape. By finding a much deeper sense of peace within me, despite living indefinitely with PTSD, there is no question that I have been helped to work through the trauma of the abuse. When I first joined AA, I had a very confused, angry and self-pitying view of God; 'if there is a bastard-God' was my usual response to the times whenever I had tried to understand what was happening in my life,

---

[9] Eaknath Easwaran, trans., *The Upanishads* (Nilgiri Press, 2007)

and to find the strength to sort myself out. I blamed God for everything that had happened during the abuse, and would say to my AA sponsor, Teacher Mike, 'If there is a God, why did this so-called fucking loving God allow the abuse to happen in the first place, and then why didn't the bastard stop it?'

After I'd been sober a few months, Teacher Mike had the wisdom to encourage me to find a Higher Power that worked for me, and to try and avoid getting caught up in the why's and wherefore's of life. I decided to revert to the experiences I'd had as a child, before the abuse happened, to try and connect to that intuitive sense of a loving presence, which I believe to be within each one of us...and that I knew I could sometimes, just fleetingly at first, connect to. Whilst I still had many philosophical questions, particularly during the first three years of my recovery and before I visited India for the first time, I eventually came to believe that this loving presence had nothing to do with the sexual abuse whatsoever. It made no sense to pray and ask for guidance and strength from a Higher Power that was, in any way, linked to the sexual abuse.

This outlook helped me greatly as I began to develop a more spiritual approach to life. At that stage of my recovery, at three years sober, I had not moved any further than what I've just described, but I had firmly rejected any notion of a divine hand directly ordaining I was to suffer, and therefore giving implicit sanction and permission for the abuse happen. I was looking for a spiritual path, without division and dogma, and something beyond what often seemed to me to be pointless ritual. Intuitively I knew the truth was inside me, somewhere deep, although my ego told me otherwise. There had to be an underlying oneness of creation, in which all beings are equal. I really needed to believe there was also something real and powerful beyond the savagery of my mind and the PTSD which crippled me; something that was non-judgemental, kind, and loving, that would help me. I needed to find a practical way to connect to this inner presence.

I had no doubt that Jesus Christ actually existed; and that he was a truly incredible soul whose life and teachings have raised the collective consciousness of mankind for over two thousand years. His message is simple. He said that we are all the same as him, we are all gods; and essentially, through practicing unconditional love we grow spiritually, and eventually come to find the Kingdom of Heaven is within us. I do not believe heaven is a place; but that it is the highest level of consciousness. I have rejected the notion that God is an all-powerful entity separate from us, and Jesus is "the one and only begotten Son of God". I now believe we are all 'sons' and 'daughters' of God, and that throughout human history several other great spiritual masters (both male and female) have come to help us realise our spiritual truth.

After an AA meeting, when I was six months sober, an AA old timer, George, pulled me over to one side and said to me, 'Matt, I know you're going through a tough time at the moment. You do realise that you are not the thoughts and feelings you have? They come and go, but you, the witness to them, remain. It's a process that takes time, but you'll learn to let go.'

He reminded me of what Dr Ron Hutchinson had said to me a few months earlier, back when I had dismissed Ron as being bonkers. But with George standing next to me, outside the meeting, it started to sink in. I knew I'd heard something really helpful. What I didn't realise at the time was that it would become one of the most important spiritual lessons of my life. This teaching also reminded me of the time when Dr Ron had said to me,

'Remember, Matt, you must never place a ceiling on your spiritual journey. Always remain teachable.'

My belief system has since become a fusion of Jesus' Sermon on the Mount, the teachings of Advaita Vedanta, and Buddhism. Buddhists do not believe in a deity as such, but rather in a Creative Force, or infinite consciousness, that permeates the whole of creation. My Higher Power is therefore a presence of unconditional love and light that permeates the whole of creation, and exists within me (and you) as the Soul or Self. It can never be separate from me, even when I doubt it, and especially when I am triggered with PTSD.

The Christian teaching that God is Love is shared by all of the world's religions. We feel love in our hearts, and this is where I have learnt to focus my meditation. I try my best to now let the thoughts and feelings come and go, to not latch onto them, and to remain focussed in the heart. (I came to learn the importance of this during my first visit to India, in February 1996).

As an adult, I love to disappear into second-hand bookshops and search for anything on meditation, spiritual healing, and travels in India and the Himalayas. In my early twenties, I became a voracious reader of the self-help and travel section shelves, where I found encouragement for my spiritual journey from, in particular, *The Celestine Prophecy* (James

Redfield), *The Road Less Travelled* (M Scott Peck), and *The Tibetan Book of Living and Dying* (Sogyal Rinpoche). One of the first books I read about India was *Autobiography of a Yogi* (Paramahansa Yogananda); there is a beautiful sacredness in its message of love and compassion. This inspired me to visit India, and to learn more about meditation.

One afternoon, I was browsing books in a charity shop when I saw on the front cover of a book, which was on top of a pile of other old books, a photo of a distinctive-looking Indian man with a huge Afro. My reaction was immediate, and the feeling behind it was bizarre; I simply had to buy the book, and I all but pounced to make sure no one else suddenly claimed it! I bought it and walked straight home, and devoured it cover to cover in one reading. The book was called *Sathya Sai Baba, The Embodiment of Love*[10]; its authors were an elderly English couple, Peggy Mason and Ron Laing, and the photograph was of an Indian Saint, Sri Sathya Sai Baba, a name with which I was vaguely familiar, although I was not sure why. Peggy and Ron were a retired couple living in Tunbridge Wells, and who had enjoyed a lifetime of searching for spiritual truth. After a series of remarkable events, they were led to visit the ashram of Sai Baba near Bangalore, South India.

The book includes illuminating interviews with Sai Baba which cover a wide range of issues I had always been interested in - the mystery of Jesus' missing years, the practice of unconditional love, omnipresence, miracles and teachings, and the authors' transformational first experience of the presence of Sai Baba. To say that their visit to Sai Baba fascinated me is an understatement, but my cynical mind needed much more evidence before I would even entertain the idea that an Avatar might be alive. (An avatar is a concept in Hinduism which means "descent", and refers to the incarnation of a deity or God on earth. Historically, Rama and Krishna are both considered to be avatars). I then thought of those who had lived at the time of Jesus, who had dismissed him as a radical or a fraud, and how many of them after his death had then learnt his true identity; that he was a spiritual master, and that he had in fact realised his Divinity whilst in human form. I had to know whether Sai Baba was an Avatar, a truly enlightened master, or a fraud perhaps, so I set about trying to find as many books as possible

---

[10] Peggy Mason and Ron Laing, *Sathya Sai Baba, The Embodiment of Love* (Pilgrim Books, 1987)

about him. Within a matter of two weeks, I had a healthy half dozen to read through, to get a better sense of what this Hindu holy man was really about.

The Holy Man and the Psychiatrist[11] by Dr. Samuel H. Sandweiss had a particular resonance for me; after all, I had met quite a few psychiatrists and psychologists in my time. The turning point, though, was *A Catholic Priest Meets Sai Baba*[12] by Don Mario Mazzoleni, which records the spiritual journey of Don Mario and his numerous interviews and interactions with Sai Baba at his ashram in Puttaparthi. It is a very personal story of inner transformation, during which Don Mario uses his theological training to examine Sai Baba's miracles and teachings. Don Mario's considerable doubts dissolve as he learns how Sai Baba's teachings mirror those of Don Mario's divine master, Jesus Christ. When the Church demands that Don Mario recant for saying that God is alive (in the form of Sai Baba) or be excommunicated, he replies, "Institutions do not accompany anyone beyond the grave. The only reality that one can present to God is one's conscience". He was subsequently excommunicated in September 1992.

Sai Baba spoke of one religion; that of love. He said there was only one language; that of the heart, He taught there was only one law; the law of karma, and he emphasised there was only one God, who is omnipresent. When I first came across these teachings something very deep down inside of me was stirred; I had the beginnings of an awakening which felt so profound I just knew this was truth. These simple teachings sums up my view of the world and the universal family to which we all belong; and that we all share this earth for such a short time of our physical existence. These words, more than anything else I'd read, convinced me to visit India. Decision made, with a mixture of fear and excitement, I considered how and when I could go. A series of seemingly coincidental events took place during the following few days and weeks which convinced me it was my spiritual destiny to visit India. Having just finished reading the Don Mario book, I was on a train to London Paddington. A lady got off the train at Cheltenham after leaving a magazine on her seat, and as I was feeling bored I leant over to have a read. As I opened it up, I saw an advert for a pilgrimage to India

---

[11] Dr Samuel H. Sandweiss, *Sai Baba: The Holy Man... and the Psychiatrist* (Sai Bhavan, 1975)

[12] Don Mario Mazzoleni. *A Catholic Priest Meets Sai Baba* (Leela Press, 1994)

the following spring. The advert read;

Sacred India Tours
to include a visit to the ashram of Avatar Sri Sathya Sai Baba

Feeling too nervous to telephone Nigel, the organiser, I decided instead to write to him with a number of questions regarding the cost, duration, and other matters such as medical cover. I wrote because I often had fears about talking to men I didn't know. I knew this was irrational, but nonetheless I felt safer writing, as I could put off talking to him and answering any questions he might have to another day. Such was my fear, I hoped he would reply in writing. In the event, Nigel soon replied by telephone, and we had a very pleasant conversation, and I gradually relaxed the longer we spoke. He informed me that the trip was the following February (1996), and the total cost for flights, accommodation, taxis, and his services as full-time guide would be £1200. I would be expected to pay for food and tips on top. The itinerary included a week long stay at Sai Baba's ashram near Bangalore, a few days at Sri Ramana Maharshi's ashram in Tiruvannamalai, and a final week resting by the Indian Ocean in Kerala. All things considered, it was a great offer.

I was desperate to go. I felt an inner calling that this was an important part of my healing journey, but I had no idea how I would find the money to go the following February, which was only five months away; and besides, I doubted my employer would allow me a month off, seeing as the theatre closed after pantomime for the last two weeks of January as usual. I would be expected to return to work at the theatre in February. Feeling somewhat deflated by this negative thinking, I said to Nigel,

'I'd really love to go with you to India. I'm interested to learn more about Sai Baba, Sri Ramana Maharshi, and meditation, but I really don't think I'll be able to get the money together in time.' Thankfully Nigel was more positive than I was,

'Well, we have a few months yet, so there's plenty of time. Besides, I've got a feeling something will happen. I'd like to put your name on the list, if that's okay with you? Let's see where we are in a couple of months, shall we?'

'Yes, that's fine, thank you', I said. 'I'm not at all sure about how I'll get the money together in time. I just want to be really up front about that in case someone else comes along to join your group.'

Nigel replied, 'That's kind of you, but that won't be a problem. I have a few spaces anyway so no one will be turned away. Let's talk again in a few weeks and see if anything has hopefully changed?'

'Okay, well, thank you. I really appreciate your call, and for all the information you've given me,' and I rang off.

Whilst I sensed Nigel was a genuinely decent man, I decided to make some enquiries to make sure I was not being duped in some way. I still had an inherent distrust of men and their motives. My intuition had always been accurate, though, which further encouraged me to trust my 'gut reaction'; I contacted a healing group Nigel had told me he was a member of during one of our conversations. The two members I spoke to confirmed that Nigel was an honest, deeply spiritual man who they would happily vouch for without any reservation. I needn't have worried about work and the money; within two weeks everything had fallen into place, and I was able to pay the £1200 in full, and make arrangements for my Indian visa. The theatre's General Manager agreed with no hesitation to my having an extended period of leave, acknowledging how hard I had worked in the past few years since I had been there; and then, a few days later, his PA called me, asking to see my First Aid certificate.

'Sure, I've got it here. I'll bring it over, but why do you need to see it? It's up to date.' I said.

'It's only routine, my darling. I just need to see it, sign the form and you'll get paid,' she replied.

My ears pricked up. 'Paid? What do you mean paid? I've never been paid to be a First Aider.'

She suddenly changed her tone, and questioned me quite rigorously. 'You have been keeping all the first aid kits fully stocked, haven't you? And making sure everyone had a valid First Aid certificate? You have been organising training, haven't you?'

'Yes, everything's been done. We're fine, completely up to date, but I've never been paid to do it. I thought it was part and parcel of my normal salary?'

'I'll call you back. Maybe I've made a mistake. I'll call payroll and get straight back to you. I'm pretty sure I'm right, though.'

The next five minutes felt like an eternity. Finally the telephone rang.

'I was right! 'she shrieked down the line at me very loudly. 'They've made a mistake, and you, sunshine, are owed a rather nice wad of money, and what's more, you owe me a drink!'

Payroll confirmed there had been an oversight, and I was owed over two years worth of monthly payments. Suddenly, I had the money to cover the costs of the India trip! I telephoned the Nigel that evening to confirm my place. He was delighted,

'I just had a funny feeling something would happen. I'm so pleased. Well, this might well be a positive omen of a fantastic trip to India; it's a magical place, and we have some very interesting people and places to visit.'

I grew more excited that somehow this trip was going to be a very special time for me. Two months later, during the week before Christmas, I bumped into an AA friend, 'Camera John', who was cycling along the Boulevard when he saw me, stopped, and called me over.

"I've been meaning to call you, Matt. I have something for you," he said. He rummaged in his rucksack and after a few moments he pulled out a tea tree candle.

"Thanks John", I said, somewhat bemused as I looked at the rather small, cheap-looking, tatty candle.

"The thing is,' he continued, 'there's a bit of a bizarre story behind this. I've been ill and went to my doctor who, after checking me over, suddenly said to me: 'John, I need to give you something else. I don't know why, maybe you will, but it's a gift from a friend and I know I have you give it to you.'

"He opened his desk drawer and gave me this tea tree candle. As soon as I touched it I thought of you, I knew I had to give it to you for some reason. And then my doctor said to me, 'it has been sent to me from friends in India, from the ashram of my Guru.' Now who's that chap you're going to see next year, what was his name?"

"Sai Baba," I replied.

"That's it, that's the name the doctor said to me, it's come from his ashram!"

I felt I was being welcomed to India, that this journey was exactly what was meant to be happening at this time in my life. Nigel and I had several more conversations on the phone before our small group met at London

Heathrow. Throughout my month traveling with him as my guide and friend, he was a mine of wisdom about all things spiritual, talking about the great teachers and teachings of all faiths. We spoke about reincarnation, the Law of Karma, the different schools of yoga, and he taught me a variety of meditation techniques. Nigel loved India, that was very clear, as was his sincere desire to share his passion for India with everyone in the group. He had lived and travelled extensively throughout the country for several years, becoming something of an Indiophile, studying the culture he loved and its traditions, and the sacred texts of Hinduism; the Vedas and the Upanishads. Our group was;

- Nigel, mid 40s, a quietly spoken man with an understated spirituality about him, and a good sense of humour; the kind, mischievous look in his eyes gave it away.
- Imogen from Bristol, a retired art teacher in her early 60s who brought her sketch pad and pencils, and whenever we lost sight of her, she would later be found sitting on a wall, surrounded by children who were fascinated by her drawings. If there were only a few children, she would sometimes sketch their faces and give it to them as a present; she looked rather like Shirley Williams, but was far gentler and less forthright in her views.
- Theo, a charity worker in his mid 50s, had grey hair, with a slight tan. Theo had a childlike curiosity about him. He desperately wanted to find something spiritual he could connect to, and he wanted evidence; a typical New Yorker, he wasn't going to be taken for a ride.
- And then there was me. Matt, early 20s, slightly bald, a son and a brother, a friend, theatre manager, rugby fan, cricket lover, recovering alcoholic, survivor of child sex abuse; feeling nervous but very excited - picture wide-eyed and bushy-tailed about the month ahead of me.

Just before leaving, a friend asked me, 'are you going to India to find yourself?' The answer was an unapologetic 'Yes'. I still believed that there had to be more than this, this could not be my life – such had been my thinking immediately after my last alcoholic drink three years earlier.

We flew into Chennai in the early hours of the 3rd February 1996, and even though it was still dark outside as we walked through Arrivals and out to our waiting car, my senses were immediately overwhelmed by the heat, the humidity, the amount of rubbish, the stench of the open sewers, the smell of incense burning at roadside shrines, and the shocking number of people sleeping rough on the streets. It really felt as if I had travelled to another world, but it had a strong sense of familiarity about it. Being there was a humbling experience; and despite the chaos around me, there was also a vibrancy which was captivating and fascinating in equal measure; a presence underlying everything my senses were trying to take in. This experience reminded me of a friend who told me of a meditation technique the Buddhists used when he attended classes in the Kings Road, Chelsea of the 1960s. They would meet for tea in the busiest cafe they could find on a Saturday morning and then, the monk would issue a command to listen to the silence. Amongst the music and psychedelic fun of the day, they would sit there motionless for an hour communing with the cosmos!

After a night at a resort in Mahabalipuram, sixty kilometres south of Chennai, with its miles of unspoiled beach, remarkable 7th century ancient rock-cut temples (including a rock-cut zoo, and sculptures of a huge elephant and other animals), we hired a jeep and travelled for several hours through jungle along dirt tracks, eventually arriving in a tiny village; literally, it seemed, in the middle of nowhere. We found the Shiva Temple, and went inside to meditate for an hour. Afterwards, we walked outside to find the entire village, of eighty people, waiting to welcome us! One of the men stepped forward and introduced himself in broken English, and invited us to have a tour of the village. We accepted his offer, and as we walked a few steps with him leading the way, we realised the whole village was walking behind us. As I smiled and acknowledged them, some of the very smallest children suddenly hid behind their mothers' legs; we may have been the first white people they had ever seen. Our guide showed us their homes, which were very simple mud huts without any electricity or water (we learnt they used a well three kilometres away, which often ran dry), and the School House, which, apart from the temple, was the only substantive building in the village.

It struck me how vastly different their lives had been to mine, in terms of their everyday living conditions, and their life expectations. When I saw their homes, I felt as if I'd gone back in time to the Stone Age. It was extraordinary to compare my typical English middle class home with the very basic structures they lived in. I had had a privileged upbringing. I grew up in a large, five bedroomed detached house in a quiet neighbourhood, had a public school education, and a two week holiday abroad each year. As I looked around the village, I suddenly realised how much I had taken for granted in life; the availability of food, electricity, gas, and fresh running (cold and hot) water, let alone the many treats which all children nag for, and often get along the way. It had never crossed my mind that I wouldn't have everything I needed in life, and this had created a sense of entitlement, which the alcoholism brought to the fore with my arrogant attitudes and behaviours. Whilst the villagers lacked material wealth, and the very basic necessities for survival, they were abundantly blessed with spiritual wealth; they were so generous and open hearted, with no desire for any reward. They didn't ask us for anything, other than our friendship.

Looking back, these observations made me consider, at length, the importance of finding a balance between the pursuit for greater material success, and deepening a spiritual awareness - not just in my own life, but in the society overall. Many of our so-called leaders; the politicians, multi-nationals, banks, and some media organisations, have embraced the path of the ego, power and economic strength as the ultimate expression of success. Consequently, as a society, we have experienced so much pain and confusion by ignoring the benefits of a more balanced, spiritual approach to life. We see this even more so at the present time, in this so-called era of post-truth, where blatant lies and manipulation from politicians, and others in positions of power and influence, are accepted in public life as the norm. The ideological end justifies the means, where the gap between rich and poor becomes ever wider, as higher financial dividends are automatically deemed more important than a genuinely sustainable living wage for the poorest workers. When people are struggling to eat, in a society as wealthy as ours, something is fundamentally wrong with our approach to life.

The goal of consciousness (the miracle of which mankind seems quick to take for granted) is surely not to accumulate even greater material wealth at the direct expense of the suffering of others. At least in my personal experience, a life without developing a greater spiritual understanding, is a life not worth living.

Back in the village, I asked whether I could take a photograph of the whole village, and when this was communicated, all the women and children disappeared; later I learned that this was so they could find their very best clothes. It was clear they were genuinely moved that we wanted to have a permanent memory of our visit to their village. The women returned wearing their best saris, whilst the children proudly wore pristine, white shirts which they would have worn for school. (It always amazed me that during my many visits to remote, rural Indian villages, without any washing machines, the children would often look so smartly dressed for school, and wearing the cleanest white shirts.)

Nigel, Imogen and Theo ushered the group together as I walked over to take up my position as photographer twenty metres in front of them. As I looked through the viewfinder, I realised I couldn't fit everyone in, so I walked another ten metres forward, only to find that they too had followed me another ten metres! With the group photograph taken, we offered to take individual photographs of each family, and of the schoolteacher with his pupils. They were once again clearly moved by this experience, judging from their broad smiles, and their applause and handshakes after each photograph was taken. A year later when Nigel, our group leader, returned with an individual set of photos for each family, he told me the welcome he received was rather like the feast offered to the Prodigal Son in The Bible. It was a humbling experience for all of us; I was so heartened by their kindness and unconditional love.

We then travelled to the ancient city of Kanchipuram, southwest of Chennai, regarded as one of the seven holiest cities in the Hindu religion. Nigel had arranged for an audience with the Shankaracharya, one of the leading and most respected gurus in India at the time. Throughout India, his organisation runs many schools, eye clinics and hospitals. The audience took place in his private interview room, and after fifteen minutes of welcome and general spiritual conversation, we were joined by fifty of the children, aged six to eleven, from the orphanage within the grounds of the ashram. The children sang devotional songs for thirty minutes, and then a few of them were encouraged to tell their stories. A few older boys spoke good English, and a monk translated for the two younger boys who spoke in their native tongue, Tamil. Several of these children had been badly beaten (one six-year-old boy showed where he had been repeatedly branded by his uncle) and abandoned by their parents. They were living alone on the streets where most had been abused again, until the ashram had taken them in and clothed, fed, accommodated and educated them.

We all found it a poignant experience to listen to their beautiful singing, and then to hear how horrifically they had been treated. I felt very privileged to be sober, and grateful that I had so much waiting for me back in the UK. It made me realise how truly fortunate I was. The coincidence was not lost on me. It took a journey halfway around the world to see that, although abuse, including child abuse, is a universal part of the human condition, so is recovery. When I learnt that these young children had been abused and abandoned by their families, I felt so grateful that I had the love and support of mine at home, something I realised I had long taken for granted.

After the singing, we played cricket. Despite it being dusk and almost pitch black outside (I could hardly see beyond a few feet in front of me), we played cricket with a wet cloth rolled up and covered with a bit of tape to make a ball, and a large stick for a bat. The children were so excited but very few spoke English, but it didn't matter as the names of Indian Cricket legends Sachin Tendulkar and V V S Laxman were met by squeals of excitement and approval. After forty minutes, the game was abandoned as a draw. Bad light stopped play.

As you live deeper in the heart, the mirror gets clearer and cleaner [13]
Jalāl ad-Dīn Muhammad Rūmī

A few days later we arrived in the temple town of Tiruvannamalai, where, nestled at the foot of the holy Mount Arunachala, is the ashram of the revered Indian sage, Sri Ramana Maharshi. Nigel had timed our visit so we could experience the holy Hindu festival of Mahashivarathri which was being celebrated at the end of the week. Also known as 'The night of Shiva', it is observed with great devotion by Hindus, with many thousands travelling from all over South India, as Arunachala is one of the most sacred places of worship for devotees of Lord Shiva. Over the centuries, many saints and sages have been drawn to Arunachala, and lived in its many caves, including Sri Ramana who lived in the Virupaksha cave from 1899 to 1916. The Arunachelaswar Temple, in the centre of the town, is also one of the most important temples dedicated to Lord Shiva in India, and Hindu pilgrims

---

[13] Jalāl ad-Dīn Muhammad Rūmī, auth., Coleman Barks, trans., John Moyne, trans. *The Essential Rūmī* (HarperOne, 2004)

travel there throughout the year to be purified and liberated from their sins. During the one hundred kilometre journey from Kanchipuram we had seen many sadhus (Hindu holy men), walking from temple to temple in their ochre robes, some covered from head to toe in vibhuti (sacred ash), as they made their way to the Arunachelaswar Temple for the festival.

As much as I was looking forward to immersing myself in the festivities, it was the life story and teachings of Sri Ramana Maharshi that really interested me. During the 1930s, the writer Paul Brunton introduced Sri Ramana to the western world in his classic 'A Search in Secret India', a book that inspired my interest in a spiritual philosophy known as advaita vedanta. Brunton had left his job as a journalist in London to pursue an inner yearning to find spiritual truth, and after many months travelling across India, he arrived at the foot of Arunachala and found everything he had been looking for, and more, at the feet of Sri Ramana Maharshi.

This was the true focus of my visit; to meditate at his ashram, to learn more about advaita vedanta, and to climb to the top of Arunachala. From what I understood at that time, advaita vedanta seemed to offer a way of bringing together the childhood experience of a 'universal consciousness' I had had as a really young boy, and the encouragement I received from Dr. Ron Hutchinson and my AA friend, George, to recognise that I am the witness to my body, and to the thoughts and feelings I have.

When we meditate, most of us are aware of our body, thoughts, and feelings; there is a general sense of 'me'. We automatically assume this is who we are.

According to Advaita, if I am aware of something, it isn't really me. The Self (or real me) is that which is aware; that which is the witness to the body, thoughts and feelings. Through a practice known as self-enquiry, we are able to ultimately connect with the Self, and discover that what we regard as ourselves (including the ego and the mind) is an illusion.

So, the core teaching of Advaita is that we are inherently divine right now. We are the universal consciousness that lies behind the phenomenal universe of matter and the mind / ego.

I found the following quote from one of my favourite teachers, Sri Nisargadatta Maharaj, really helped me to grasp this concept.

Finding My Truth

The source of consciousness cannot be an object in consciousness.[14]
Sri Nisargadatta Maharaj

Whilst I could, to some degree, understand intellectually what this meant when I first came across it twenty years ago, on a more practical level it seemed completely and utterly beyond me! The more I tried to meditate back then, the more thoughts would flood into my mind and drive me crazy. I would quickly fall into old behaviour and either replaying worn out tapes of the past in my mind's eye, and feel angry and upset, or I would project into the future and start fantasising about a girl I really liked. There was very rarely, if ever, any stillness in my mind at all, and this was even without the PTSD being triggered. Despite my upheaval I sensed there was something genuine and profound about advaita vedanta that might help me. I was attracted by the fact it dealt directly with the mind, and my experiences with cognitive behavioural therapy convinced me the mind was the filter to my world, and the key to my happiness. Sri Ramana's words gave me huge encouragement; I knew in my heart as soon as I read them that I had found my spiritual truth. This was, after all, my true reasons for visiting India in the first place.

The world is so unhappy because it is ignorant of the true Self.
Man's real nature is happiness. Happiness is inborn in the true Self.
Man's search for happiness is an unconscious search for his true Self.
The true Self is imperishable; therefore, when a man finds it,
he finds a happiness which does not come to an end.[15]
Sri Ramana Maharshi

I intuitively knew that in Sri Ramana's teachings I'd found something I could study and learn from when I returned home. I understood what the goal of consciousness is; to realise the Self, or in western terms, to become spiritually enlightened, and I knew without doubt that this is indeed possible.

---

[14] Maurice Frydman, trans., *I Am That: Talks with Sri Nisargadatta Maharaj* (The Acorn Press, 2015)
[15] *Abide as the Self, The Essential Teachings of Ramana Maharshi*, DVD. (Inner Directions Foundation, 2006). Narrated by Ram Dass.

Then there was the presence and personality of Sri Ramana Maharshi himself. I felt an incredible stillness and peace when I looked at his photo. From it emanated such a gentle, graceful power. I saw a Christ-like quality in his eyes. When he spoke of realising the Self I trusted he spoke the truth. He gave me hope.

Sri Ramana Maharshi was probably the most famous sage of the twentieth century, both in India and throughout the rest of the world. At age 16 he realized the Self spontaneously (he became enlightened) and ran away to Arunachala, one of India's traditional holy sites, where he stayed for the rest of his life. He was renowned for his saintly life and for the powerful spiritual transmissions that often occurred to visitors in his presence. Sri Ramana said that his most important teaching was done in silence. His core teaching is that self-realisation - or enlightenment - is not an alien or mysterious state, but the natural condition of humankind, and can be discovered by undertaking a spiritual practice called self-enquiry.

He directed people to look within rather than seeking outside themselves for Realisation, as 'God resides in your Heart as your true Self'. He described the nature of the Self as 'Existence-Consciousness-Bliss'. So many people came to receive his teachings that an ashram was built which to this day welcomes thousands of visitors from all over the world. He passed away in 1950, but has remained hugely influential to many spiritual seekers ever since. His core teaching "Who am I?" is widely used by the foremost spiritual teachers of recent times including H. W. L. Poonja (Papaji), Robert Adams, Mooji, and Eckert Tolle.

Peace is your natural state. It is the mind that obstructs the natural state.[16]

The mind will subside only by means of the enquiry 'Who am I?'. The thought 'Who am I?', destroying all other thoughts, will itself finally be destroyed like the stick used for stirring the funeral pyre.[17]
Sri Ramana Maharshi

---

[16] Ramana Maharshi, *The Spiritual Teaching of Ramana Maharshi* (Shambhala Publications Inc, 2004)
[17] David Godman, ed., *Be As You Are: The Teachings of Bhagavan Sri Ramana Maharshi* (Penguin, 1988)

I loved the peace and stillness in the ashram; there was something so timeless about the place; it was almost as if Sri Ramana was still there. I could feel his presence as I meditated in the hall. Whilst the implications of advaita vedanta teachings were too vast and intimidating (that 'at my highest level of connection I am divine') for me to comprehend in any detail at that time, I took encouragement from the fact that, at least intellectually, I could understand the principle behind them. By focussing all my attention on the awareness, rather than grasping and following the thoughts, I would find more peace within myself.

> *The highest teaching in the world is silence.*
> *There is nothing higher than this.*
> ....
>
> *Quietness, silence, total stillness, it is the greatest teacher.*
> *Reality shines through where there is silence.*
> *If you want to experience reality just keep quiet. That is all you need to do.*
> *Shut up. Stop talking. Stop thinking. Stop imagining. Leave it all alone.* [18]
> Robert Adams

It was the beginning of a very long (ongoing) journey. Whenever I had tried to meditate in the past, my mind felt as if it was being 'hit' by an avalanche of thoughts, feelings, hopes, dreams and fears; I was far too interested in my fantasies and my fears to stop 'looking' at them; I always allowed them to develop in my mind, which would often ruin much of my day. This understanding alone was a good enough reason to keep practising meditation. The more I read about Sri Ramana's life and teachings on advaita, the more I thought there must surely be a symmetry between his experience of realisation, and what Jesus Christ meant when he said, 'behold the kingdom of God is within you'. I was also struck with Jesus' other biblical statement: 'I and my Father are one'. He was surely referring to the divinity within each one of us, and inviting us to follow his teachings and

---

[18] Robert Adams. *Silence of the Heart: Dialogues with Robert Adams* (Yogi Impressions, 2012)

realise our own inner divinity.

Sri Ramana commented on the importance of silence when he quoted from Psalm 46, Verse 10; "The Bible says: 'Be still and know that I am God'. Stillness is the sole requisite for the realization of the Self as God". I had so many questions I wanted answers to, and with a myriad of sadhus and spiritual-looking people wandering around the ashram, I hoped I might meet an enlightened master who could bring some living evidence of these teachings. I needed to see and feel the truth of what I had read about advaita vedanta.

With the festival of Mahashivarathri later that week, the ashram and the town were getting busier each day with thousands of pilgrims from all over Southern India arriving on foot, by road and rail. During the festival pilgrims observe fast and keep vigil all night, and at full moon start the fourteen kilometre circumambulation of Arunachala from the temple, walking past the Sri Ramana Ashram along the way. Known as Giri Pradakshina in Sanskrit, pilgrims are encouraged to walk barefoot, and slowly in silence or meditation or by repetition of God's name, or singing devotional songs, and thereby think of God all the time.

There was absolutely no silence as we joined tens of thousands of Hindus inside the Arunachelaswar Temple to receive the blessings of Lord Shiva before we began giri pradakshina on festival night. The atmosphere was vibrant, joyous and very welcoming. The fact that we were not Hindu did not matter in the least to the devotees, and it was a magical experience walking around the foot of Arunachala, alongside hundreds of Sadhus, and the many thousands of Hindus of all ages singing devotional songs and attending religious ceremonies to Lord Shiva at the roadside temples we passed. Our fellow pilgrims were open and generous with their food and conversation. We felt like honoured guests. At daybreak, having completed giri pradakshina in just under five hours, the sun started to rise as we began our ascent of Arunachala, and to hopefully meet the famed Hindu holy man who we were told had lived there for many years in complete silence. The energy on Arunachala was very powerful. As we climbed, each of the four of us commented how we could feel what I described in my diary that evening as 'a tangible vibrating energy beneath our feet'.

After three hours of a fairly steep climb, we reached the top and received the blessing from a Sadhu. We sat quietly to savour the moment, and to enjoy the glorious views across Tiruvannamalai and far beyond. Beneath us I could see hundreds of pilgrims still doing giri pradakshina; some were singing and some dancing, and as they made their way into the centre of the town to the temple, the positive energy was palpable, and life affirming. The view from the top of Arunachala to the Arunachaleswarar Temple below stunning to behold. (The temple complex itself covers 10 hectares, and is one of the largest in India. It has four beautifully ornate gateway towers known as gopurams, the tallest of which is 66 metres, or 217 ft, and dates back to the 9th Century).

I don't know what it is about sitting on the tops of mountains, but it always seems to inspire from within me some form of spiritual musing about the meaning of life, consciousness, and my connection with the divine. Over the course of the next few days, I tried to get my head around my understanding of spiritual truth, and made notes as a number of ideas and realisations came to me. I wrote these in my diary, and have condensed them into what has been written below.

As I sat watching the many thousands of pilgrims walking around the foot of Arunachala below me, I found myself contemplating what a stark contrast there is between spiritual devotion in the east compared to the very traditional, conservative and emotionally restrained religious practices I had experienced during my childhood in the west. Here in India I was witnessing and taking part in a vibrant, energetic, heartfelt celebration of God's presence, which (accepting the tensions that have existed since time immemorial between Hindu and Islam) bring together communities of young and old, as a way to raise the consciousness of participants and to invoke a greater awareness of the presence of God within.

Looking back at my life in England, I remember as a child feeling that religious practice was too formulaic in its prayers by rote; that a non-academic approach to understanding God (how the importance of blind faith often seemed the easiest answer to a difficult question; the 'God works in mysterious ways' response) was, at least to my young, active mind, very boring. As I thought about this more, I realised that perhaps my reticence with the teachings of Christianity was due to the externalisation of God; the notion of separation between God and creation, which didn't sit comfortably with me as the truth. To the Christian mind, to say 'I am God' is the ultimate heresy, and after the looks of shock and dismay have passed, the straightjacket is quickly called for. In Eastern mysticism, however, any sense of individuality is deemed to be an illusion. It's not that we are not real, or that we are not responsible for our thoughts, words and deeds, but rather that we are not distinct from God or each other. The presence of God permeates the whole of creation, of which we (the body, mind and spirit) are an intrinsic part. Over many lifetimes we realise our highest consciousness, and we gradually release the need for a body and mind, and live eternally as awareness.

Whilst Christianity teaches us to love our neighbours, Advaita teaches that at our highest level of consciousness, we are our neighbours. There is, ultimately, no other. All is one. Thus the two essential teachings of Christianity — sin and salvation — are both absent in eastern philosophy. The Law of Karma deals with the deliberate acts of harm we may have committed, so there is no need for salvation in the Christian context. There is only enlightenment. In the east, whilst there are many festivals which honour and celebrate our inner divinity, spiritual practice is primarily focused on quieting the mind to allow enlightenment to naturally happen. In the west there are, of course, religious festivals such as Christmas and Easter that honour the birth, death and resurrection of Jesus, and prayer and meditation are also important, but Christian spiritual practice is often focussed on developing and maintaining a personal relationship with an external God, and only through his one and only son, Jesus Christ. The key difference, and one which I have since come to realise is the crux of my attraction to advaita, is that in the east we are regarded as divine, whilst in the west, we are regarded as inherently sinful, hence the need for a saviour and salvation.

For all my musings on spiritual matters, the simple message of AA helps me to keep my feet firmly on the ground, for the most part! I am reminded that first and foremost, it's simply about not picking up an alcoholic drink one day at a time, and doing my best to help those who are trying to get sober. We call this our primary purpose; to stay sober and help other alcoholics achieve sobriety. Whenever I get too carried away with my spiritual search, my sponsor often asks me, 'have you called an AA newcomer today?'. Offering support and encouragement to someone who is struggling (be it to stop drinking, or with life problems) is a cornerstone of the AA programme. We have a saying for this; 'to keep it, you've got to give it away'. To see a newcomer settle in to recovery; to gradually regain their health, their sanity and their sense of humour is a privilege, and a potent reminder for me of where I come from. The experience, strength and hope in an AA meeting inspires me to learn more about myself, and to recognise how changing my attitudes and behaviours, by working the 12 Step programme, is so emotionally, mentally, and spirituality rewarding.

Whether an AA member believes in a deity of any kind is a personal matter, and regardless of this, there is a common spirituality at the very core of the AA 12 Step programme. It took my reading of M Scott Peck's classic self-help classic *The Road Less Travelled*, and his subsequent writings on the spirituality of the AA programme, to recognise this at the very beginning of my recovery, and to recognise my alcoholism as a blessing rather than a curse.

> *The quickest way to change your attitude towards pain is to accept the fact that everything that happens to us has been designed for our spiritual growth.* [19]

In his 1991 book, *Further Along the Road Less Traveled: The Unending Journey Towards Spiritual Growth*, Dr. Peck outlines his belief that all that alcoholics (and all addicts for that matter, whether affected by drugs, gambling, sex, food etc) are really yearning for is a connection to God. Dr. Peck takes the view that, at birth, at some level of our consciousness, we are all aware of being separated from God, but some are more sensitive to it than others, and this creates a sense of profound, visceral emptiness within, often referred to as "a hole in the soul." At some point alcoholics and addicts find something that eases their inner demons (fear, anxiety, resentments, guilt, shame etc), which changes how they feel and brings about an immediate sense of relief. Whether alcohol, drugs, gambling, sex, compulsive spending, or internet porn, such is the impact of this psychological, emotional and physical reaction, that the addict is convinced he/she has found the elixir of life, and the answer to the problems. Dr. Peck recognised this existential reaction in the many

---

[19] M Scott Peck, *Further Along The Road Less Traveled: The Unending Journey Towards Spiritual Growth* (Touchstone 1998), 24

alcoholics and addicts he treated over many years as a psychiatrist, and concluded that addiction is a deeply spiritual hunger, and, as such, a sacred disease which requires a spiritual solution:

> *Thus I believe the greatest positive event of the twentieth century occurred in Akron, Ohio, on June 10, 1935, when Bill W. and Dr. Bob convened the first AA meeting. It was not only the beginning of the self-help movement and the beginning of the integration of science and spirituality at a grass-roots level, but also the beginning of the community movement. That is the other reason why I think of addiction as the sacred disease.* [20]

I am sure you will not be surprised that I agree with him; after all here I was, a recovering alcoholic and addict, sober through the fellowship of AA, sitting at the top of a mountain yearning to know God! The essence of his statement, however, goes much further than being just a powerful endorsement of AA and all other 12 Step Fellowships, of course. Dr. Peck states unequivocally that the core of AA is the spiritual community, and it is this community approach to spirituality which will be the salvation of us all. The core tenets of all the world's religions (the importance of love, honesty, kindness, sincerity, charity, forgiveness, generosity, and prayer) are embodied within the 12 Step programme. The key difference between AA and religion is that AA members are encouraged to find 'a power greater than themselves'. Thereby, the door remains genuinely open to all, including avowed atheists and agnostics. Indeed, one can be a deeply spiritual being, and an atheist after all! I sometimes wonder whether the word 'God' is so loaded with misconception and prejudice that it can sometimes be a barrier to spiritual enquiry.

Sitting at the top of Arunachala, we searched but didn't get to see the holy man. He may have been there. There was another sadhu who kindly offered us a complimentary cup of tea, and joined us for an hour of meditation, after which we climbed down to the ashram. As we arrived, Nigel heard that a direct disciple of Sri Ramana, a highly revered self-realised master in his own right, Sri Lakshmana Swamy, was giving darshan

---

[20] M Scott Peck, *Further Along The Road Less Traveled: The Unending Journey Towards Spiritual Growth* (Touchstone 1998), 150.

at his ashram nearby. (Darshan is an opportunity to see a holy person or the image of a deity in a temple. Hindus attach great importance to a darshan, and believe that by paying respect in this way, they will receive the spiritual blessings). After several years of intense meditation, Sri Lakshmana Swamy realised the Self (he became enlightened) in 1949, when he was still a young man in his early twenties, at the ashram in the presence of his guru Sri Ramana Maharshi. It was a swift five minute walk to his ashram, and when we arrived, there were already sixty people, crammed into a small hall, sitting in silence as they waited for the Master to arrive. Recognising us as visitors from overseas, the Indians kindly allowed us to sit near to the front. They gestured to us to climb over several rows of guests who had arrived before us and were already sitting on the floor. All four of us somehow managed to squeeze into a tiny space in the middle of the second row, where we sat cross-legged and meditated for a few minutes until darshan began.

The Master walked in, and he radiated the most extraordinary, magnetic presence – I was mesmerised by his energy, his aura, and looking into his crystal, clear, blue eyes I felt he was completely connected to the Universe. It was as if the rarest, most exotic, most beautiful of birds had been brought out of the forest for the first time in a few hundred years, for a brief moment, for all of us to see that enlightenment is possible, even whilst we inhabit our human bodies. He sat down on a chair, looked around the room and smiled at everyone, and then said nothing for an hour. And yet I noticed how, after a few minutes, I was receiving teachings in my mind which clarified a number of spiritual issues that had been confusing me; about the nature of the ego, fears, and how to meditate without the avalanche of thoughts, and so on. The teachings entered my consciousness as an easy flow of information to questions I had recently considered, even though I had not thought of these questions whilst I was in his presence. My mind was completely passive; it did not pose any questions, it only 'received' information in his presence. The teachings I received, during the silence as I looked at Sri Lakshmana Swamy, were noted in my diary that evening;

Concentration is much easier when you focus on the breath. When you are aware of a thought, bring all attention back to the breath. As you do this, you can focus on the name and form of a God in the heart. This will help concentrate the mind. Keep up this practice until you have achieved a state of inner calmness.

The mind is merely thoughts. Of all thoughts, the thought 'I' is the root. Therefore the mind is only the thought 'I'. Ask yourself, from where does this 'I' arise?

Focus all attention on the 'I'-thought, on the inner sense of 'I am', and ignore all other mental activity. With constant practice, the 'I'-thought will stop identifying with thoughts and ultimately subside into its source, the Heart. The illusion of the individual self vanishes, and there is eternal peace and bliss.

Thereafter, for the remainder of this period of silence, I felt a beautiful peace emanating from the Master and entering me, which I felt throughout my mind and body. He then did a fake yawn, which made everyone laugh, and started a verbal teaching for perhaps twenty minutes. His verbal teaching was brief, direct, and very powerful. He remained seated as he taught, and spoke in a quiet, clear voice. Such was his presence and the vocal clarity with which he spoke, his voice naturally filled the space.

"You are not this body, you are not thoughts, you are not feelings, your true Self is far, far greater". He then said; "Kill the mind, destroy the ego and know truth. Realisation is nothing new; you are realised now. It is only the mind that is making you think otherwise. In reality it is non-existent. It is giving you all this trouble because you do not look within to find out where it comes from. The mind has no beginning, but it can be ended by realising the Self. Kill the mind, and the Self will remain and you will be in internal peace and bliss."

Throughout his teaching, both silent and spoken, The Master radiated a powerful energy which, rather likes the waves of the ocean reaching the shore, I experience as waves of energy emanating from his heart throughout our time with him. With each 'wave' I felt a greater sense of peacefulness within me, and my mind started to quieten, until it was completely still and free of thought. I knew without any doubt that I was in the presence of an enlightened being. I had read these teachings so many times in books by Sri Ramana Maharshi, Sri Nisargadatta Maharaj, and several other teachers of advaita, but when it was spoken by such a powerful self-realised teacher, it penetrated one's beingness at a depth and with a force which gave it a legitimacy, an authenticity. I knew how privileged I was to have experienced a rare audience with a self-realised master.

After receiving his Darshan, we left the room in silence and walked a few hundred metres before anyone in our small group spoke. When we approached the busy road next to the Sri Ramana Ashram, Nigel suggested we go to a café (one we had visited several times and was only a short walk away), and share our personal experiences of darshan. After we had sat down in the café and ordered some tea, it soon emerged that we all wanted to sit quietly and hold the energy within us for as long as possible; there is often a tremendous power in silence. After a further ten minutes of contemplation, Theo broke the silence, and we began to compare notes, so to speak (e.g. verbally, not in writing), during which we discovered we had each received similar intuitive teachings, specific to each one of us, during the period of silence in darshan from this remarkable being. This was how his own teacher, Sri Ramana Maharshi, had taught.

Theo described his experience with the master, and the sadness he felt was very real to all of us, as he spoke.'I watched him very carefully for a few minutes, and began to feel very peaceful. He definitely had a calming presence, I could, ah, just feel this energy coming from him, it was radiating from him, wasn't it? Anyway, after a while, I closed my eyes, and saw myself in my mind's eye as a really young boy. I was, maybe, eleven years old, and even then, I knew that I was.... that I was gay. It wasn't the kinda thing you admitted to in the fifties, but I knew I was, even at that age, and so did my father. He got it, you know? I've always felt I hadn't lived up to my father's expectations; he wanted grandkids, and of course, that was never going happen. I need to think more on this, I know.'

Nigel's eyes and mine met, and we smiled at each other. I think we were both wondering how best to reply to Theo's emotional response. In the event, Imogen spoke first; 'I'm not excusing his attitude, Theo. My parents also had a very rigid, conservative approach to life, and wouldn't accept anything they thought was not the 'norm', if you'd excuse the word?' Theo nodded that he understood what she had meant.

'But thankfully we live in, at least I hope we live in, more enlightened times about many things now. Are you able to forgive your father, Theo? I'm sure if you could forgive him, it would help you.' She held his hand gently as she spoke of forgiveness, and she then embraced him, which brought tears to his eyes, and he mouthed a silent, 'Thank you'.

Imogen next spoke of her experience at darshan. 'I felt very peaceful in the Teacher's presence. My mind is rarely if ever quiet, but it became so after a few minutes just sitting there, looking at him. I could feel his energy coming towards me in waves -I think that's the most accurate way to describe it? I felt drawn to close my eyes, and as each wave of energy 'touched' me, I saw, in my mind's eye, the beautiful colours gently changing from white, to light blue, to a pink and so on. I was aware of a lovely, gentle buzzing energy around my third eye, and then I saw the most stunningly beautiful landscapes; it was rather like traveling to a heavenly place. I could try and paint some of these places later, but I don't think I will; I'd never do justice to them.'

Nigel's experience was very similar to my own. He had felt the energy pulsating from the Master and creating the peaceful atmosphere in the room. He had absorbed the energy into his heart, and as his mind stilled, he had focused all of his awareness on his heart.

'I feel very, very peaceful,' he said, with a beaming smile. 'My mind became still almost as soon as Sri Lakshmana walked into the room. I felt the energy was being generated from his heart; that's where I sensed it was being transmitted from, anyhow, so I quite naturally focussed my awareness on my heart and, with the mind so quiet, I felt a beautiful sense of wholeness come over me. I'm not aware of receiving any particular teachings other than, I would say, the importance of living in the present. Which is to say, to live, as far as we can, with a still mind, and with love in our hearts.'

A few days later, we left Tiruvannamalai and travelled two hundred kilometres north, by car, to the city of Bangalore, the suburb of Whitefield, and the Brindavan ashram of Sri Sathya Sai Baba. Our driver warned us that the roads were bumpy and treacherous, and had numerous potholes, but this did not stop him driving like a maniac. He must have been fantasising he was winning the Indian Grand Prix as he drove at suicidal speeds before suddenly braking to avoid yet another lethal pothole in the road.

From one extreme to another, the Brindavan ashram in Whitefield was an oasis of peace and calm in comparison to the journey we had somehow survived.

Sai Baba would stay here for about three months each summer, and during the rest of the year, he lived at his larger ashram, Prasanthi Nilayam, near where he'd been born in 1926, three hours north of Bangalore. Having settled into our guest house, opposite the ashram, we walked around the Brindavan ashram after lunch. It was much larger than I had ever imagined, with a sprawling campus which included an institute of Higher Learning, General Hospital, Institute of Higher Medical Sciences, an old peoples' home, a hostel for the students studying at the institute, and several accommodation blocks for visiting devotees. There was also a huge auditorium for cultural events and conferences, and the Sai Ramesh Krishan Hall, with a seating capacity of six thousand, where Sai Baba met his devotees. It was clearly a huge administrative operation. I subsequently learned that his charitable trusts run schools, hospitals, colleges, stadia and a planetarium, as well as a piped-drinking-water project serving more than 750 villages in the surrounding areas. Remarkably, there is no cost for medical treatments at his hospitals, nor any cost for the residents who live at the old peoples' home.

It had been a magical time for me in India so far, exceeding all of my hopes and expectations, but meeting Sai Baba was the real reason for my making this journey. I couldn't write off, as purely coincidental, the sudden, unexpected way that the money 'arrived' to cover the entire costs for my trip, and the candle the Sai Baba devotee had given to my AA friend, Camera John, who had felt compelled, as soon as he touched it, to give it to me.

This had been the catalyst for my interest. From the two dozen books I had read, and numerous conversations with Nigel and others during the past few months, I was subsequently attracted by the simplicity of Sai Baba's teachings. He spoke of the importance of love and service, and he used simple but direct instructions for his devotees to follow.

I gradually started to incorporate these teachings and positive affirmations into my morning meditation, and used them as a guide during my day. It helped me to believe that within each one of us there is a presence of love, however difficult it can often be to recognise it in ourselves, or others. I was also encouraged that his followers were not required to adhere to any specific set of beliefs, or to renounce worldly possessions. They didn't need to change their religion. He encouraged the Hindu to be a better Hindu; the Christian a better Christian; the Moslem a better Moslem, and so on. I liked the inclusivity of this message; intuitively it rang true for me that all men and women, regardless of religion and faith, could live in peace, and get along with one another. With such high expectations, I hoped

I wouldn't feel disappointed when I finally met him.

The following morning we arose very early, near 5.30am as I recall, and made our way to the ashram to queue for Sai Baba's Darshan. Several hundred devotees had arisen even earlier and had been performing Nagar Sankirtan. (circumambulating the ashram) chanting the Vedas (Hindu scriptures). There was an atmosphere of reverence, excitement and intrigue as we walked through the ashram gates and made our way to the waiting area, where we were guided to sit in lines by a Seva Dal (volunteer). The Seva Dals had the unenviable task of organising the several thousand devotees who were waiting for Darshan. A system of lines were used, whereby the person at the head of each line collected a numbered token from a bag which would tell us how early we would enter the Sai Ramesh Krishan Hall, and therefore how close we might be to Sai Baba when he came out. I counted that there were at least forty, perhaps fifty, lines, on the mens' side, with seventy people packed tightly in each line. Number 1 line was the line to be in, as this line went in first.

As the bag with the tokens was brought out, I could feel the excitement among the devotees suddenly move up a few notches. The head of each line, in turn, took out a token, and everyone sitting behind him would immediately lean forward wanting to know whether they had a high or low number. Nigel was at the front of our line; he would be the tenth person to pull a token from the bag. I was sitting behind him, and Theo was behind me. As he pulled our token out of the bag, he calmly looked at it, and slowly turned and looked at us both, with a broad smile, and said, 'We are line one'. I felt elated. I wanted to be as close to Sai Baba as I could. I wanted to experience his presence and get a real sense as to who he was. I also hoped to have an opportunity to talk with him. In accordance with Indian custom, the men and women sit separately for Darshan, and between us there was a five-foot-wide carpet on which Sai Baba would walk. We sat cross-legged, and I soon learnt how important it was to bring a small cushion, as sitting for over an hour on the hard, marble floor could be very painful on the ankles after a while.

As we waited for Sai Baba to leave his house, which was next to the Sai Ramesh Krishan Hall, I could feel a tremendous sense of excitement and expectation build up within me. I knew he was coming out before I could even see him; there was a tangible change in the atmosphere within the hall.

At my first sight of Sai Baba, my heart exploded with an immense feeling of joy and I saw a powerful, bright aura of white, like a five inch crown of brilliant light around his head. (Needless to say, this is not my usual reaction when seeing a man!) I knew without doubt that I was in the presence of an extraordinary being. He wore a full-length, orange robe which dropped to the floor, and often covered his feet as he walked. He had a huge, black Afro hairstyle and looked exactly the same as he did on the first photograph I'd ever seen of him, which had been on the cover of the book, *Sathya Sai Baba, The Embodiment of Love*. This was the book I'd felt compelled to buy as soon as I saw it in a second-hand bookshop the previous year.

He gently and gracefully moved along the carpet raising his hand in blessing, receiving letters, talking briefly to a few people, and even manifesting vibhuti (sacred ash) which, with a couple of twirls of his right hand, he effortlessly poured into the outstretched hands of a few people near to him. (Although Sai Baba faced some accusations of being a fraud, many books and first-hand accounts have been published since the late 1940s which attest to the fact that he had the ability to create, at will, objects and substances, such as vibhuti, from 'thin air'. He often played down their significance, referring to them as his 'calling cards' which he used to attract attention to his teachings).

As he came closer to me, within twenty feet, I felt such an intense rush of energy through my body; I knew I was in the presence of an extraordinary man. My mind, which had previously been filled with so many questions, felt still and peaceful. Nonetheless, a few questions gently arose;

'I just want to know, is it true? Is everything I have read about you true? The healings, the omnipresence, the manifestations; the claims you are the Cosmic Christ? Is this all true?'

As I was thinking these thoughts, I watched him move slowly and gracefully along the carpet. He was now standing opposite me, with his back to me, talking with a few ladies. He suddenly turned and walked straight over to me, and stood one foot in front of me. I looked up at his face and felt tremendously powerful waves of love flow from him to me; and as our eyes met and he looked directly at me, I felt the greatest experience of unconditional love I have ever known. I felt inside of me, and all around me, the most beautiful presence of love. Whilst he was obviously a physical being, I saw his body as a vibrating energy which I could feel was healing me.

It's very difficult to describe, but when he stood in front of me I saw his body as shimmering energy, rather than 100% bone and muscle. My understanding of this perception was that we are not essentially physical beings, but rather energetic vibrations that give the illusion of physicality. There is some scientific backing to my experience.

I don't pretend to understand either science or quantum physics, but scientists have discovered that everything in the universe consists of vibrational energy which includes, of course, our physical bodies. Quantum physics has also shown that physical matter is the manifestation of a certain vibratory rate of energy. Matter and energy are two different manifestations of the same primary energetic substance of which everything in the universe is composed, including our physical bodies. Perhaps this vibrational field is the underlying principle of oneness I heard about during the sermons in church as a child where, in 1 Corinthians 8:6 it is written 'yet for us there is but one God, the Father, from whom all things came and for whom we live...'

I had no doubt whatsoever that Sai Baba was operating at a level of consciousness beyond anything I had encountered before. Looking into his eyes, I knew he was more aware of a much higher state of consciousness than I certainly was; I glimpsed for a split second the entirety of it all. It felt like everything I had ever been through, through every lifetime, was to bring me to this place, at this time. It was the single most profound experience of my life; in fact I cannot compare it to anything else, such was its remarkable impact on my psyche, on my soul.

Over the years, I have sometimes joked with friends that if Sai Baba hadn't moved, I would still be sitting there, all '*blissed out*'! I have no idea how long he stood there looking at me; it may have been only several seconds, but it felt timeless. As he walked away, I closed my eyes and automatically sank deep within myself to a place of silence from which I had no desire to leave.

When Darshan had finished, I didn't speak to anyone for fifteen minutes. I wanted to savour the whole experience and hold on to the energy that had been transmitted to me. We slowly arose from our seated positions, and took a few moments to stretch and allow the blood to run back to our leg muscles, which had been squashed under our weight for almost two hours. We walked out of the hall, and joined the thousands of other pilgrims who were slowly making their way to the ashram gate. It took several minutes to negotiate our way through the crowds, and get across the busy road to a small café nearby, where we had agreed to meet Imogen (who had been sitting in the womens' area during darshan). Nigel sat down next to me on a bench outside the café. He smiled at me, and said, 'You've been well and truly zapped!'. I smiled and laughed, agreeing with his accurate assessment, saying, 'Yes, I'm in the zone, as they say!' There were hundreds of people milling around outside the ashram. Many were having breakfast at one of the numerous small roadside cafes in the area. Imogen and Theo spotted us outside the café, and sat down, and as we spoke among ourselves, an American joined us. He was a cheerful, open and good-humoured man. He had, however, the most obvious and awful blonde wig I'd ever seen. You couldn't miss it, and it seemed so out of place to wear a wig at an ashram!

A group of monkeys had gathered on the tree branches above us, and they too were somewhat taken aback by the appearance of the wig. They chatted among themselves for a minute or so, and then one of them moved like lightning. He charged along a branch, and then bolted down from the tree and sat directly in front of the American as he spoke. Feeling somewhat disconcerted by this surprising interruption, he stopped talking in mid-sentence and stared in disbelief, with his mouth wide open, as the monkey very slowly took the wig off the poor chap's head, and then raced back up the tree and decided to wear it. It was such a funny moment; we were all in hysterics, and thankfully even the American laughed as well. Theo, however, was keen to talk about his mixed reaction to seeing Sai Baba.

'He's a very interesting guy. I can't say I've ever been at anything quite like that before. The atmosphere at the Yankee games is very different, you know! I could feel his presence, he has a very real energy about him, for sure. As he walked closer I really felt it, it kinda surprised me but it was real, I felt it. I don't know... he's obviously helping a lot of people, through his charitable work, but I... you know I have a problem when he says he's God. I have a real problem with that, it's too huge a statement. I'm not so sure about that.'

Imogen had been listening, whilst she carefully dissected her two bananas with a sharp knife... and before suddenly deciding to mash them up with a spoon into a bowl, interjected,

'But he says we are all God as well. I don't think he means he alone is

God?'

Nigel nodded, and quietly added, 'It's a statement most people, at least initially, have a problem with. Imogen is correct; what Sai Baba actually said, in response to being asked the question, was, "Yes, I am God and so are you. The only difference between you and I is that while I am aware of this fact, you are not." That's an important point to understand. He's reminding us of our spiritual truth, that we are divine.'

Theo replied, with a look of incredulity on his face, 'Okay, that's helped, thank you. But I struggle with the idea that I am God! I've got to work a helluva lot more on myself before I'll accept that!'

'Don't we all?' I replied, with a chuckle.

Imogen continued, 'He has a lovely presence, that's what I took from the darshan. I felt a beautiful feeling of Love when I looked at him, which is what his message is all about; Love and service. I'm impressed by the charity work his organisation does and how well organised everything seems to be here. I don't really think it matters whether Sai Baba is labelled God, a Saint, or simply a very good man. It's only a label, and what he does, and encourages others to do, is far more important.'

I agreed with Imogen, stating, 'The label wasn't important, and in fact, for me it creates a barrier to think of anyone as 'God'. At some level, I accept there have been spiritual teachers, such as Jesus, who have lived at a much higher level of consciousness, and perhaps Sai Baba is at a similar level. I've got to say, he blew me away. I had such a profound experience in there, one which I need more time to process before I can understand what was going on. But what I can say is that he is an extraordinary being; his consciousness is at a level I've never come close to experiencing before, and that, in itself, has opened my mind up to the fact that, there is so much more going on.. I felt an immense spiritual consciousness within a physical body, and I felt the body was purely a necessary convenience as that level of consciousness, that we are so much more than we 'think' we are. There's so much more going on.... It sort of feels like this experience is the tip of the iceberg, so to speak.'

'Wow, you really did get zapped!' said Nigel, with a broad smile. 'Tell us more, what else did you get from your experience?'

I took in a very deep breath and released it, as I tried to put into words what I had seen and sensed earlier.

'For me, Sai Baba is a highly evolved spiritual being. He must be: I saw a very bright aura around his head, from forty metres away, and I've never even seen one before. As soon as I saw him, I felt powerful energy emanating from him enter into my heart; it was almost like an explosion of power was shifting something inside of me.' I paused and took another deep breath, as I felt very emotional at the experience I was describing, 'and when he stood in front of me, I had an incredible feeling of bliss, of unconditional love in me, and all around me. The God thing is irrelevant; I just see him, and everyone else for that matter, as spiritual beings having a game in consciousness. Sometimes it's very painful, sometimes it's the most amazing thing ever.'

Nigel, Imogen and Theo all told me how pleased they were I'd had such a positive experience, with Theo adding, 'I want some of what this guy's got!', which made us all laugh. Nigel was a devotee of Sai Baba, though his approach was always understated, and he had never put us under any pressure whatsoever to follow him. Nonetheless, he was clearly delighted we'd enjoyed darshan so much, adding,

'I also resisted any idea that 'God' might be alive on the earth. I think it is a particularly challenging concept for us, who live in the west, and have been influenced by Christianity to accept. So I took the same view as Matt, in that we are all spiritual beings, and some people are sufficiently advanced to live at a higher level of consciousness than the rest of us. You might call these old souls, saints, masters, teachers, or, perhaps they are everyday people who are kind, open and generous; they simply love helping people.' He paused to take a sip of his chai, before continuing,

'I've become convinced, over a number of years of visiting Sai Baba, of his divinity, and I believe him when he tells us that we are all divine. He gives a message of hope, and the guidance how to realise our divinity. I've had several interviews with him over the years, and witnessed his omniscience and omnipresence. All my questions have been answered, all my doubts have been removed. But it's a personal journey ... you might feel a stronger connection to another spiritual teacher, which is absolutely fine. We all come from God, and to realise this, we are taught to practice love and service. The simplicity of his message is just that. It's beautifully simple.'

Our conversation about Sai Baba helped me to understand more about what I had experienced. I'd felt an immediate connection with his teachings by reading several books about his life in England several months earlier, and now having met him I could readily acknowledge he was an extraordinary being. Just being in his presence had somehow brought about an opening in my consciousness; I now knew that there was so much more going on beyond the physical universe, and this knowingness was linked with the childhood spiritual experiences about wholeness I described in an earlier chapter.

The most significant realisation I learned in that brief moment in front of Sai Baba, and one which has been essential to my spiritual growth, is the knowledge that there are men and women who have genuinely attained higher levels of spiritual consciousness, and that this awakening to higher consciousness is ultimately why we have awareness. The experience also galvanised my commitment to AA; I could see that the spiritual programme of AA was an ideal platform upon which I could learn and grow. Everything I needed had been laid before me. With this understanding of a spiritual context to my life, I further understood at a much deeper level that my role in life, above all else, was to connect to the love within me. This meant I had to work on myself to remove the mental barriers that had been erected and which prevented me from feeling comfortable to give and receive love.

Sri Sathya Sai Baba passed away on 24th April 2011. He is revered as a great spiritual leader, whose life and message attracted many millions of followers throughout the world. His core spiritual teachings are the same as advaita vedanta. He encouraged everyone to recognise that we are all embodiments of God, and that our goal as human beings is to realise our inherent divinity, and to achieve "enlightenment".

As a survivor of CSA it was, at first, very challenging to accept how any man could have such a profoundly positive impact upon my life. Yet I cannot deny the power, the immense spiritual healing, and the unconditional love I received in Sai Baba's presence in February 1996, and indeed on several other occasions when I visited his ashram during the following fifteen years. He has also come to me in several vivid, prophetic dreams and visions. Over twenty years later, I still regard how the 1996 darshan brought about a profound change to my consciousness. I think it's also worth stating that I do not consider myself to be a devotee.

Indeed, my encounter with the legacy of another holy man, at the southernmost tip of the Indian subcontinent, convinced me, as it had Nigel before me, that one didn't need to be a devotee of any one individual to awaken spiritually. We left Sai Baba's ashram and travelled six hundred kilometres south to the town of Kanyakumari. It was on a small island, just off the mainland, that a wandering monk, who became famous throughout India as Swami Vivekananda, found enlightenment. In the course of his short life of thirty-nine years (1863-1902), he promoted peace and human brotherhood on the spiritual foundation of the Vedantic Oneness of existence, the same philosophy as taught by Sri Ramana Maharshi. In 1970, the Vivekananda Rock Memorial was built in his honour, and over a million pilgrims visit every year to pay homage to the man who many believe brought about the spiritual rebirth of India.

After a ten minute boat ride to the temple, I left the others and decided to meditate alone in the meditation hall in front of the huge AUM symbol. Aum, or Om, is the most sacred spiritual icon in Hindu religion, and it is also a mantra in Hinduism, Buddhism and Jainism. There is considerable significance and depth to what AUM represents to Hindus, but in essence and for the sake of brevity, the sound and symbol of AUM represents the Atman (Self or soul) and Brahman (ultimate reality or God).

A stands for Creation
U stands for Preservation
M stands for Destruction or dissolution

This is representative of the Trinity of God in Hindu teachings; Brahma, Vishnu and Shiva. I sat in the traditional lotus position for meditation (cross-legged with my feet on the opposing thighs), and began to consciously breathe very gently. Within a matter of ten seconds or so, I was aware that my consciousness was going deeper within myself very easily; with each in-breath I was losing awareness of my body and my breathing was so infrequent and shallow, it felt I was hardly breathing at all.

My mind was completely still; there were no thoughts at all, and I stayed in this thought-free state for an unknown period of time. At some point, I had the most incredible experience. I felt and heard my physical body dissolve into the ether from the head down to the soles of my feet. It was a sudden, utterly painless, beautiful experience. The dissolution was 'heard' as a fast, but gentle fizzing sound; the only comparison I can think of is from the TV series *Star Trek* when the crew are vaporised to a different location, with the immortal line, 'Beam me up, Scotty!'

This experience was observed without any thought or emotional reaction. Thereafter the consciousness was from the heart and there was a oneness with all; there was no separation in mind or body for I had no awareness of either existing. There was no thing there. There was no mind, no thoughts, no judgment. Only pure awareness and a love for all as I was the all. It was a wholly natural, blissful state of consciousness.

After ninety minutes of meditation - only when I became aware of thoughts was I able to judge how long I had been in this state - I started to become very gently aware of 'having' a body. With an awareness of a body, the thought very quietly and gently came- 'I have a body' - and immediately disappeared. There were no more thoughts. The mind remained still and completely silent. I slowly rose to my feet and felt I was in a state of utter bliss. I gently walked outside of the meditation hall and stood by the 'wall' looking at what we call the 'sky' and what we call the 'sea', but I did not label them 'wall', 'sky' and 'sea' as I was not separate from them. There were no labels, and there was no sense of any separation at all.

My consciousness was unconditional love. There was nothing but unconditional love. Rather like the water from a river entering the sea does not identify itself as a separate entity, so too did I feel a oneness. There were no labels; only love. When I saw a person, I saw an embodiment of love. My consciousness and everything in it was an expression of love. I saw a body, but it was a manifestation of love in the form of a body. Whilst I was aware of 'my' body, I viewed it as nothing more than a vehicle to be used in a physical dimension. I didn't recognise the body as 'me' or 'mine'. I knew that I existed without it, at a higher level of consciousness.

After a total of two hours on the island, I caught the boat to the mainland and on arrival felt immense love for all beings I saw. Everything I saw was treated exactly the same; the love was unconditional from the heart, to the goat, and to the children playing in the street. There was no judgement, no labels. My awareness was love. I was not aware of anything else. There was no mind, and no thoughts, to create the illusion of separation. This continued until I became aware of a few thoughts tentatively appearing and starting to evaluate these experiences. And with this, very gently and gradually came the labels, the illusion of separation. There were the slow beginnings of a subject / object relationship.

"That was amazing", a thought said. "You really loved the feeling of oneness. Go back and feel it again!"

And so I did. I caught the boat to the island, and sat once again in the meditation hall and meditated, but it wasn't the same!!

It is very difficult to describe oneness. Words are not able to do justice to the extraordinary bliss one feels. However, the quote below comes as close as I have found. I believe I had a moment of grace which is available to anyone willing to be open, and to realise the truth that is in each one of us.

God is pure knowing itself. God is beyond everything that can be conceived or thought about. Words cannot describe it. God is beyond space and time. God is infinite Being, infinite Consciousness, and infinite Bliss.
Author unknown

February 1996 was the life-changing month of my life. I was aware that my consciousness was changing, and that I was being gently introduced to a new, more dynamic, profound approach to life, and remarkably (given my life history, and approach to life), I had so little inner resistance to the experiences I was having. There were intellectual challenges, and some fears, of course, as there often is when one doesn't fully understand what one is experiencing, but I had no PTSD triggers. In fact, I have always felt very safe, both physically and emotionally, during my numerous visits to India.

I knew I was in the right place, at the right time, and with the right group of people for my spiritual journey to open up, which, in itself, felt so empowering. My time in India revealed a new paradigm for living; western society, for all its advantages, is so materially influenced, at the expense of the pursuit of spiritual truth, which I know is the ultimate reason we are playing this game of consciousness. India's gift has been the reminder of this sacred, eternal truth. Whilst I have faced a number of challenges during the following twenty years living with complex PTSD, the spiritual experiences that took place that month have never left me, and have driven me forward through life, especially when the PTSD has been so crippling. Meeting these self-realised souls, Sri Sathya Sai Baba and Sri Lakshmana Swamy, and having the brief experience of oneness at the Vivekananda Rock, brought alive a reality that had been buried so deeply within me. Its presence consciously reminds me of my spiritual destiny, and serves as a powerful, magnetic invitation to go further.

Advaita Vedanta offers a unity amongst the diversity of the world's religions. Equally I have witnessed it to be a means for the atheist and the agnostic, if they do desire, to find a profound inner peace.

> *A quiet mind is all you need. All else will happen rightly, once your mind is quiet. As the sun on rising makes the world active, so does self-awareness affects changes in the mind. In light of calm and steady self-awareness, inner energies wake up and work miracles without any effort on your part.*[21]
> Sri Nisargadatta Maharaj

---

[21] Maurice Frydman, trans., *I Am That: Talks with Sri Nisargadatta Maharaj* (The Acorn Press, 2015), Chapter 65.

6

TREADING THE BOARDS

The consciousness in you and the consciousness in me, apparently two, really one, seek unity and that is love. [22]
Sri Nisargadatta Maharaj

After my spiritual experiences in India during February 1996, I returned to the UK in a much more positive frame of mind. I was keen to explore and develop my understanding of all things spiritual; whether this be my relationship with God, or the Divine, or Higher Consciousness. The name was immaterial to me; I just knew there was a benevolent, loving and healing presence, and I needed to know how to consciously connect to it – that's what really mattered. I knew I was so much more than just the body I saw in the mirror, the thoughts I had, and the feelings I felt. I realised that to have an awareness of a body, of thoughts and feelings, I couldn't BE these things. Instead of centring my life on obsessing about these three imposters, I wanted to explore what this awareness was; and how it might enable me to find more peace and understanding in life.

I prayed for guidance to learn more about my true self, and to grow spiritually. My understanding of prayer changed from being a somewhat abstract yearning for some entity outside of myself to give me help, to now evolving into a more focussed relationship within myself to some form of Higher Consciousness. It was becoming, very gradually, a more direct,

---

[22] Maurice Frydman, trans., *I Am That: Talks with Sri Nisargadatta Maharaj* (The Acorn Press, 2015), Chapter 21

personal experience. I found myself spending a lot more time in nature, as I pondered the vastness of the universe (of which we know so little, it seems), and of societal norms which are so restricted in their ambition to living one life in this body... and then at some point, this body dies and we are told that's it - it's either heaven, purgatory or hell. This view of consciousness seemed so limiting and immature to me. As a child I instinctively rejected this view of life; I'd always sensed there was so much more going on beyond the physical universe and an afterlife, but I had no context with which to explore it.

After India, I sensed a greater depth to myself; I felt I had a stronger foundation to who I was, and I intuitively felt more able to handle life's challenges. I'd found something tangible which would help me learn, heal and grow. The experiences with Sri Lakshmana Swamy in Tiruvannamalai, Sri Sathya Sai Baba in Bangalore, and in the meditation hall at Vivekananda's Memorial Rock at Kanyakumari, India, had brought about a change in my consciousness; I was aware there was so much more to 'me' than what I had previously believed. I explored meditation with the certainty that it could genuinely help me to open up spiritually.

I returned at the beginning of March 1996 to the Empire Theatre as Front of House Manager with a renewed sense of optimism for the future. I started to really enjoy my work, and was keen to learn more about the business. I also became much more involved supporting new members of AA and organising conventions, both of which were hugely rewarding. Over the next few years, life was a really busy but exciting mixture of work, AA, rehearsing and performing in several plays, developing my spiritual understanding in a meditation group, and escaping for long weekends with friends to Majorca, Paris, Stockholm, Vienna, Prague, Amsterdam and Berlin.

In the spring of 1998 there were a number of key staffing changes at the theatre but the loss of several senior figures also meant new opportunities for my career. I was summoned to the Town Hall and the powers that be promoted me the position of Programming and Marketing Manager. I was now responsible for negotiations with theatre promoters and for the programming of the shows. I was thrilled to accept. I had a pleasant flashback to a few years earlier, when I was promoted to Front of House Manager and I recognised how far I'd come since that time. Now promotion felt exciting; it was not something to be paralysed with fear about or intimidated by. It was the reward for my efforts over the past few years, and an opportunity to use my experience and energy to develop the theatre further.

Within a few weeks I had appointed John and Sean to support me with the programming and marketing; the three of us quickly settled into a productive team, and we all clearly enjoyed working together. The theatre already had an experienced, much respected technical crew, and with the arrival of my replacement as Front of House Manager, the senior management team had been formed. My successor, Paul, was another excellent appointment, and under his leadership, the Box Office, ushers, bar staff, and many volunteers, made for a very talented, passionate, hard-working theatre team.

In my new position I didn't want to reinvent the wheel, so I studied what other theatres were doing regarding the programming of shows, ticket prices, special offers, group bookings, and marketing strategies. I was, in particular, keen to learn how other seaside theatres programmed shows during the summer months, when, although the towns were packed with many thousands of day trippers, very few ever stayed on to see any shows. I contacted a number of other theatre managers from beyond our catchment area, and we informally agreed to work together to share ideas for shows, financial deals, promoter reputation, new box office systems, and how the development of the internet was an opportunity to be embraced. This informal relationship sometimes made life easier for promoters, as they could book five other theatres and contract for shows in the same week in the same geographical region (thus saving on travel times for the performers and the cost of petrol) during the course of thirty minutes, rather than approaching each theatre individually over the course of several days.

Whilst John, Sean and I each had our specific areas of responsibility, there was so much crossover of roles and responsibilities it was essential, working in such a busy environment, that we were well organised, and enjoyed each others' company. Thankfully we got on really well, and the theatre office was therefore a very productive and positive environment to work in, which I found so supportive. We set about improving the design and quality of the theatre leaflet from a simple, eight page concertina-fold leaflet with small images and very limited information, to a twenty-four page

A5 glossy booklet which allowed for more information about the theatre facilities, the shows, and which had the space to include a selection of images for each show, if we wanted to. We also decided to increase the print run and distribution networks, taking advantage of our army of passionate and energetic volunteers. At the same time we dreamt up a list of the star names and shows we wanted to book for our first year, and my main challenge was to get their promoters to sign on the dotted line.

John was the numbers man. When I sometimes wasn't sure about a provisional show deal I was negotiating, the three of us would talk it through and agree what we thought, as a team, was a fair deal to go back to the promoter with. John would then create a marketing strategy and a spreadsheet which would estimate the financial breakeven for each show, taking into account ticket sales, merchandise commission, printing and advertising costs etc.. so we'd know our profit and loss account on a weekly basis. Unless there was an emergency, twice a week we'd discuss sales figures and decide what our focus needed to be to boost audience numbers.

This was before e-marketing was the norm, so sending an e-promotion to a specific market on our e-database or advertising on social media or via SMS had yet to be invented. Our options were limited to sending mail shots to existing customers (the old fashioned way; with a letter, leaflet, envelope), adverts, interviews, and competitions in the print media, along with interviews and competitions on local radio. Sean was our media man. He came from a media background with excellent contacts, so he focussed on developing a closer relationship with our key media channels within the region, to improve our overall media profile; this meant regular interviews, competitions and reviews. Our aspiration was to be regarded as a regional theatre, not just a local one, and along with attracting big names, our ability to secure regional media interest in our shows was crucial to widening our catchment area.

My challenge was to attract the biggest names I could to a theatre which offered a good reputation that had been established over many years; excellent technical facilities and a respected crew; a pro-active marketing team; a warm welcome (which is not to be underestimated), and 700 seats. The comedian Bob Monkhouse described the theatre to me in a letter as 'a comedian's playground', a quote I often used when negotiating with a new promoter. However, less than thirty miles away we had our closest competitor, a theatre that offered 1800 seats and a much larger catchment area on its doorstep.

Nonetheless, over the course of the next six years we developed closer relationships with a number of key national promoters which brought many great names to our theatre for the first time. We enjoyed several record-breaking seasons and critically acclaimed pantomimes, which was hugely satisfying. There was a real buzz about the theatre as our audiences grew year on year. With our business developing so well, I felt more confident to develop news ideas for events, and in 2002 and 2004, as Festival Director, I organised two national festivals. Working with a local team of volunteers, and a national committee of experienced theatre professionals, the 2002 festival had a four-day programme which included exhibitions of original theatre posters and costumes, talks by expert speakers, circus skills workshops, merchandise stalls, black-tie gala dinner and cabaret, a children's variety show one afternoon, followed by a Variety Extravaganza the following evening. The 2004 festival followed the same format but was extended to a five day programme, such was the success of the first festival. Combined, the two festivals raised over £45,000, which was donated to a wonderful entertainment charity.

In 2003 and 2005, I co-organised two seven-day festivals which each brought in over two hundred professional entertainers from more than seventy countries including the US, Mexico, Cuba, Russia, Australia and Malaysia. The programme included a Grand Parade which attracted an estimated twenty thousand spectators, followed by a four hour outdoor party with al fresco entertainment and a live orchestra in front of another eight thousand spectators. There were organised visits to the General Hospital, entertainment in nursing homes, workshops in primary schools, and free circus skills classes for children and young families. There were also several theatre shows, and street performances every lunchtime in the town centre. To cap it all, we held a charity auction in aid of the local hospice.

Creatively this was the most exciting period of my career to date, and I take great pride looking back at what we, as a theatre team of experienced professionals and many dedicated volunteers, collectively achieved during this time. We'd enjoyed sell-out shows with many of the biggest names in show business, including Derren Brown, Lee Evans, Al Murray, Harry Hill, Paul Merton, Jimmy Carr, Rich Hall, Michael McIntyre, Jack Dee, Jethro;

clairvoyants Colin Fry and Sally Morgan; and the Chinese State Circus. There were concerts with legendary musicians such as Bruce Welch from The Shadows, Peter Green of Fleetwood Mac, Richard Stilgoe and Peter Skellern, Humphrey Littleton, Helen Shapiro, original 50s stars Joe Brown and Marty Wilde, and skiffle king Lonnie Donegan. Being a fan of variety theatre since I was a child, it was such a privilege to work with great variety stars such as Sir Ken Dodd, Sir Norman Wisdom, Des O'Connor, Victoria Wood, Dame June Whitfield, Roy Hudd, Sir Cliff Richard, and Jools Holland.

Despite the stress and pressure of running the theatre, and organising the festivals, each of which were a huge undertaking, the PTSD was very rarely triggered in my professional life. There were times, particularly during the first year, when I was striving desperately to book the best names and when struggling I felt a fraud inside, and feared I was setting myself up to fail. There were periods of workaholism, especially in the months leading up to each festival, when I felt the pressure to prove myself; that I was worthy of the positions I had been entrusted with. The difference was that whenever I came up against a dilemma or some seemingly immovable block on my journey, something inside of me would kick in, and push me through it. There were times of fear, panic and confusion, of course, but previously these stressful challenges would have triggered the PTSD, and the appalling abyss of shame, self-hatred and self-condemnation would have crippled me, at least for a while. During this period of success, that was not the case.

Looking back, I am in no doubt that it also helped me hugely to be working in a healthy, professional environment, with colleagues who, like me, loved their jobs and shared a very similar vision for the theatre as I did. I had also maintained a structure of regular AA meetings each week, which helped me to have a greater balance in my emotional life. I rarely, if ever, went a few days without talking through any concerns I might have with my sponsor or another member, which enabled me to live my life with a much healthier perspective. The 'old me' would have been too proud to admit I needed to talk through my fears and confusion. I would have denied them, until the pain was so great that I'd either break down, or start to drink.

I learnt in AA that I couldn't afford to live in such intellectual and emotional isolation. The well-known phrase, 'No man is an island' ran so true for me, and I embraced and held AA close to me. In truth, I had gradually realised how important AA had become; not just in keeping me sober, but also as the foundation to my spiritual journey. There was now an inner resolve, a place of calmness, which, before going to India, I had previously never really been aware of. The more aware of this presence I became, the more I learnt to trust the intuition I received. It gave me strength, peace, and a much greater mental clarity. It helped me 'keep it real'.

My experiences in India and in AA have been vital to my developing a greater understanding of this underlying presence. Beneath the external chaos of Indian life (the noise, the volume of people, and the sights and smells of street life), there is a tangible stillness I have discovered. It is similar in AA; when you walk into a meeting you hear the buzz of members talking and then, when the meeting begins, there is a powerful silence, which I love, as the Preamble (the introductory statement of welcome) is read. When I am able to fully let go and live in the moment, there is an intuitive wisdom and profound feeling of connectedness in the silence.

In time, I realised this intuition was best sensed, or experienced, in meditation and so after a year or so in my new position I started to mediate on a more regular, structured basis. During the summer of 2005, I realised I needed a break from work. The last six years had been so rewarding professionally I'd had loved to have continued, but I sensed it was time for change. I made plans to return to India for a few months during the spring of 2006 and then to Brazil, where I hoped to develop my relationship with the Divine, my understanding of spirituality through the lens of spiritual healing, and through being in the presence of a remarkable man I had recently heard of, known to many as John of God.

7

IN HEAVEN AND EARTH

*There are more things in heaven and earth, Horatio,
Than are dreamt of in your philosophy*
William Shakespeare, Hamlet, Act 1, Sc V

During the first year of my recovery, I met who I would later learn were a spiritualist couple. They had lunch most days in a café near where I was working at the time. I had noticed them looking in my direction on a few occasions and smiling at me. I would politely smile back, hoping they wouldn't join me. I felt self-conscious and uncomfortable around strangers, worrying what I would say if they approached me.

One lunchtime they walked in, saw me sitting nursing a coffee in the corner, smiled and walked over. They asked if they could join me. I said 'Yes', feeling it would be rude to say no even though I felt defensive. They were a lovely, softly-spoken older couple, from Yorkshire originally. Over lunch, they told me about their lives, how they had recovered from some challenging physical illnesses, and how their spiritual beliefs had opened up their ability to connect with others. They said they were spiritualists, and told me that when they first saw me, they had seen lights around my head.

'The lights were very bright. Has no one mentioned this to you before?' enthused the lady, who I soon learned was named Kay. Her husband, Paul, gently nodded in agreement as she said this. They were both in their mid sixties, of slight build and dressed conservatively. They didn't look at all like typical spiritualists who, in my mind, wore hippyish, well-worn corduroys, had long hair, and probably had an old Volkswagen camper van on the drive. Paul had grey, receding hair and reminded me of a young version of the actor Peter Sallis, who was most famous for playing Cleggy in the long-running BBC comedy series Last of the Summer Wine. But in truth I had at first hardly noticed what they were wearing, such was the impact of Kay's statement.

I had also completely forgotten my experience at university, with Helen and tarot cards in the pub, and as soon as they mentioned the 'lights around my head', I felt suspicious of their motives, and wondered if they were perhaps loopy. Whilst they seemed to be a genuinely nice, gentle couple, I was paranoid enough about my appearance, without the idea of any lights above me! Paul then said to me, 'I don't know whether anyone has told you this before, but you are a healer.' They both smiled at me, and Kay added, rather delicately,

'It won't happen straight away. You will need to have healing for yourself first.' She then smiled more broadly, and said, 'But it will open up over the years.'

Paul concurred, and probably in response to the look of fear and incredulity on my face, he gazed at me with an encouraging look of understanding and kindness in his eyes, and said, 'There's no need to worry. It will become a very easy, natural gift, that you will share with others'.

I smiled politely, but what they had said was so removed from the reality of my recent past. I thought back to the times, not so long before, when I had head-butted walls and shouted at myself in the mirror; the idea that I was a healer was as remote, to me, as walking on the moon. Nonetheless, I did acknowledge to myself that I felt a peaceful, calming energy in their company, which was healing in itself. I shared with them that I was at the beginning of my own spiritual journey, and that I knew I needed to develop some connection with a power greater than myself. Kay looked at me, with a sincerity and a genuineness that touched me, and whispered,

'You will be shown, I know, without any question. You will have the evidence that the spiritual world is real. I promise you.'

If nothing else, I reflected, I felt safe and relaxed in their company, and that was reassuring to me. After we'd finished our food, I thanked them for their company, and for their words of encouragement. In parting, Paul said,

'What we've said might not mean anything to you now. But in time, you'll come to know we've told you the truth.'

I felt moved by the sincerity of his words, and not wanting to reject or upset them in any way, I replied,

'Thank you. What you've said seems so far away from where I am in my life, at the moment. I love the idea of helping people, but I'm finding it tough myself.'

Kay gently touched me on the arm, 'We know. We could have spoken to you a few weeks ago when we first saw you, but we felt it wasn't the right time. You will be okay. Of that, I have no doubt whatsoever.'

With that we smiled at each other, shook hands and went our separate ways. I don't recall ever seeing Paul and Kay again.

The idea of spiritual truth has fascinated me since I was a child, as I've written about earlier, and throughout my adulthood I have searched for it in many places. Whilst Paul and Kay were gentle, kind and encouraging with their spiritualist beliefs, in contrast when I was in my early twenties a friend and I were attracted by the teachings of an outfit that was, (unfortunately, it turned out) driven by a desire to control its members, and get as much money out of them as possible. It was a cult of ego, power and money, in the guise of offering spiritual 'enlightenment' at a price. For the first twelve months, however, I enjoyed travelling every weekend to a centre in the south of England, and studying its teachings. Then, one Sunday afternoon, I was invited to a meeting with the manager, Thomas, who questioned my commitment to my spiritual journey, and how my resistance to their teachings showed I had an even greater need for the courses and counselling they offered.

When I explained I had very little disposable income, and I couldn't ask my parents for money, Thomas suggested I consider taking out a bank loan for £30,000. I replied,

'I'm sorry, I don't understand? Surely a bank wouldn't agree a loan for 'counselling'?

Besides, I don't have the income at the moment to cover the cost of the monthly repayments'.

After a pause and a smile he replied with carefully chosen words,

'This is the challenge we have, with the important work we are doing here. We live in a lost, bewildered society that doesn't understand the true value and importance of the knowledge we have. Those who are spiritually gifted, who have a strong desire to change this world for the better realise this.' He paused to gauge my response. I politely nodded that I understood what he was saying. He then continued,

'You are correct, the bank will not understand this. You see, what happens here is so important to the spiritual growth of our society, and the world, there is a justifiable need to be flexible with what is written on the form, so that our efforts are not limited, or even destroyed, by society's resistance to the knowledge we have. We have a responsibility to raise the consciousness of society, with the knowledge we have.'

He then went on to impress upon me that this investment in my future would enable me to be free from pain and suffering. He explained in detail how I could become what might be described as 'enlightened', and it would cost £30,000!

'This is such an exciting opportunity for you. With these teachings you will bring about so much positive change to your life, and to your family, and friends.' His next statement sent chills through me, 'If you invest in yourself now, it's a given, there's no doubt you can become one of the most effective people on the planet.'

Whilst my ego loved to hear this, I was appalled by the assuredness with which he spoke. Thomas showed me a typical loan application form, and suggested how I might fill it in. I left his office promising to have a think about what he had said. In truth, I felt so angry and disillusioned with our conversation and the implicit encouragement to be dishonest with the bank. Soon afterwards, I started receiving regular telephone calls from this organisation to both my work and home, trying to get more money out of me. Whilst the calls were not specifically threatening, they were persistent and caused difficulties at my workplace by their regularity. The Theatre Manager told me he was concerned at the number of personal calls I was receiving, and that it must stop immediately. I was Front-of-House Manager at the time, and they were often using the box office telephone number to contact me, and therefore preventing customers from buying tickets. Typically, the calls were from very friendly and enthusiastic young women.

'Hey, is this Matthew? Hey, how are you today? We've got some really exciting, ground breaking announcements coming out in the next few weeks, and I wanted to make sure you are in the loop on what's going on.'

When I replied that I was thinking of leaving the organisation they sounded really surprised, and then gave me explicit instructions on what to do. They would suddenly change their tone of voice to sound very strong and authoritative; they tried to assume the 'power' position, it was no longer a conversation of equals. I was now listening to someone who was completely and utterly convinced they were correct, and fully justified telling me exactly what to do.

'Matthew, there must be someone in your life who is a negative influence on you. Someone who is clearly holding you back from realising the success which is there for you to enjoy. We can help you identify who this is, and show you how to deal with them. When you do this, everything comes into play. You will be a winner in life, for sure.'

This approach usually meant questioning in detail my relationships with family and friends to identify the negative influence that needed to be eliminated from my life, or demanding that I go straight to the centre for counselling. It was never, ever, of course, the organisation itself that was at fault! Whilst I admit some teachings helped me, at the beginning, the constant harassment was challenging my sobriety and I became increasingly depressed and fearful at times. Their behaviour was wearing me down; I felt shame that I was doing something 'wrong' when they questioned my judgment, and more depressed and scared I might start drinking again.

Despite warnings from family and a few close friends, I remained in denial of their tactics for a few weeks after my conversation with Thomas, until the continued pressure to send more money (for courses, books and counselling) from their incessant telephone calls and letters helped me to finally see the light of day. I'd had enough of their attitude. I decided to write and ask for the return of monies I had already paid, and for which I had not received the teachings and books. I heard nothing from them for three weeks. There was no acknowledgement of my letter, and surprisingly no telephone calls at all, from anyone. Then, all of a sudden, I received even more telephone calls and letters from members I didn't know (mostly pleasant in tone and 'surprised' that I wanted to leave, and varying between interrogating me about my relationship with family and friends, or inviting me to meet them in a centre), but I just wanted to get my money back, and get the hell out.

One afternoon, I was drinking a coffee in a cafe near the theatre where I was working when a friend of a friend, Joseph, approached me and gently asked me how I was.

'You don't seem your usual cheerful self? You look as if you're carrying the weight of the world on your shoulders. Would it help to talk it over, perhaps?' he said, as he sat down in the booth opposite me. I told Joseph in vague terms what was going on, and then, when I felt the anger come up, I told him straight,

'I've got involved with..., well I, I guess you might call it a counselling or a self-help outfit. It was fine at first but it's now just 'pressurising' me to spend more and more money. They call me at home, at work. It's really stressful talking to different people who question my decision to leave, they ask me ridiculous questions about my family.... I just want my money back, and for them to piss off.'

He told me he had had a similar experience some years earlier, and eventually took them to court to get his money back. He named the organisation. It was the same one! Joseph said to me, 'You have a few options. You can walk away without your money, and they will continue to call and write, no doubt, for several months, and then eventually they'll give up. But this will be stressful, as they don't like anyone leaving; it's a sign that it isn't working, and they cannot or perhaps will not accept it isn't working, so they will persist to keep you involved.'

'Or you can take the legal route. If you do this, it will force their hand, and they'll react in a much more predictable way.'

'I don't understand,' I replied.

He went into detail about the mind games that would happen if I started legal proceedings, which I had been considering.

'The calls and letters will initially stop, and then, after a few weeks of nothing, you'll be contacted by different members from this country, and perhaps elsewhere, who you won't know, have never met, and they'll pretend they know nothing about what's happened, and will take the soft approach to encourage you to stay.'

'Okay', I said, 'but I want to leave, I want my money and I want to get out'.

'Well, this soft approach will continue until they are convinced that you definitely want to leave. At this stage, perhaps six months or so after you initiate legal proceedings, it'll go quiet again, for a few weeks or maybe slightly longer. Then, you'll suddenly get more direct, slightly aggressive calls, demanding to know why you are being so awkward, why you are deliberately undermining the organisation. They'll say your behaviour is unacceptable;

they'll probably demand to meet you, but you will refuse, of course.'

'God, will this ever end?'

'Don't worry, you're in the home straight now. When the date for your hearing is only a few days away, at the eleventh hour, the person you name on the legal papers will call you out of the blue, for the first time. Then you know you've won.'

Joseph continued his detailed description of what would happen,

'When he calls, the chap you've named on the papers, he'll suggest a meeting in a public place, probably at lunchtime or during the afternoon, but he won't turn up. There's no point even going, it's all part of the plan to manipulate and undermine your confidence. This chap will arrive at your flat late at night, probably about 11.00pm or 11.30pm; he'll say his car broke down or something like that, and he didn't have a telephone number to call you. That sort of thing. The whole game is to catch you off guard, to wear you down... You just need to stand your ground and eventually he'll pay the money over; they're desperate to avoid legal proceedings for the bad PR they'd get.'

He finished with, 'Don't underestimate how much of a problem you are to them. It is the worst scenario for them, someone effectively saying 'I don't want this. This doesn't work for me'. They can't, or won't, accept that. So they'll try everything to convince you to stay.'

I sat there somewhat stunned by what Joseph had told me, and amazed at the remarkable synchronicity of our conversation. Just when I needed guidance, the Higher Power had sent me an angel who described in detail what would happen next. I asked him how he knew so much, and he told me,

'I went through exactly what I've described to you.' It was extraordinary to meet someone who had experienced what I was going through, and who could give me advance warning of the games that would be played against me. It gave me a feeling of empowerment to know what to expect. As soon as I started legal proceedings, during the following eleven months, the process happened exactly the way Joseph had described, until I finally received a cheque which covered what they owed me, and the court costs. Writing this I hope will in turn empower other survivors, or anyone in a similar vulnerable position, to not fall into the hands of such controlling groups and organisations. When you have a huge ego and chronic low self esteem, such groups and their promises can be very attractive.

In 1999, a few years after having spoken with Joseph (and five years after I met Paul and Kay, the spiritualist couple), I found myself standing in the express checkout queue in the local Tesco. I was holding a five pound note in my right hand, and completely out of the blue, I had a powerful burning heat in the palm of that hand, which shocked me. It was so hot I wondered what the hell was going on, and I moved the note to my left hand, which was of a normal body heat. I then felt an energetic connection with the person standing behind me in the queue, so I turned and gently smiled at the lady who was there. She was in her late forties, small of stature, with dark blonde shoulder length hair, and her eyes were wide open like a rabbit in the headlights, and still red from what must have been her recent tears. She looked in shock, and whatever had happened had left her so utterly lost and bewildered. There she stood in the queue, with her arms folded tightly to her chest, as if she was trying to hold herself physically and emotionally together. I felt an overwhelming compassion for her. I didn't know her, I'd never seen her before, but I felt such a love for her. I wanted to tell her how special she was; how much she was loved and respected. She had clearly been recently broken in some way.

There was nothing sexual about this connection; it was strictly compassionate, and the energy reminded me of my experience a few years earlier, with Gemma and Richard at a friend's wedding reception, when healing energy suddenly flowed through me to help them. Despite my mental reservations in that Tesco, the experience those years ago encouraged me to trust my intuition.

Knowing most strangers would probably freak out if you suddenly told them you felt love for them, and have energy in your hand, I sent up a prayer to the powers that be, asking: 'what do I do with this energy?'. I intuitively sensed I was to channel all the energy I felt flowing through my right hand directly to her, and to visualise her feeling stronger within herself, and more peaceful. I did what I had sensed was correct (at the same time as I was questioning my sanity, even though the energy was definitely very real to me), and hoped that it might help in some way. All this, from the awareness of the heat in my hand through to channelling the energy, happened in the space of, perhaps, twenty seconds. I turned again, and said to the lady behind me,

'Hi, how are you today? Have you had a good day?' It felt such a lame way to start up a conversation with her, although my intention was genuine. In my heart I hoped to develop a connection with her, to hopefully encourage her to open up. She looked stunned as I spoke to her; as if she was miles away, lost in her thoughts.

'Are you okay?', I asked her, knowing of course she wasn't, but just trying to see if she would open up about her problem. She swallowed, and replied in a very quiet voice, but with considerable candour, 'It's..... it's been a tough few days.... We've had a sudden family crisis, which has shaken us all.' She stared in front of her as she spoke, and after a pause of possibly ten seconds, she looked up at me tears in her eyes, and continued.

'Everything's just happened all at once. Dad had a stroke on Friday afternoon, after lunch. He was fine, one minute he was his normal self, there were no signs or anything to warn us. Then the next he was on the kitchen floor.....He went down so fast.... We all panicked, we didn't know what the hell was going on. He's in hospital now, in ICU.... He had a massive stroke...'. As she described the trauma she and her family were going through, she broke down in tears, placing her hands on the side of the checkout conveyor belt to steady herself. Her emotional pain was obvious to see.

'We don't know how badly damaged his brain is.... how badly it's affected him. He hasn't been able to speak since it happened...' she whispered through her wracking sobs.

The queue had moved forward whilst we had been speaking, and it was now my turn to be served at the checkout. I didn't want anything to interrupt her flow, so I gestured to allow a few customers behind us in the queue to be served instead. I wanted our conversation to continue for as long as she felt she needed or was willing to talk. She took a deep breath and steeled herself, and I could feel her anger rising,

'.....My two kids and I moved down from Walsall five weeks ago, to stay with Mum and Dad. My marriage broke down a few months ago....' Her face was now much harder, her eyes focussed in front of her as if she was imagining her ex. 'He told me a few months ago he'd been having an affair.... I was devastated, but tried to make it work.....for the kids really...but I couldn't trust him anymore. He broke me completely.' Her face looked so much more aggressive as she was speaking. She seemed almost ready to spit the words out.

'I couldn't stand being anywhere near him. Everything about him was revolting to me; his voice, smell, his fucking arrogance..... A few weeks ago, he suddenly announced it was time for me to get on with it. He kept telling me that he'd admitted he was wrong, and that I was using it against him. It was as if I was at fault. He wanted me to feel that I didn't have any right to be upset. He sounded like a bloody saint, and I was just being pathetic for overreacting.... But he had broken me. I loved him once....for a while... at the beginning. I wonder now... maybe he was always like this. Perhaps I had imagined he was something so special, I believed his bullshit for so long... I thought it was true......Maybe I was kidding myself all along.'

She broke down once again, and tried to talk through the tears.

'I'm sorry.... God, I'm so sorry to dump all this...... all my crap on to you,' she suddenly blurted out, with a look of embarrassment on her face.

We had by now moved slightly away from the queue, and were standing next to a pillar where we had more privacy, and could not be so easily overheard. Throughout our conversation there was no physical contact between us, other than a few involuntary gentle touches to her shoulder to offer some comfort and encouragement. (Physical contact during healing is not necessary, although when asked whether it's a preference, I have found most people prefer it).

'It's alright,' I replied. 'It takes so much courage to be able to be open, to talk about it, to try and get it out. It's such a lonely place if we bottle everything up. We need people we can trust around us. We need to know we're not alone.'

I had thought of the paedophiles as soon as she had described her ex-partner's attitude and behaviour. There were similarities in the arrogance, the sense of entitlement, the need for control, and the lies. I could feel my body tensing up as the memories came back to me. I could feel my consciousness drifting and I felt lightheaded, which scared me. I momentarily feared I might have a panic attack and collapse, so I forced myself to stay present by repeatedly digging my thumb nail into a finger, and touching the pillar to make sure I was more conscious of my physicality. I hoped she wasn't aware of this as I didn't want to interrupt her flow.

She straightened herself up, showing greater trust and confidence, and continued with recalling her life with her ex, 'It's not the only time I've walked out, but I've gone back. Twice. And he knows that. He's waiting for me to go running back again to him. He's waiting for me to be weak. But it's different this time., with what's happened to Dad..... You see, he <u>has</u> to have it his own way... He spoke to our daughter earlier, told her he wants to come down here... He'd turn up and play the knight in shining armour, and act as if nothing had happened between us. He'd do what he always does; spoil the kids rotten with presents and promises, and tell me what I need to do. It's gone too far now... I'm not going back.. I can't.' She had a determination in her eyes as she spoke, and I could see how strong she really was beneath the trauma of recent events.

'I'm sorry. I'm sorry to hear you've having such a difficult time.' I paused, and then continued, 'I...You're going to be alright, you know. As difficult as it is now, as horrendous as it all feels right now, you will get through it. You don't realise how strong you are. Just telling me, a total stranger, what you've been through shows you how strong you really are. You need to connect with people you can trust, people who've shown they have always been there for you, and you for them, in the past.'

As I said this to her I'd no idea if this was helping. (What I said to her sounds so trite, as I recall the conversation now.) It just felt the right thing to say at that time. She looked up at me and was still clearly very emotional, with tears in her eyes, and said,

'Thank you, I needed someone to tell me that. Thank you....' She paused, and looked at me as if questioning herself. 'I don't ever do this. It's so strange... I don't ever talk about my life, about what really going on underneath. I've been a closed book for years. I suppose I always have been....except with a few of my oldest friends. I have never, ever spoken to someone I don't know like this.... But today of all days, I felt safe to do it. It felt... it felt in an odd way, natural to talk to you. I don't know how else to describe it...I felt safe.'

I smiled gently at her. 'I just felt you needed to talk with someone, and I happened to be here. I know I can't say anything that will take your pain anyway, but I guess.. you need to know you are not alone, you need to know you have the strength inside of you to deal with everything that is coming at you, even if your heart and mind tell you it's all too much.' She looked up and nodded as I described her innermost feelings and thoughts.

I continued: 'I think that's how the feeling is, isn't it? That things are 'coming at you'? It's a time of change in your life, but you will be okay. Something inside of you will push you forward. You'll become much more aware of an inner presence. I promise you.'

She grasped my forearm, looked up at me with tears in her eyes, and nodded. I could see she had a strong determination to move on. I said, 'You take good care of yourself.' She mouthed a 'thank you', and smiled at me. I turned to be served at the checkout, aware that the energy in my right hand had now dissipated. As I walked away, I felt a calmness throughout my body, and momentarily a peacefulness within my mind which was comforting and encouraging. As I approached the exit I instinctively turned to look back at the lady one last time. She was looking directly at me, and as our eyes met we both gently smiled at each other. I felt very emotional, and momentarily tearful.

Then the internal critical voices started up, telling me I was a fraud, and accusing me of having ulterior motives. The cynical mind can easily dismiss such occurrences, as mine certainly had done for years. At first I thought I must be imagining things, and tried to ignore these feelings and sensations, but when they kept occurring on an increasingly regular basis over the next few months, I knew I had to explore what was happening, and reach out to friends who I thought were 'spiritual', and wouldn't therefore judge me.

Essentially the experience of feeling the healing energy was only sensing an opportunity to genuinely show someone some love and kindness, without placing any conditions on it; it's nothing more complicated than that. During these months I felt physical pain, other times I felt heat again in the palms of my hands. On the few occasions I plucked up the courage and initiated conversation with the strangers I had felt a connection to, to try and find out whether this was my overactive imagination or perhaps some spiritual connection, it was invariably confirmed as the latter. It was much easier (than being in an unfamiliar place) to start a conversation at the theatre with an audience member, as small talk about the show was an easy ice breaker. If the pain I'd sensed was physical rather than emotional, it wouldn't take long before I mentioned during the conversation about my having a pain in the area of the body where I sensed they were suffering. One time I sensed a pain in my shoulder, and as I stretched to try and shift it, the chap behind me commented he'd done something to his shoulder as well.

Once they concurred, as was the case on most occasions, I'd continue making small talk with them about the show or the theatre, whilst mentally focussing the energy I was feeling on the location of their pain. I didn't tell them I was doing this; I was too embarrassed that I would either be called a nutter, or felt that I would be putting myself under pressure to heal them (my ego hadn't realised at that stage that I wasn't the healer). Over a period of several months, there were more than a dozen occasions when I felt the energy, started a conversation and focused the healing energy as described above. On four occasions the audience member would come up to me after the show with often an incredulous look on his or her face. I remember one couple in particular, with whom I'd discussed my back pain before a performance. As they walked through the theatre foyer at the end of the show, I noticed the lady pulled on the gentleman's arm, looked at him and nodded in my direction. My heart immediately sank as I feared some adverse comment about the performance. He looked over and smiled shyly. I nodded and smiled back at him. He then walked towards me, with his wife behind him. He stood next to me, and very discreetly said to me,

'I hope you don't mind me saying, and I know this sounds very odd, but I've had some pain in my back for some time now, for a number of months, and have tried various ways to deal with it. Well. Since talking with you before the show, it seems to have gone.'

These moments were admittedly very few and far between, but always felt very special when they happened. They prompted me to think about the spiritualists and our conversation about healing, which had taken place many years earlier. I decided it was time to join a meditation group run by a lovely medium, Jessica, the partner of an AA friend. I knew intuitively that if I learnt how to meditate, and could thereby detach from the savage thoughts and obsessions that so often dominated my mind, I would be more at peace and happier within myself, and therefore more able to help other people.

Jess was a very warm, kind, genuine lady in her mid-forties. As I grew to know her better I grew to love her like a sister; I saw she had a beautiful soul. There was a gentleness and an innocence about her which reminded me of a young girl who loved helping people. It was her raison d'être to help people. Her sense of humour was warm and infectious, and we'd openly laugh at the dafter things of life whenever we met up for coffee. After her family, the most important thing in her life was her spiritual awareness, and she opened her home each week to a small group of new and experienced seekers, and openly shared her considerable spiritual gifts. She was really important to my growth at that time of my life, and It was so sad when she passed on only a few years later.

After a few weeks of group meditation at her house, Jess invited me and a few other regular members to an informal Reiki Healing workshop at her home the following week. I hadn't mentioned my recent healing experiences to anyone but decided, with some nervousness, to go along and see if anything 'happened'. After a welcome and a few minutes of silent meditation, Jess briefly explained the history of Reiki and its core principle that an unseen "life force energy" flows through us and is what causes us to be alive. The underlying assumption was that if one's "life force energy" is low, then we are more likely to become ill, and if it is high, we will feel more healthy and peaceful. By using a simple, traditional "laying on of hands" method, the healing energy brings about stress reduction and relaxation which, in turn, heals the body, mind and spirit.

As she spoke I felt encouraged to believe that Reiki treats the whole person, similar to what AA refers to (as alcoholism being a threefold illness: physical, mental and emotional) which constitutes our spiritual wholeness. I was also attracted by the fact that Reiki is spiritual in nature; it is not faith healing, and a belief in a deity is not required for healing to take place. Whilst I believed in a power greater than myself, I felt a sense of freedom in the knowledge that I could explore healing without needing to understand how this fit into the structure of a faith or religion. From how Jess described Reiki, it seemed to offer a simple, straightforward way to feel a deeper level of peace within myself, which others could, I hoped, benefit from.

This was akin to my recent experiences at Claire's wedding reception with Gemma and Richard, and with the lady in the checkout queue at Tesco. My awareness was that the energy I felt had emerged from within my body, and the intuition to channel it also came from within me; I was not aware of any external influence which suggested to me that the healing presence emanated from within. Perhaps it had always been there. It was just a matter of becoming aware of it. Jess finished her talk by saying that healing is not dependent on belief at all and, in fact, works whether one believes in it or not. I felt the pressure lift from my shoulders when she said this. I'd always endured a mental battle as I tried to understand how and why the healing worked, and would beat myself up if it didn't work. Furthermore, whenever I felt the energy within me, my mind would immediately reject and ridicule any notion of my being a channel for healing.

After a brief demonstration showing us how to stand appropriately (basically to relax; to keep a straight back, and to not bend our knees), and how close to hold our hands over the body, we were then grouped into pairs and encouraged to practice on each other. I quickly disappeared to the toilet and when I returned my healing partner, Leo, was lying on a massage table on his front, with his face down and his arms lying by his sides, waiting for me. Jess motioned to me to stand at the side of the table. She whispered;

'Just relax, close your eyes and ask for the healing energy to work through you, and then trust what your intuition tells you to do. Just let go and let it happen.'

I did what she told me to do, and felt like a complete idiot. I stood listening to critical voices in my mind telling me how stupid I looked, and how this was all a waste of time. I tried to concentrate on my intuition as best I could. After a couple of minutes, with my hands face down hovering about three inches above Leo's shoulders, I felt 'something' in the middle of the palms of my hands. I ignored this, thinking my mind was playing games with me. I then moved quickly to place my hands over the back of his head, near the brain stem and the top of the spinal cord, and felt some more tingling in my palms. It was definitely stronger than a few moments earlier. My hands felt more 'alive', or sensitive, in a strange way. After a further few minutes, I unmistakably felt heat in my palms, and as I moved my hands slowly over Leo's body, I sensed the need to stop at a certain point. It was not a mental thought, but an inner sense of some kind. My mind, at this point, was much quieter.

Just then, in my mind's eye, and with my eyes closed, I 'saw' what looked like a vague x-ray of a spine, and a red mark which I intuitively knew was the centre of the pain. My hands hovered over this red mark for a few minutes, until it faded. I opened my eyes, very curious as to what had happened, and then dismissed it as an overactive imagination... feeling somewhat idiotic and very self-conscious again.

Leo stood up, stretched, and walked around the room. He then told me his back pain had completely gone! I wondered whether this was a setup; my cynicism and distrust of people was still my dominant attitude in such situations, and I hated the idea of anyone making a fool out of me. I hadn't

In Heaven and Earth

known Leo had a problem in his spine; he'd always looked a physically fit, healthy young man whenever I had seen him. I liked Jess a great deal and trusted her. She certainly wasn't in it for the money. I only gave her £1 each time I attended the group, and during the three years I went to her weekly group, more often than not we had to remind her about the donations!

When Leo had sat down, after stretching, she asked each one of us in turn to describe our experiences of reiki healing to the group, which made me want to shrink away in the corner. Other members said that they had also sensed energy, but no one else had 'seen' a screen per se, in their mind's eye. (By screen, I mean that with my eyes closed, I would see a wide screen on which I saw the x-ray projected. The 'screen' was not a figment of my imagination; I've experienced seeing a screen on several occasions over the years, and have always felt it had been placed there beyond my conscious control to guide and educate me). In front of the group, I felt embarrassed to admit what I had seen, for fear of being challenged about it and ridiculed, possibly, but Jess eventually coaxed it out of me.

'Matt, you saw something didn't you? What did you see during the healing? It will help other people to know how spirit works to help us to help each other,' she asked.

'I ehh. Well, it sounds really strange, but ehh, after about a minute, I felt the energy in my hands like everyone else did. It was steady for the most part until right at the end when it started to decrease, and I realised it was time to stop. There was a time towards the end of the session when its intensity suddenly increased, and I saw very clearly in my mind's eye what looked like an X-ray, as crazy as that sounds. It's the only way to describe it really.'

'Can you tell us where you were when this happened? Where were your hands?' asked Jess.

'They were over the base of his spine. I saw an X-ray showing his spine and hips and I noticed a red spot or mark in a specific area. I knew I had to focus the healing right there. I did this until the red mark faded away.'

Everything I had said was true, but I still questioned my sanity even though Leo had confirmed the pain had been removed. At the end of the session, I thanked Jess for her time and guidance, and said I'd really enjoyed the evening and hoped to see her again soon.

In the event, I avoided the group for a few weeks as I struggled to accept something positive and beneficial could work through me. The experience of feeling the healing energy had opened up something within me which would take years to come to terms with, because it challenged the deepest level of my psyche. This was the perception I had always held of my body; that it was filthy, disgusting, and tainted.

It is interesting to note that several years later, when I was running a Healing and Meditation group, I still found it very difficult to allow anyone to practice healing on me. To lie with my eyes closed, and to trust, was very painful. I felt the others' physical presence so close to me to be a threat, even though these were people I knew really well and consciously trusted. Nevertheless, my mind would immediately go back to the toilet cubicles, and the abuse. I think there was something there about allowing myself to receive healing as well, of giving myself permission to heal. Shame is such a powerful, toxic emotion, and at some level I think I denied myself the healing because I didn't feel I deserved it.

A few weeks after the Reiki workshop, I was auditioning for a play and I heard my friend Janet, who was standing at the back of the auditorium, complaining she had sore shoulders from gardening earlier in the day. Without thinking about it, I walked over and placed my hands on her shoulders, more as a gesture of kindness than any conscious desire to help, and she immediately commented on how warm they were. Then she said 'you do know, don't you, you are draining the pain away from my shoulders?' The healing had worked again which, as before, scared me.

Just before the dress rehearsal a month later, the lead actor, Peter, arrived complaining of a bad back. He said he had pulled a muscle and had tried deep heat but it hadn't made any difference. I felt obliged to at least offer help, but I said nothing; I was scared it might work again, but also feared it wouldn't. A fellow actor, who had witnessed the pain from Janet's shoulders being healed, said,

'Let Matt have a go, see if he can work the magic...' I cringed with fear and embarrassment, and felt forced to see if I could help. I asked Peter to sit on a chair leaning over the upright so his back was fully exposed. I placed my hands at the base of his spinal cord and pleaded in my mind for the healing energy to help him. I soon felt a 'connection' between my hands and his back, and felt an energy was being transmitted between us. After a minute, Peter commented on the energy he felt, and that the pain had started to decrease. He described that pain as being 'pulled out'. After five minutes, he suddenly stood up and said 'job done, he's done it'. He shook my hand, thanked me, and said to me, 'I think it's time for a cuppa before we crack on with the rehearsal, don't you?'

I felt relief to have not been made to look a fool, but I also felt really confused. The healing went to the core of my shame and fear of being 'found out' as a fraud and a liar.

Because I didn't understand it, I couldn't control it. As I didn't know when and how it might work, it scared me. The times that it didn't work felt humiliating; they confirmed everything my thoughts were telling me, and I would stop helping people for a while. The irony was, of course, that the healing energy was also slowly and gradually healing me. It was triggering my deep seated assumptions about myself being a worthless individual and a fraud, (none of which, of course, were true). By connecting to my heart, and allowing love to come through, I do believe overtime I have received healing and all but transcended these corrosive, damaging false beliefs.

I had thought it impossible that anything benevolent could be channelled through my body; at a deep, psychological level I still felt a sense of disgust and embarrassment about my physicality. Despite these mental and emotional reactions, I was fascinated by spiritual healing. During my free time, I would often disappear into second-hand bookshops looking for books written by and about spiritual healers to learn how they came to accept the healing energy flowing through them, and whether they had struggled with the psychological and emotional challenges, as I most certainly had. I became fascinated by the healing work of the eminent 20th Century healers Harry Edwards, George Chapman, and Ted Fricker. Their experiences helped me to understand the need to let go, to remove myself, along with my hopes and expectations from the healing experience, then allow the healing energy to flow, and to accept the outcome, whatever it might be. I've found the slogan Let Go and Let God, so often seen on the wall at an AA meeting, has really helped me when healing is involved.

Beyond Jess's small group, I had only mentioned to one of two other friends my interests in healing, for fear of being challenged to heal someone, or of being ridiculed. Thankfully, they did neither; they were far more open about healing than I was, which surprised me. One of them gave me a book about a Brazilian healer known as 'John of God'. I thanked her, and made a mental note to read the book the following week, but in the event forgot all about it. Then a month later someone else gave me a copy of the same book, *The Miracle Man. The Life Story of John of God* by Robert Pellegrino-Estrich, so I took the hint and started to read it. A week later, I was having a clairvoyant reading with Jess (who knew nothing of my recent interest in John of God), when she described to me that she 'saw' a large, heavyset man, with black hair and kind eyes, who had 'appeared' next to me. She said she could feel a strong connection between this man and me. She went on to say that he had placed his arm around me, and was telling her that he and I would meet shortly. I interrupted her and asked, 'Have he and I met before?' to which she replied, 'No, he's telling me that you have never met in person, but that you know all about him.'

She went on to say, 'He's saying he's from South America. He's told me, Brazil. His name is Joao but you know him as John'. I felt a rush of energy flow through me as she said this, and I thanked her, asking her to acknowledge my gratitude to John of God. This clairvoyant reading gave me the boost I needed, and that evening I continued reading the Pellegrino book with a feeling of excitement. After a dozen pages, I placed the book face down on my bedside table and plugged my earphones in to listen to Pink Floyd's *Comfortably Numb* on full blast.

I was imagining myself playing Dave Gilmour's famous guitar solo in front of 100,000 fans at the Glastonbury Festival, when I heard the most enormous thud to my right. Startled, I immediately ripped the earphones out and looked to my right to see the book was now face up on the bedside table! I looked for every rational possibility for the loud noise even though I knew the book had definitely moved. The thud had been so loud, I even looked to see if any shelves had collapsed. There was no one else in the flat, so it wasn't a door slamming and besides, as mad it it seemed, the thud had happened right next to me. I decided to continue reading, and within a few hours had read the remaining pages.

The Miracle Man. The Life Story of John of God[23] was the first book written in English about Brazilian medium Joao Teixeira de Faria, who is known by many as John of God. It has been translated into sixteen languages

---

[23] Robert Pellegrino-Estrich, *The Miracle Man, The Life Story of John of God* (Publisher not specified, 1997)

and has guided hundreds of thousands of people seeking help from this remarkable healer. Since publication in 1997, many other books and DVDs have been released honouring the remarkable life of John of God. In recent years his fame has reached a much wider audience through his interview with Oprah Winfrey,[24] and the testimonial of Dr. Wayne Dyer, who credited the healing he received through John of God as having cured him of leukaemia. In fact, when Dr. Dyer passed away several years later, his autopsy confirmed there was no trace of leukaemia in his blood.[25]

For more than four decades, John of God has channelled healing energy and achieved extraordinary success helping people heal from AIDS, cancer, paralysis, blindness, mental illnesses and a host of human infirmities. João himself says, "It is not me, but God who heals". He encourages research into his healing abilities, and has been studied by teams of legitimate scientists from Russia, Germany, the USA, Japan and France. Pathology tests has revealed that the tumours, substances and tissues that are removed from the sick during healing are indeed human tissues from the individuals operated upon.

There is a room, next to the entrance to the main hall at his healing centre (the Casa de Dom Ignacio in Abadiânia, Brazil) which is full of discarded walking frames, sticks, splints, old wheelchairs, and crutches. These bear witness to the fact that he is a gifted and powerful medium for healing. Often over a thousand people per day, sometimes many more, wait in line to see him at the Casa for healing. Such has been his success as a healer, the neighbourhood around the Casa has developed over the years to support the healing centre, with numerous hotels, guest houses and longer-term accommodation providers welcoming visitors each week from all over the world. The healing one receives may be physical, emotional, mental, spiritual or all of these. It is a personal and transforming process which often unfolds over a period of time, and whilst some experience almost immediate results, others recover over time, as they may require several visits. I was attracted to the idea from my reading about John of God that through prayer

---

[24] Oprah Winfrey, *Oprah's Experience with John of God - Oprah on life's journey*. From the June 2012 issue of O, The Oprah Magazine. www.oprah.com
[25] *Who Is John of God?* God Heals: My Meeting with a Spiritual Healer, from www.drwaynedyer.com on September 8, 2015.

and meditation it was possible to connect with the love of God to the extent that healing physically, mentally and emotionally was possible. To this extent, I believed in the Church of England faith I had been brought up in.

Where I veered away from the traditional teachings of Christianity was my belief in karma and reincarnation. Whether healing took place, and to what extent, seemed to me to be a karmic issue, although I hadn't fully accepted or understood this teaching at that time. But I knew there had to be some law of consciousness which governed why it seemed some people acted with impunity and 'got away' with dreadful crimes whilst others who lived moral, ethical lives often suffered immensely. Karma — the universal law of cause and effect across many lifetimes — offered a possible explanation for this unfairness. Equally I was attracted to the similarities between Advaita Vedanta and Buddhism, and the focus on the importance of the mind being the gateway to truth, and enlightenment. It seemed to me to be a very practical approach to spirituality, and was aligned with the fact that so many of my problems lay within the mind after all! I sensed my truth ultimately lay somewhere within the teachings of Christianity and Advaita Vedanta, which are, at their core, somewhat different. Both believe that there is one supreme, eternal, infinite God, the Creator of heaven and earth, but thereafter Christianity teaches that God is a separate being, which can only be experienced through his one and only son Jesus. "I am the way and the truth and the life. No one comes to the Father except through me." (John 14:6).

Whilst I was drawn to Jesus as a great Master whose teachings of Love and service were so emphatically correct to leading a moral, ethical life, I could not accept it was only through him that one would gain salvation or enlightenment. It was too narrow and restrictive for me. I accepted his life was the ultimate example of the way to spiritual awakening, but not the only way in the sense that one had to accept Jesus and Jesus alone as one's Lord and Saviour. Advaita Vedanta teaches us that this idea of separation from God (or the divine) is an illusion, and that we are all intrinsically divine here and now, and that our purpose on earth is to realise this. Some advaitists take the view that this is what Jesus meant when he said "I and the father are one". (John 10:30).

Brazil is predominantly a Catholic country (with an estimated 125 million followers, 64 per cent of the population), but is also home to a growing Spiritist movement with almost 3.8 million devotees. Unlike traditional Catholics, Spiritists believe in reincarnation, karma and the ongoing improvement of the soul until it reaches perfection. They also believe in God as 'The Supreme Intelligence,' and the presence of spirits and the existence of other life forms in the universe, which can be communicated with for the good of mankind by spiritual mediums.

For many in Brazil, John of God is regarded as one of the foremost spiritist mediums alive today, and this also intrigued me. I could readily accept that spiritual beings at higher level of consciousness (such as angels and spirit guides) existed to help mankind to grow.

As I studied more about John of God and Spiritism, I pondered how this way compared and contrasted with those I had found in India. After I had visited both countries, the main difference I found between my experiences in Brazil and India was that in Brazil the belief is that one prays to an external being for healing, whilst in India (following the tenets of Advaita Vedanta) one seeks to connect within oneself to an inner divinity which is deemed to be the gateway to a higher consciousness, or what many refer to as God, of which we are already intrinsically at one with. I decided I had to visit the Casa and meet John of God, but during the spring of 2005 I was in the middle of organising a second international festival, so I knew it would be at least a year before I could go. Nonetheless, I had to find out whether these claims of such remarkable healing were in fact true. I thought that there had to be some credibility to his reputation, especially after so many years of helping people. I'd also read that he has been recognised by His Holiness the Dalai Lama and several other eminent religious and political leaders, including a former President of Peru (for healing his son).

The fact that there were a number of occasions when visitors had not received the physical healing they had hoped for struck me as being real and genuine. It had a ring of authenticity about it; for being so honest that sometimes healing does not 'work', at least not in the way one expects or hopes it will. I have often witnessed other spiritual benefits when physical healing has not taken place. The healing can be a catalyst for a change in one's attitude to the problem; instead of fighting the disease the healing can bring about a greater acceptance, and with that a sense of peace. The same principle applies with alcoholism; it is only when one accepts the problem exists (instead of denying or trying to control it through using drugs or damaging behaviours) that the healing can begin. When I first visited Abadiânia and met some of those who had not been physically healed, they invariably stated they felt a deeper-level acceptance and peace about their condition.

Sometimes there is a delayed effect to healing for reasons that are difficult to understand. When I returned for my second visit to the Casa I spoke with an American lady, Val, who looked very familiar to me. As we spoke, something was confusing me; we obviously knew each other - and something had changed since we had first met but I couldn't put my finger on it. She recognised my confusion, and told me her story. She had been living in a guest house close to the Casa for over a year, hoping for healing for her condition; some form of horrendously painful muscular illness, which was crippling her physically. In the US, where she lived, she had seen various experts but none of the treatments she had tried had made any difference, and she remained in constant, physical agony which no pain killers, including morphine, could help ease. Val was desperate, wheelchair bound, and on the point of giving up – and this was how I now remembered her, when we had originally met on my first trip several months earlier. (Auth: I had enjoyed my first month at the Casa so much, I had decided to return as soon as possible to experience the healing energy and develop my meditation). But here standing before me, looking so healthy and happy, was a completely different woman! She told me her remarkable story of healing.

One morning she went in front of John of God and was told the healing could help her. She went into meditation hoping to feel some improvement. Over the course of the next few weeks, the pain started to leave her and enormous amounts of energy began flowing through her body during each healing session, which was at times very painful. Eventually, after a few months, Val was for the first time in many years absolutely pain-free. This process had started eight months earlier, and as if by a miracle I watched her as she walked around; a free woman in every sense. Being a witness to such remarkable healing creates a shift in one's consciousness. I could not deny that the healing had taken place.

My visits to India and Brazil were an integral part of my search to heal from the abuse in my childhood, and to develop a greater understanding of spiritual truth which would help me to live more ably and with an acceptance of the PTSD, and to understand what life was really all about. My desire for a change of scene and new healing, in 2005, prompted my plans for visits to both India and Brazil the following year. Having tendered my resignation from the theatre in December 2005, I worked my notice, and on February 3rd 2006, I flew to Mumbai for four months of travelling around India and Nepal (some of my experiences are described in the chapter called *A Revolution In My Head*). After a few months back in the U.K, that October I flew to Sao Paulo and then onto the capital, Brasilia, the nearest international airport to Abadiânia, the small town where John of God's healing centre is located.

Ever since I was a small boy, I had sought answers to the perennial question that has challenged mankind, and has been sought by spiritual seekers for millennia; what is the meaning of life? A year into my sobriety, I started reading as widely as possible in an attempt to find some answers, from the teachings of Jidda Krishnamurti, the Theosophical Society, Bhagavad Gita, Spiritualism, Gurdjieff, Buddhism, and of course the Bible, in particular the Gospels and the Sermon on the Mount. In Brazil, I hoped that Spiritism might help me understand more about spiritual healing and the power of prayer.

I booked into a guest house, the Amazonis, which was next to the Casa, and after settling in, I decided to explore the Casa de Dom Ignacio. Set in beautiful and well-tended grounds, the energy of the Casa felt very powerful; I could sense it as soon as I entered the grounds.

Perhaps it might help to clarify what I mean when I use the word energy? The only way I can describe my experience of energy is to compare it to when you walk into a room for the first time, and you pick up the powerful vibrations, and immediately sense either a very warm or a very cold atmosphere. I've walked into hotel bedrooms before and straight away felt a dreadful vibe, and was really uncomfortable being there. Other times, when I've visited a friend's house, and walked into their meditation room, I've felt so peaceful straight away.

My experience of the energy at the Casa (and a number of other places I have referred to in this book) is feeling the positive vibes in a place, to the extent my immediate reaction has always been 'Wow! This feels so beautiful'. It feels as if you are in a cocoon of sacredness. The mind knows, without question, something extraordinary is going on. You sense a loving, holy, powerful, healing presence all around you which enters into you. You become one with that healing energy. There was also a similar sense of energy surrounding me the evening before the first healing session when I attended a brief orientation in the main hall. The energy was almost bristling. One way or the other, you know something's happened in there. The energy reminded me of when I was in New Delhi a few months earlier when it was 118 degrees; it was as if I was walking in a huge oven with constant heat all around me, which also affected the body temperature inside of me.

Back to my first visit to the Casa in 2006. After a brief talk about John of God by one of the volunteers, about what we could expect the following morning, we had a Question and Answer session, followed by a guided tour. We were shown the Main Hall, which had a small stage where John of God and his team of healers welcome everyone, and where they also offer prayers of healing and spiritual guidance. Those requesting healing are then invited to line up and, when instructed, the first room they walk through is the Meditation room. Here people sit and meditate while a medium reads a guided meditation and universal prayers for healing. This room opens up into the second room, the Current Room, where John of God receives all those who have requested healing. From my experience the following morning, I can vouch for the fact that when you walk through the Meditation and the Current rooms, where perhaps two hundred people have been meditating for over an hour, the healing presence is very powerful. We were also shown a small infirmary in a side room, where a registered nurse is based for insurance purposes. In recent years, as a precautionary measure, the Casa has employed a nurse. It is inevitable that some visitors to the Casa cannot be healed, and sadly some, who are chronically ill, die whilst they are on their visit to Brazil. As a precautionary measure, everyone who receives a physical healing is seen by the nurse before leaving the Casa to assess their fitness or wellness, and to determine whether they are strong enough to go to their accommodation. After the tour had finished, we were asked to consider what our requests for healing might be. After considerable thought, I decided I would request healing to:

1. Help me to open up emotionally.

I was still scared to allow any woman close to me, either emotionally or sexually. This, of course, meant I needed to allow a deeper healing to take place within me, addressing the abuse. I knew I had to finally let go of the resentments I had towards the paedophiles who had abused me. The fantasies to hunt them down and execute them had continued throughout my adult life, and I knew intellectually how this was damaging me, not them. But I didn't know how to let go. As much as I had prayed for the strength to let go, whenever the PTSD was triggered, the fantasies would start all over again. They would then play obsessively, like groundhog day, no matter how much I tried to stop them. Looking back, I can also see that these resentments blocked me from being able to connect with the young boy who was abused; so long as I focussed my rage on the paedophiles, he and his deeper healing remained ignored.

2. Help me to open up spiritually.

I wanted to understand more about my relationship with God, the Divine, or the Higher Consciousness (I had yet to decide on a label.) I had always sensed there was so much more going on than 'met the eye'. I knew intuitively of this and had occasionally experienced a higher level of consciousness, but these experiences had been fleeting.

3. Help me to be a more effective Healer.

I wanted to understand more about the experiences I was having with healing. I wanted to find acceptance and be as open as possible to allow whatever healing might come through me to be as powerful as possible. I didn't want to hinder it in any way through my own ego, energetic blocks, or doubts. I wanted to enjoy the whole process of healing. My experience had been very clear; when I let go and meditated, the healing energy was more powerful than when I doubted and questioned it, and the energy was typically less powerful.

The following morning these requests were given on a piece of paper to a volunteer who translated them into Portuguese, and then handed the paper back to me. I then stood in the main hall and waited with three hundred people for the opening prayers and spiritual guidance from John of God and his team of healers. After prayers were concluded, John of God walked through to the main healing room, and sat down in a chair to meet all those who had requested healing. There are three ways to receive healing at the Casa:

- During meditation. I can vouch for feeling energy buzzing in and around my body, particularly my head, which made me feel relaxed. I had very few thoughts during the meditation.
- Sometimes, the healing is given through natural herbs which can be purchased at a small cost and are taken with water.
- Through a physical operation, whereby the healing is directly channelled physically by John of God to the recipient.

During my visit to the Casa, I saw a number of physical operations, perhaps the most delicate being a lady who appeared to be in her seventies, having her eye scraped with a scalpel. I watched from five foot away, from the side of the stage, and could see considerable force being exerted, and yet the lady's face remained calm, and she showed no sign of any pain. Describing myself at this time in my life as a bit of a spiritual junkie, I decided I would have a 'physical' operation if I had the option. I wanted to experience the healing energy as much as possible, and a physical healing seemed the best way to do this. It had been explained to me that the healing I received would be just as effective through meditation, but in looking back I am so pleased I asked for a physical healing. However nothing, absolutely nothing, prepared me for what was to happen during that afternoon. After receiving a bowl of free soup, which is available to everyone at lunchtime, I sat in the meditation room with other visitors who had also requested specific healing. After a short period of meditation, a volunteer asked whether anyone wished to receive physical healing, and I put my hand up to confirm that I did.

I was led into the main Healing room where I stood in front of a four foot high by two foot diameter-wide amethyst quartz crystal, with a dark grey sharp, rugged edge on the outside, which gave way to a lighter purple-white six inch deep hollow inside. I had been told the crystal had been dug up nearby some years previously and gifted to the Casa. A volunteer asked me some medical questions (for insurance purposes) regarding my overall health. I was asked whether I had diabetes, epilepsy or any heart conditions, or if I was on any medication. I answered 'no' to all his questions. He then said,

'Please close your eyes, place your hand over your heart and pray to the God in your heart for the healing to take place'.

I followed the instructions and after a minute I felt the most extraordinary power surge through the ground beneath me, and flow up and into my body. It felt as if I was standing within a huge vortex of energy. Experiencing the reality and strength of this immense force brought tears of joy to my eyes. My head dropped down, and my chin rested on my chest, and as I wept with gratitude, I became aware on my right-hand side of a hand holding mine. I opened my eyes and saw John of God standing next to me and smiling at me. Now aged seventy-four, Joao is physically quite stocky in build, about six foot tall, with brown eyes which I've always felt, at least when he's in trance, to have an 'otherworldly' sense about them.

He also has what might be described as 'presence'. I have worked with certain actors, who are magnetic to watch on stage. Even when they are doing 'nothing' they have such a dynamism you can't take your eyes off them, as their inner power is so compelling. They connect to a source of energy within them, when they are on stage, which often creates such a compelling experience for an audience. Whilst John of God is no actor he has, by the power of his nature, a similar presence about him. He led me through the meditation room to the stage in the Main Hall, and as we walked through this room together I had a powerful sense of déjà vu. I knew that I had been here before, and what was taking place was exactly what was meant to happen at this time in my life. This was hugely reassuring for me twenty minutes later, when the healing took place.

My consciousness had changed since I experienced the vortex of energy, and whilst I could see the people and hear the voices around me, I felt somewhat detached from the events taking place. I felt very relaxed physically, and I knew I was in an altered state of consciousness, but I was fully aware of who and where I was. I recognised the hall and a few friends. John of God led me onto the stage in front of two hundred people who were listening to prayers and spiritual teachings spoken in Portuguese, a language I do not understand.

I want to state unequivocally that I come from a place of deep cynicism about spiritual healing. My distrust was certainly influenced by the sexual abuse. As a teenager and during my early twenties I was convinced that spiritual healers, and those who followed them, were deluding themselves (and others) and on the make. I fully appreciate that what I describe next will be, as it once was for me, in the realm of Star Trek and science fiction for many readers. Nonetheless, this is my truth. This is what happened, and it was witnessed by many people, including several friends.

After ten minutes of prayers and spiritual guidance (my eyes remained closed throughout the healing session), I sensed a change of atmosphere in the hall. There was an anticipation that something was about to happen. With that, I felt someone hold my nose, and all of a sudden, what I later learnt was a haemostat (a surgical instrument that stops bleeding by clamping the blood vessel) was forcefully inserted into my left nostril, and twisted quite forcefully several times. I heard an outward gasp from the people watching, and as it was pulled out, I felt a trickle of blood settle on my upper lip. Then I felt my t shirt being lifted above my chest, and a sudden, sharp inch-long cut to my skin was made, below my heart. Throughout all of this, there was NO adrenaline rush; no fight or flight response; no impulsive reaction to open my eyes and resist in any way; in fact there was no tension in my body whatsoever. My mind, however, was racing at 300 miles per hour trying to grasp what the hell was going on! I repeated again and again; 'Thy will be done, Thy will be done'.

The one inch cut created only a trickle of blood, and was stitched up in front of everyone by John of God. My friends, who were watching, told me afterwards that he used forceps, a needle and a suture. Throughout both 'operations' I remember him talking to the audience, although I have no idea of what was said. After a few other people (who I was later told were already on the stage by the time I was led out) had received healing, I was invited by a volunteer to sit down in a wheelchair. I asked if I could open my eyes, to which he replied 'yes'. As I did so, my consciousness returned immediately back to normal; I was fully aware of everything taking place around me.

I saw two hundred pairs of eyes staring at me, and I felt absolutely incredible; it was a feeling of euphoria throughout my body, and the most enjoyable buzz I had ever felt; it was far better than the alcohol had ever been! I was then wheeled into the infirmary next door where the registered nurse looked me over whilst I rested on a bed for a couple of hours. One of the healers came in to say hello, asking how I was feeling. He gently tickled the soles of my feet to wake me up. 'I feel great', I said, 'absolutely fantastic'

– this said with a huge smile.

An hour or so later, I walked back to my guest house, The Amazonis, one hundred metres away; this is regarded as a no-no after any operation at the Casa. I had been told during the orientation the previous evening to treat any spiritual operation in the same way as a conventional physical operation you might have in a western hospital. I should have taken a taxi, or at least asked someone to push me in a wheelchair. I rested in my room for the next forty-eight hours, as suggested by the healers, and friends kindly brought me food and water. During the following two nights, I had incredibly vivid 'dreams' including, during the first night, one of me flying a plane over the desert during the Second World War; it was so real that, as I flew really close to the ground I could smell the smoke coming up from fires below. During the following afternoon, I was dozing when I physically felt an invisible presence open my air passage by moving my head backwards, and then my right leg was lifted up four inches. For a period of thirty seconds I saw a dark energy leave through the sole of my right foot.

As bizarre and extraordinary as these experiences were, the most profound, significant healing took place during the fourth (final) week of my stay. Towards the end of a three-hour morning meditation in the main healing room, our guide invited us to visualise a beautiful waterfall and to feel the crystal clear waters healing all emotional, mental, physical and spiritual ills. I did so, and felt a deep feeling of peacefulness within me. After perhaps five minutes, we were then invited to visualise all those we loved – our family and friends, both those alive and those who had passed, and to visualise them in the crystal clear waters of the waterfall, and to see them receiving unconditional love from our hearts. We were then invited to visualise all those we had had any disagreements with, anyone we felt any anger or fear towards, and to also visualise them in the crystal clear waters of the waterfall, and to see them receiving unconditional love from our hearts. We did this for a further five minutes.

Then, we were invited to visualise anyone we hated, anyone we wished harm towards, and to visualise them in the crystal clear waters of the waterfall, and to see them receiving unconditional love from our hearts. I knew this was the moment I'd been waiting for, for so many years. It felt the right time and place to forgive the men who had raped me as a child. It was time to release the pain, to let go of the fantasy I had whenever the PTSD was triggered - of hunting them down and torturing them - that I had been carrying all my life.

It is very difficult to explain how I felt at that moment of 'forgiveness' in the meditation. Even the word forgiveness doesn't sit well with me when trying to describe what took place. In a religious sense, I have not forgiven them, as forgiveness implicitly suggests the slate is wiped clean. I much prefer the psychological definition of forgiveness as being a conscious, deliberate decision to release feelings of resentment or vengeance toward a person or group who has harmed you, regardless of whether they actually deserve your forgiveness.

Just as important as defining what forgiveness is, I found it crucial to understand what forgiveness is not. Forgiveness does not mean forgetting, nor denying the seriousness of what happened. Neither did it somehow excuse what happened, or release the men from legal or criminal accountability.

I did this for me, for my healing, so that I could completely disconnect myself from any energetic connection to them. I knew I needed to release the rage I felt towards them; I knew that whilst it crippled me, it would not affect them at all. By refusing to forgive and continuing to nurture the resentments and fantasies, I had an irrational idea of some power over the men and could terrorise them, but I remained chained to the suffering of my past and effectively lived it over and over again. I knew something had to change within myself for healing to take place, and when I heard the invitation during the guided meditation, I knew this was the time; this was the opportunity that might bring me peace, and enable me to love more openly. In a moment of what some might describe as grace, I distinctly heard a very calm, peaceful inner voice confirm that this was the time, and which encouraged me to let go. Whilst the words were few, its presence felt wonderfully empowering.

'It is time to let go. Now is the time to forgive and let go absolutely.'

As I heard these words, the intention in my heart in doing this was for my own healing; it was nothing to do with them. I have since adopted an attitude of emotional ambivalence on the rare occasions I now consciously think of them. When the PTSD is triggered, a subconscious rage is still released and I feel overwhelmed, so this emotion is somehow trapped within the buried memories...but nevertheless, even when triggered there is no desire to hunt them down and torture them. At the moment of forgiveness, I connected to the memories of the abuse; memories that I could recall from that time, and tried to visualise as best I could the paedophiles in the crystal clear waters of the waterfall, and to see them receiving unconditional love.

I prayed to the God of my understanding to help me release all the emotional and mental pain within me. As soon as this prayer had manifested in my mind, I felt a dark, toxic energy leave my body through my shoulders – the resentments, nightmares, and visceral fantasy to find and torture these men have never since returned. This healing happened over ten years ago. The forgiveness has since brought about a long process whereby I have found peace of mind and feel free of the corrosive anger I'd been carrying for so many years. It has empowered me to recognize the pain I suffered, without letting that pain define who I am.

It would take me another seven years before I would fully forgive myself for 'allowing' the abuse to take place. At some level of my psyche I was raging with the small boy inside even though, since my early twenties, I have understood (intellectually, at least), that I could not have stopped it. Looking back, I can see how these resentments served as a device or a diversion to keep me from acknowledging the shame I felt about my actions, and what I perceived I had done to 'allow' the abuse to take place. By focussing all my rage, understandably, on the men, I was keeping myself from seeing how ashamed I was of myself, and of my actions as a young boy. Connecting to this shame was far more painful than dealing with the rage I felt to the men.

This was their greatest crime against me; I thought the small boy, hidden away deep down in my psyche, deserved to be detested and rejected. With regard to the paedophiles, I take solace in the Law of Karma. I trust that they will, at some point in their spiritual journey, pay the price for their crimes, but I see this as none of my business. I have no opinion or judgement about what this should be. This universal law of justice and fairness works for me. Ultimately, we are rewarded for the good that we do, and punished for the bad. It means everyone is ultimately equal. No one is 'above the law'.

On my last day at the Casa, after a month of prayer and meditation, during lunch I saw one of the mediums, who supports John of God with his mission, walking in the garden. I decided to thank him for his service, and for what had been a powerful month of spiritual learning and healing. He smiled and hugged me; then he stood back and looked above my head and suddenly said: 'You're one of us!' he said. He had read my aura, and told me he had seen healing spirits around me. He confirmed that I, too, was now a channel for healing; this meant so much to me, although it also frightened me at the same time as I still felt such a fake and fraud inside. This was to become apparent when I started practicing healing after I returned to the UK.

Visiting the Casa was hugely significant to my journey of healing. I arrived with many questions... including the efficacy of prayer, and how our thoughts affect our perception of both our internal and external worlds. As much as I may have resisted the practices of organised religion since childhood, the sincerity of devotion I witnessed at the Casa was inspirational, and this helped me to feel a deeper connection to a loving presence within me, and consequently I felt much better about my life.

As simplistic as this sounds, it is worth stating again and again because it goes to the core of spiritual awakening; it was at the Casa that I fully realised that when I focus on love with all my beingness, I feel much more loving to myself and to others. My views on life automatically change. Some might call my approach to be a form of prayer; and essentially it is, but the intention to live a spiritual live, I have learnt, is far more important than pledging allegiance to a religion. The mechanisms of prayer work regardless of faith in a particular God. The love of God is, after all, unconditional.

> *In this intelligent system that you're a part of, everything arrives from the field of intention where the infinite, invisible life force flows through everyone and everything. This includes you, and everyone else as well. Trust in this invisible life force and the all-creating mind that intends everything into existence.*[26]
> Dr. Wayne W Dyer

The presence I felt at the Casa was similarly one of unconditional love, compassion, and reverence for all beings, regardless of religious belief. This

---

[26] Dr. Wayne W Dyer, *The Power of Intention* (2004). Hay House, INC., Carlsbad, CA.

healing presence had brought about the letting go of my deep-seated resentments to the men who had abused me, which in turn created an awakening of my spiritual consciousness. The forgiveness was profoundly healing for me; it has (since it is ongoing) empowered me to move beyond a certain level of pain, suffering, and a desire for vengeance, which in turn has inspired me to have a stronger desire to be of service to others. Back at the Casa I felt, at a deeper level, I might be able to genuinely help others. Consciously, I still felt a shudder inside when I thought of this, but something inside of me was becoming more real to me, and I knew I couldn't ignore it no matter how much fear I would often have, in the months ahead. Something inside of me was pushing me forward, of that I had no doubts. I left Brazil with the understanding that sincere positive intention, regular meditation, and a focus on love for all beings was the key to spiritual growth. No tall order to follow!!

> *Happiness is your nature. It is not wrong to desire it.*
> *What is wrong is seeking it outside when it is inside.*
> Sri Ramana Maharshi

8

HEALING AND MEDITATION

Your vision will become clear only when you look into your heart...
Who looks outside, dreams. Who looks inside, awakens. [27]
Carl Jung

After visiting John of God's healing centre in Brazil I felt an overwhelming drive to practice healing. I had sensed for several years before this trip I had the capacity to channel healing energy, even though the idea seemed so utterly ridiculous to me. I'd struggled with low self-worth all my life, and somewhere deep inside of me was the belief that my body was dirty, defective and broken in some way. The notion that anything beneficial might work through me was ridiculous to me.

Subconsciously my reaction to healing felt like 'beauty and the beast' territory. There were plenty of times when I felt the whole experience was beautiful, but it triggered the beast in me, and after the healing session had finished (and invariably there had been a positive outcome) I'd often feel ugly, deformed and vile. This savage internal reaction to healing went directly to the core of how I viewed myself, emotionally, physically and psychologically, and my relationship with my body. The idea and practice of healing brought up immense shame, and a fear of being humiliated and ridiculed. I set the bar very high, and would beat myself up mentally and emotionally if the healing energy was not strong enough to bring about the

---

[27] C. G. Jung, auth., Gerhard Adler, ed., Aniela Jaffé, ed., R.F.C. Hull, trans., *C.G. Jung Letters, Vol. 1: 1906-1950* (Princeton University Press 1973).

desired effect (meaning as close to, if not total, healing). Even when the recipient walked away with improved health and there was evidence of physical healing; even if they had sincerely thanked me, I felt crippling shame.

I came to realise only more recently that my mental and emotional resistance was due to the PTSD being triggered by the physical touch during the healing sessions. I was physically closer, when healing, to another human being than I had been at any other time in my life, since the abuse. Everything from touch, breathing, smell and even silence felt very uncomfortable. I wouldn't accept that a loving energy could flow through a body I detested so much. To put this into perspective, during that time in my life, when I was in my early thirties, I often felt uncomfortable kissing and hugging even family and close friends.

Lastly, the positive results of healing were a massive challenge for my ego. I needed to understand everything that was going on. I'd been intellectually arrogant, as a defence mechanism, all my life, but without really knowing why healing sometimes didn't work, I felt completely exposed, and naked. I felt I had to understand what was going on, so I knew that it was real, and not imagined. And yet, despite all of these reservations I felt compelled to continue. I knew I couldn't walk away. The idea of healing and the positive results fascinated and horrified me in equal measure. I loved the idea of being able to help people, and developing a relationship with a loving spiritual presence was so compelling, I felt powerless to ignore it.

There were times during this time of practicing healing, when all those painful reactions fell away and I was in the zone, so to speak. Those occasions when my mind would shut down completely, and I was able to be fully present, brought the most immense feelings of bliss and peace as the healing energy flowed through me naturally. These were the truly transcendental experiences of unconditional love I needed to have, and which spurred me to keep going. I gradually became aware through the practice of healing, over the next few years, that deep within me, far beyond the feelings of fear, shame, and rage, and at the very core of my beingness, is a place of peace, strength, wisdom and love. I learnt that it is within our spiritual heart that we find our salvation.

A few days after returning from Brazil, I took a deep breath, tried my very best to ignore the savage thoughts which were ridiculing my intentions, and decided to invite a few friends to have healing. My intention was to carefully record their, and my, reactions to whatever happened during the healing session as some form of informal study from which I hoped I could find some encouragement. I looked through my address book and noted those friends I thought unlikely to laugh and reject me out of hand. (It didn't occur to me what a low opinion I had of my friends! In truth, of course, it was my low opinion of myself I was projecting onto them). I selected twelve possibles based on their openness to life, their honesty, and my belief they wouldn't snigger behind my back. I then called each one in turn, explaining my thinking;

"Hi! I've just come back from travelling again. Brazil this time. Yes, to a Meditation and umm a ... Healing Centre."

"Had an amazing time thanks, and I feel, I am thinking, I want to... practice healing. I wondered whether you would be open to some sessions, perhaps?"

All twelve friends readily agreed to at least three sessions in the first instance, which surprised and terrified me in equal measure. The healing sessions began the following week and were held in my lounge, with its high windows overlooking a bay. My good friend Freda was my first willing guinea pig. Freda was in her early seventies; a healthy, attractive, spiritually-open lady with a terrific sense of humour. I felt safe with Freda. We'd known each other since I was seven years old, through my great-aunt, and she had always encouraged me to be positive, and to trust my intuition.

As with everyone I worked with, I explained that I would not charge a fee for my time (I thought I might be wasting their time, anyway!) and that my intention was to channel healing energy which I hoped might ease or remove any physical, emotional or psychological problems they might be facing. I stressed I could not promise anything. In return I asked only for their honest and sincere feedback regarding their experience of the session, and indeed any developments that might take place during the following few days, if they thought this was relevant to the healing.

My friends came with a variety of issues; some with long-term back problems, shoulder pain, stress, anxiety, migraines, and other emotional issues - and all seemed at the very least, at the end of the healing sessions, to feel a deeper sense of relaxation, which was encouraging...even if I sometimes wondered if they were just politely humouring me. I could definitely feel the energy flowing through my body and out through my hands, which would usually be very warm (sometimes even very hot) but my mind would try and savage my sincere intentions to help, telling me I was wasting their time; that I was imagining it. But then at the end of the sessions some of my friends stated quite emphatically that they had had a significant reduction in physical pain, which in some cases had lasted several weeks. Of the original group, some have since told me the healing has been, to date, absolute. They also confirmed what I had experienced; feeling heat and energy within their body throughout the healing session, whilst some also reported what they described as 'work' taking place within their auras. I knew I wasn't the 'healer'; I didn't have a clue what on earth was going on, or what would happen!

The 'method' of healing, however, was always the same. The friend would sit in an upright chair and I would stand behind them, say a simple prayer for their well being in body, mind and spirit, and start by gently placing my hands on their shoulders. The idea was, as Jess has told me during the reiki workshop, to just let go and intuitively sense where my hands should be placed, and for how long. Sometimes in my mind's eye I would see an image of their lower back or 'hear' in my mind 'right knee', for instance, but this was rare. More often I intuitively sensed what to do, and was drawn to a specific area. There were times when what I 'saw' or 'heard' in my mind did not correspond to what they had told me when they arrived. I gradually learnt to trust this inner guide, even when the evidence was to the contrary, because at times it was spot on.

Despite the successful healing that had taken place, I was struggling to deal with the emotions being triggered within myself, and mentally I was not in a good place at all. Several weeks after starting these sessions, on a Friday afternoon after a busy week of healing, I decided I couldn't live with the inner trauma of shame and self-loathing that was coming up. I decided that was it: I wasn't doing this anymore, and I would cancel all the remaining sessions. That weekend was probably the most emotionally painful I'd had in years. By ignoring the inner guidance, as extreme as this reaction might sound, I felt as if I was suppressing a lifeforce in some way. I once described my reaction to deliberately ignoring the healing energy as something akin to having deliberately locked a small child in a cupboard and, despite knowing full well he was suffocating in there, deciding to leave him there to suffer.

When I described this reaction, several months later to a psychologist, she suggested to me that I was that small boy... and that I too needed healing.

The emotional pain I felt that weekend forced me to seek help with the healing process. In the first place, I had to learn to just let go and accept that the outcome of each healing session was exactly as it was meant to be. Secondly, I had to accept that the feelings that were triggered would pass, and that my awareness of them was not relevant to the actual healing taking place. The healing worked regardless of how I felt about the healing. During that weekend, I delved into a few books written by the great twentieth century English healer Harry Edwards, which I found really helpful. Edwards made it clear in his writings that the key realisation for a beginner is that 'he or she does not heal'; a belief which he considered a stumbling block for many in their early stages of healing. He went on to say that 'reception from the Spirit World takes place when the ordinary mind is dormant' and that one must attune oneself to the spirit world, rather than learn how to become a healer.

I felt more comfortable with this approach than others I knew of. There was an implicit humility and passiveness to it. It also encouraged me to meditate during the healing session, as this was the only way I knew how, to some degree, to silence the mind. I resolved to pray, and then meditate during the healing sessions the following week, with a rather belligerent attitude of 'we'll just see what happens'. It is also interesting to note that even when I settled into healing and was much more at peace with it, it took considerably longer for me to allow others to practice healing on me. Lying with my eyes closed was akin to being unguarded and vulnerable; in the same way as, during my twenties, I remember forcing myself to stay awake on long train journeys, just in case someone tried to molest me. Whilst this was not a wholly conscious thought, it lay deep down in my mind, quietly influencing my behaviour.

Reading Harry Edwards' writings on spiritual healing helped me to realise my resistance was not to do with the idea of healing, but that my mental trauma had rejected the notion that I could be a channel for it. This awareness encouraged me to continue with my new approach. I absolutely believed in the possibility of healing; when Jesus said '...behold, the kingdom of God is within you.'(Luke 17:21), he laid out our spiritual destiny; that life's ultimate truth lies within us. However daunting that may be in the light of Jesus' miracles, I think this statement goes to the core of his teachings, and gives a prospective healer, and everyone else for that matter, hope and strength. Through meditation we are able to connect to a healing energy, which can be channeled for the benefit of ourselves and others, and which can bring about profound healing.

After several months of practice it became clear to me, at first intellectually and then emotionally, that the principle of all healing is unconditional love. It was this love which I learned triggered off emotions and thoughts locked within the memories of the abuse; memories of something which were, of course, the opposite of love. It triggered the shame, disgust and rage which I felt later in the day after the sessions had finished. Whilst these were not transferred to anyone I 'worked' with, this was the context with which I started to practice healing. I didn't realise for years that whilst the healing for others was, of course, important, I was also a beneficiary, even though I didn't know that at the time. The healing energy therefore served to heal me of the belief I had, amongst other false beliefs, that my body was to be detested, and rejected through self-hatred and shame.

Talking with friends who practiced spiritual healing helped me to accept I was simply channelling Universal Healing Energy, and despite the fact I always seemed to focus on the times when it did not 'work', they encouraged me to have a more balanced approach mentally. I was not doing anything wrong, immoral or unethical, they convinced me, and indeed most of the people I worked with reported a deep feeling of relaxation, improved health overall, and often an awareness of inner peace.

After my first session with Freda, using my technique of letting go, I somewhat nervously asked her how it felt. She replied, 'What are you doing differently? It felt so much more powerful than the last few times.' To which I answered in a gentle but slightly defiant tone, 'Oh, I'm doing nothing. I'm not involved at all. I did my usual prayer, then I tried meditating for a while before I drifted off and thought about what was happening in the test match.'

Freda roared with laughter, saying, 'Ha, I love it. Good for you. Well, if that's what works for you, keep doing it. It's definitely made a huge difference compared to our earlier sessions.'

Adopting this new approach to the healing sessions brought about immediate results, as I soon discovered the flow of energy to my friends was almost always considerably stronger than before, and they invariably commented on this the first time we worked together after the new approach had begun. With my lesson learnt, I made the conscious decision in prayer at the beginning of each session to let go and allow the energy to flow, thereby ignoring the ego mind which had previously challenged and questioned it. The difference was clear; when I was involved, putting myself under pressure to achieve a certain outcome, it could be fragmented and the energy would not flow as smoothly. When I got out of the way, it was a much more enjoyable, rewarding experience all round.

Over the course of the first six months my confidence with the healing grew, and I was slowly becoming more open in conversation with friends about my spiritual interests, and particularly the subject of healing. It was so obvious from their body language and positive comments and that everyone else was really relaxed about it. I was the only one who sometimes felt awkward and uncomfortable. One morning I was having coffee with Alex, a good friend who ran a spiritual centre in the town, when he asked me,

'You've been all over India, meditating at various ashrams. You've met John of God in Brazil and had healing there, too. Have you not thought of running a meditation group, and passing on what you've learnt?'

'It's too soon, my friend, I don't.... Ummm I don't feel I'm ready to teach meditation yet. Perhaps a few months down the line?' I instinctively replied, from a place of fear. My need for control (to fully understand everything about meditation so I would not feel humiliated if I was asked a question I could not answer) sprung up immediately, and I recognised later that day my specific fear was whether I would be able to answer the questions the group members might have, and feeling a fraud again.

'Okay, I understand. I'd love you to run a group whenever you feel you are ready. I think you'd do an excellent job, but you must feel comfortable, of course. The offer is always open.' I felt flattered and relieved at the same time. A few days later the telephone rang, and it was Alex.

'I've decided to run the meditation group we discussed the other day. I was thinking perhaps on Wednesday evenings? I'm hoping you might join and support me?'

'I'd love to be involved', I replied, and agreed to attend the following week at 7pm.

Alex led the group that first week, and I ended up leading it every week for the next six years! My good friend knew I needed a gentle push, and I'm so grateful that he did. It created another opportunity to confront and to let go of my fears.

> *We are here to awaken*
> *from our illusion of separateness.* [28]
> Thich Nhat Hanh

For the first two years the group was held at Alex's centre, and then, when he and his wife Ann decided to move home, it was held in my front room, which could comfortably accommodate twenty people; our maximum number. The group evolved through word of mouth, and for those members who attended almost every week, a feeling of intimacy and continuity soon developed. I was keen to protect this feeling, and so decided to keep our number at twenty overall.

The group had a simple structure. We opened with a universal prayer of peace and healing, followed by a ten minute guided meditation, after which we sat in silent meditation for a further fifty minutes. Thereafter, those who wished to practice healing would pair off for thirty minutes, whilst those who wished to continue meditating were welcome to do so. We all convened again for a brief closing prayer just before 9pm, and then had coffee and biscuits in the kitchen. Whilst a prayer might include the word 'God', members were invited to interpret this as they wished; after all, the benefits of meditation and healing do not require any belief in a religious deity. During the first few months, members arrived fifteen minutes before we started at 7.30pm, but as the energy within the group started to build up, several asked if they could arrive slightly earlier and sit quietly in the energy. Others would often stay later for coffee and conversation, so the running times of the group were extended accordingly. We opened the room for individual meditation at 6pm, group meditation and healing 7.30pm - 9pm, and everyone would leave by 10.30pm. The energy in my flat was revitalised by the group each week, and after everyone had left I would sit quietly in my front room and allow myself to be immersed in its healing presence.

---

[28] Wendy Johnson, *A Floating Sangha Takes Root, Early days in Plum Village with Thich Nhat Hanh* from www.tricycle.org (Spring 2015)

The vibes within the room were tangible. There was a presence within this space which was felt as soon as one walked into the room. We all commented on it. It was created by the positive intention of the group members, and their heartfelt desire to connect to peace and love. Consequently, the healing brought about a much greater mental clarity and a peacefulness within me. Leading the group also normalised the healing process for me. It was simply about creating a safe, clean, comfortable environment for friends to relax in, enabling them to connect to that beautiful presence that resides within each one of us, and then to let go and ask for healing to be shared with another. I received so many benefits as group leader, not least the quality of the new friends I had made, and the opportunity to learn from them, as their collective experience removed the element of mysticism I once believed about healing. I no longer bought into the notion that healing was a gift. I came to realise it was the most natural thing in the world, and if more people would let go and practice healing, how much more would positive change automatically come about in our world as our minds become less aggressive, and more peaceful? It really is that simple and straightforward, in my experience.

We all have the capacity to heal. One does not have to have a faith, or believe in God or a power greater than oneself for healing to take place. All that's required is an open mind to accept the possibility that healing can take place, and to have an intention to receive and send love. For a healer, the initial challenge is to let go of any notion that one is the doer.

Healing has certainly changed my perspective on life, and I now understand that all the answers are within me. Leading the group also encouraged me to find new prayers and practice different meditation techniques, so it gave me the platform to learn and be teachable, and to find out for myself what felt helpful and what didn't. Group members were encouraged to share ideas for meditations, spiritual writing, prayers, poetry, and music. One very good friend of mine, Tom, was often inspired to perform original musical compositions on his flute after meditation most weeks. He has since become a much respected musician, particularly with followers of 'spiritual music'.

The Meditation and Healing group continued each week for several years, which, with my continued involvement with the 12 Step programme of AA, helped me to develop a deeper spiritual awakening. The individual healing sessions also continued every Sunday. I had, by this time, practiced healing for a few years, and had worked with clients with a wide variety of physical and emotional problems. Sometimes the intuition was very clear, and I followed this inner direction accordingly; at other times I 'saw' and 'heard' nothing... but I had, by then, learned to trust the process and let go. I was asked to offer healing to a lady member of AA, and this was one occasion when I initially had no inner guidance at all, but then I suddenly 'saw' what needed to be healed.

Louise had unfortunately suffered with anxiety and depression for several years. She approached me after a meeting one evening for healing, and we arranged to meet the following evening at her flat. She sat on her dining room chair and I positioned myself behind her, and placed my hands in her shoulders. I felt the energy flow through my hands which were gently moving from the top of her neck to the base of her spinal cord. I sensed her energy was much weaker at the base of her spinal cord. I then 'saw' in my mind's eye what looked like an x ray of her lower spine, and a mark specifically over her coccyx noting where the focus of healing needed to be. My hands were placed there for five minutes or so, until I sensed the energy in my hands decrease. It is interesting to note that Louise had not told me she had an inflamed coccyx, and yet the healing energy was guided to relieve her of this pain, which she confirmed it had done. Whilst these intuitive moments or inner visions had started to happen more often, they were not common... though I welcomed them as evidence of a higher consciousness that seeks to help us.

My own healing had greatly improved during this period of my life and I would often feel so connected and peaceful when channelling the healing energy. It was an empowering experience which stayed with me throughout the day. On another level, a deeper healing was taking place. I was being physically intimate with another human being in a way which, under everyday circumstances, I would shy away from. I still felt uncomfortable with being touched, with being kissed or hugged, unless I could see it was going to happen and had time to prepare myself - yet when healing, these barriers seemed to be removed, and a true sense of love and peace was my conscious reality. This felt enormously liberating. Feeling healing energy flow through my body and out through my hands was also healing me. My body, which I had viewed for so many years at a deeper level as being dirty and disgusting, actually had the capacity to channel something that could often help people. I began to consciously realise that physical touch could be mutually healing, and was a natural expression of love for another being.

Another friend, Natalie, had been depressed for several years following the breakdown of her marriage, and the stress of struggling with crippling debts that had built up as she tried desperately to cover the cost of her children's school fees whilst maintaining the family home. She told me she had tried drug therapies, counselling and hypnotherapy, but for whatever reason these had not worked for her. I must admit I felt somewhat nervous working with Natalie as I could see how vulnerable she was and I worried I might be raising her hopes when conventional modalities had not made any difference. However, she was desperate to try anything, so we arranged a weekly session over the course of six weeks, initially to see whether there would be any improvement. Progress was slow at first, as can often be the case with mental health issues, but over the course of two months, Natalie began to feel more relaxed within herself, and slowly gained confidence. Over six months she continued to improve, and I was later encouraged to learn that she had attended the theatre several times that year, something she had not been able to do for a number of years.

Whilst there were inevitably times when the healing did not reduce or remove any pain, and I always struggled when this happened, there were more times when it did work. As my acceptance of this grew, I started working with more people who had come to me through word of mouth. A devoutly Catholic lady contacted me for a session, and when she arrived it was clear she felt very distressed, both physically and mentally. I asked her what the problem was. She told me;

'I've had a chronic back problem for twelve years, and have tried everything to help alleviate it; pain killers, acupuncture, massage, but nothing has worked. I nearly didn't come here today, but I knew I had to try it. I have come here as a last resort.'

She continued, 'I am a devout Catholic, and I am not sure how you work, but if you work with spirits I would feel very uncomfortable as my faith only allows healing through Jesus Christ.'

I assured her I did not go into trance, I did not become possessed or speak in tongues, and that I often prayed to Jesus for healing. The only difference between us, I explained to her, was that whilst she recognised

Jesus as her Lord and Saviour, for me he was a Great Master. She then said she felt more relaxed, and thanked me for what I had said. After a brief explanation from her regarding the location of her pain, I took the precaution to explain that sometimes with physical healing the pain can feel worse as it is being removed from the body, and that if this happens if she should focus on her breathing - this would help her handle the discomfort. She nodded in agreement, and the session began.

I felt the energy, which was like a sensation of heat flowing through my body, as soon as we started and I let go and began meditating, as was my usual practice by now. I had enough awareness of any intuition I might receive during meditation to move my hands to certain positions, and I trusted it was what was needed. After fifteen minutes the energy decreased and I came out of my meditation. The lady opened her eyes and, looking very shocked, stared at me for a few moments and then she slowly moved to sit on the sofa next to the couch. I waited for her expression to change, feeling somewhat nervous about her reaction. She then spoke very slowly and deliberately. Her face now had an expression of utter calm and peace, and with eyes wide open she looked at me with what I felt was an acceptance of a new feeling of health. After a few moments composing herself, she said,

'The pain in my back has completely gone. When you started the healing, the pain became excruciating, but I remembered what you had said and focussed on my breathing, which did help.'

'What has really shocked me though, is that as the pain was leaving me, I had a vision on a screen in my mind; it was so real I was taken aback by how vivid it was. I saw my family home, which I loved living in as a child, but in the vision there was a very tall hedge all the way around it. I walked around the hedge from the outside. I knew the house was on other side, and I tried to find a way to get into the house but I could not. There was no way through. Then the vision stopped.'

I asked her whether she had thought of anyone in particular during the vision, and she replied, with considerable emotion, 'My mother'. I asked her to tell me about her mother.

'Mum died over ten years ago. I think about her every day, I miss her so much. Between bringing up the children, looking after my husband, and making sure we had what we needed at home, Mum and I would somehow find the time and talk on the phone for hours, about anything and everything'. She sobbed gently as she spoke.

I asked her, 'When did Mum pass away?'

After a brief pause, she replied, 'Twelve years ago.' I then asked her, 'How long have you had the back pain?' She thought about it, and then gasped in recognition. Through her tears she said, 'Twelve years'. I said it was time to allow the emotions to be released. She needed to allow herself to grieve.

'I've tried to cry, but whenever the tears came up I felt so selfish', she said. 'Life has been so busy being a Mum to two teenagers, and being a wife. I've got on as best I can, looking after my family'.

She broke down and wept quietly, and after a minute, was calm enough to continue.

'Whenever the tears did come up, I would shove them back down again. There was always so much I needed to do. I know I can't go on like this'.

I suggested it was now time to allow herself to grieve. 'Perhaps it's now the right time to speak with your family and to let them know how you are feeling. Allow them the opportunity to support you with their love.'

We spoke for a while longer, during which she agreed that it would also help her if she contacted Cruse Bereavement Care, a national charity for bereaved people, and which offers professional counselling for people who have suffered bereavement. As she left, she thanked me, and then hugged me and cried a little more. I never saw her again, but she recommended me to several of her friends over the next few years, which was touching.

The following week a female friend, Tara, called me and was rather embarrassed to tell me that since she had had sex on a recent holiday, for the first times in ages, she had felt painful bolts of 'electricity' shooting up and down the inside of her spinal cord.

'I've been to my GP but she can't find anything wrong with me. She is as baffled as I am!'

We arranged to meet and I prayed for guidance as to what to do. I sensed Tara had inadvertently released the kundalini energy at the base of her spine. Kundalini is a Sanskrit word that literally means 'snake' and is an energy which, according to the teachings of yoga, lies dormant in the first chakra (spiritual energy centre), located at the base of the spine. The ancient yogis discovered that by meditating on the chakras, the kundalini is activated

Healing and Meditation

and as it begins to rise through the energy body, higher states of consciousness are experienced. So the teachings go, when the kundalini reaches the seventh, or crown, chakra, it develops its full majestic force and brings about enlightenment.

On a more practical level, it is said kundalini is also released during orgasm through the second chakra, as the body attempts to create a child. It is experienced in life-threatening situations, enabling people to suddenly develop hitherto unknown strength to save themselves or others. However, when released there is sometimes an explosion of power, and without proper direction, it can be very uncomfortable and possibly damaging. When my friend arrived for her appointment a few days later, she was clearly in considerable pain, and looked exhausted.

'I've hardly slept for several nights. I find it really difficult to walk properly, as when these bolts happen, it feels like I'm being attacked from my inside each time I try and move. It's really unsettling. Driving is a nightmare, as sitting down for any length of time is also excruciating. It feels like electricity shooting inside my spinal cord. It shoots up and down all the time. I've hardly slept since I.....well, since I had sex. I've been off my food.'

As she spoke, I noticed how she kept shifting in her seat, and then standing up. Her quality of life had been greatly damaged by her condition.

'The sex was great, but I didn't expect this!' she said with a rueful smile.

She had practiced yoga for many years and when I suggested it was probably kundalini she told me she was familiar with the principle of it, but had never experienced it before. I asked her to sit and lean on the back of a dining room chair, with her back exposed, so I had easy access to her spinal cord. I prayed and asked for guidance and intuitively 'saw' a waterfall of fresh healing energy falling from her brain stem to her coccyx. I asked her to visualise this, to see the 'water' moving the energy back down to settle at the base of her spinal cord. As she visualised this, I gently placed my hands on her neck, and focussed the healing energy in the usual way, and thankfully within a few minutes the discomfort was completely healed, and she could finally relax. It did the trick. I asked her to call me later that week to let me know whether it had worked, longer-term.

Five days later, Tara called and confirmed the healing had been definite, and then she suddenly said, 'Does this mean I can have sex again now?'. I didn't know what to say, and stumbled around for a few seconds umming and aaahing, before she burst out laughing at my embarrassment. As much as possible I used the same space for both the meditation group and the individual healing sessions. I found the more I meditated or practiced healing in a specific room, the more energy seemed to remain – there was a distinctive change in the vibration or atmosphere in the room – and I felt it become like a cocoon of peace, a safe and sacred space. After several months of healing in my lounge, a friend visited for the first time in over a year, and as he was about to enter the lounge, he stopped in his tracks and asked me:

"What's... what has happened in here? It feels so different! It feels so peaceful."

The benefits of meditation and healing on a regular basis in the same space can be felt long after the actual practice has taken place. I experienced this when I visited the renowned Indian sage Sri Ramana Maharshi's ashram for the first time, in February 1996, and looked into his private room. The power in that space was palpable; it was as if he was still there generating the remarkable energy that is so evident in his eyes when you look at his photograph. This, despite the fact that he was not physically present in the room, having passed into spirit over forty years earlier.

It was in my lounge, in May 2010, that one of the most extraordinary experiences of my life took place, and one which I know will bring people, no doubt, to question my sanity (if they haven't done so already!). A good friend, Hamish, who has a very peaceful, gentle presence about him, was visiting and in the course of a long conversation about spirituality we got to the topic of unconditional love, and the challenge of practicing this in everyday life. As we spoke, a thin, smoke-like manifestation could be clearly seen between us approximately five feet in height. We both looked at it, and then at each other, with our eyes wide open in amazement. Hamish spoke first, speaking slowly as he tried to describe what had appeared.

'Ermm. What is that? It looks like a very thin smoke, but it isn't smoke. What is it? It wasn't here a few seconds ago...'

'I've no idea. How bizarre! I don't understand it', I replied, as I tried to work out what it was and where it had come from. I knew in my heart that this was a spiritual experience, but my practical mind demanded a logical answer. I went through a list of possible sources.

'Well,' I said. 'There's no incense burning, in fact I've haven't lit any

Healing and Meditation

incense sticks or candles since yesterday morning. No one smokes in this flat. The windows are all closed, and nothing has been cooked in the kitchen.'

Hamish interjected, 'Besides, there's no trail from anywhere else. It's just hanging there! And there's no smell, so it couldn't come from something burning anyway. It just suddenly appeared, out of the blue.'

My attention was suddenly drawn to the lounge door on my left side, and there I saw what looked like a very small child with wings, hovering in mid-air about four foot off the floor. All around this supremely beautiful spiritual being was a six inch wide, completely pure, radiant, crystal-clear aura of pulsating light which exuded a very powerful healing energy. Whilst its form was as real to me as my friend Hamish was, sitting opposite me, it was not physical, in the sense that if I had been close enough to touch it, I didn't think I would have felt any bone or muscle. I saw this most beautiful angel move towards my friend.

'Oh my God! Hamish, can you see....? The most beautiful angel is very slowly moving towards you,' I said, with a feeling of privilege and utter amazement in my voice.

Hamish replied, with his eyes even wider open and a touch of incredulity in his voice, 'No, no, I can't see anything, except the 'smoke'... But I can definitely feel something is going on. There is a presence here. Something has definitely changed in this room, there's no doubt about that.'

As he said this, the angel was moving directly towards him, and I felt that the healing energy it brought was specifically for my friend. With that the angel simply disappeared into thin air, as they say. The whole experience, from both of us noticing the 'smoke' to the angel leaving lasted no more than perhaps thirty seconds. I wished he had also seen the angelic vision, and not just the smoke, but unfortunately he had not. Our conversation continued and we both understandably made several references to what had just taken place, trying to make sense of it all. Hamish and I came to the conclusion that maybe it had happened because our hearts were both open, we felt very peaceful, and we were talking about the importance of unconditional love. Who knows? I've been all those things many times since, and nothing has happened!

Several years ago, I used to enjoy watching the television programme, *This Is Your Life*. On this particular episode, broadcast on 8 November

1999, the presenter Michael Aspel was honouring the remarkable courage of Britain's most decorated serving lifeboatman and recipient of the RNLI Gold medal, Hewitt Clark MBE. As coxswain of the Lerwick lifeboat, Hewitt had served 34 years and saved 319 lives. At the end of the show, the captain of a trawler, whose life had been saved by Hewitt, described him as 'sometimes angels come in the guise of men', a phrase which has stuck with me ever since.

I have had many earth-bound angels throughout my life to help and encourage me along my journey, but it's very difficult to put into words the intensity of the emotions I experienced from what I saw and felt during the angelic vision. I've used the words 'peace', 'love', and 'gentleness' many times throughout this book. It was all these emotions and more, much more than I can describe. With the vision came a purity I cannot do justice to with words. They are woefully insufficient to describe the spiritual beauty I witnessed. After the immediate shock of the vision, I remember my first flash of thought was, 'It is true. Angels really do exist'. In my cynicism towards organised religion, I had often wondered if angels had been created as a tool to encourage the faithful. Now I had received confirmation of what I had hoped in my heart might be true. I know I can only fail to do justice with my description of the experience. After Hamish had left, I sat down and meditated. As I thought about the vision, the words of Jesus from the Gospel of Matthew (18:3) came to mind: 'Truly I tell you, unless you change and become like little children, you will never enter the kingdom of heaven.' It struck me that there was a childlike radiance within that angelic vision, as well as a physical resemblance to a small child. My interpretation of heaven differs from the traditional teachings of the Christian church.

My personal view, for what it's worth, is that 'heaven' is the state of highest consciousness, and our ultimate spiritual destiny. I know many will scoff at what I have written about the angelic vision. I was once one of the cynics about clairvoyance, and I can only share my truth.

At the end of October 2011, a lady came for healing one Sunday evening, and brought a friend to support her. I always encouraged anyone new, who I didn't know, to bring a friend with them. Apart from providing them with emotional support if they needed it, it also created a safer environment all round. Whilst I had taken out Public Liability Insurance for some years, one has to be careful when inviting vulnerable people into your home. Over a mug of tea in the kitchen, she told me she had been in a car accident a month or so previously which had left her in considerable neck pain from whiplash. The injury also prevented her from being able to play with her eighteen month old daughter since the accident, as she had difficulty lifting and carrying her. This was obviously very upsetting for both of them, and particularly for her daughter. As I usually said to anyone who came for healing, I told her I would do whatever I could to help, and that the healing might alleviate some, perhaps even all, of the pain... but I couldn't promise anything. She then told me she had a dilemma.

'I have a meeting with my solicitor on Wednesday to talk through the insurance claim. We will be going through the specific details of the accident, and then describing the physical pain I've been in since it happened. I'll then be expected to sign the document.'

She added, 'If the healing works, I don't know where that leaves me... with signing the form?'

'Okay', I said, ' I'm not sure what to suggest, to be honest with you. With healing, I never know what will happen. The healing might work 100%; it does sometimes happen that the pain is completely removed in one session. But often several sessions are needed, and the pain might not completely go. If it decreases today, it might return tomorrow. I never know what will happen.'

I continued, 'What you decide to do regarding the insurance document is not for so me to say. But if the healing removes 100% of the pain, and your solicitor says you can't sign the document for some reason, I cannot put the pain back!'

After a few moments of thought, she said, 'I've had enough of it, I want to play with my daughter. Let's see what happens.'

'Are you absolutely sure you want to go ahead? The alternative is you meet your solicitor, sign the document, and then come here for healing.' I looked to her friend, who suggested it might be best to talk with her solicitor first, and then come back. She had made up her mind. 'Let's give it a go, I can't live like this anymore.'

She then sat on a dining room chair and I gently placed my hands on her neck. The energy felt so immediate and smooth I knew instinctively it would help her. She looked surprised by the heat and looked over to her friend, saying, 'My God, it's really powerful.'

After a few minutes, the energy dissipated and the session finished. I knew it must have helped. I know when there is a special connection; the whole process feels so natural and easy. As the channel, you are doing nothing but asking for love to come through and help. She turned and looked at her friend, with her eyes wide open and a smile across her face as she moved her neck and shoulders through various twists and turns. She announced, 'the pain has completely gone!' Her friend then replied with a laugh, 'so, what you gonna do about the form, then?!'

I asked her to call me after she had seen her solicitor, and to let me know if the healing had been permanent, and what her solicitor had advised her to do regarding the form. We happened to bump into each other a few days later in the town centre, and she recounted her conversation with her somewhat bemused solicitor.

'I told her I'd met you and that the healing had worked, and that the pain has completely gone.' As she said this to her solicitor, she noticed a look of incredulity appear on her solicitor's face, and he said;

'I've never really come across a situation such as this one before. I really don't know what to suggest.'

Shortly thereafter I had another experience that confirmed to me that I was not the healer; that I was only the channel. I was working with a good friend, Lisa, who had no physical issues but wanted a relaxing thirty minute healing session, which I happily agreed to. She arrived in her normal chatty frame of mind and after the usual chit chat between good friends she climbed onto the massage couch and lay face up and closed her eyes. I stood at her feet and was about to say a prayer asking for healing energy to come through when I saw, to my left, the unmistakable form of the Indian saint, Sri Sathya Sai Baba. It was unmistakably Sai Baba. The figure was very short and had a slender build, (Sai Baba was only five foot, two inches tall). He wore an orange robe which hung down to cover his feet, and had a huge bush of black hair, rather like an afro.

My heart exploded with energy, and I felt in awe of this incredible experience. The vision of Sai Baba stopped me in my tracks. He walked directly to the massage couch and placed his hands over Lynne's heart for perhaps thirty seconds, and then disappeared as quickly as he had appeared. His form was not entirely physical in the sense of how I would have described Lisa lying in front of me, but his form was much more substantial than a hologram – as crazy as this will sound to many, he was definitely there! After the healing session, Lisa got up from the massage couch and stared at me, smiling. She then sat down on the sofa next to me, and I asked, 'how do you feel?'. I didn't want to lead her with my questions; I wanted to know exactly what she had experienced before I said anything about what I had seen.

'I feel amazing', she replied. 'As soon as you started I could feel this immense healing energy in and around my heart...I.... I've never felt anything, anything like it before. The healing that's come through you is much more powerful now than it has been before isn't it?' She then had what can only be described as verbal diarrhoea for the next five minutes; speaking so quickly and without seeming to draw breath that I found it hard to understand everything she was saying. As well as describing the experience itself, Lisa commented on how much emotion she was releasing. It was an extraordinary experience to listen to her steam of consciousness flow through her, and even she said,

'This is bizarre. It's as if the play button in my mind is permanently stuck. I can't stop talking'. And off we went again at 300 mph! She always loved talking a lot but this was comically ridiculous for both of us. We both had a giggle fit as she continued to talk and giggle for a few more minutes. When she finally stopped talking there was a gap of ten seconds as she stared at me. She was forcing herself to keep her mouth shut, but finding it very difficult not to talk. She took several deep breaths, but then she was off again for another minute or so, which made us giggle even more. She couldn't control herself!

'What the hell have you done to me?' she asked, with a smile on her face.

'I haven't done anything at all. And I was nowhere near your heart during the healing session. I didn't move an inch from your feet.' I replied. She was having none of this,

'Yes, you were! As soon as I closed my eyes, I felt you standing right next to me, and then your hands were above my heart; they were like red hot irons!'

I said to her: 'That wasn't me. Sai Baba suddenly came in and it was his energy you felt.'

Although Lisa has never met Sai Baba (at least in the conventional sense), she had heard me talk about my experiences in India, and knew he had been a considerable influence on my spiritual journey. After a pause, and with a wide smile, Lisa replied;

'Well, he certainly knows what he's doing, doesn't he!'

As I have previously mentioned, I have visited John of God's healing centre, in Brazil, on two occasions, and stayed for a month each time. The night before my second visit, in October 2006, I went to see a very dear AA friend in a nursing home. He had been diagnosed with cancer several months earlier and I knew this would be our final goodbye. Peter had been instrumental in my sobriety; he had a wonderful gentleness about him which was heartfelt and genuine. He had helped so many people in AA over the years. During the last few weeks of his life, when he was still able to attend meetings, the number of AA members who travelled considerable distances to see and thank him for his love was truly remarkable. From this outpouring of love and affection, it was clear that Peter was a very special friend to so many people in AA and Gamblers Anonymous. He had been sober for over twenty-five years, and had dedicated much of his time to encouraging new members of the fellowship. In AA, we have a phrase: 'Our leaders are but trusted servants: they do not govern'. It is the highest compliment, in my opinion, to be acknowledged as a 'trusted servant' of the fellowship, and Peter was certainly a trusted servant.

As we sat beside each other, I asked whether I might channel some healing energy and he thanked me, accepting my offer. Channeling healing for someone you love can often be difficult, as it is easy to 'get in the way' in the sense that you so desperately want to help them that you are in the frame of mind of being the 'doer'; you are not letting go and letting God, as we often say in AA. Nevertheless the energy came through and Pete acknowledged it was helping him, which meant so much to me. I held his hand and then placed my fingers against the cancer nodules on his neck. I didn't know whether the energy would alleviate any of the pain, but the intention to help was there. After we had spoken on and off for an hour during the healing session, Peter said he needed to lie down on the bed.

I helped him get up from his chair to walk over to the bed, and took his weight as he carefully lowered himself onto the bed. I stood at the side of his bed for a few moments, and we said our goodbyes. I remember standing two feet away from him when something totally unexpected happened. Without any deliberate intention on my part, I suddenly found myself very gently hugging him, and kissing the cancer nodules on his neck.

I opened my eyes, realising where I was, and thought to myself, 'how the hell did I get here?' It was as if I had momentarily had a loss of consciousness, and yet I had not collapsed in a heap, or fallen on to the bed. I hadn't been ill with the flu, nor dizzy from having stood up quickly. There had been no warning, and my body was in a very specific position to kiss the nodules. I stood up feeling somewhat bewildered; Peter smiled and thanked me. We held hands, and I thanked him for everything he had done for me and so many others over the years. We looked at each other for a few more seconds in silence, then I quietly left the room.

Twenty-four hours later I was flying from London Heathrow to San Paulo in Brazil, and as I sat there in my seat, the right side of my neck started becoming increasingly painful. I flashed back in my mind to when I had kissed the right side of Peter's neck where the cancer nodules were. By the time we landed in Brazil, I was using my right hand as a vice to give my neck as much support as possible.

After a further flight from San Paulo to Brasilia, and a taxi journey to Abadiânia, (where the healing centre is), I was now in agony. I had a sleepless night and went for healing the following morning. After ten days of meditation and healing the pain was finally released. This, in itself, was dramatic. I was lying on a massage couch and after twenty minutes of healing, a very heavy, dark energy left me through my right leg which shook violently as the energy was released. It felt as if exhaust fumes were being expelled from my cells; I was very relieved and grateful the pain had gone.

Back in the UK, I received the news that Peter had passed away a few days earlier. I have no idea whether the healing he received alleviated some of his pain. I hope that it helped my dear friend in some way. During the early months of practicing healing I had sometimes felt physical pain pass through my body, as the pain was released from the client. I hoped that I had taken on some of his pain, at least temporarily.

Healing is, after all, about helping. The agony in my neck has never returned.

9

LOVE LOST

*Your Heart
is the light of the world.
Don't cover it with your mind.*[29]
Mooji

    Since getting sober and continuing to work the AA 12 Step programme, I have developed a more spiritual approach to life, and with this change in attitude has come much reward. I enjoy a close, loving relationship with both my parents. For almost fifteen years we lived only a few miles from each over other, and every Sunday we enjoyed a traditional family meal, and a good catch up on what was happening in our lives. As a family, we have also shared many holidays both in the UK and abroad, and every Christmas for over twenty years, we've all come together.

    My brother and sister both got married, moved away and had children when I was in my twenties, and we meet up regularly throughout the year. Being an uncle to their three children has been an important part of my own healing process; it's brought out the child in me, and I love being around their energy for, and their fascination with, life. Our time together has helped me to re-evaluate my own childhood, with regard to the abuse, as memories have gradually come back of myself when I was their age. When my eldest niece was four years old, and my sister was visiting my parents for the day, I left work early to see them. As I opened the lounge door, I heard

---

[29] Reference: www.twitter.com (@moojiji) Posted on May 17, 2015.

my little niece say,

'When will he be here, Mummy? I can't wait to see him!'

I felt incredibly emotional as her words sunk in. Until I was in my early thirties, I would automatically mentally filter everyone when they were kind or friendly with me, as an instinctive self-protective mechanism, but I knew her love was real and genuine. At home, and on my own that evening, I cried. There is so much to be grateful for; my family life, a great circle of friends, both male and female; friendships of quality I hugely value, and an enjoyable, rewarding career in theatre. All combined, life is busier than ever what with the meditation and healing group, and my forays into amateur dramatics. As often as work and cash flow permit, I continue to travel extensively in India, my spiritual home, which helps me develop a more rewarding spiritual life and which, as well as my active involvement with AA, is so important to my recovery.

Personal relationships and dating have been an area of my life which for many years have crippled me. Since reaching puberty I rarely allowed myself to date, let alone have a relationship. The ultimate legacy of the sexual abuse was my inability, until the last six months, to allow any woman, towards whom I have been attracted, to get close to me. Be it physically, emotionally or sexually, the PTSD would be triggered, and I always ran away from any form of intimacy. It has until very recently terrified me. For as long as I can remember, I have wanted to get married and be a loving husband, a good father, and have a family of my own. Over the years, I have questioned whether I am capable of allowing a lady to get close to me, in order to realise this lifelong dream. I've occasionally spoken about this with my family but until I was willing to comprehensively face the trauma and release the shame, there always came a point during our conversation when I would shut down, change the subject, or make some excuse and leave the house.

Perhaps this is the main purpose of this book; to be a catalyst for such a profound healing within me that I am able to develop a loving, intimate, sexual relationship with a woman I love, and who I know loves me. After the chapter describing the abuse, the one that now follows has been the most painful to put onto paper because it goes to the very core of how the sexual abuse affects me to this day. Ever since I first became aware that I was sexually attracted to women, I've had a feeling of terror and shame running through me whenever I've felt that attraction. During my teenage years, whenever I saw or was in conversation with a woman I considered to be attractive, I felt intimidated. I immediately felt 'less than', ugly, and vile.

I avoided any opportunity even for friendship if I was sexually attracted; the PTSD would be triggered and the mental and emotional reactions that followed would be crippling, and I would, in my teens and early twenties, regress to the scared nine year old boy, and admired the woman from afar where I felt safer... though increasingly I was feeling more and more isolated. As friends from school started dating and I saw young relationships starting to develop, it seemed so out of my reach. I felt as if I was on another planet; I didn't have the emotional vocabulary to understand how it was possible. When I was fifteen, a good friend from prep school days, Alice, one day saw me on the seafront and grabbed my arm, pulling me close.

'Hello! How are you? You know I've always really liked you, Matt. Well, shall we? Shall we go out one day, you know, on a date?'

I felt horrified. Whilst I found her very attractive, fun company to be around, and I knew she was a nice person, my instinctive reaction was the feeling of an abyss that had suddenly opened up in front of me, and as the ground gave way, in I would fall. I nervously mumbled,

'Thanks, that'd be nice but I've just started seeing someone, and we're getting on pretty well as it happens. Sorry.'

'Oh. Okay, I didn't know you were seeing someone. I asked Ben, who told me you were single so ... Well. Good luck. Umm. Bye.' She turned and walked away.

I felt ashamed of myself for lying to Alice so brazenly, but relieved at the same time. Lying to protect myself had become normal, and I had a fictitious girlfriend on and off throughout my teens and through university. I felt so angry with Ben for 'setting me up', and I avoided both of them for a few months; they went on my mental 'not to be trusted' list. Intimacy and relationships were mystifying and dangerous to me, and I completely avoided dating, kissing or hugging any woman I was attracted to until I was in my mid-to-late twenties.

I was twenty-four years old when I first managed to masturbate. Until then I had suppressed any sense of sexuality as it was so rare to get an erection; the sexual energy triggered the PTSD and as I tried to masturbate I would feel the paedophiles were in the room with me, watching and threatening, and I would immediately stop in horror at this vision. Those moments I would sit at the end of my bed, bent over with my head in my hands, with an erect but useless penis, were probably the most excruciatingly painful, emotionally and psychologically, of my life. I felt sub-human; a dirty, disgusting runt. I would get visual and emotional flashbacks, a stiff neck, nausea in the stomach, and images in my mind of the front door being kicked in by a gang of men who were angry with me. At my absolutely worst state of mental torment, with the groundhog day flashbacks playing obsessively in my mind, and an erection which could not be brought to ejaculation, I would want to kill the sexual energy. I would feel like cutting my member off to instantly destroy the sexual energy I felt in the body. Thankfully, I never made any attempt to do this, though I do remember punching it in frustration.

I finally was able to ejaculate when I developed a crush on a really tall blonde woman who had moved in nearby. I found her overwhelmingly attractive, and I forced myself to get into conversation with her whenever we saw each other, to get a real sense of her physicality. She always smelt really nice; she had a way of walking which was naturally sexy, and she would flick her hair in a certain way when she looked down and spoke to me. I would replay in my mind all these physical details to the extent that I had created a very real 'film' of her in my head that I could fantasise about. I needed something so real in sight and smell to counter the flashbacks. One night, after several attempts, it worked and I ejaculated for the first time ever.

'What the hell have I been missing?', (I said to myself!)

It was in every sense a momentous occasion. I always knew that being able to finally masturbate was a hugely significant step for me to take, if I was ever to be able to be intimate with a woman; to ultimately be a loving husband in every sense; and to be a good father; and to have a healthy, happy family. That had always been my dream.

My catalyst for healing has been my long-held desire to be in a loving relationship. I've always known I had to fully confront the abuse and let go of the trauma for this to happen. This has been one of the main driving forces throughout my life. Yet, I knew I had first to learn how to be intimate with myself; to have a loving relationship with myself emotionally, sexually, psychologically and spiritually. This was the first step in a long journey of psychological and emotional healing with my body. I had for years detested my own physicality, and could not understand why anyone would be attracted to me. My inability to masturbate left me feeling sub-human in so many ways.

It often took me a while to even recognise I found a particular woman attractive; I developed a strategy of conscious denial as a means for 'survival' for most of my life. I could kid myself that if I saw a girl I found attractive in a shop, and followed her in, that I was only really there to look for a particular book. That way, it seemed to me, I could suppress the feelings of shame I always felt when I scurried away, too scared to say 'Hello'. I convinced myself I wasn't there to see her, I was there for the books. When I 'allowed' myself to acknowledge that I found a woman attractive, and decided to find out whether she was 'safe', I would hang around wherever she had lunch or coffee; not with the intention of saying anything (I considered that far too confrontational and dangerous), but to try and get a better sense of who she was; whether she was a kind, decent and caring person, or someone who would turn on me and hurt me. I was terrified of being attacked. I couldn't go through it all again.

I would try and engineer opportunities when we might 'accidentally on purpose' bump into each other – anything more than that at this stage was too much for me to deal with – so if I saw her in Tesco on a Monday at 6pm I would be there every Monday at 6pm for the next few weeks, feeling sick to my stomach, but hoping I might see her, even if it was just for a fleeting smile as we walked past each other. If I fancied a woman in an estate agency I was, for a few weeks, interested in leasing a flat; I hate DIY but was suddenly the world's most prolific enthusiast when I had a crush on a girl who worked weekends in Homebase, and so on. At the moment of wanting to say more than a simple 'hello' and start a conversation, however, my body would tense up, I would be in fight-or-flight mode, and looking for ways to get out if I suddenly needed to. Being close to a woman I was sexually attracted to was never, ever a pleasant experience. It triggered off so many symptoms of the PTSD.

After a few weeks of trying to force myself to actually ask one of these fantasy women out, I would hit a wall of such overwhelming shame and self-disgust, I would have to give up and walk away. These were moments of such crippling pain and self-loathing that, in my early twenties, I would briefly taunt and punch myself in the face again. I would listen to the voices in my head;

'You are a fucking c*nt. Why the fuck would such an attractive woman want anything to do with a c*nt like you? Stop kidding yourself. Have you just shit yourself? Can I smell something? Stop wasting your time with her, she's way, way out of your league.'

Or...

'How fucking pathetic. Why are you kidding yourself? This woman is vastly more worldly-wise, and why would she date an ugly runt like you?'

I'd imagine her wanting to be with someone really good-looking with a better job, and would play out scenarios in my mind during which even if I did manage to say 'hello' she would look so shocked and appalled, I'd feel humiliated. If I knew her, I imagined her brothers or father coming around to the house and threatening me. Counsellors often talk about baby steps, and by God this felt like I was crawling to connect. This avoidance behaviour started in my mid-teens and continued through my twenties and into my early thirties. In my late twenties there were a few excursions into what felt like 'enemy territory' when I managed to psyche myself up, block out the fears, and go on a few dates. Even on those handful of occasions I did go on a date, I behaved like a good friend as opposed to a potential boyfriend. I would assume the role, rather arrogantly, of a pseudo – counsellor with my date, as some form of compensation for my considerable lack of sexual experience which was, masturbation aside, nil. By assuming the role of a pseudo-counsellor, rather than the potential boyfriend, I'd be able to momentarily quieten these savage voices as there was no risk of any physical intimacy, even though I was attracted to the girl I was with. When I spoke in some depth about these fears a counsellor said to me,

'You almost have a phobia of relationships, almost'.

My behaviour with women I found attractive became very predictable, and I would never tell anyone else for fear of being ambushed or pressurised in some way to do something about it. I had to have absolute control, so I could protect myself. After these fleeting encounters with women, the emotional and physical symptoms of the PTSD would be triggered and I would feel dirty, ashamed and overwhelmed with panic and fear, which would be felt throughout my body in the form of nausea, sleeplessness, stiff neck, palpitations, and sometimes panic attacks. I tried my best to consciously change my avoidance behaviour once I had acknowledged I was too scared to allow anyone to get close to me. I used the CBT techniques to challenge the irrational fears, and to think more positively, but the whole process was emotionally and psychologically exhausting. Excepting perhaps the dozen dates I went between the age of fifteen and thirty-five years of age, this pattern of avoidance behaviour was repeated every time I felt sexually attracted, until I was in my mid thirties. Typically, I would;

1. Realise I found a woman attractive, and often feel depressed with a sense of resignation of what would happen. (I.e the PTSD would be triggered and I'd run away again)
2. Admire her from afar, and create a fantasy in my mind of a loving relationship. I would see myself as being a devoted husband, a good father; confident, kind, successful, and good in bed. I would see her being happy and enjoying life, and we would have happy and healthy children.
3. 'Fall in love' with the fantasy.
4. See if she responded to my shy smiles, or if she looked shocked, and fearful.
5. If she responded positively after the first encounter, I would usually respond in a more direct way with my smiles the next few times we saw each other (I'd be too ever scared to say anything beyond a nervous 'Hi'), but a shift would happen inside me whereby I would feel more overwhelmed with panic and fear as the PTSD kicked in. I would start distrusting her motives, and fear she was setting me up to be hurt.
6. When this happened, I would avoid her at all costs; changing my routes to work, or my regular shopping habits. If we happened to see each other, I'd pretend I hadn't noticed her.
7. If, when seeing her again, she then started to ignore me, I'd feel upset by her rejection, and start briefly flirting again.
8. Whether she responded or ignored me, I'd convince myself I didn't really like her after all, suppress my interest, and blank her entirely.

I was aware this behaviour was not healthy, but what I didn't know at that time was that I had many symptoms of sexual anorexia. A good AA friend of mine, Jennie, who was one of very few people I talked to about my intimacy issues, suggested I join a 12 Step fellowship called Sex and Love Addicts Anonymous (SLAA). I did some online research, and felt a horrible pang of shame and recognition when I read a description of a love addict on a treatment centre website;

'Love addicts live in a chaotic world of desperate need and emotional despair. Fearful of being alone or rejected, love addicts endlessly search for that special someone – the person that will make the addict feel whole. Much like sex addicts, love addicts are searching for something outside of themselves – a person, relationship, or experience – to provide them with the emotional and life stability they feel they lack. In other words, 'love addicts use their intensely stimulating romantic experiences to (temporarily) fix themselves and feel emotionally stable'.

These words summed up my behaviour since my mid-teens in a nutshell, although my romantic experiences have been, almost entirely, in fantasy. SLAA offers support to those who suffer from an addictive compulsion to engage in or avoid sex, love, or emotional attachment. Joining SLAA gave me the strength to first acknowledge, and then learn how to change my thinking and my behaviour regarding intimacy and sex. It also helped me recognise I was still holding onto a lot of pain, which needed to be released. I learned, once again, that I wasn't alone which, in itself, helped me to heal.

At my first SLAA meeting I was asked to read a document called the 'The Characteristics of Sex and Love Addiction'. It summed up what had been my attitude and behaviour for so many years. Painful to acknowledge, it was yet a relief to know I was not alone. Four of the twelve characteristics triggered immense feelings of shame as I read them out loud:

- Having few healthy boundaries, we become sexually involved with and/or emotionally attached to people without knowing them.
- We become immobilized or seriously distracted by romantic or sexual obsessions or fantasies.
- We avoid responsibility for ourselves by attaching ourselves to people who are emotionally unavailable.
- To avoid feeling vulnerable, we may retreat from all intimate involvement, mistaking sexual and emotional anorexia for recovery.
The Augustine Fellowship, S.L.A.A., Fellowship-Wide Services, Inc.

My heart sank as I read from the page; this described so precisely my behaviour for the best part of twenty years of my adult life. However, I was encouraged to learn that SLAA groups outside of the larger cities are usually much smaller and more intimate than a typical AA group, with on average ten to twelve members. This suited me fine; I much preferred a smaller group where I knew everyone, as I found it easier to talk more openly about my psychological and emotional history. SLAA members are often, though not exclusively, members of other 12 Step programmes as well, and SLAA offered me a structured programme to help deal with the emotional blocks (my fears and fantasies, projections, and typical patterns of behaviour), and to learn how to change my thinking and actions, and develop a healthier relationship with myself, and those I am attracted to.

Whilst I have briefly spoken about relationship and intimacy issues in AA meetings, and the importance of emotional sobriety as a foundation to my physical sobriety, this has been more of an overview rather than an in depth analysis of my behaviours. Our primary purpose in AA is to stay sober and help other alcoholics to achieve sobriety, so deeper issues are usually discussed with a sponsor. An AA meeting is, typically, more focussed on keeping away from a drink one day at at a time, and offering support and encouragement to new members, than talking in depth about protracted emotional issues. At the same time, members are free to talk about life challenges that directly affect their sobriety.

Whilst the memories of the abuse remained buried as deep as possible in my mind, somewhere within my psyche I had desperately held to the belief that when this beautiful woman finally walked into my life, the trauma would magically dissolve away, and we would live happily ever after. However, it became clear to me in SLAA, after so many years of running away, that I had to feel the pain to be able to heal. The challenge was not just being willing to face the trauma, but how to actually remember what happened during the abuse in enough detail so the trauma could be released. The flashbacks during the episodes of the PTSD were often sudden and very aggressive, and when they passed they seemed to lock the memory away without any change in its impact on me. It took until my late thirties, when I had a breakdown (I prefer the word breakthrough), that the flashbacks became less savage, and I felt a great deal of rage and shame leave me. Thereafter I started to remember in more detail what had happened. (Note: these events are covered in the *Underlying Triggers* chapter).

I often wondered whether the paedophiles had cast some sort of spell or practiced hypnosis on me, as I just couldn't get access to so many of the memories until after I had had the breakthrough.

I subsequently learnt that one of the psychological and emotional causes of sexual anorexia is sexual abuse and rape. People with sexual anorexia avoid, fear, or dread sexual intimacy. It is also known as sexual avoidance, or sexual aversion. The main symptom of sexual anorexia is a lack of sexual desire or interest, and often when the subject of sex arises, sexual anorexics feel afraid or angry. Much like a food anorexic, a sexual anorexic refuses or rejects emotional and sensual experiences in a desperate attempt to keep chaotic feelings, anxiety, and trauma at bay.

Sexual anorexics, as I can personally testify, effectively starve themselves by denying the pleasure of relationships, of dating, of allowing a loving touch, and of the opportunity for a genuine connection with others. The possible rejection or humiliation is just too threatening, and whilst the loneliness of isolation is a continuous agony, it feels so much safer. I've had many platonic friendships, and I've not been a recluse. Far from it, the confidence I developed when I was Front of House Manager at the theatre encouraged me to be friendly and out going; I knew many people, and had a wide circle of friends, but very, very few were ever allowed to get close to me. If anyone tried, the shutters came down very forcefully. I learnt I had been sexually anorexic since puberty; in the sense that I avoided the possibility of either physical or sexual intimacy in any way. Other signs in my life that are common among sexual anorexics included:

- Feelings of shame and self-loathing during and after masturbation.
- Rigid, judgmental attitudes about sex. I feared that people, when sexually aroused, would undergo a change in their personalities, whereby they would become aggressive, selfish, and humiliating.
- Excessive fear about sexually transmitted disease. Linked with the above issue, I feared people could be so predatory that their animalistic desire for sex meant they might dupe or con me in this way. I had an HIV test at the beginning of my AA recovery, for peace of mind more than anything else, as I was terrified the ultimate legacy of the paedophiles might have been to have infected me in this way.
- Obsessive self-doubt about my ability to 'perform' sexually.

At the SLAA meetings I got to know the fellow members on a deeply emotional level, which was profoundly healing. The honesty within the group was inspirational, and made me realise that by sharing about even our very darkest, most painful experiences, we can also help someone else to heal. We allowed ourselves to be open about our innermost pain, and helped each other to grow. I spoke about as much as I could remember from the abuse. A typical share, in my first few meetings was along the lines of;

'I've been running away from intimacy all my life. The idea of sex terrifies me. My mind goes back to my childhood and I'm scared that if I allow a woman to touch me I'll be back in those toilets. When the flashbacks are triggered, it's so real and I can't stop re-living the abuse again and again. It all comes back, like an avalanche or a tidal wave of fear, disgust, rage.. I know I'm not alone, and that's really helps me. I know it passes, but afterwards I feel exhausted and want to hide away.'

I was encouraged by the more experienced members in SLAA that by facing my deepest fears about intimacy, and the actual act of sex itself, anorexics, like myself, can move forward and develop healthier, sustainable and rewarding relationships. Despite the emotional and psychological trauma I had experienced as a child, I had managed to half-convince myself that my lack of intimacy was perhaps due to my profound spirituality! I reasoned that monks somehow transcend the sexual urge as they develop their spiritual awareness. The reality was, of course, I was terrified to re-live the abuse. I could understand why I felt scared of being hurt, why I was so distrusting perhaps, but not why the idea of intimacy was so specifically overwhelming. I would rarely even allow someone to kiss me - especially on the lips, where I had an irrational fear I might suffocate.

It certainly wasn't all doom and gloom in the meetings. There were often moments of dry, stoic humour among us as we spoke openly about our thinking, and our behaviour. Whilst doing so we learnt to be more forgiving of ourselves, acknowledging where our boundaries needed to be, and how to avoid 'acting out', which had created so much more pain in our lives. For years my default position was to hide my feelings in a series of fantasy relationships with emotionally unavailable women. I think I knew subconsciously there was no risk of these relationships ever developing, so it was like enjoying the rehearsal knowing there's no pressure of a live performance. On those few occasions I did go on a date, I hid behind a very convincing mask of confidence; it's the natural actor in me, the chameleon who feels so much shame and fear that I would focus all my energy on trying to 'save' them, in the sense of trying to help them with their issues, and thereby avoid my pain. This wouldn't usually work as, if they were of a similar mind to me, they would also be running away and would not want to be 'saved'. There'd therefore be two people with avoidance strategies, which is hardly the recipe for a healthy relationship.

I got momentary pleasure from being considered physically attractive whenever a woman made it clear she liked me, but at the point I realised I had to do something about it, I would panic and shut down. I would then feel immense relief that I was now 'safe', and then feel self-loathing at my cowardice. I was convinced: "no one can hurt me if I don't let anyone close to me," and yet by running away I was becoming increasingly isolated. I remembered back to after the last time I had been abused, when I told myself 'I will never, ever, let anyone hurt me again'. I had kept to that solemn oath, made by a terrified ten year old boy, but was now finding it so difficult to let it go, in my adulthood.

I thought I was looking for a loving relationship, but I soon realised in SLAA I had been seeking infatuation and nothing more, hence my attraction to emotionally unavailable women. When I saw a woman and felt a sudden rush of adrenaline and excitement through my body (the 'going weak at the knees' scenario), I thought this was 'love'. In SLAA, I came to realise I had been acting out from a fear of abandonment. I was attracted to women who were truly unattainable but who intrigued me, in order to avoid developing a genuine opportunity for a relationship; I desperately feared I'd get hurt or be abandoned. As bizarre as it may sound, I found a negative attraction far, far more compelling and intriguing than a positive one as, at a subconscious level, it kept me 'safe'. Rather like my initial attraction to alcohol, I bought into the lie that these internal chemical reactions were a sign that she was 'the one', that she had the 'magical qualities' and being with her I would feel whole.

I was attracted to any woman who aroused this physiological reaction within me; it was a powerful aphrodisiac, which created an intrigue in my mind, and which I understood to be love. The longer I fantasised about these unavailable partners and kept the romantic intensity on the boil, the more I became neuro-biologically addicted to the feelings of excitement and danger I felt. If I met a woman who was genuine, friendly and fun company, but didn't feel these yearning, craving sensations, I thought it meant there was no possibility of love, and that she was probably boring. I associated these cravings with love.

I remember being utterly infatuated with one particular woman for several months in my late twenties. Every time I saw her I suddenly felt so alive. I never told anyone, and certainly didn't mention how I felt to her. It so happened that she and I had mutual friends, one of whom told me that this lady really liked me. The inner change immediately started to take place, and at a theatre party a few weeks later we were introduced, and I felt absolutely nothing. The fact she was potentially available made me shut down automatically. She looked amazing, she was great company, but there was no chemical reaction at all, (and without this physiological reaction there was no infatuation), so I lost all interest. Another time, I asked out another lady, to whom I was very much physically attracted; she had really turned me on whenever I saw her. Yet after a few dates, I became very bored and couldn't understand why I was no longer physically attracted to her. We got on really well, we shared similar values and the same approach to life, but I was not turned on anymore.

Becky was beautiful, intelligent, sexy, and popular, and whenever I saw her I felt intimidated. I had held a light for her since our school days, when we were aged fifteen, but I never had the courage to tell her that I really liked her. I didn't tell anyone. She was so far 'out of my league', that if anyone knew, they would laugh at me. I feared being humiliated for having the audacity to be attracted to her. After university, she moved away and developed a successful career, and once in a while her name would pop up in conversation with mutual friends, and I would feign mild interest to avoid any uncomfortable questions. Every Christmas, for several years, I desperately hoped we might see each other, as her parents still lived in the town. My 'ideal' Christmas Eve would be to bump into her and say a shy 'Hello, how are you?', but beyond that I dared not imagine any further conversation because the emotions I felt were too physically powerful; they frightened me. The rush of energy I felt through my body when I saw her I thought must be 'love', and this convinced me that she really 'was the one'. I felt quite shaky, light-headed and sometimes feared I might faint. At a subconscious level I was looking for the perfect woman; someone who was beautiful, successful, kind and loving, and with a sense of humour. Someone who would be a great Mum, and who would come into my life and somehow miraculously solve all my problems. I became convinced that Becky was 'the one'. Whilst the fantasy relationship felt wonderful, the reality of my fear and naivete with women and my low self-esteem would hit me and I would question myself again and again:

'Why would she ever agree to go out with me?'

I challenged this negativity, and used fantasy as a form of positive mental thinking. I'd imagine Becky and me in various scenarios enjoying each other's company (as loving parents, on holiday, dinner with friends etc..), so I'd be ready to psyche myself up and ask her out when the opportunity arose. Whenever I enjoyed success in my career, I secretly hoped she might somehow find out, and think well of me; I felt I needed material or professional success to be eligible in her eyes, to date me.

In the spring of 2009, a mutual friend told me Becky was moving back to town in a few weeks time. I felt really excited, but daunted at the same time. I hoped this might be the opportunity I'd been waiting for, and that we'd get to know each other again. I prayed for guidance; I really wanted to know if she really was the love of my life. Such was my fear of getting humiliated again (although I couldn't admit it to myself at the time, it is so obvious to me now that this infatuation was a desperate attempt to run away from the trauma of the abuse), I looked for clues in dreams and 'coincidences' which might help me feel more confident to ask her out, when I saw her next.

On one occasion, in September 2006, I was visiting John of God's healing centre in Brazil, and during meditation I had a vision in which Becky and I were on the opposite sides of a huge hedge which was part of an elaborate maze, like the one at Hampton Court. The hedge suddenly parted and we ran into each other's arms. I felt so alive and happy as we held each other, in the vision; I was convinced this was a positive sign. Another interesting coincidence was when the Royal Mail delivered a letter addressed to her mother to my letterbox, which was one of six letterboxes on the front door. To explain the bizarreness, her mother lived approximately a mile and a half from me, in the town centre! A few weeks after Becky moved back, I had lunch with a female friend called Kate.

'Are you going out with anyone at the moment?' she asked.

'No, I haven't been on a date for a while,' I replied, as I munched through my jacket potato...

'But an old school friend has recently moved back to town. I've always had a bit of thing for her, so I'm hoping we might meet up for coffee, and, well, I'm, I'm hoping something might happen.'

'Would I know her?', she asked.

'No, I doubt it. She moved away after university well over ten years ago now. You moved here, what, four years ago?'

'Yes, that's right. Now ... tell me about this mystery woman!' Kate replied. 'What's her name?' I replied 'Becky', to which she said 'Becky? And she's just moved back into town? Actually, I think I do know her!'

I was taken aback by her response, and tried to put it into some perspective,

'We live in a town of over 100,000 people; Becky moved away maybe fifteen years ago, and has only just moved back; you moved here four years ago. How could you know her?'

Kate asked me a few more questions, and it turned out they had lived in the same neighbourhood and frequented the same bar in a nearby city a few years earlier. It was the same girl. I took this to be another sign.

The most convincing sign, however, at least as far as I was concerned, was a sequence of events that took place in India in the Spring of 2006. I was flying between Chennai and Bangalore to visit Sai Baba's ashram in Puttaparthi, and during the flight I had a conversation with a man called Duncan who was sitting next to me. I had regularly had a number of 'out of body' experiences for some weeks previously, which had become disconcerting. Every time I closed my eyes I felt a sudden, powerful rush of energy leaving through my head and then I was above a beautiful valley somewhere. I could feel the freshness of the air, I could smell the trees; it was a very peaceful, serene place, but every time I went there I was always above, looking down into the valley. I never descended to the valley floor even though I sensed there was something very important there which I needed to learn. During my whole time in India, I had not mentioned these experiences to anyone.

Our conversation on the flight moved to meditation, and then our

Love Lost

mutual interest in Sai Baba. Duncan told me of his spiritual awakening with Sai Baba in 1985 and that he had, since that time, developed psychic abilities. He learnt towards me and said somewhat emphatically, 'You must go into the valley and talk with Sai Baba'!

'Wow', I replied, 'You really are psychic. I haven't told anyone about the valleys!'

Several weeks later I was trekking in the Himalayas near the border with Nepal; a stunning, challenging trek from Darjeeling to Rimbik via Sandakpur which, at 3636 metres, is the highest peak in the state of West Bengal.

There is an irresistible, mystical quality to the Himalayas, as far as I am concerned. It stimulates from deep within me a feeling of awe and wonder which is inspired by the powerful, physical presence of so many snowcapped mountain peaks, the differing shape and personality of the deep valleys, tropical jungles, glaciers, rivers, and rich mosaic of colours in its flowery meadows. If there is a physical heaven on earth, for me, it is the ancient Singalila forest and the tiny hamlet of Gurdum, which is a few hours trek from Sandakpur where I had been thrilled to enjoy stunning views of the magnificent Kangchenjunga which, at 8586m, is the third highest peak in the world.

Gurdum is one of the most beautifully picturesque and peaceful places I have ever visited. It seems to have been untouched for over a hundred years with its old fashioned wooden chalets and uninterrupted views of the valley and the Singalila forest below. There was no music, no mobiles ringing or people shouting into them, no airplanes; nothing but the delicate sounds of the birds playfully darting between the trees, and the animals of the forest below. I sat meditating with my eyes open, breathing in the freshness of the air, and looking at the hundreds of trees on the opposite side of the valley from my chalet; each had its own personality, its own particular shape and shade of green. It all felt so alive.

It was in Gurdum that I had two vivid dreams which were so real I felt I was actually there, in the dreams. In the first, I saw Sai Baba standing on the floor of a valley. He was smiling at me and said, 'In time, not yet', and then gestured to a woman a long way behind him. I could see it was Becky, looking so beautiful my heart exploded, and I remember saying in my dream, 'Thank you, thank you.' My understanding of the dream at that time was that this was a sign confirming Becky and I were meant to be together. It is clear to me now why it was important that I believed that to be absolutely true. The following night I had another lucid dream in which I could see a very large plant, with wide, shiny green leaves and very long roots, being pulled slowly out of the ground. I was not shown who was physically doing this, but I intuitively sensed a kind, loving presence was teaching me an important lesson. The roots were being stretched as the plant was pulled in its entirely from the earth, and at the place where the plant and the earth were finally joined, a very sharp, clean knife was used to sever all connection.

Then I heard a voice in the dream say, 'There is no way that God would ever hurt you.'

Looking back, and with the knowledge of what has since happened, my interpretation of first dream has changed. I thought it meant that Becky and I would definitely get together, but this did not happen. The dream helped me to believe that it really would happen, which encouraged me to take the risk and be willing to let her get close to me. When I realised this was not going to happen, I understood the second dream was to encourage me to realise that what might, at first sight, seem to be the worst possible outcome, actually has a deeper purpose, which I have since come to realise was absolutely necessary for my healing. The second dream released a deep seated belief that God had punished me in life. This false belief has been permanently cut away from my subconscious mind. It was a powerful lesson in the challenge, and the necessity, of letting go. At the moment when the knife is used, the roots are stretched to their very limit before the cut or letting go finally takes place. Both dreams served a definite purpose, and were experienced in order for a reason which became evident a few years later, and which I cover at the end of this chapter. When I returned home to the UK from India I felt refreshed and with renewed hope that I might finally have a relationship with someone I had liked for so long, even though in my heart I knew I didn't really know her.

A really exciting job opportunity came up shortly after I arrived home. The local authority had been awarded £1.8 million of funding over three years from the Arts Council of England to develop cultural opportunities for children and young people. I needed to get my teeth into something new and challenging; my work in the theatre had always been really important for me as I loved the variety it offered, and the structure it brought to my life, so this position was ideal for me. My role was to engage with local schools, youth centres, theatre groups and all possible settings that already worked with children and young people, and support them to develop a wide range of cultural projects with local creative artists, and a number of nationally recognised organisations including The Royal Shakespeare Company, National Portrait Gallery, National Trust, and Rambert Dance Company.

Becky and I kept bumping into each other, usually in the High Street or the local Marks and Spencer, and I practiced chatting her up as best I could, feeling all the time really self-conscious that she was out of my league... so I never went so far as to ask her out. In my mind, I was playing out the fantasy of us being together - happy, healthy, successful, and having three beautiful children.

'Hi Becky! How are you. It's really nice to see you. I like your jacket.' I would say, with my heart feeling like it would explode out of my chest.

'Hey, I'm good. It's so nice to see you as well. How's your week been?'

'Busy, lots going on. I'm working on a new project with the Arts Council which is really exciting.'

By this time, I needed to get away. Albeit very brief, this exchange was a major success for me at that time but, by now, I remember feeling overpowered by the physical anxiety, and my mind would become increasingly negative and fearful that I'd say something stupid, and she would be angry with me.

'Anyway, it's so lovely to see you again. Hope you have a great weekend.' And I'd escape quickly, and find a quiet, safe place to analyse in far too much detail what had just happened, and hope I didn't see her again for at least a few days as I felt much too intimidated to know what to say. My mind would be going at 300 hundred miles an hour trying to handle all the thoughts and fears that had been triggered by this brief encounter.

A few days later a mutual friend, one of only two I really trusted and therefore knew I really liked Becky, mentioned to me that they had spoken about me in a bar one evening, and my friend got the sense Becky felt something for me as well. My heart raced even faster. I decided to send her a card, to let her know I really liked her, and that I wanted to take her out for dinner one evening. Despite my nerves, I felt it was time to tell her that I really liked her; I hoped my directness would elicit a clear, unambiguous reply so I would know where I stood. I hated the uncertainty of not knowing what would happen next; it went back to the mind games the paedophiles used when they promised to let me go if I did what I was told, but then recanted and piled on even more pressure by claiming I was not trying hard enough. I traded in black and white; I found the grey areas confusing and intimidating. It was a control issue. I needed to know exactly what would happen next, so I could prepare myself for it.

It reminds me of the time, during my drinking, when I said to a friend, 'People who are overtly friendly scare the hell out of me far more than those who are openly hostile. At least with the latter you know you're going to be attacked; the other bastards keep you waiting.'

I wrote the card several times, and eventually decided on words I thought were honest, friendly but not heavy; whilst I didn't want to scare her off, I wanted her to know how much I liked her. A friend walked over as I was signing it and asked me,

'Birthday card? Anyone I know?' I told her an abbreviated version of what is was about;

'An old school friend has just moved back home, and I've always had a thing for her, but I've never actually told her. I think she knows, as we keep bumping into each other, and I do try and make it obvious... Anyway, I've decided to go for broke, and send her a card telling her how I feel.'

'Wow, good for you, I'm sure she'll love it. Do I know her?' she asked. I was alright until that second she asked if she knew her, because then the shame hit me and I felt intimidated that she would laugh at me if she actually knew her. I reluctantly said,

'Well, you might do. Her name is Becky.'

'Paul's sister? Yes, I know who she is. I'm not a close friend or anything, but I know who she is as I know Paul and their family a little bit.'

Relieved that she hadn't laughed at me, I asked her to read the card and let me know whether I'd got the right tone for the circumstances.

'It's really well written, Matt. It's open, friendly, honest about how you feel, but not OTT.' She then had a sip of her tea, and said, 'I think she'd love to receive a card like this.'

After another sip of tea, she continued,

'I saw her with a guy in town, the other day. I don't know her, as I said, so I don't whether they are together, but something wasn't right. I don't know. You may have a chance with her. She's a beautiful woman, but she looked so unhappy.'

Her reply was the final clincher, as far as I was concerned. I am not the type who gets involved with other people's relationships, but this convinced me that as long as I was open with my intentions, at least she would be made aware someone else really liked her. I posted the card. I expected either an immediate polite but negative response, or perhaps nothing at all. I felt there was a very slim chance of a positive reply. After two weeks of waiting, I had started to give up hope... until one Friday evening, I received a text,

'Thanks for your lovely card. Be great to have a catch up, but am really busy at the moment. I'll be in touch. Take care, talk soon.'

My heart exploded with joy, and then a huge amount of fear that I would have to let her possibly get close to me. She would then find out how completely screwed up I was. A few weeks of intermittent, friendly texting followed, and then she called me a couple of times and we agreed to meet for dinner the following Monday evening at a local restaurant. I had a mixture of excitement and visceral fear in the pit of my stomach as the evening approached. My mind built it up to be possibly one of the most important nights of my life, which did nothing to ease my nerves!

I arrived ten minutes early, and asked for a table by the window. She arrived on time, and looked so attractive as she walked into the restaurant. She always dressed with great style. That evening she was 'smart but casual' with black jeans, a black top, and short blonde hair. We kissed on the cheek, which felt nice. Despite my nervousness, it was a very pleasant evening. Our conversation flowed really smoothly as we recalled school days, spoke about mutual friends, our careers and current affairs. It was towards the end of the evening she mentioned her boyfriend. She said nothing negative about him, other than 'he has his issues like everyone else', but I knew this was an opportunity to tell her how much I liked her. I thought I knew what I wanted to say; I'd been rehearsing this moment in my mind for over twenty years. It was supposed to be something like, 'I do respect the fact you have a boyfriend. At the same time, I need to be honest with you and let you know I really do like you. I have done for ages now'.

But with her sitting in front of me, showing me photos of her cat asleep in daft positions, I was too scared and confused to say anything. I didn't know what to do. She had been friendly and engaging throughout the evening; I'd really enjoyed her company, but maybe, deep down, I knew I didn't really know her. I knew deep down that the incredibly positive experiences I'd dreamt us having together, over so many years, were a delusion. I felt as if I was existing in a no-mans land between a fading fantasy of the love of my life sitting in front of me, and the reality of a young woman whose company I'd enjoyed, who I found attractive, but perhaps nothing more. As we were leaving, she suddenly suggested we meet up again soon, which confused me even more.

'Mondays are good for me,' she said. I felt excited, I think, but didn't understand what this meant, and was too scared to ask, so I bluffed and said,

'That would be really nice. Shall we text each other in the week to arrange another time?'

She smiled and nodded, 'Yes, let's do that,' and we kissed on the cheek and left.

I was too caught up with myself to let her know how I felt. I also knew, deep down, that I didn't really know her, and neither did she know me... but she still intrigued me. I left the restaurant feeling downhearted and confused. I texted her the following day. 'Thanks for such a lovely evening. I really enjoyed our conversation and catching up on old times! Be great to meet up soon.' She was out of town for business and sent me a really friendly, positive reply later than evening. Neither of us followed up with any further texts. We spoke once on the telephone and I heard she had some personal issues so I backed off. I found myself trying desperately to keep the fantasy alive, but its hold was starting to weaken and the reality was slowly dawning on me. I questioned how I felt about everything. There was still a part of me that wanted to call her, text her and play the fantasy game, but that felt so horribly false now. I shared my emotional turmoil in SLAA, and these meetings gave me the strength to see the truth, for a short while at least (as I was not willing to let go quite yet);

'I'm beginning to see how I've gone from one fantasy to another all my life, to keep running away from myself, and my past. This feels the same lie as the drink. It's empty, hopeless but something keeps pulling me back for one more go – just as the drink did years ago. I'm slowly seeing how this fantasy, with this woman, needs to be smashed, for me to go deeper and heal properly. But the intrigue is so powerful.... I've written down the fantasy of how I thought I would feel, and the reality of what I felt when we met for dinner, and it's so obvious on paper that there's nothing there. It's not about her and me, it's about me with me.'

Other members shared back their similar experiences, and crucially their practical guidance which helped me to change my thinking. My friend Frank said,

'What's helped me, when I find a woman whom I don't know attractive, is to acknowledge the feelings I have, but then recognise I do not know her at all. She might be a very nice woman, but until I get to know her (if indeed she welcomes an approach), I cannot have an informed view of her. I stop the intrigue at its root immediately, so a fantasy cannot develop. I have to keep it real. It has really helped me to relax much more, and stay in the present moment.'

I knew at some level in my psyche that it was either / or if I admitted to myself the fantasy was a sham and a lie. I would have to face all the feelings I'd been running away from. In those moments of acknowledging the lie, I felt such immense pain being unearthed inside of me. I wasn't willing to face it yet; it terrified me.

A few months after we'd had dinner, I heard that Becky and her boyfriend were engaged and would be getting married the following year. I felt distraught. I decided to write and tell her that whilst I respected she was getting married, I regretted not telling her how much I was in love with her. I reasoned if I was honest and she rebuffed me (as I fully expected her to), I could then let go and move on. I told her I'd had a crush on her ever since we were teenagers, and that since she moved back home, my feelings had become even stronger. I remember writing the line, 'whenever I see you my heart melts and all the lights go on'.

I delivered the letter by hand and waited for a response, during which time I dreaded bumping into any mutual friends for fear of being ridiculed. I felt an anger deep within me (not towards her- I didn't think she'd done anything wrong), but particularly with a few mutual male friends even though nothing at all had happened to justify such an emotional reaction. It was the feelings of shame and rage from the childhood trauma being triggered off again.

After a few weeks without a reply, I still couldn't walk away. I composed a text message, saying I hoped she was okay, that I'd heard she had decided to get married to her partner, that I had accepted her decision, and I wished her well. I think I even said I'd always been there for her. Before sending it,

I prayed for a sign to show me it would be okay to send it. I didn't want to hurt anyone, and I didn't want to make a fool of myself. I was exhausted, and suddenly fell into a deep sleep still holding my mobile – with its unsent text. I awoke suddenly and saw a figure in white standing at the foot of my bed. I heard a voice clearly say 'you can send it', and later that morning I did. The figure had not promised I would like the reaction!

Becky's response was short, strong and straight to the point. I recoiled with shame and panic as I read it. I felt completely broken, but looking back now, what did I expect?

As I read the text I immediately felt a dirty and revolting energy throughout my body, and I went into shock. Not shock at being surprised by her reaction, but mental and physical shock as the PTSD was triggered off. I felt overwhelmed with shame, anger and fear which, for a while, poisoned everything; my view of life, my desire to live, and my attitude to people. I avoided as best I could anywhere I might see her, or any mutual friends who I thought would be talking about me. I knew this reaction was about the abuse; it was nothing to do with Becky. I had needed someone to serve as the catalyst to destroy the fantasy I'd been using to run away from my childhood. Subconsciously I'd hoped she would be the magical one who would make everything right – and the irony is that the pain and humiliation of the rejection helped shatter the false belief that someone else could save me. I had to take responsibility and be willing to talk about the deeper emotional trauma I'd been avoiding all my life. I needed to remember more about the abuse. My subconscious mind held the secrets my conscious mind now needed access to, so I could heal.

As soon as I received the text, I began having intrusive thoughts and imagery in my mind's eye of extreme violence against me from her male friends or associates. There was no basis in reality for any of these fears, but nonetheless I imagined myself being threatened in front of a group of people, and my losing it and smashing a bottle into someone's face for humiliating me, and then going on the run and being hunted down. I'd feel the rage in my stomach building up with this vision, and then, as the reality of committing such a dreadful act dawned on me, I'd feel scared by the power of my rage.

Whilst I never acted on these thoughts, I knew I was retreating further within myself to a place where no one could hurt me. I distrusted people

'Hello..... are you okay?'

I couldn't understand what she said at first, she was hysterical and smelt of alcohol, but after a few attempts she managed to say,

'They've taken my two kids away from me. I'm never going to see them again. They won't let me, I've tried to hold it together, but I can't....' She became more agitated as she spoke, and kept looking down at the concrete below, which really alarmed me.

'I can't live without them, there's no point anymore.'

I asked: 'What exactly have social services told you? Are you sure this is not a temporary thing so you can get some help for yourself?'

She replied, 'they told me I had to stop the drinking and 'using', but I've tried so many times, I don't know how to. I can't handle life without it. I was... I was abused sexually when I was a kid, and it all comes back when I try and stop drinking. I can't live with it, it's too painful. But they've said I have to stop if I want to see my kids again.'

Throughout everything she said, she kept looking down to the tarmac beneath her, and I knew her trauma had triggered the PTSD. I felt myself going into a deeper sense of shock as the seconds and minutes of our time together ticked on. I decided nevertheless, despite my own shock, to tell her my story.

'You may not believe me, but we've got a lot in common. I'm an alcoholic, and I used to drink aftershave when I had the shakes. I stole to get drink, I've had black outs. At the beginning I loved the buzz it gave me, but then it destroyed me. I hated the person I became. I eventually went to AA. That's how I stopped drinking.'

She finally pulled her eyes away from the tarmac below, and stared at me. 'But you don't look like an alcoholic! How long has it been since you had a drink?'

'It's been a long time, it's about eighteen years now. I stopped when I was really young.'

'Oh my God'.

'I drank to block out all the pain from the times I was abused. I was raped several times when I was about nine and ten years old, and for a while booze took it all away. But no more, it doesn't work anymore, does it? I used to punch myself in the face, shout at myself in the mirror 'you fucking c*nt..'. I really hated myself. It's different now, it takes time, but it is worth it.'

She looked really shocked as she listened to me. Her one hand remained holding onto the railing, but her body had moved slightly closer to the railings. At least she was not leaning away from them and looking at the car park as she spoke to me.

'I've never told anyone I was raped as a child. I didn't think anyone would believe me. I hate myself, I get into a frenzy and start cutting myself'. She showed me the blooded bandages around her wrists. 'I feel so dirty and disgusted with myself.'

'So did I,' I replied. 'I felt like I had fungus under my skin. I never told anyone either, for many years, I was so ashamed. But it's time to talk, for you to heal. There are plenty of good women who have been through exactly what you've been through, and can help you.'

'Are there? Really?', she asked, and for the first time with a hint of hope in her voice.

I asked her, 'what are the chances of you and I meeting like this, here on this bridge? We have so much in common. What are the chances of this happening? It's unbelievable isn't it?'

She agreed, and stayed silent for a few moments.

'I can't promise you anything about your children, but I know a number of mums who have got clean and sober, and have got their kids back. They were convinced it would never happen, but you've got to get sober first. And you're not alone. It's really important to know that. There is help out there; I know, I've had it.'

At that moment, an AA (Automobile Association) recovery van slowed down as it was passing over the bridge and the driver gestured with his mobile, and I knew he would call the police. The woman and I continued talking about how we felt, how the drink and drugs didn't work for either of us anymore, and how scary the idea of being clean and sober was. By now, she was standing with both hands on the railings facing me, and though still clearly traumatised, she had not leant away or looked down for a while. Throughout our conversation I had not moved at all. I sensed I would only do this if she moved away from me. Whilst I feared any sudden move on my part might preempt her jumping, I needed to be close enough to try and grab her if I could.

After a few more minutes, I noticed that both sides of the bridge had been closed by the police. A police car suddenly pulled up, two officers jumped out, walked over to us, and pulled her over the railings. She sat in the back of the police car looking dazed and confused, as if she was trying to take in everything that had just happened. Standing next to her outside the car, I felt exactly the same way. She looked up and asked me,

'What do I do now?'

'Go to AA meetings, get the professional help you need. Talk to the women, and allow them to help you. You are not alone, however much you feel you are. I promise you, you are not. It has worked for me, it can definitely work for you.'

She then asked me my name. 'Matt', I replied. 'Thank you,' she said, with a very weak smile. She was clearly in shock, and looked so scared.

I felt such hope when she asked me my name. Something in me told me she had some hope, and with this I sensed she would get sober. I think of her quite often and hope that she is indeed sober, and her children are with her. I spoke with my AA sponsor about this incident later that evening.

'I met her very briefly,' he said. 'She came to church this morning and a few of us tried to help her, but she was so distraught she ran away.' I subsequently learned from a sponsee that she had gone to the lunchtime AA meeting, and he and his girlfriend had both offered support. The day after the incident on the bridge, I had met with another sponsee, who is a professional working in the field of addiction; he had taken her to a treatment facility for detox and therapy that morning.

As I hoped I had helped her in some way, she really helped me. I realised that, in spite of the chaos in her life, she was being more honest about her trauma than I was about mine. Her agony was in full view whilst I was still desperately suppressing my deepest pain. I needed to find the courage to go inside myself, and talk with others about everything I was running away from. Since meeting her, though, the PTSD symptoms had been triggered off with more venom and aggression than I had experienced since I was in my late teens. I went into physical shock; I felt as if my body had been run over, and the visual flashbacks became a regular thing, which in turn caused sleepless nights, and a deep depression. I was standing on a figurative bridge, looking down into an abyss. There was now a visceral, existential pain in me which I now recognise as my final barrier, behind which the suppressed memories were hidden, and these were being ripped away from my subconscious mind and the truth of my childhood was starting to become more real to me.

A week after talking with the girl on the bridge, I was sitting on a train on my way to speak at an AA meeting. The feelings of shame and fear were such that I could feel energy moving physically within me, which scared me; I felt an internal rearrangement was taking place, of which I had no control over. Trauma, which had been locked inside my body since I was a child, was finally shifting, and I felt a sense of bewilderment and shock. My arms and legs would sometimes jerk involuntarily, and I felt deep pain in the pit of my stomach...and a sensation that my heart was broken. Not in any romantic sense, but because the full impact of the abuse was being physically manifested in my body.

During the autumn of 2012 I felt a significant change taking place within me. It was as if the thick concrete of the PTSD had been smashed into smaller pieces and I was at last allowing the suppressed energy, that felt so powerful and that had been pushing from underneath with such strength that it scared me, to finally be able to force its way through the cracks.

With hindsight, the rejection from Becky and talking to the suicidal lady on the bridge were two of the hammers I absolutely needed to help smash the 'protective' wall behind which the trauma was buried; this in turn enabled a much deeper healing to take place. Looking back, it was as if the shame and anger locked up in the PTSD were the cement and bricks holding the wall together, and that Becky's rejection worked like an electricity bolt flashing through the cracks in the wall of the PTSD. By later feeling the trauma of the suicidal lady I was able to connect to my trauma, buried deep within my subconscious, and which I had been running away from all my life.

However, it took another three years before the memories of the abuse would finally come up in enough detail for me to talk about what had happened, and to heal. I needed a few more hammer blows to the 'protective' seal. Only then could the rage, shame, guilt, and confusion finally be released. These blows were essential to my finding an inner peace. (I'm hugely grateful for all these challenges, although I certainly didn't feel anything like gratitude at the time).

Reaching out for help through the SLAA programme was essential for my overall recovery; it made me realise that in this specific area of my life I was not alone, and this strengthened my resolve to seek the professional help I also needed to deal with the memories that had been triggered. As I began to open up a little more, the need to act out in fantasy began to gradually decrease. I had always found myself attracted to emotionally unavailable women, but I now recognised the futility of this, and started to follow some very practical suggestions to help me change my thinking and behaviour. For instance, whenever I am attracted to a woman, it helps me greatly to;

- Acknowledge to myself and to a friend whether I am seeking the emotional high of a fantasy romance or a trusting, honest, loving relationship.
- Keep it real. Accept that whilst I am physically attracted, I do not actually know her. Go beyond the physical attraction. If the circumstances are appropriate, get to know who she really is.
- Accept that it often takes time to develop a friendship, which must come before any relationship might develop.
- Be wary of wanting to 'save' or change anyone else, especially if I find them physically attractive.
- Learn from the pain of my past, and remain vigilant that the intrigue and fantasy does not creep back into my thinking.

A friend once asked me what it was about Becky that first intrigued me. I thought about it for a few moments and then recalled a couple of experiences when I was drinking. I was walking past a group of six guys (including a few I'd had a fight with as described in *The Centre of Attention* chapter), and they started jostling and threatening me;

'Here he is. Alright tosser? You're going down tonight. We haven't finished yet. We'll see you later, sunshine....'

Becky happened to be standing close to them, and on hearing this she walked directly over to me, smiled, and asked me if I was okay. I replied, 'Yes', and she said, 'Are you sure?'.

Another time, I'd been drinking all day and after last orders I staggered to an all night party in the woods near the town. As I was throwing up by a tree, she came over and asked a friend if I was okay. Besides finding her very attractive, I think it was those two brief moments of kindness that triggered off a twenty year fantasy.

Alongside my regular AA meetings, I continued attending both a weekly SLAA meeting, so I could talk through in some depth the abandonment issues, and my fear of intimacy. I had first, however, to confront my own 'long dark night of the soul', and this would eventually happen during the Spring of 2016. As the saying I'd heard in AA goes, 'we can bury our demons but we bury them alive'. Looking back, I do believe that these spiritual experiences (the combination of the fantasy with Becky being smashed and meeting the suicidal woman on the bridge) were to guide me to this emotional rock bottom. I needed the fantasy to be shattered for the core trauma to be revealed.

In September 2011, the Arts Council contract was suddenly terminated by the then Chancellor of the Exchequer, George Osborne, and so I was at a loose end. I yearned that I would connect to a power greater than myself, to escape from my hometown, and receive the healing I needed along my journey. It was with this mental and emotional background that I decided to fulfil a lifelong ambition, and walk the Camino to Santiago de Compostela.

10

THE WAY TO SANTIAGO

Once you realize that the road is the goal and that you are always on the road, not to reach a goal, but to enjoy its beauty and its wisdom, life ceases to be a task and becomes natural and simple, in itself an ecstasy.[30]
Sri Nisargadatta Maharaj

Despite the turmoil in my private life, my professional life was thriving. But then something happened... I had loved every minute working on the Arts Council funded programme with my colleagues Simon, Jason and Amanda. Between September 2008 and August 2011, we supported over 200 cultural projects and involved more than 40,000 children and young people.

We collaborated with nationally recognised organisations, including the Royal Shakespeare Company, Welsh National Opera, National Portrait Gallery, London College of Fashion, and engaged with many local professional creatives; writers, actors, producers, and musicians. The projects we funded included many that were devised and managed by young people themselves, with the adults acting as facilitators, and they involved a wide range of genres from dance, music, drama, poetry, heritage, museums, to media/digital art and film, podcasting and pervasive media, and the built and natural environment. The programme had certainly been inspiring for

---

[30] Maurice Frydman, trans., *I Am That: Talks with Sri Nisargadatta Maharaj* (The Acorn Press, 2015). Chapter 83.

me; it had offered the opportunity to co-create and manage a wide variety of multimedia, creative projects and to make so many new contacts within the industry. We were devastated when the newly elected Conservative / Liberal Democrat coalition government decided to shut the national programme down due to their austerity drive. We had been forewarned to budget for a 20% cut in funding; as a precaution we planned for 30% and 50% cuts, so it was a shock when the Chancellor of the Exchequer stood up in the House of Commons on the 17th June 2010 and closed the whole programme down, effectively sacking us on the spot! We had a number of existing contracts to be honoured, and so the programme eventually closed in August 2011.

Out of work and with nothing in the pipeline, I decided to fulfil a long-held ambition and walk the Camino to Santiago de Compostela. The Camino is a series of pilgrimage routes, the most popular being the Camino Frances which stretches from St Jean Pied de Port in the French Pyrenees across Northern Spain to the shrine of the evangelical apostle St. James the Great in the Cathedral of Santiago de Compostela.

The Camino has been walked by millions of people for over 1200 years, including St. Francis of Assisi, King Ferdinand and Queen Isabella of Spain, the moral philosopher Dante and the English poet Chaucer, author of *The Canterbury Tales*. In recent years, the numbers walking the Camino has grown dramatically, not least because it has caught the imagination of writers and film makers, the most notable book being Paulo Coello's international bestseller *The Pilgrim* published in 1986; and *The Way*, released in 2010, starring Martin Sheen and Emilio Estevez. For many pilgrims, walking the Camino is a very personal religious or spiritual experience; for some it is to find clarity regarding a life issue; whilst for others it is the physical challenge to walk 500 miles. My purpose was very clear to me; it was first and foremost to be, as clichéd as it sounds, an inner journey; that of the soul.

I had been inspired reading Shirley MacLaine's book *The Camino*,[31] in which the celebrated actress describes not only the considerable physical challenges of her journey, but more significantly for me, her remarkable spiritual experiences of visions of her past lives stretching back to the origin of the universe. I had also read somewhere that the path of the Camino

---

[31] Shirley MacLaine. *The Camino* (Pocket Books, 2001)

Frances lies directly under the Milky Way and that it reflects the energy of the star systems above it. The incurable romantic in me loved the idea of this profound cosmic connection!

The physical challenge to walk 500 miles appealed to the sense of adventure in me. I loved the outdoors and the beauty of nature; the sights, smells and touch of nature is, in itself, a spiritual experience for me. Being in the countryside has always helped me come out of myself. On those occasions when I let go of my 'monkey mind' (my mind would jump around from thought to thought like a monkey jumps from branch to branch) and truly live in the moment, I feel connected to the miracle of consciousness, and feel a deep inner peace. When these magical moments happen, they remind me that I, too, am an intrinsic part of the cosmos. There is in truth no separation, and having that knowingness is so empowering. It reminds me of my spiritual awakening at Vivekananda's Rock in South India almost twenty years earlier.

For several years during the summer months, when I had finished work for the day, I would leave the theatre and walk along the beach and watch the glorious sunsets over the sea; I love connecting with nature. I felt, during those moments, a tremendous feeling of peace within me as I watched the tide breaking gently on the beach, and the light of the fading sun glistening over the water; it is a conscious connection to something more powerful than myself. It works the same way as an AA meeting often does; meetings help me to clean my filter on life, gain a greater mental clarity on issues, and gain a healthier perspective.

After the emotional turmoil of the previous year, I needed the space to let go of the baggage I'd been carrying, and find an inner peace, and a new sense of direction for my life. The AA 12 Step programme encourages me to be honest with my emotions, so I made a list of my fears to help acknowledge and process them. Most were thankfully only fleeting, and the acceptance that they existed helped me to let them go.

My fears were...the physical proximity to others in the dormitories and toilets; not finding a bed for the night; dirty mattresses and bed bugs; talking in my sleep; not attending AA meetings for a while; loud snorers; blisters; getting lost; wild dogs; and the limited menu available in rural Spain for a fish-eating vegetarian.

I also listed my hopes and intentions; what was I was looking forward to? What did I hope would happen? ... the opportunity to understand the emotions I had been feeling during the past year, and to find a deeper feeling of acceptance, and a greater feeling of inner peace; experience the healing energy of nature; live in the present moment, rather than replay the past or project the future; feel the terrific sense of freedom and adventure to explore a countryside and a history I didn't know; meet kindred spirits from all over the world; and find the love of my life!

I wanted to make the very most of the opportunity in front of me. I meditated and asked for inner guidance, and had a strong feeling that I needed to have a regular spiritual practice. Prayer and meditation had always helped me feel a deeper connection to my Higher Self, and consequently I find I can manage the PTSD symptoms more effectively. The problem was, I was often too lazy to maintain the meditation on a daily basis, especially when the memories of the abuse had been triggered and I would feel overwhelmed with anxiety, irrational fears and often insecurity about my personal safety.

When I started to prepare for the Camino during July 2011, by reading online articles and travel blogs, I decided It made sense to follow a few simple spiritual practices;

1. Breathing Meditation

Rather than rush the physical journey, I wanted to relax and be fully aware and appreciative of the world around me. My mind went back to when Dr Ron Hutchinson taught me the concentration techniques in his garden, shortly after I had been diagnosed with PTSD. These helped me focus on the physical world around me rather than the drama in my mind. This would help me as a forerunner to a simple breathing meditation, if the PTSD was triggered. I made a mental note to start each day with a brief prayer, and a breathing meditation so I could be 'present' as much as possible, and allow the mind to become still. I particularly like Mahatma Gandhi's prayer for peace, as it is a prayer of offering from within myself.

I offer you peace.
I offer you love.
I offer you friendship.

The Way to Santiago

I see your beauty.
I hear your need.
I feel your feelings.
My wisdom flows from the highest Source.
I salute that Source in you.
Let us work together. For unity and peace.
Mahatma Gandhi

Whenever I had maintained a daily meditation in the past, I had experienced an inner silence which, though very fleeting when I had begun meditating years earlier, in time had helped me with my healing. When it really clicks, I feel awake, free of thoughts, fears, hopes or expectations. I am present; there is no past or future. I can just BE. I have lived two extremes in my life; I am blessed to have experienced a profound inner peace on many occasions through meditation, yet also lived with the symptoms of PTSD for over thirty years.

2. Write a daily journal and a gratitude list. (When I joined AA my sponsor encouraged me to write a gratitude list each day. This simple practice has definitely helped me develop a much more positive outlook on my life).

3. Listen to my body, and respect its needs.

In AA we refer to this as HALT; Hungry, Angry, Lonely, Tired, and we use this acronym as a guide to help us maintain our physical, emotional and spiritual wellbeing. I decided to practice a visualisation meditation which had been popular in the meditation and healing groups I had been running for the last seven years. Known as the light meditation, it can take various forms, but I would visualise in my mind's eye a powerful golden light entering through the top of my head and moving very slowly and gently through my body, healing each part of my body in turn; I would consciously release any tension, and thereby create a deeper feeling of relaxation within me. I would focus on the words 'Peace, Love, Gentleness, and Joy', and with each breath, I would hear a beautiful voice invoking these emotions.

4. Connect with fellow pilgrims and local people.

I looked forward to meeting kindred spirits along the way, and to hear their stories, their hopes and their dreams. From my experience of the AA Fellowship my fellow pilgrims would, I fully expected, play an important role in my inner and outer journey. With my emotional and spiritual needs considered, I called an AA friend, who had served in the Special Forces, for his guidance regarding the practical things like walking boots, rucksack, sleeping bag and everything else I would need for the journey.

The list was comprehensive and somehow, after several attempts, I managed to squeeze into my rucksack: zipable waterproof long trousers, shorts, two t-shirts, two shirts (light weight, quick drying), two pairs of socks, one lightweight, squashable sleeping bag, two pairs underwear, poncho, fleece, sandals, pain-killers, sunscreen and sunglasses, hat, toiletries, travel towel, mobile phone and charger, camera and charger, earplugs, and a small torch. I also took needle and thread for blisters. There is a risk of infection (although I've never had a problem), but I've found it a direct way to deal with blisters when I'm on a trek. You pierce a threaded needle through one side of the blister and push it the through the other side, so that only thread remains in the blister. Then, cut the thread so that there's some thread on either side. The liquid will drain out slowly, allowing time for the new skin to harden underneath.

Apart from two walking sticks, which I decided to buy in France, I was ready to go. Those two simple sticks of wood proved to be my sturdy, reliable companions throughout!

At the end of August 2011, I flew into Biarritz, and after a few hours exploring the elegant seaside resort I took a bus to Bayonne and then a train through the beautiful mountains and ancient forests to St Jean Pied de Port, fifty kilometres south of Bayonne, where the Camino Frances traditionally begins. Nestled at the foot of the French Pyrenees, St Jean Pied de Port is a small picture postcard Basque town with steep, narrow cobbled streets and many albergues (also referred to as refugios, or hostels), hotels and guest houses for the 250,000 plus pilgrims, from all over the world, who walk this route each year. I arrived in the late afternoon feeling both excited and daunted by the reality of what was about to start the following morning. Tomorrow morning at 6.30am, I really was going to start a 500 mile walk to

Santiago, in all weathers, come what may.

I walked into the Municipal Office on La Rue de la Citadelle to receive my Pilgrim Passport and to book into the municipal hostel. The system of pilgrim hostels is a unique feature of the Camino, especially the Camino Francés. There are over 300 alberques along the Camino Francés, and for €3 - 10 per night pilgrims share sleeping quarters, usually on bunk beds in mixed-gender dormitories, and many provide a shared meal, basic washing facilities, and most importantly the opportunity to connect with people from all over the world. Staying in an alberque offers each pilgrim the unique experience of being right in the heart of the pilgrim community, and it was here on my first night I met fellow pilgrims with whom I was privileged to share so many wonderful hours of conversation along the way. They were Warren (United States), Lucy and Paul (Germany), Darren and Sam (Sunderland, UK), and Olla (Poland). After introductions, we all decided to take a walk through the old town and then have dinner together.

I felt a tremendous sense of history in the town; I thought of the millions of pilgrims who had walked this way over the centuries. I spoke with my newfound friends about this over dinner, and it was clear that we all felt a powerful spiritual energy no doubt created by the ancient pilgrims, a spirit which had been revitalised each day for over 1200 years by all those who were, like ourselves, quite literally following in their footsteps.

The first day of the trail from St Jean to Roncesvalles passes over the rugged and beautiful Pyrenees Mountains. As we left St Jean Pied de Port, we climbed through the mountains where the views were stunning. As we went higher and higher, we could see for miles; looking up, there were eagles soaring above us, and looking down, in the distance, there was low lying mist and a dense, silent forest in the valley below.

Over the next few weeks, on my hike along the Camino I would pass through gorgeous orchards and vast vineyards, across open plains, at times alongside busy highways, and then I would weave my way through small villages, towns and even cities such as Pamplona, Burgos and Leon. Pamplona was of particular significance to me. During my teens I had been fascinated with the famous drunks of yesteryear; actors such as John Barrymore, Errol Flynn, and James Dean; and the writers James Joyce, William Faulkner and Ernest Hemingway.

Hemingway had first visited Pamplona in 1923, arriving at the height of

Los Sanfermines; the (in)famous running of the bulls festival. His first experience of the festival, together with the city, its people and traditions made such an impression on him that he returned a further eight times and made Pamplona the backdrop to his semi-autobiographical novel, *The Sun Also Rises*. Hemingway's alcoholism had fascinated me when I too was drinking so desperately. I felt he was a comrade in arms, and I could strongly identify with the novel's themes of aimlessness, insecurity, sexual jealousy, and drunkenness. With James Dean, I had felt a similar affinity; the 'live fast, die young, and leave a beautiful corpse' attitude, often attributed to Dean, felt like a mantra during my late teens as I descended into alcoholism and depression.

 The challenge along the way, though, was to share my space with my fellow pilgrims. The snorers in the dormitories were the greatest irritation and threat to my sleep and sanity. I could accept the early starts and walking long distances in all weathers; I could forgive myself for getting terribly lost on a number of occasions; I even learnt to walk with blisters without moaning too much; but nothing prepares one trying to get a good night's sleep with what sounds like wild animals mating in the surrounding bunks. The inconveniences and annoyances of the dorms gave me many opportunities to practice patience, tolerance and detachment, but it was a good set of ear phones and Pink Floyd usually did the trick.

 After a few days' walking, I noticed how well organised some pilgrims were. They might be best described as 'professional walkers'. They may have had limited time to walk the Camino, and they always seemed to have the bunk bed nearest the exit; and they would typically be the first to bed; they had ear plugs and eye covers; they would be up as early as possible (5.00am) and would look rather like miners, with lights strapped to their foreheads as they packed their rucksacks and escaped into the darkness outside.

 Whilst these early risers would be almost guaranteed a bed each night, my typical day was to get up at 7.00am, risking a later start, with less assurance of a place to sleep at the next alberque (despite the large number of fellow pilgrims I always found a bed). After washing, dressing, packing and re-packing my rucksack several times to squeeze everything in, I would be on the road by 7.45am. Despite the urge sometimes to join them, I decided not to rush my journey. My default position, since childhood, was to 'win' for the sake of winning, for the buzz of coming first, ... to be ahead of the game, so to speak. I had to remind myself that pilgrims have walked the Camino for over 1200 years, so I needed to let go of any notion of a competition and focus on relaxing and deepening my connection to the natural beauty around me, and to connect with the innate wisdom within me (and, I believe, that of everyone else) which all too often lay hidden behind my fantasies and fears. I wanted to let go of all limitations in my mind so I could be entirely free.

Had I rushed the journey I might have missed the many acts of kindness and selfless love between pilgrims, not only when walking but often during the evenings at the alberques. I was moved to see pilgrims offering a listening ear to a fellow pilgrim who was obviously physically and emotionally exhausted from the journey; another time I witnessed someone treating a stranger who had severe blisters, and afterwards gently and lovingly washing their feet, which reminded me of the story of Jesus washing the feet of the disciples. One afternoon, I came across a group of four chaps who were cheerfully carrying an older man up a mountainside in a human sedan chair after he had badly twisted his ankle. They carried him all the way to the next refugio, some six kilometres away, and were singing as they went! Then there was Olla from Poland, who had injured her foot but battled on bravely through the pain. For the best part of a week, a few of us slowed down and walked with her until she had fully recovered.

Another time I came across three of the most jovial and quick-witted Irish guys you could ever wish to meet; they had only two weeks' holiday from work to walk the 500 miles, so to make sure they did not lose any time they had decided to sleep outdoors, in all weathers, all the way to Santiago. You come across many people with remarkable stories to tell along the way. Anna's was certainly the most spontaneous I've ever heard. She had suddenly decided over breakfast, in her home in Vienna, to walk the Camino again. She made her sandwiches, filled a bottle of water, dusted off her walking boots, grabbed her bank cards and some cash, sleeping bag and passport - and left her very comfortable Viennese suburban life, and started the long, long walk to Santiago; over 1600 miles!

She told me she had missed the wonderful sense of freedom it had always brought her. Anna was, in fact, following an ancient tradition; as with most pilgrimages, her Camino began at home and ended at the cathedral in

Santiago de Compostela.

Though I enjoyed exploring the small villages, historic cathedrals and getting to know my fellow pilgrims along the way, after a while I felt the need for solitude. Between Burgos and Astorga, the Camino passes through the Meseta (the flat, mostly barren plateau of central Spain, which stretches for over 200 kilometres), most of which I walked alone. I had been warned to carry plenty of water as the temperature on the plains can reach 34 degrees centigrade. This in itself was not a concern, but there is very little shade and some sections of the meseta have few villages for rest and refills.

Walking on my own was initially a very lonely exercise, but after a day or so I started to feel a deep connection with the landscape. There was less of a sense of separation than before; where I had seen space and felt within me a vast emptiness, I now saw the creative beauty of nature, which developed more and more the further I walked. I felt I was an intrinsic part of what I could see, and there was a profound and calming awareness that everything was connected. As the wave is to the ocean, so too was 'I' to the forest beneath, beside and above me. At its most basic level, energetically, there was a sense of wholeness, a feeling of wonder at the miracle of consciousness. The following statement, from the Chandogya Upanishad, describes this experience in far more eloquent terms that I can.

> *As the rivers flowing east and west*
> *Merge in the sea and become one with it,*
> *Forgetting they were ever separate rivers,*
> *So do all creatures lose their separateness*
> *When they merge at last into pure Being.*[32]
> Chhandogya Upanishad. 10:1-2

The fact that I didn't know where I was going opened up a wonderful feeling of freedom, and a childlike sense of adventure and curiosity within me. It was during this part of the Camino that I had several very powerful, emotional dreams. Whilst I knew my fears were largely irrational, they still felt very real to me. I felt an overwhelming sense of panic and tension

---

[32] Swami Krishnananda, *The Chhandogya Upanishad* (Divine Life Society, 2004)

throughout my body whenever I thought of dating and intimacy. I hadn't realised how much shame was within me, and how toxic it was in my relationship with myself and in my relationships with others, and particularly with women. I wanted acceptance and approval from women (especially women I was sexually attracted to), and yet I would immediately suppress these feelings whenever the shame was triggered.

The shame of being abused as a child had destroyed any confidence I had in myself; I felt 'less than', and could not understand why any woman might like me. I thought there must be something wrong with them! My mind would project incidents where I would be threatened and humiliated by the male friends, brothers and fathers of any woman I found attractive, and had asked out. I would see, in my mind's eye, mocked up images of men ridiculing and laughing me, and women looking shocked (in the sense they knew they were way out of my league, and it was almost insulting that I had even asked them out) when they realised I liked them.

It isn't anything any woman has actually done to me; they just trigger off the shame I was already holding within me. With the women I admired during my teenage years and into my twenties, once I realised I liked them, I would avoid talking to mutual friends, as they were, in some way, 'tainted' or a potential threat to me. When I see a woman I knew during my teens, my immediate, instinctive reaction until recently was to recoil from talking unless I really had to.

Something in my subconscious mind fears being ridiculed and threatened, but my conscious mind knows this is so unlikely to happen. My dream world was helping me to accept this positive reality, and to let go and heal. Each one was a variation on a theme being played out each night, teaching me. I always saw myself, in each dream, as a very shy, nervous teenager desperately wanting to communicate with the girls I really liked, but was too ashamed to say hello them. In the dream, the girls would be genuinely kind and friendly to me. In one, I was in a hallway at a house party, and feeling intimidated about saying hello to a girl in the next room. I decided to quietly leave through the backdoor, and as I walked past an open doorway, the girl I liked recognised me, and said,

'Hey, how are you? It's so lovely to see you. I've been meaning to ask you about a show I want to see at the theatre?'

And then the dream fast-forwards to me sitting on a sofa, with her and her two friends, and I am clearly feeling relaxed and enjoying their company. I have told a joke, they are laughing, and the one girl I particularly like leans closely to me, and says,

'You know, I didn't want to come this evening. I almost talked myself out of it, but it's great now I'm here with you guys...I'm glad I gave myself a kick up the bum, and came.'

In another dream, I am fifteen years old, and walking along the street towards the town centre, and I see some girls I like in a car driving past. I want to wave and say hello but I am too scared by what I anticipate will be their reaction, so I don't. I pretend I haven't seen the car. Then, a minute later the car has turned around, and is coming towards me. As it approaches it slows down and pulls up next to me. The door is opened, and I see the welcoming, smiling faces of the girls I really like leaning over in my direction, as I bend down to speak. One of them jumps out, hugs me and says,

'Hey! We thought it was you. Jump in, are you going into town as well? Come and join us for a coffee.'

After experiencing these dreams I woke up with tears in my eyes the following morning. In the dreams I had experienced what I had deeply craved for all my life; to openly accept and to enjoy the attention of a women I am sexually attracted to without the PTSD being triggered off.

I also dreamt of my father as a young man doing his National Service in Hong Kong. When he spoke to me, in the dream, I intuitively sensed he was speaking from his highest self (or his highest level of consciousness), and that he consequently knew about everything that had happened to me as a child. With this perspective in mind, it was a very powerful healing dream for me.

'I'm so proud of everything you have been, and everything you are, achieving with your life.'

These words were said with such an openness of heart, I remember feeling very emotional as I dreamt it. In real life, my father has a quiet integrity about him. He had what you might call a Victorian upbringing to some degree, and so is not given to grand emotional statements. In the dream I sensed he was saying what he actually wanted to say to me in real life, and it was this awareness that made me feel so much closer to him. I told him I loved him and that despite anger towards him during my teenage years we had developed a really good relationship, which he agreed was the case. The dreams highlighted a core fear I realised I had been carrying since I was a teenager - I desperately did not want to become a sad, lonely, single old man. This was in itself an awakening; I knew I needed to go deeper and talk about the abuse again (with a professional trauma therapist) to release this shame and rage, if I was to ever have a chance of a relationship, marriage and a family.

Whilst I could intellectually challenge these thoughts, the energy within them, from the abuse, was so powerful I would feel exhausted; and it seemed so much easier to pretend I wasn't interested in whomever I was attracted to, than to work through the trauma. I was evidently not yet ready and willing to feel the rage within me and to get the professional help I needed. In truth, the specific fear was this: if I felt the such intensity from my rage and shame, what would I be capable of doing, who would I become, and to what lengths would I go to seek retribution? I buried these thoughts as quickly as they came.

Deep down, I knew I had to go deeper, if I was to ever realise my dream: I wanted to allow myself to be emotionally and sexually intimate with a woman I loved, and one who I accepted loved me, and to embrace and enjoy it. One morning, whilst walking alone through a beautifully peaceful wood on the Camino, an inner voice spoke to me;

"You can leave everything you do not want here."

I mentally asked for the following to be removed:

- The shame and fear from my childhood
- The anger and rage I was carrying
- The frustrations I felt in my personal life

The philosopher Jean-Paul Sartre so accurately described the physiological effect of shame as 'an immediate shudder which runs through me from head to foot without any discursive preparation.' For most of my life, every time I saw a woman I found physically attractive, I would immediately experience this reaction, which crippled my ability to talk with them.

I walked into the small village of Ages just after lunchtime one afternoon, and was welcomed with a friendly smile from one of the local men who was sitting on a bench. We struck up conversation and over a coffee he told me his life story; how he had fought in the Spanish Civil War against General Franco, had travelled the world in the merchant navy as a young man; met the love of his life and finally settled in Spain where he was enjoying his retirement. He had thin, white hair, with a pencil moustache. He was small in stature, even more so I suspect in his old age as he was slightly bent over. He wore thin, gold rimmed glasses, and was casually dressed in dark trousers, braces, and a white, collarless shirt, with the sleeves rolled up. Now in his later years, (he must have been in his late eighties), he had discovered a passion for drawing elaborate mandalas in biro. It was, for him, a regular form of meditation.

I had once stayed in a remote Buddhist monastery in the Himalayas and watched the monks create mandalas using coloured sand. They spent a few hours very gently and methodically creating the most intrinsic and beautiful designs by pouring the sand through their fingers, as they meditated on the impermanence of everything. Regarded as a spiritual and ritual symbol in both Buddhism and Hinduism, a mandala represents the universe, and once created it is traditional to ceremoniously destroy it and release the grains of sands into water as a sign of the impermanence of life.

I felt blessed, as I soon recognised the good timing of our meeting. It was soon after the dreams I had been having the previous nights, and related to their meaning to me, and my need to let go. He asked whether I would like to see a selection of his drawings. I agreed, and off he bounded home with a spring in his step. He returned with a bundle of rolled up papers under his arm, a huge smile on his face, and proceeded to tell me how a gallery in Bilbao had heard of his work, and were sending a representative to view his portfolio the following week. He showed me an extraordinary collection of hand drawn work, and over a coffee we discussed our spiritual views.

'I lose myself whenever I draw. My mind becomes very still, and I focus on the drawing I am doing, and nothing else. It's my own way of meditating. The process of drawing is more important than what I create. I feel very calm when I put my pen to the paper.'

'They are fantastic,' I replied. 'And you had no interest in art or drawing as a younger man?'

'No. I sometimes doodled when I was bored on a train, perhaps, or waiting for a bus, but nothing as intricate as these. I see it as a blessing in my old age that I have found this. It keeps me out of mischief!' he replied, with a laugh.

When it was time to go, we exchanged addresses and I promised to send him something from home (I later chose some fudge), and he promised to send me something as well. A few months later, I received a long tube inside of which this kind, wonderful gentleman had drawn my very own personal mandala, in biro. Inspired by the dreams and my meeting with the artist, I asked in prayer to the Higher Power to allow me to live each day of my life with a greater awareness of Peace, Love, Gentleness, Joy. For the remaining days of the Camino, I focussed much more on these higher emotions.

I had a tremendous sense of achievement as I finally walked through the busy streets of Santiago to the Cathedral on the 23rd September 2011. Whilst many pilgrims headed for the Cathedral pilgrim office to present their pilgrim passport and receive their certificates, I decided to visit the Cathedral, give thanks to my Higher Power, and look out for friends who had arrived in Santiago before me. I was amazed to see, within the swirling mass of pilgrims and parishioners, the lithe figures of Darren and Paul from Sunderland. They welcomed me like a long lost brother, and we shared our news over coffee, before attending Mass with perhaps 1500 other pilgrims inside a packed cathedral.

The atmosphere was highly charged, especially when the famous swinging censer - the botafumiero - was lowered into position at the end of service, and then swung in a huge 150 foot arc across the nave with incense pouring out. To a battery of camera flashes, this was a truly spectacular sight to behold, despite several near misses as pilgrims leaned across its path as it flew past, to get a better angle. I soon learned that there were several unofficial welcoming committees of pilgrims who waited in the square in front of the cathedral every day for their friends to arrive. It was so moving to see the many joyful reunions taking place; it underlined the genuine friendships that had developed along the journey.

After a few days resting in Santiago, I felt the urge for some space away from the crowds, so I packed my rucksack, checked out of my digs, and walked another ninety kilometres to the Atlantic Ocean, along the Finisterre Way, to what was once regarded as the 'End of the World'! Finisterre

(Fisterra in Galician) was, for many centuries, the final destination for many pilgrims who made the journey to Santiago, until Columbus' exploits somewhat changed the way we look at the world. The ancient pagans would head to Fisterra on the Costa da Morte (Coast of Death) where they believed the sun died and the worlds of the dead and the living became closer. Prayers would be said and offerings would be made to please the gods. Fisterra is also believed to be the place of Ara Solis, a magical place and altar dedicated to the dying sun.

Few modern day pilgrims continue beyond Santiago, so after the hustle and bustle of Santiago, I appreciated the greater sense of freedom; and the peacefulness and tranquility as I walked through the picture-postcard Galacian villages and open countryside before reaching the sea cliffs of the westernmost point in Spain, at Cape Fisterra. There I joined thirty fellow pilgrims as we sat on the rocks underneath the famous lighthouse, and waited for the sunset. As the sun started to go down I could well understand why the ancients must have thought this was the 'coast of death'. The view from the rocks to the sun looked as if the sun was literally dropping off the end of the world. There was also the most beautiful channel of golden light across the ocean between the sun and the rocks, which no doubt supported the ancients' illusion that this was the meeting point between life and death.

The Finisterre Way continues along the rugged coast to the sanctuary of A Virxe da Barca in Muxía, which was the most beautiful walk of my entire 1300 kilometre Camino. The route passes through forests of eucalyptus trees, among others, and along old walled lanes, woodland tracks, and old forest paths. I could hear the breaking of the ocean waves to my left for several miles before the path opened to a most wonderful, expansive view of the Atlantic ocean. Stretching before me, so silent and still; it literally took my breath away.

It was one of those moments in life when one wants to embrace and honour the whole experience and hold it close to oneself. There is a sacred, timeless presence within such moments, which is divine, and connects us to a higher consciousness in a way that words so often fail to achieve. I sat in silence, eyes open, in meditation for a few hours. I wondered how it might have been in ancient times for those who lived in dense jungle so far inland that they had never seen the vastness of an ocean. How, at some point in their lives, they may have travelled nearer to the coast and heard, for the very first time in their lives, in the distance, the frightening roar of the breaking waves. As the ocean came into their view, they too must have be blown away by its immense presence.

As the sun began to set, I started my final journey into Muxia. I felt a strong, loving presence within and around me, like I was within a cocoon of peace and wisdom, for the next few days. An issue would arise within my mind regarding the spiritual path, work, or love, and I would receive clear, concise intuition as to what I needed to do, which was ultimately to connect through love and meditation to the stillness deep within me. The healing I felt, with this intuition, was not so much what I was guided to do (which was often to pray, or to talk to someone in particular about an unresolved issue), but rather to feel a greater awareness and acceptance of the powerful presence behind the wisdom itself. I felt I was in a stage of grace.

In this state of connectedness, my mind kept returning time and again to the statement Jesus had made. 'Be ye as little children to enter the kingdom of heaven'. I had always thought of heaven as an eternal state of spiritual enlightenment, and it seemed to me the sense of unconditional love, wonder and awe that little children express is what we need to connect to as adults, but we have become too caught up in ego, competition and power.

After dinner that evening, in a small, quiet restaurant, I went for a walk around Muxia, and I knew I needed to connect to the child I had ignored, rejected and despised for so many years. I felt a pang of shame, physically inside myself, inside my groin, stomach and heart, and took a deep breath. After a day in Muxia, I returned to Santiago, and then flew home.

Looking back, beyond the physical beauty of the landscape along the route of the Camino Frances, there's so much to admire in its architectural heritage as well: Gaudi's Episcopal palace in Astorga, the magnificent cathedral in Burgos and the monastery of San Millan de la Cogolla, both UNESCO World Heritage sites; Ponferrada, home to the mysterious Templar Castle; the remarkable San Marcos monastery and the stunning Gothic cathedral in Leon; and finally Santiago de Compostela, with its famed cathedral and grave of Saint James. More than anything, I loved the fact that I was among so many kindred spirits. My fellow pilgrims were open to talking about their lives, loves, faith, dreams, careers and everything else in between. This extraordinary intimacy is what makes the Camino such a powerful spiritual experience. I had witnessed so many uninhibited, spontaneous acts of kindness.

Whilst walking the Way, at times I could feel the presence of the millions who have gone before. I am sure we must experience the same bonds of camaraderie across the generations. We must no doubt face many of the same emotional, physical and spiritual challenges as those who came before, and for me it is this historical depth which enhances the spiritual journey; I'm walking the path of countless others over many, many centuries.

On another level, the Camino is like an extravagant treasure hunt played for over 1200 years by many millions of pilgrims. You get up early and walk through unknown countryside looking for the way markers; the elusive yellow painted arrows or scallop shells which can be on trees, buildings, barrels, pavements, and which guide you to the next place of rest, food and shelter. One walks through deserted streets, along country lanes by dim moonlight, searching for clues. Somewhere - on a wall, barrel, tree, or pavement - is the way marker pointing the way to Santiago. I saw them as elaborate graffiti on the wall of a café; stones arranged as an arrow on a forest path pointing the way; a pair of discarded walking boots with Santiago scribbled on them, with an arrow; and at the top of a mountain path, as a road sign showing the ways to Jerusalem, Rome, Paris, London, and, of course, Santiago.

My experience of the Camino had fallen into three distinct sections, in terms of the geography of the landscape and my emotional journey. The first week or so I walked over the Pyrenees Mountains and through the regions of Navarre and La Rioja, and I felt the excitement of meeting new people and the adventure to explore of exploring the beautiful countryside. The second week was spent crossing Spain's barren, table-top plateau, the Meseta, which as previously mentioned I walked mostly alone, thereby experiencing a period of deep introspection and emotional turmoil. The final week was through the luscious and fertile region of Galicia to Santiago de Compostela, which brought about feelings of acceptance, letting go, and overall a more positive attitude for my future.

Whilst the PTSD has connected me to the lower levels of consciousness, the underlying trauma creates a powerful yearning for spiritual truth. This, in turn, has enabled me to heal myself through the AA 12 Step programme, and to do what I can to help others. I have been linked to these two extremes for most of my life. It reminds me of the beautiful lines of the Rūmī poem:

Out beyond ideas of wrongdoing and rightdoing there is a field.
I'll meet you there. When the soul lies down in that grass,
the world is too full to talk about. [33]
Jalāl ad-Dīn Muhammad Rūmī

I recognised that I needed to be able, willing, and strong enough to go into the depths of the abuse and acknowledge everything, with professional support, in order to release these lowers energies, and live in the higher consciousness more often. I knew there was more work to be done on myself. I knew I had to:

- Accept the truth of what actually had happened to myself and get the help I needed.
- Release the shame and sense of responsibility I was still carrying.
- Let go of the fear of judgement and condemnation I anticipated I would receive from others if they knew the truth.
- Somehow let go of the rage without hurting myself or anyone else.

The SLAA programme helped me to identify and talk through many of these emotions, insofar as they affected my relationship with myself and others, but I still had many blocks to the deeper-seated emotions, and so few developed memories, and these were where the core of the trauma was trapped.

My Camino had brought clarity to a number of truths. I know I am intrinsically connected to God / Higher Self at my highest level of consciousness. I also know that I have, at times in my life, experienced a profound sense of peace and love that transcends my normal consciousness.

---

[33] Excerpt from a poem called 'A Great Wagon'. Jalāl ad-Dīn Rūmī auth., Coleman Barks, trans., John Moyne, trans. *The Essential Rūmī* (HarperOne, 2004)

11

UNDERLYING TRIGGERS

*Even in its darkest passages, the heart is unconquerable.
It is important that the body survives,
but it is more meaningful that the human spirit prevails.*[34]
Dave Pelzer, A Child Called "It"

I returned home from the Camino feeling refreshed and enthusiastic to move forward with life. It took me a while to adjust back to so-called normal living, after such a nomadic month, and if truth be told I didn't want to slip back into running away from my emotions and living in a fantasy. It was time for change. The Camino had opened up a deep sense of the need to be proactive and positive, and I awoke most mornings in my flat feeling restless and looking for new things to do, and thinking of new places to explore.

After a few weeks I eventually settled back into my routine of meeting up with my family and friends, attending regular AA meetings, daily meditation, catching up with my AA sponsor and sponsees, and going for walks on the beach. I started looking for work in theatres all over the country; I felt it was time to move away from my hometown and start afresh somewhere else. I felt I needed to re-invent myself, and let go of my recent past.

After a few weeks of filling in endless application forms for jobs that didn't really interest me at all, I received a telephone call from an old theatre

---

[34] Dave Pelzer, *A Child Called "It"* (Health Communications, Incorporated, 1995)

Underlying Triggers

friend at the end of October 2011.

'I want to tempt you with a real challenge!' he said, somewhat teasingly, but it worked; he had my attention straight away. 'I'm trustee at a wonderful old theatre which needs someone with your passion and skills to grab hold of it, and turn it around,' he continued. 'It's lost its way in recent years, and is struggling financially. It'll be a huge job, I'll be honest with you, but I know you can do it. There's a great group of volunteers down there who really want to make it work. I know they'll do everything they can to support you.'

Whilst my friend didn't know specifically what I'd been through, he did know I'd been needing a break and had been on the Camino. It made me wonder whether he was reaching out to give me a clean start, or was he making this offer purely on the basis of my reputation? Either way, the timing was fortuitous, and loving a challenge I grabbed hold of it with both hands.

With my ego flattered and a new opportunity potentially before me, I contacted the chairman of the Trust and six weeks later, with a packed van and the help of a few friends, I moved lock, stock and barrel to the other side of the country where I hoped I could make a new start and perhaps finally settle down.

The theatre I was now managing had opened in the late 1800s and was reminiscent of a Victorian concert hall. During the heyday of music hall and variety it had enjoyed an illustrious history, but as with many seaside theatres the postwar years had been difficult, what with the rise of television, and cheaper holidays abroad in the sun. Nonetheless the theatre had bucked the trend in more recent years with a successful summer season variety show, which offered holidaymakers and locals alike two different shows each season, playing to full houses, for many years. Whilst the good times rolled, the borough council was happy to offer financial support for the summer season show, but during the winter months the theatre was mostly closed, offering only a handful of dates to community groups and amateur dramatic societies. As soon as the council withdrew its subsidy, and the summer season audiences started to dwindle to paltry numbers, the theatre inevitably faced a financial crisis.

A few years before the subsidy was withdrawn, a trust had been set up to run the theatre on behalf of the local council. It had, under the most challenging circumstances, done an amazing job keeping the theatre open, and in such good physical condition. It soon became clear to me what a huge challenge it would be to make a success of the theatre. There were so many issues which needed to be urgently addressed, and it was a question of.... where the hell was I to start?

By the time I arrived, the theatre was not receiving any external funding from the local council or any other public body such as the Arts Council, nor from business sponsorship. Its income came from theatre hires (which a financial audit showed did not even cover its daily running costs), the percentage share of the box office income from professional shows (which, due to their infrequency and low ticket prices, was very small), the bar, and from the considerable fundraising overseen by the theatre volunteers. It meant that the theatre had been drawing on its reserves to cover its running costs, and there was considerable concern that the theatre would close unless it could address its critical financial issues. I drew up a list of the issues I felt needed my immediate attention:

- The programme of events was mainly community productions, and a few professional shows. The view was that professional shows 'went to the bigger theatre' nearby which offered two hundred more seats, and a considerable subsidy from the local authority. The theatre I was going to consequently lacked much profile within the town or the surrounding area, especially with audiences under forty years old.
- Due to financial constraints there was no quality theatre brochure, just a black and white photocopy. The old-fashioned, hackneyed website often crashed, and offered only limited online booking facilities. The box office system was also old-fashioned and was not used to develop any marketing opportunities. There was no e-marketing, and direct mail letters were not even sent to groups, societies, or other potential audience members. There was no marketing beyond posters outside the theatre and around the town, so the theatre relied very much on local volunteers leafleting and promoting shows at large events.
- Due to the lack of shows, media releases were not sent on a regular basis to the print media, so interview opportunities and articles promoting the shows were rarely created, and the theatre had very little profile. The advertising looked like we were promoting a jumble sale rather than a theatre show.

- The technical crew were all volunteers (with full-time jobs elsewhere), so the number of shows that could be booked was, in theory, limited.

Despite these concerns, I could see how passionate the trustees, the small team of employees, and the army of local volunteers were to keep the theatre open. It was a question of channeling their energy in the right direction if we were to create and then implement a business plan with which to create a financially secure theatre. In fairness to the Trust the subsidy it had once received only covered the basic running costs of the theatre, leaving little to cover the cost of further staff, to invest in new box office systems etc.. so whilst I felt overwhelmed by the magnitude of the challenge before me, I could get inspired by the remarkable job the trustees had done to maintain the building to such a high standard during what were, financially, very difficult times. It also became clear to me after a few weeks how many positives there were:

- The Trustees and existing theatre staff (one full time, two part time) were experienced, professional people who were committed to keeping the theatre open. They each had specific responsibilities for the theatre including Treasurer, Health and Safety Officer or Technical Manager, so almost every day, several trustees would be beavering away in the front office.
- The technical crew were all volunteers, and without question they were highly talented, and passionate, and were the core of the theatre operation. Their commitment and expertise were crucial to the success we came to enjoy during the next eighteen months, and were the reason why many shows enjoyed playing the theatre each year.
- The Friends of the Theatre worked very hard to raise funds for the theatre, and were always offering to promote shows at events across the district, and to send me programmes from other theatres they had recently visited.

Over the course of the next year and a half, we set about the huge challenge to devise and implement a business model that would serve the theatre's immediate needs whilst creating a more secure financial foundation. The Trust backed my business plan for the next twelve months, despite some tough meetings, as one would expect when making decisions which affected the balance sheet so dramatically. Difficult issues were discussed and resolved, and within the first six months we had invested in a brand new online booking system, a new fully interactive website, and found sponsorship to cover the costs for a glossy 36 page theatre programme. I needed to put all this into place whilst booking the shows I knew from experience would bring a travelling audience and would therefore sell well straight away. We had the minimum of advance promotion compared to our competitors, as our existing resources for marketing was almost zero.

The first year we welcomed some great names to the theatre, including Fairport Convention, the Chinese State Circus, comedians The Chuckle Brothers, Rich Hall, Andy Parsons, and Jethro; The Military Wives, Marty Wilde and the Wildcats, Joe Brown, as well as the established mix of good quality amateur dramatic and community shows that were regular bookings. In working crazy hours to turn the theatre around, the stress I put myself under was triggering off the PTSD to the extent I started getting flashbacks to the abuse once again.

The underlying triggers were all there, and I tried my very best to ignore them and carry on, but I felt the road was now getting much narrower, and I would soon have nowhere left to run away to. My office was a small, decaying, depressing room with an old carpet and no clear window, which reminded me of the toilet cubicles I had been abused in. The walls felt as if they were closing in on me when I felt stressed, and this, of course, made me feel even more depressed. The flashbacks were more aggressive than before and brought up a lot of shame and rage, so I became a workaholic in an attempt to suppress them as I was too scared to face them. There comes a time, though, when every attempt to run stops working, and you come face to face with yourself. The long dark night of the soul.

With so much change to turn the theatre around, I put myself under intolerable pressure to succeed. I felt I had to prove myself – my feeling of self worth was directly linked to how successful I felt I was at my job. No one else put me under this pressure; and the trustees and volunteers were incredibly supportive of the changes I was making. I made sure they were with me all along. Nevertheless, despite the support of a committed team to raise funds and promote the shows, I deliberately worked very long hours, both at work and at home, in an effort to block out the memories; but this inevitably led to more anxiety and exhaustion. Whilst in this state of mind I taunted myself that, if the theatre did not succeed my reputation in the industry would be ruined. My thinking was that, as it had been my word that encouraged many of the promoters to risk playing the theatre that had struggled for business over several years, if the shows failed (and they lost money), they wouldn't trust my judgment in the future.

To help support my recovery, I had been attending AA meetings each week since I had moved into the area and had developed a strong network of recovery friends in the town. Our regular meetings, frequent telephone calls, and lunches and coffees, had without question helped me keep sober, safe and relatively sane during this traumatic period of my life. It also helped my self worth to listen to other people's problems rather than just focussing on my own all the time, so I made sure I was offering support to AA newcomers. It helped me to remember how far I'd come from my days of active alcoholism, and the serious consequences to my health, and to know that my experiences could help someone else to get sober. Over a period of years, it is surprising how even the most painful and humiliating of memories can fade, to the point where the alcoholic can forget how bad it really was, and then often start to drink again. I was determined not to let that happen.

Mark walked into a meeting one evening. He looked like a dead man walking; his face red, blotchy by alcohol and battered by violence. He had sad, lonely, sunken eyes, and a few days' stubble. He always wore the same pair of old, dirty jeans, trainers with holes, and a thick, dirty grey top with a hood. He had been broken by the addiction. Though in his early fifties, he walked like an old, arthritic-riddled man in his eighties. He had been to university and gained a 2:1 in Law, and had enjoyed a stellar legal career, eventually becoming a partner by his mid thirties in a large, internationally renowned legal firm in London. His alcoholism developed in his mid-twenties, and he'd managed to hide it for many years. He had since destroyed everything in his life, and he was now existing in a bedsit, just about surviving on benefits and vodka.

'My name is Mark, I'm an alcoholic. I've been trying to stop drinking for years. I've been in treatment three times, but I've always gone back to the drink. I've got to stop, but I don't know how; life without it terrifies me, even though I'm hating every second I'm drinking. It's insane. I hate what its doing to me. I hate the person I've become. There's no enjoyment in it, I hate everything about it, it's full blown desperation drinking....'

The group listened with understanding and compassion as he continued, 'I'm hardly eating.. I can't remember what I did yesterday; I was in blackout, and this scares me!'

He paused and stared at the floor in front of him. After perhaps ten seconds, he took a deep breath and continued,

'I.... I sometimes punch myself in the face,' and he clenched his fist as he said this, and it reminded me so much of my behaviour (so many years before when I had drunk and then punched myself in the face and taunted myself). ' I can't stand looking at myself in the mirror. I stare at myself and shout, 'Who are who? Who the fuck are you? What the hell have you become?' He broke down as he continued, stumbling over the words. 'I come here every day and can get a few days away from drink, but then the obsession is on me again, and I go back.'

There was no self-pity in his voice; he was simply stating the appalling reality of his life which he felt powerless to change. It helped me to listen to someone share like this, as it reminded me so much of my past, and how I had behaved; the mental torture, the self-hatred, and the self-harming of my active alcoholism. It helped me to see how truly fortunate I was to be sober, and to be in long term recovery.

I offered support and encouragement to Mark during the summer and autumn of 2012 (as several members did) as best I could by meeting him for coffee, talking with him, and buying him some food every now and then. When you see a newcomer getting sober, and starting to enjoy life once again, it really is an amazing feeling. The reality is that so many alcoholics tragically never stop drinking. They don't know it is possible to live without alcohol, and what's more to enjoy living a sober life.

An AA meeting is a microcosm of life, and you hear a wide variety of stories, encompassing the whole gamut of births, marriages and deaths, and everything else in between. There is plenty of hope and encouragement, as well as the everyday challenges of life that everyone has to face but there are, inevitably, the tragedies, and a few years ago, I was upset to learn that Mark was one of those unfortunate souls who had died from alcoholism. Listening to people like Mark helped me to grasp an important perspective; that regardless of how difficult my problems were at the moment, I knew I was

Underlying Triggers

not alone, and there were always others in a tougher place than me. The AA slogan *Together We Can* became a constant and reassuring reminder that there was hope, so long as I did the simple things:

- Don't pick up a drink each day
- Attend regular AA meetings and share honestly
- Continue to pray and meditate
- Talk to my sponsor, and maintain contact daily with AA friends
- Offer support and encouragement to the AA newcomer

It's a powerful experience when a newcomer, in particular, attends an AA meeting, as their presence reminds me of my first meeting, and how broken I was when I first walked through the door. Seeing a newcomer, or any alcoholic for that matter, in the throes of their addiction reminds me how fortunate I am to be sober. A few years ago, I was telling an old AA member about a mutual friend, called Ian, who had after several years of sobriety sadly started drinking again, and had become very ill, mentally and physically... very rapidly. He had been hospitalised at least four times during the previous month.

'Alan, it's so tragic to see him in such a dreadful state. He's a good man, and he helped so many people over the years.' I said.

Alan replied, 'It's very sad, Matt, to hear what's happened to him. And yes, he went out of his way to support many people, including myself, but it isn't tragic.' I was shocked, and thought him uncaring, and it was only when he qualified his statement that I understood exactly what he had meant.

'Don't misunderstand me. I'll do whatever I can to help him. We both will, I'm sure. This is my point. He had over nine years of good quality sobriety. He had achieved so much during that time in his life; his family had returned, his health and business had greatly improved. Yet, he decided to pick up a drink. That is very sad, I agree. But remember, the tragedies are those alcoholics who never, ever stop drinking. They have no idea it is possible to live for a day, let alone a week or a year without alcohol, and more than that, actually learn how to enjoy life without it. These poor souls, and there are so many of them, are the real tragedies.'

The mind is a cunning foe at times. The memories of my drinking have faded so much over the years that without regular attendance at AA, it would be so easy to forget how destructive it really was. Then the inevitable, I am sure, would happen and, like Ian, I would start drinking again. After a while the mind creates a very alluring and convincing picture of how enjoyable my drinking was, of how good I felt when the buzz used to rush through my body, of how much fun I really had, and how much better my life would be if I had just one drink. Unless I get honest and challenge my thinking straight away, the dreadful reality of active alcoholism is soon edited out completely; it's as if that hell had never existed.

 Listening to Mark's pain helped me to be completely honest with a few AA friends about what was really going on, and the support of these fellow members was so important to my getting through those difficult months. The miracle was I did not want to drink; I knew it wouldn't work fast enough to kill the mental and emotional pain. Their love and the regular AA meetings gave me the strength to make sure I didn't finish myself off in a far more immediate and brutal way. Posh John really helped me, during this time in my life, when he said,

 'You've been through harder times than this, Matt. The difference now is that you know it will pass, and you'll grow through it, and you'll be so much stronger for it. You don't want to drink, which is amazing in itself, you just want to change how you feel.'

 I felt too much shame and confusion to let my family in, so I edited out the core issues when we spoke so they were only aware (or so I thought at the time), that I was finding the new job stressful and was feeling exhausted. I called Mum one afternoon, when I was feeling stronger, and said,

 'I'm okay. It's just really busy at work. There's so much to do, it's hard to know where the hell to start some days, but we are moving forward.'

 'Are you getting the help you need from the staff and the volunteers? You're not taking it all on yourself, are you? Do make sure you don't overdo it and burn yourself out, my love.'

 'There's a good team here; they're keen to turn the place around, but some of the changes are so fundamental, they are, I guess, nervous at the same time. I'm getting there,' I replied. 'I'm feeling the buzz of booking the strong shows I know will sell well, and seeing the advance bookings come in; that's a great feeling. It's just the infrastructure is so basic and old fashioned. There's so much potential here, but it's an enormous job. I'm still a bloody perfectionist as well!'

'You must switch off though. You must take time out and relax. Make sure you have two complete days off each week, when you don't think about it at all, and do something you really enjoy.'

My family were really supportive, of course, but I always felt a mixture of encouragement and depression after speaking with them, as my inability to be really open about the abuse brought into plain view the barrier that existed between us, which was shame.

Why did I not tell my family exactly what was really going on for me?

I knew my family loved me, but the intense shame locked within the PTSD drowned out the ability to feel, and sometimes to even accept, that I was worthy of their love. Because I was carrying such a huge secret, I felt at a very deep level that the love was conditional. The fear was, if they really knew the truth about what had happened, would they still love me? This was not about their capacity or desire to love me, but much more about the impact shame had in my life. I had placed this impenetrable barrier around me, not them. Besides, I was still too ashamed and confused to acknowledge what had happened to myself, let alone anyone else. I was also struggling to remember details of the abuse, beyond the memories I'd spoken to Dr Ron Hutchinson about in 1993/4. Whilst the flashbacks were sudden, fast and overwhelming, I 'saw' enough to know that they related to different incidents of abuse to those I had received counselling for, as the locations were different. The shock of the memories and the flashbacks were such that I could not imagine I would be able to hear, listen or to deal with my family's emotional reaction as well. I feared too that Mum and Dad, in particular, would feel they were responsible in some way for having not protected me, and all these issues just added more and more to my emotional confusion.

The levels of exhaustion I felt were such that I could only just about handle my own issues. I anticipated my family's pain, concern and questions rather than their love and kindness. I felt too uncomfortable within myself to accept their love and support at this stage; I felt it would exacerbate the shame I was already feeling. I was struggling to come to terms with what I was remembering about the abuse, so I felt it was too overwhelming to let them in at this stage as I knew it would open up so many questions for them, including: Why didn't we notice? What could we have done to stop it ever happening? Who were these men?

I did not want to involve my family until I was in a better place, even though at times I genuinely doubted I could get through this traumatic period of my life. I have since found out that my family and closest friends were really concerned I might start drinking again.

A few of the theatre trustees noticed I was feeling stressed, and would discreetly drop by my office for a chat on a more regular basis than previously, and my line manager, Karen, who was wonderfully supportive throughout this time, met with me on a weekly basis. Although they sensed I was under extreme pressure, they didn't fully know the source of it, nor the extent to which I was suffering. Karen was a retired NHS senior manager (so, by her own admission, she knew a thing or two about anxiety and stress), and she often had practical ideas to help with the workload, which really helped me;

'I don't think any of us realised quite how much work was required to turn the theatre around, and we all think you're doing an amazing job. Can we delegate some of the initial IT developments to someone else, as you told me the research was particularly time-consuming when we spoke last week? My husband is willing to work to any briefing document you create. He could do all the leg work, and report back to you directly?'

The pivotal moment in my breakdown came whilst I watched the daily horrific revelations on the news of the abuse that Jimmy Savile had done to so many children and young adults over many years. I would obsessively watch Channel 4 news and imagine hunting Savile down, had he still been alive, and executing him. Every time I saw his vile, smug face on the television I felt a rage within me I had never, ever felt to such a degree before, and I could no longer suppress it. Even though he had died, I fantasised about hunting him down, and putting a bullet between his eyes.

Even now, I do not like using the name 'Jimmy' as it implies some kind of familiarity and friendship.

As I watched the news reports about his offences, the memories of abuse I had suffered became more real and clear to me. In another incident, one evening alone I was watching the film *Taken*, starring Liam Neeson, and more of the main flashback memories came to me during the scene when Neeson's character is on the telephone with the man who he has abducted his daughter. He threatens him, saying;

'...I will look for you, I will find you, and I will kill you.'

As I heard this, I had a sudden visceral surge of emotion flash through my entire body as I remembered what the main paedophile had said to me as he leaned down and held me on that final occasion;

'We know where you live, we know who your father is. If you tell anyone what has happened, we will find you and we will kill you.'

I knew there was something else he did immediately after he threatened me, but as I struggled to make a connection after watching Taken I found that the memory was buried so deep in my subconscious mind I could not remember what it was... but I had reached, at last, my emotional rock bottom. As horrific as the memory of this was, after a few weeks it was a relief to know why I was so terrified of any form of intimacy. I had known many people who had been abused in the same way as myself, but they had somehow managed to form relationships with a partner, and to be intimate emotionally and physically. I struggled for years to understand why I was so incapable of achieving this.

All of the symptoms of the PTSD were now a daily experience for me. As much as I tried to suppress the emotions of shame, fear, and rage within me, I became more obsessive at the theatre; its commercial success became the be all and end all. As the energy of the PTSD became increasingly powerful, I felt a rage I had never ever encountered before, erupting from deep within me. Previously, whenever I had been triggered I would feel a tension and a sensation of dirtiness in my genital area, and then the rage would rise up from the pit of my stomach and my whole body would be overwhelmed with shock.

As soon as it reached my chest area, I would mentally 'flick a switch' in my mind, and focus my attention on something; anything else, so as to not feel the intensity of it. The energy terrified me. I convinced myself I had to keep it in; if I allowed the energy to come out, I was scared I would completely fall apart, have a mental breakdown, during which I might commit some horrendous crime, such was the rage I felt inside. The regular visual and emotional flashbacks to the abuse, which followed on with the rage, fear, suicidal thoughts, sleepless nights and regular nightmares, and the physical tension throughout my body became the norm. The rage manifested with me punching the walls and desks in the office, and kicking the cupboards as hard as I could. I would also shout and scream as I did this; I felt like a wounded, terrified animal as the emotions overwhelmed me physically, mentally and emotionally.

I felt a dirtiness under my skin, and my thoughts were of snakes and horrible, dark places. I feared I was having a breakdown. I didn't trust myself, I was fearful about most situations; it felt as if the ground beneath me might give way. Sometimes I would pace up and down the dressing room next door to my office, and stare at myself in front of the mirror pleading with myself to cry and release the pain.

"Cry, just fucking cry please.... Get this crap out of you..."

But I couldn't shift it. When my body felt riddled with the shame and disgust I was tempted to throw myself down the stairs outside my office. At home, I remember standing on my third floor balcony looking down, telling myself if I did decide to jump I would have to go head first to make sure I broke my neck as I feared if I survived I would be in a wheelchair. I would play the suicide scenario in my mind over and over, and would then think how much I would be hurting my family and friends, and reminding myself that the intensity of these emotions and thoughts would pass.

"Hang in there, just hang in there. You've been waiting to get this crap our for so many years, you knew it would be difficult. Just hold on', I would tell myself.

Bizarrely enough, the thoughts of suicide helped me; there was an immediate way out if I was really desperate. In a weird way, it seemed to release some of the tension. I thought of Saville, and thought to myself I wouldn't give him the satisfaction. Although I had never met him, he had come to represent all the men who had ever abused me. In truth, the rage really scared me. I genuinely feared for my sanity. I feared;

- What would I be capable of doing if I feel the full intensity of this rage?
- Who will I become?
- Will my personality change to become someone who enjoys hurting people?

I had frequent thoughts about the serial killer Michael Ryan, who massacred sixteen people in Hungerford in 1987; I've no idea what motivated Ryan to commit such a dreadful crime, but these intrusive thoughts really scared me – such was the rage inside of me, I feared that in a moment of madness, I might be capable of committing a similar, horrific crime.

Underlying Triggers

Finally, one Tuesday evening, just after seven o'clock, I broke down on the floor of the lounge and cried, and cried for the first time in many years. I had felt the emotional pain building up within me during the day; it felt as if the cells underneath my skin were about to burst with the pressure, which made me feel very uncomfortable, but I knew I had to let it happen. I couldn't have stopped it if I had wanted to; the energy was so powerful I felt as if a shift was taking place within my body; a cleaning out of the emotional toxins I had been carrying for nearly thirty years was finally taking place. On that first night of several that particular week, I lay naked in foetal position with visceral pain surging through my body as it writhed around. I was exhausted in every sense; emotionally, physically and mentally.

At last, there was an emotional release taking place. These experiences took place most evenings for the next few weeks, and I could feel the intensity of the rage gradually passing over a period of several months. An enormous amount of energy, which had been suppressed for so many years, was now shifting and finally gave way to the tears. With the avalanche of tears, the venom in the PTSD started to drain away. The dirty, rusty tin which in my mind symbolised my PTSD, and which had been full of snakes, darkness, rage and shame, had been opened, and at last light could come in and heal me.

With this healing I became aware of some of the false beliefs I had been subconsciously holding onto all my life. I was relieved to recognise and release them. They were:

- If I tell my family everything that happened to me during the abuse, they will be so ashamed of me they might not love me anymore.
- If I tell my family everything that happened, they will not believe me, as it is so horrific.
- I will only be able to let go of all this pain when I become a father, and have children of my own.

For many years, whenever my parents told me they loved me, I felt very uncomfortable inside and with a shudder of shame my immediate emotional reaction was 'but you don't know everything about me'. This period of my life was the most difficult part of my journey in sobriety, but one I can see was entirely necessary to experience if I was going to find a place of acceptance about my childhood. After eighteen tumultuous months, I decided it was time for change. It was, ultimately, a period of transition, both personally and professionally.

We managed to breathe new life, over a period of eighteen months, into a lovely theatre, with credit to the trustees, friends of the theatre, my three members of paid staff, and the legions of volunteers who helped bring this about. At the end of the financial year, the theatre reported a net profit on ticket sales of almost £80,000, the first reported profit in living memory (and perhaps ever, so the chairman informed me recently.)

Looking back, and please forgive the crass cliché, I can acknowledge the rather bizarre symmetry between both the old theatre and myself undergoing a rebirth of sorts, and building for a brighter, more positive future. In my early days working there, I did identify with the theatre, feeling we were both broken, but with so much potential.

12

A REVOLUTION IN MY HEAD

Yesterday I was clever, so I wanted to change the world.
Today I am wise, so I am changing myself.[35]
Jalāl ad-Dīn Muhammad Rūmī

By the spring of 2013, my life in England had started to become tense on the work front, and I was beginning to feel that a change of scene, if only temporary, was needed. I first looked for this change in my career.

I had noticed a theatre management job advertisement in *The Stage* newspaper, in March 2013, and my gut reaction, which is so often correct, was to wait for something else to come along. I trusted my intuition until I saw a second advertisement for the same job a few months later, and by this point I was so desperately unhappy in my present job (due to the challenges of living with PTSD and the flashbacks to the abuse) that I decided I had to move on. It didn't go to plan, however. Even at the interview the warning signs were clearly there, and everything about the experience rang alarm bells for me, all of which I ignored. From the intense rambling and highly stressed demeanour of the main interviewer (who was to briefly become my line manager), to what seemed to me to be the wildly unrealistic business strategy they wanted to implement, everything screamed at me: this is not for me. I was not in the right place, either emotionally or psychologically, for this position.

---

[35] Jalāl ad-Dīn Muhammad Rūmī, auth., Coleman Barks, trans., John Moyne, trans. *The Essential Rūmī* (HarperOne, 2004)

Even when a few friends in the theatre business offered me their honest feedback about the theatre and its recent issues, I continued to feel I should take the job; a flashing red light was that a number of good quality, experienced staff had decided to leave in recent years, and by all accounts there was much unhappiness among the remaining staff. But I ignored these warnings and blindly pursued the job. My pride and failure to listen proved my undoing. It quickly turned out to be a case of jumping out of the frying pan and into the fire. In short, I had no confidence to do the job whatsoever. I felt broken inside, and I was teetering on the verge of a nervous breakdown. Looking back, I can see the state of my mental health had been deteriorating during the previous two years, since the PTSD had been triggered by Becky's rejection, and meeting the suicidal girl on the railway bridge. I am not blaming either of these events for my mental health challenges. In fact, they were entirely necessary for the most painful memories of the abuse to be finally triggered during the following twelve months.

The new job exacerbated what I was already feeling inside, and the work environment I inherited was very unhealthy. I lacked the energy to change it. I felt lost, confused, and deeply depressed, and after six tough months I gave my notice. The following week, when my workaholic line manager was placed on gardening leave, the Chief Executive asked me to reconsider my decision. He was really keen for me to stay, but I was finished. I had to walk away. Yet in the midst of this period of changing jobs and locations, I was also organising what became a hugely successful three-day festival in London, attracting audience members from all over the UK. In one sense the timing was not ideal; the festival took place during the third week of my new job. Playing to full houses each day, the packed programme included several nationally respected star names, and over twenty four hours of expert speakers, interviews, archive films, exhibitions, and live shows. Despite the considerable amount of work necessary over several months to organise and promote the festival, it became a safe haven for me to temporarily escape into. I had an amazing team of good friends to work with, all of whom, like me, were passionate to make it a huge success; and in the end, it most definitely was. In another sense the timing was impeccable; whilst I felt my life was falling apart emotionally and psychologically, the festival was without doubt the professional high point of my career to date. It gave me something positive to hold onto for a while. The reality began to dawn on me, though, that where I had been able, for many years, to use work as a means of escape this was no longer possible. It was as if the Higher Power had now removed this last obsession of work from the reality I had to confront.

I had abused alcohol and drugs in my late teens, and been a workaholic at times during the last twenty years. I'd also lived in fantasy relationships with women I hardly knew, denied being a sexual anorexic, and now my final crutch was being removed and I had to face my past.

In February 2014 I had just about enough money in my savings to get away and decided I needed a few months out and to return to India. I headed off once again to a country I have come to regard as my spiritual home, a place which had so often helped me in the past to find an inner peace (I have visited India for extended periods five times during the last twenty years). I booked a room for a month of resting, reading, writing, and meditating in the spiritual community of Auroville, twelve kilometres from Pondicherry in South India.

Founded in 1968, Auroville was inspired by the visions of the spiritual teacher, Mirra Alfassa, also known as The Mother, who was spiritual partner of the revered Indian sage Sri Aurobindo. His ashram, in Pondicherry, remains a popular destination for spiritual seekers from all over the world. Auroville is now a community of just over two thousand permanent residents from forty-three countries, with an influx of approximately five thousand (mostly international), visitors each year. It has seven schools, five outreach schools, and two health centres supporting 10,000 patients. The residents and visitors live on just over one hundred small settlements with names such as Hope, Aspiration, and Peace, across an area of eight square kilometres. When Auroville was first developed, this land was completely barren and its original residents set about implementing an ambitious plan to reclaim it. To their credit, almost fifty years on much of the land (over 1250 acres and 1.5 million trees) is now covered in thick jungle interconnected with roads and cycle paths.

For most people, including me, it is the remarkable Matrimandir that dominates the consciousness of Auroville and keeps pulling me back there. It is "the soul of Auroville", as the Mother called it, and a very special place to meditate. The main, outer structure of the Matrimandir is twenty-nine metres high and has a diameter of thirty-six metres. It looks like a huge

Terry's Chocolate Orange. It has, around its base, twelve meditation chambers which are, collectively, shaped like a fully blossoming lotus. The Inner Chamber in the upper hemisphere of the Matrimandir is fifteen metres high at its centre, has a diameter of twenty-four metres, and is dodecagon in shape. It is completely white, with white marble walls and white carpeting, and represents the Supreme Consciousness. Within the Inner Chamber itself, and directly underneath an opening to the sky, is a huge translucent, crystal globe, seventy centimetres in diameter upon which the meditators can concentrate. When a ray of electronically guided sunlight falls onto the globe, the light within the chamber symbolises, according to the Mother, divine grace.

Since my first visit to Auroville, in February 1996, I have come to appreciate the spiritual ideals of the community, and enjoyed the peaceful, relaxed atmosphere and community living it offers. There is a busy programme of artistic, educational and spiritual events which take place throughout the year. One can choose from classes in yoga, dance, language, pottery, and healing; to film showings at the town hall; volunteering opportunities in schools and on farms; or sign up for the conservation initiatives in the appropriately named Buddha Garden, and Sadhana Forest. I had first visited Sri Aurobindo's ashram in 1996 on my first trip to India, and felt very much out of my depth in these surroundings. I had the notion that everyone else, particularly those dressed all in white and who looked pious and thoughtful, had reached some high level of spiritual consciousness way above mine, and had attained the ability to perform siddhis (spiritual 'gifts' such as clairvoyance). I have thankfully since learnt that this view is erroneous, and even more so that it is far more important to be open, loving and kind than to attain any such spiritual gifts.

It was in the early evening when we had arrived on my first visit, and straight away I could feel an atmosphere of deep peace and serenity as we paid our respects at the beautiful Samadhi or shrine to Sri Aurobindo and The Mother. As I meditated I felt myself becoming immersed in this presence' with a strong sense of gratitude for the creative energy that had manifested during the day. I had an inner vision of the natural beauty of the earth in my mind's eye; the trees, mountains, rivers, and a whole range of different species of wild and domestic animals... these flooded my consciousness. It felt as if a deeper consciousness within me had been awoken to remind me of the miracle of creation, and that I was an intrinsic part of it. I felt a natural healing taking place, an experience I know is always within me (and I believe within everyone else) at all times. We just need to be able and willing to allow it to happen.

Eighteen years later, in 2014, when I meditated in the Matrimandir, any notion of being less than everyone else had disappeared completely from my life (apart from those times when I am in PTSD mode), and I genuinely felt I was an equal with everyone else, so was able to be 'present' and relax into the energy. I focused all of my attention on my breathing and after a few minutes felt a different presence in and around me from the ashram experience many years earlier. Perhaps the Inner Chamber, which I have always sensed has a profound universal presence within it, influenced my perception, but I began to feel more and more immersed in the cosmic energy of the universe. It felt humbling to feel such a connection to the vastness of the universe, and to let go, for a while at least, of this sense of the small 'me'.

At my everyday level of consciousness I am fully aware and identify my body as 'me' and therefore 'see' myself as a separate entity to everyone and everything else. But on those occasions when I am able to connect more deeply through meditation I feel immersed in a higher consciousness where there is no notion of any separation. It is in this place that I can often feel, as it says in the Bible, 'a peace that passeth all understanding'.

> *Your task is not to seek for love, but merely to seek and find all the barriers within yourself that you have built against it.*[36]
> from *Jesus' Course in Miracles*

It is in these moments that I can feel at one with a higher consciousness, I lose all sense of being a separate entity, and there is no connection to 'my' story, and specifically there is no notion of 'my' trauma. I feel free, completely free. If only it lasted! As ever the challenge is to let go of thoughts and allow the mind to be still, which is not easy. If thoughts come up, the

---

[36] Helen Schucman and William Thetford, *Jesus' Course in Miracles* (Course in Miracles Society; Hugh Lynn Cayce ed., 2000), Ch. 16 The Forgiveness of Illusions, 162.

goal is to let them pass, and not follow, judge or evaluate them in any way. Over the years, I have found meditation in India to be a much more powerful experience than it is in England. Despite the external chaos of Indian city life, where one feels one's senses are overwhelmed, I've always felt that underneath there is a tangible spiritual presence and this creates a more healing environment for meditation.

Meditation is also much easier there because the PTSD is very rarely, if ever, triggered in India, and I am therefore able to connect more easily to a higher level of consciousness for longer periods of time. With a structure of regular meditations, I am much more at peace, and less aware of any trauma within my body and mind. The 11th Step of the 12 Step programme is 'Sought through prayer and meditation to improve our conscious contact with God, as we understand him, praying only for knowledge of his will for us and the power to carry it out'. It has been through following the guidance of this step that I have ultimately gone from being a 'punch myself in the face drunk', to someone who has experienced a conscious contact with an inner loving presence which inspires me to live with peace and love in my life. It is a journey from the inner torment of active alcoholism and self-abuse to an awareness of an inner peace.

I do believe 'once an alcoholic, always an alcoholic', but that it is my karma in this lifetime to use my experience of alcoholism and sexual anorexia as a catalyst for my own spiritual growth and that I have been guided to both India (and the spiritual teachings of advaita vedanta) and AA to help me with my healing journey. AA is my foundation for this spiritual journey, and for that I am eternally grateful. Whenever I am travelling I make a point to attend AA meetings. Even after so many years of sobriety, I can find myself, once in a while, thinking back and questioning my drinking and wondering 'how bad, really, was it?', and then thinking 'it would be different now, I've had therapy, and other life-changing experiences etc...'

These thoughts used to really scare me, as I feared I would start drinking again, but now I recognise them for what they are, and remind myself of the reality of the devastation of my drinking for myself and my family. The old timers I met when I joined AA talked about the need for 'eternal vigilance'. I never want to revisit the psychological, physical, and emotional agony of active alcoholism, and to remain sober I have followed their guidance with a regular, structured involvement with AA, especially when I am travelling. Besides helping me to maintain my sobriety, it also is a great way to meet local people.

It's much easier for AA travelers now as we have online meetings when we are not able to attend a meeting, but these are not, in my experience, a substitute for the real thing. Before the Internet came along, if you were abroad and didn't know the address of an AA meeting, you would call the nearest American Embassy. Attending an AA meeting when you are travelling also underlines, in my opinion, that AA is one of the most remarkable stories of the twentieth century. From its beginnings in Akron, Ohio in 1935 when AA's founders Bill W and Dr Bob first met, it is now a truly international fellowship with meetings all over the world. The number of people, and indeed their families, who have benefitted from the 12 Step programme during the last eighty years must surely register in the tens of millions. I've been fortunate to have attended AA meetings in many cities over the years, from New York, Barcelona, Paris, and Kraków, to Berlin, Prague, Stockholm, and Kathmandu. It had been a long-held dream, since my childhood, to visit Kathmandu.

Ever since I had recited a famous poem as an 11 -year- old at a Junior Arts Festival, called 'The Green Eye Of The Little Yellow God', visiting this famous city was on my so-called bucket list, and on my second visit to India (in the spring of 2006), I decided it was time to realise my long held dream. In my young mind, the name Kathmandu conjured up exotic images of a Shangri La suspended in time; a lasting testament to a bygone age of expedition, exploration and discovery.

> *There's a one-eyed yellow idol to the north of Kathmandu*
> *There's a little marble cross below the town*
> *There's a broken hearted woman tends the grave of mad Carew*
> *And the yellow god forever gazes down.*[37]
> J. Milton Hayes

The guidebooks I had read since childhood described the remarkable architectural heritage in the city, confirmed by the fact that in the

---

[37] The first verse of the famous poem '*The Green Eye Of The Little Yellow God*' by J. Milton Hayes (1884 - 1940). Reference: www.allpoetry.com

Kathmandu valley alone there are seven UNESCO World Heritage Sites. I was really keen to see whether the city would meet my expectations, and fulfil a childhood dream. I had been traveling through India for several months and, when possible, following the news reports of the political unrest in Nepal. Whilst the BBC reported that foreign journalists had been arrested and beaten by the Nepalese Army, the UK's Foreign and Commonwealth Office was not discouraging tourists visiting, but rather advising against trekking in the foothills, or visiting any remote areas, where abduction by the Maoists had become a political tactic. I decided to go; I hated the idea of not being allowed to do something. I caught a train for the eight-hundred-kilometre journey from Old Delhi railway station to Gorakhpur, and then took a taxi for the final six hours to the border town of Sunauli, which is very close to the Nepali border. At the border crossing, sitting on a bench, I met a rather nervous-looking French woman, who told me of her misgivings about visiting Nepal,

As I sat down next to her, she looked at me, and asked, in a jittery voice,'Have you read the news reports on the internet?'..

'I've read them as well and I do feel a bit nervous about what's happening, but then again the British government isn't advising tourists not to visit, at least not yet,' I replied.

'I've always wanted to see Kathmandu, but I'm worried it might get worse very quickly, and I'll get caught in the middle of it. But I might never be here again! What do you think? Are you going to cross the border?', she asked.

'I'm going to Lumbini first, and I'll keep an eye on the news before I decide about going to Kathmandu. But like you I've always wanted to see Kathmandu, since I was a kid, so unless it gets a lot worse I'm going to give it a go, and hope for the best, I guess!'.

We stood and watched a hundred tourists walking over the border from Nepal into India, and apart from two dozen Nepalese returning home, we were, as far as I could see. At that time, the only tourists travelling in the opposite direction. Seeking some reassurance, we asked a tall guy who, with his very long beard, looked like one of the 80s band ZZ Top, what was happening in Kathmandu, and he was quite relaxed about it,

'Overall it's fine, we didn't have any problems,' he said, speaking with strong German accent. 'You can get into all the temples really easily. And there are no queues. It's relaxed in Kathmandu during the day, but in the early evening, leading up to the curfew, I could feel the tension building up.'

His older friend, who reminded me of a wide-eyed, rotund version of Ken Livingstone sounded a more cautious note,

'You don't know when it will change, it could happen very quickly. There are no queues, which is really good, so we saw everything we really wanted to, and then decided to leave a few days early. There was no point hanging around any longer. You might be fine, but who can tell what happens tomorrow?'

We listened to a few others, and the received wisdom was that it was only a matter of time before there would be more violence. One or two were more positive, and took the view 'you might never come this way again', which certainly played to my sense of adventure. The French girl decided against crossing the border, but with some apprehension I decided to trust my gut, paid my $50 entry visa and walked the fifty or so metres across the border into Nepal. It was already early evening and the sun was starting to go down, so I hired a bike rickshaw to take me directly to Lumbini, which was over an hour away. Our route through the Nepali countryside was mostly along flat, dirt lanes, with green, luscious open fields and palm trees either side lining our way. I admired the determination of my rather aged rickshaw peddler as he struggled to pull both me and my bags. He was probably in his early sixties, as thin as a rake, with a wide, beaming smile, which revealed a solitary tooth in the middle of his mouth.

We stopped every few miles to give him a break, which coincided with me watching local children playing cricket in the fields near the villages we passed through. I caught ten minutes of four different games, and each time, as soon as the children saw me watching, they automatically waved and shouted 'Namaste'. Namaste is a traditional saying of welcome meaning literally, 'May the God in me bless the God in you'. Their spontaneous friendly welcome felt very special. Watching the children playing, and feeling their wonderful energy and enthusiasm for life, immediately brought back memories of me playing football in the park near home when I was their age, and being abused in the toilets. The contrast between their spontaneous enthusiasm for life contrasted so starkly with the memories of the abuse. I remembered how the men had been initially welcoming and friendly, as part of the grooming, and then how violently their attitude changed and the abuse began. A child's innocence can be so easily destroyed. As these memories came to mind, I realised my body had tensed up, I felt hyper-vigilant and I had also instinctively scanned the area, several times, for any men 'hanging' around.

I started to suddenly distrust my rickshaw man, and to question his motives. So many irrational thoughts suddenly flashed through my mind. Knowing they were irrational helped me to process them, but the physical reaction in my body was immediate nonetheless; the feelings of nausea in the stomach, the tension in the groin and, in this occasion, the lower back pain. The gist of the thoughts were,

'I don't know this guy. How the hell can I know whether I can trust him? How do I know he's not taking me somewhere else?' I had several visions of being attacked in an old, dirty room by different men I didn't know. These weren't memories, just my mind creating images of violence. I prayed for these thoughts to go, and to be connected to the inner peace. I blocked out the thoughts and was carried forward on my journey. We eventually arrived in Lumbini, the traditional birthplace of the Buddha, by nightfall. Lying in the foothills of the Himalayas, Buddhist monasteries and temples had been built at Lumbini until the 9th century when the arrival of Islam and later Hinduism made these, in turn, the more dominant religions. Buddhism declined from the 10th century and the importance of the site was all but neglected for a thousand years until, in 1895, a German archaeologist came upon Ashoka's Pillar, identified by its inscription.

This brought about a renewed interest in the site, and whilst the area around Lumbini has remained entirely Hindu, many Buddhist temples and shrines from various nations have been built around the holy site itself. Designated as a UNESCO World Heritage Site in 1997, Lumbini typically attracts thousands of visitors from all over the world each year. It was to feel rather odd, therefore, to visit the many beautiful temples, shrines and pagodas on my own, and meet only half a dozen tourists in total during the five days I was there. The Maoists were clearly having a devastating effect on the economy and lives of the ordinary Nepalese. After a rather lonely week in Lumbini, I flew from Bhairahawa, thirty kilometres from Lumbini, through the mighty Himalayas to the capital of Nepal, the city of Kathmandu.

Flying through the Himalayas took my breath away. I felt in awe of the magnificence of the terrain beneath me; the mountains were a rugged carpet of snow-laden peaks and deep valleys spreading for miles and miles. I thought of the energy that had created, and was within, everything I could see and the fact that I, too, was made of energy, but in a different form. I was reminded of a quote from The Mother;

When I was a very young girl, I was told everything was atoms. They said 'You see this table? You thinks it's a table - it's solid and it's wood – but it's only atoms moving around.' 'I remember the first time I heard that, it caused a kind of revolution in my head, coupled with a feeling of the complete unreality of all appearances. All at once I said, 'But if it's like that, then nothing is true. [38]

Spread across five countries - Bhutan, India, Nepal, People's Republic of China, and Pakistan – the Himalayas are over 2,400 kilometres long, almost the same distance as the crow flies between London and Moscow. I've been blessed to have visited and trekked in many regions of the Himalayas over the last twenty years, including Gangtok, the capital of Sikkim, Shimla, Manali, Kalimpong, Ladakh, Darjeeling and Dharamasala, where His Holiness the Dalai Lama officially lives, and where the seat of the Tibetan Government in Exile resides. Nothing prepared me, however, for the experience of flying around Mount Everest a week after arriving in Kathmandu. The one hour flight cost only $100 and the pilot allowed the twenty of us, one by one, to go into the cockpit and take the most stunning photos of Everest as we flew around it. It is so hard to believe that any human being could climb to its peak. Being a witness to the immense physical presence and the majesty of Everest, and the hundreds of miles of mountainous terrain as far as the eye could see, stirred something deep within me; it reminded me of the miracle of consciousness, something I can take so easily for granted in everyday life. The experience made me consider once again how truly awesome the creative power of God, Higher Power, or Mother Nature is, and that we are all, energetically, an intrinsic part of this whole.

---

[38] *Mother's Agenda 1951-1960* (Institut de Recherches Evolutives, 1979)

I thought to myself, 'I wasted a lot of money on some powerful crap to feel this stuff.' Nothing, but nothing compares to feeling such a deep connection to nature, clean and sober. The real deal is so much better than any falsely generated, alcohol or drug-induced high. When I had flown through the Himalayas and into the Kathmandu Valley a few days earlier, I was nervous as to how tense the political situation in the capital, Kathmandu, would be when I landed. My nervousness was coupled with the same excitement I get on a rollercoaster at Alton Towers as I was not at all prepared for how low we would fly over the mountains to be able to land.

The events of June 1st, 2001 at the Royal Palace in Kathmandu have all the hallmarks of a Shakespearean tragedy. Whilst the entire story behind the massacre will probably never be known, it has become the accepted version of events that Crown Prince Dipendra, deeply resenting his father and other family members for disapproving of his relationship with a woman from a rival clan, in a drunken fury gunned down ten members of his own family, including his father, King Birendra Shah, before shooting himself.

King Birendra was regarded by many native Nepalis as the living incarnation of the Hindu God, Vishnu. When the king's middle brother, Prince Gyanendra, was declared the new king in the wake of the massacre, to a country deeply shocked and saddened by the events, this was not a popular decision. Immediately after the killings, there were mass riots throughout the country as conspiracy theories flourished. The Maoists rebels, who had long sought to overthrow the Royal Family, took full advantage of the political turmoil, and led an upsurge in violence. A state of emergency was declared in November 2001. A seven-month truce failed in August 2003 and two years later the new king imposed direct rule, stating the Nepali government had failed to defeat the Maoists. In April 2006 an alliance of seven opposition parties organised a series of general strikes and protests throughout the country, which led to a violent crackdown by the police and army.

The following month, the Nepalese government approved a plan to curtail the king's powers, obliging the royal family to pay tax and hand over control of the army to parliament which would also name the king's heir. Since my visit to Nepal in April 2006 the political and constitutional changes have been profound. The Maoist rebellion found its way into power, transformed the kingdom into a republican democracy and abolished the monarchy altogether on the 28th May 2008.

This was the tense and uncertain political climate I flew into, and I must admit I was excited by it.

It was quickly apparent as soon as I left the airplane that the airport and city were under emergency martial law. The security was heavy, and there was a tangible atmosphere of tension in the air. As my taxi drove from the airport to the city centre, there were very few vehicles on the roads, but there were regular army checkpoints with many soldiers, some obviously barely out of their teens, sitting on open-topped lorries, with guns pointing. My friendly guide informed me that the army was on high alert due to an increase in Maoist communist attacks in recent weeks, and that there was continued unrest among the Nepalese towards the newly instated Royal Family.

It might seem strange that whilst I felt anxiety about being in this tense political situation, there was also much excitement about what might happen, such was the unpredictable nature of the crisis. In truth, I got a kick out of the buzz I felt, and being in Kathmandu at this time reflected a side to my nature that loves being on the edge, and taking risks. I must admit I have a rather defiant, 'fuck it' side to my personality which has stood me in good stead over the years, when I've found life tough going. It's not an 'eff it and run', but a deep breath 'eff it and just get on with it'. For the most part in this setting of turmoil in Kathmandu, I had an egotistical, 'Boys' Own' attitude to what was going on around me. (There was a magazine called *Boys' Own*, which was published between 1879 and 1967 and which often ran stories describing men doing incredibly brave exciting things, like a hero in an adventure story. It was originally written to instil Christian morals in young boys during their formative years).

I did experience some PTSD triggers (for instance, there was general anxiety and hyper-vigilance when I suddenly came across a tense demonstration one afternoon, with a few hundred angry Nepalis standing off on my left, and the Army positioning themselves to deal with it on my right, which I got away from immediately), but I did not feel at any time a genuine fear of being physically attacked or sexually violated, so the PTSD did not limit my desire to explore Kathmandu and to make the very most of my visit. The challenge, as anyone with PTSD will tell you, is that it could have been a very traumatising experience had a combination of triggers taken place. There are times when I can see imagery in my mind's eye of me being violently attacked, but I have enough awareness to know I am witnessing this imagery; I know it's my mind reacting to some external trigger. Whereas some years ago, the imagery was much more real to me, and I interpreted it as a warning about what could and sometimes definitely would happen unless I escaped to a safe place. Over the years, I have learnt that I have to live life as much as possible, and as the power of the imagery has decreased, I have learned to trust my intuition more.

The army had recruited teenagers to swell its ranks, to deal with the ongoing threat of the Maoist Communists. Seeing these fresh-faced young boys thrown suddenly into potentially life-threatening circumstances was especially poignant; I saw the parallels of their predicament with my own childhood experiences and how you never know what life will throw at you and when.

The Maoists were threatening local businesses and forcing them to go on general strike. The goal was to undermine the King's power and that of the Royal Family, and they were evidently succeeding. The army had a presence on almost every corner, and my guide told me that the use of vehicles in Nepal was strictly limited to the government, security and emergency services, and some tourist companies. In fact, I saw very few tourists during my time in Kathmandu. In this way, the government hoped it could limit the opportunity for protests to suddenly take place; they had also imposed a strict curfew at dusk each night. My hotel, *Hotel Tibet*, was close to the centre of Kathmandu, and a throwback to the 1930s with its wonderful, traditional architecture, and old fashioned internal decor. I absolutely loved it. I was one of only four guests staying there, such was the devastating effect of the Maoist insurgency. As I checked in, I met a stunningly attractive American girl called Amy in reception and we discussed what we had both seen so far. We agreed to meet for dinner later that evening, after we had reported to our respective Embassies.

Amy was such a beautiful woman, and I fancied her like mad. She was 5ft 8" tall, with a slim build, long blonde hair, and gorgeous green eyes. She had the looks and the walk of a catwalk model. Beyond all this, she also had 'presence', and a natural confidence about her which I found irresistible. She had a way of leaning in towards me as she spoke, which made my heart race so fast. However, she was not a tease. She seemed to be self-effacing as far as I could tell. I took her tactile nature to be her way of engaging more enthusiastically during conversation.

She explained, as we spoke that evening during dinner, that the US Embassy had already taken the decision to close completely. Thankfully the British Embassy was still open, and only a few hundred metres from the hotel. The staff were very helpful, and particularly blunt with their appraisal of the political climate. I was told, in no uncertain terms, to avoid any groups or crowds under all circumstances. I was also warned that the Nepali army had banned demonstrations or any small groups gathering together, and were ruthless dealing with anyone getting involved. The BBC website had reported that some journalists had been attacked by the Nepali Army in recent days; this might have been the actions of young recruits but nonetheless it highlighted how volatile a situation might be if I came across any potential political demonstrations. The Embassy confirmed that almost all non-government vehicles had been banned throughout Nepal to make it harder for any such demonstrations to take place. If I inadvertently got caught up with a demonstration, however innocently, there was nothing the Embassy could do to help me. They also advised me not to:

- buy any drugs;
- go trekking, even in the foothills, as the Maoists had kidnapped some tourists for ransom in recent months;
- have any contact with the Army for any reason unless they communicated with me first;
- and to respect the dusk curfew without fail.

I was advised to report to the Embassy every other day in case there were any political developments, and let it know of my intentions to leave the country as soon as I made them. I was assured that if there were any urgent changes to the political situation, they would contact my hotel immediately. I returned to my hotel much more aware, my adrenaline pumping with a mixture of both fear and excitement. I'd never experienced a situation like this before, and I had to admit to myself that part of me loved the energy I was feeling, even though I could see what a devastating effect this situation was having on the livelihoods of ordinary Nepalis. That evening, Amy and I had dinner in our hotel. She was from Georgia in the

United States, and had been travelling on her own... and abroad, for the first time ever, for several months. I found her so attractive, both physically and personally. She was intelligent, funny, engaging and seemed to have a very natural inquisitiveness about life, which I shared.

I was far too intimidated by her looks, however, to tell her how gorgeous she was. The negative thinking was there as usual; I had decided that she 'was out of my league', and so assumed the role of the older, calm, experienced traveller.

'Do you think you'll stay a few more days?' I asked her.

'Now I know for sure the US Embassy has closed I feel I might have to get a flight as soon as possible. I don't want to go, I'd love another couple of days here. It's sometimes tense on the streets, but the Nepali people are so friendly. I feel really safe.'

'Well if it helps, and you decide to stay, if the political situation suddenly gets much worse and we're told to leave immediately, you can come with me to the British Embassy. We can make out we met in India and have been dating for a few months?' I put to her in an inquisitive, hopeful voice. I was smitten with her, no question. I fantasised about the political situation getting worse, and me being her 'knight in shining armour' which we would talk about in our old age, after we had fallen in love, married, and had three beautiful children.

'Ahh, thank you', she replied. 'That's so sweet of you. I'd like to stay at least two more days, but I'm really not sure. Maybe it's not worth the hassle. I'll sleep on it and decide what I'm going to do in the morning I think. I dunno, maybe it's time to go home?"

Feeling slightly gutted I asked her, 'What will you do when you go back to the States?'

She spoke with an obvious love for her father, but I sensed she felt he was a little too protective of her.'Dad wants me to focus on my career. He's very conservative, and he'd love for me to settle down, get married, have kids, do all the normal things you're supposed to do. He's a great guy; I know he wants the best for me, but I'm still his little girl.'

She added in a quieter voice, with a sudden sense of the mischievous, 'He's no idea I'm here in Kathmandu, he'd go nuts if he knew. He'd probably charter a plane and come and rescue me if he knew the embassy had closed!'

We both giggled and I asked, 'How about your Mum? What does she think about your travels?'

She looked at me with a smile. 'Mom's much more laid back. She'd worry if she knew where I was. Mom tells me to keep on the road if that's what I really want to do. She keeps telling me I'm only young once and to enjoy my freedom before I get married, have a family. My folks are quite different in their outlook on life'

As soon as she mentioned marriage and kids, in my mind's eye I could see the two of us on our wedding day; a posh, elegant resort somewhere in the US, an outdoor ceremony overlooking a lake, with a hundred guests, a small orchestra.... The fantasy had been re-fuelled. It was deflated very quickly the following morning when, over breakfast, Amy told me she had decided to book a flight to Delhi that afternoon, and then fly home. My heart sank, and I felt gutted to hear this news. I'd hoped we might hang out more often, and I'd get the confidence to get to know her more. Despite convincing myself she was far too attractive to date 'someone like me', I felt a few more days together would help me to relax more in her company.

'I understand. I'd love for you to stay a few more days and we could explore Kathmandu together?' I replied.

'Ah, that's so sweet of you. I'm tempted to stay, but Dad emailed me last night. He and Mom are really worried. I eventually told them I was in Kathmandu. They've seen the news reports. As soon as they knew the American Embassy had closed, well, they've kinda told me to leave Nepal today. Dad told me quite bluntly 'don't delay any longer, you go now.'

I felt upset when she told me that she had decided to leave, but at the same time I wasn't at all surprised by her father's position. The closure of the US Embassy seemed a hasty decision to me, but I also had to admit to myself that there were concerns lurking in the back of my mind that perhaps it would be safer to leave the country after all. But I'd wanted to visit Kathmandu for so many years, I had decided I wasn't going to leave until I absolutely had to. We said our goodbyes, with a gentle hug and a kiss on the cheek, and Amy went to her room to pack. I walked to my room wondering if I ought to tell her how much I liked her. I felt scared of making a fool of myself and so I quickly suppressed these emotions. I daydreamed of flying to the States and visiting her, and fantasised about us getting married and having children together.

When Amy checked out, in part due to my feelings about her I felt lonely, as I was one of only three remaining guests in a hotel with over fifty rooms. Nevertheless, I decided to explore Kathmandu on my own. My advance impressions of Kathmandu had been inspired by the J. Milton Hayes' poem I recited as a child, the articles and books I had read, and from friends' first-hand accounts of their travels to this usually bustling, chaotic city. I had imagined an exotic Shangri-La; a remote, romantic hideaway, high up in the Himalayas, with hundreds of narrow alleys opening up to reveal gloriously old-fashioned buildings, ancient temples and palaces, and other faded architectural gems. My imagination wasn't so far-fetched and I loved Kathmandu for all these reasons; it was no hideaway as I'd hoped, but it was such a fascinating city to explore, even if it was eerily quiet. There were so few tourists.

As I walked through the old city, I could easily imagine how packed full of pilgrims Kathmandu must have been, just a short while ago, before the political crisis had developed. I could imagine my feeling overwhelmed by the thousands of people slowly edging their way along the heaving streets; the incessant noise, the pollution, the piles of rubbish, the non-stop honking and hooting of the taxis as they tried to cajole their way through impossibly narrow alleys packed with tourists, sadhus, and street vendors; and then amongst all this chaos, the remarkable calmness of the cows as they wandered, as if in deep meditation, blissfully unaware of the crazy world around them.

Throughout my travels in India, I'd been somewhat envious of the nonchalant way the cows aimlessly wandered around without, so it seemed, a care in the world. I needed to know their secret of detachment. As much as I enjoy the buzz of a crowd, I am often uncomfortable when hemmed in or physically restricted in any way. I need to have an escape route; if not, the PTSD is often triggered when the physical bodies of a crowd are pressed up against my own. Instead, it was an eerie and sad feeling to wander through this fabled city, where there were so few tourists, and sometimes be a solo witness to its vibrant traditions, its rich, architectural heritage, and the fascinating synthesis of Buddhist and Hindu cultures, which that have peacefully co-existed for so many years. Whilst the temples and tourist attractions were all open, and desperate for visitors, many smaller businesses had been forced to close, due to pressure from the Maoists.

A Revolution In My Head

I understood what the Embassy meant by avoiding any sudden demonstrations. With such narrow streets and alleyways, it was easy for a crowd of people to suddenly congregate. On one occasion, my guide and I inadvertently came across a very tense standoff between the police and demonstrators, which later developed into violence and many arrests when the army intervened. Back at my hotel I found that Mum, still thinking I was in India, had emailed me.

Dearest Matt!
Many thanks for your email and, as always, it was so good to hear from you and know that all is going to plan and that you are feeling great. I expect you are in Jaipur now, which I have discovered from the internet is not too far from Delhi. Dad and I love the photos of Varanasi, it looks like an amazing place to visit. Are you eating properly? You look much thinner in the last three photos? Have you lost much weight? Thanks for your phone number which I've made a note of and will find out the code for India.
Will stop now and go to bed.
With lots of love from us both always,
Mum xxxx

Needless to say, I didn't tell her where I was or what was happening outside my hotel window! Not wanting to worry her, I sent an edited version of events.

Hi Mum!
I hope you and Dad are well, and thanks for your email. I'm glad you like the photos, I'll upload the others to Facebook when I get a chance. Despite the 'Delhi belly' a couple of weeks ago, I don't think I've lost much weight! Your eyes are deceiving you...! I'm thinking I may go to Ladakh in a few days, but will let you know my plans when I've decided what I'm doing. I'll call in a couple of days for sure.
Much love
Matt xx

Within Kathmandu itself, Durbar Square, the religious and social heart of Kathmandu's old city, had an amazing complex of elaborately carved temples, well-preserved shrines, and statues and courtyards built between the 12th and 18th centuries by the ancient kings of Nepal. Tragically the earthquake on 25th April 2015 devastated so much of the old city. Amongst the stunning architecture, I found Brahman priests and Sadhus performing elaborate yoga rituals, and charging tourists for photos; it was the Nepali version of the street entertainment at Covent Garden on a Saturday afternoon.

The most poignant place I visited was the Pashupatinath Temple, one of the most sacred Hindu shrines in the world. Stretching alongside the banks of the Bagmati River, the temple attracts thousands of Hindu pilgrims who come from all over Nepal and India to find shelter for the last weeks of their lives, to prepare for death, and to be cremated on the banks of the river before making their last journey with the waters of the sacred Bagmati, which later meets the holy Ganges. As non-Hindus are strictly forbidden to enter, I took up my vantage point on the opposite side of the river, which has several temples, shrines, statues and pagodas, and watched the funeral pyres being built and a body being prepared for cremation. There is absolutely no pretence about life and death when you watch a body being cremated so openly; whilst it is a profoundly shocking sight to behold, it creates a sense of clarity about the reality of death and opportunity of life; it cuts through all the 'crap' we tend to worry about.

Death is not extinguishing of a light, but the putting out of the lamp because the dawn has come.[39]
Rabindranath Tagore (1861-1941)

Acknowledging that I and everyone I know will die within the next 100 years is a great leveller, and an immediate reality check. Beyond this practical benefit, it's also made me think about life, death and what consciousness is, and I've pondered its significance in terms of my life

---

[39] From the poem, 'Say not in grief that she is no more, but say in thankfulness that she was. A death is not the extinguishing of a light but the putting out of the lamp because the dawn has come.' Rabindranath Tagore, auth., Herbert F. Vetter, ed., *Heart of God: Prayers of Rabindranath Tagore*. (Tuttle Publishing, 2004)

beyond the existence of a physical body. In short, I've always been fascinated by the meaning of life and death.

Albert Einstein's understanding of death is made clear in a letter of condolence he wrote to the sister of his closest friend Michele Besso, who had recently passed away; 'Michele has left this strange world a little before me. This means nothing, as people like us, who believe in physics, know that the distinction between past, present and future is nothing more than a persistent, stubborn illusion.' [40]

For most of us, the idea of death can be very upsetting to consider, not least because we are reminded of loved ones who have gone before. We may have complicated and painful issues yet to be resolved with those still alive, and there are often emotional wounds that need to be healed. The idea of being parted from those we love is also frightening, and then there is the fear of the great unknown. It is for all these reasons that a meditation on death is so powerful, although when I first started practicing it, I found it very painful. It brought up a tremendous fear of losing my family, friends and, of course, my own mortality. But when the intensity of these feelings passed I felt a much greater clarity about who and what I valued most in life, and in that sense, it was an enlightening experience.

This approach helped me develop a deep feeling of compassion for my fellow beings, as physical death is of course, a reality we all share. As my understanding of Advaita Vedanta started to grow, I felt an even deeper empathy and love for the world around me. The belief is that within our hearts is the source of consciousness, or God, or higher self, which connects us all. As Einstein intimated, the external universe, and the concept of time, is only 'a persistent, stubborn illusion'. This relates to what we believe about life and death. The details of the memory of when the paedophile was threatening to kill me, which were buried for years but then resurfaced a few years ago, (specifically what was actually said and the threat of the scissors) must have been some sort of catalyst for my spiritual journey.

Perhaps it was this specific threat, the panic attacks in my early recovery (when I was convinced I was going to die, as I had difficulty breathing), and

---

[40] Carlo Rovelli, *Seven Brief Lessons on Physics*. (Allen Lane, 2015)

the desperation from the PTSD, that prompted my consideration of what death, and therefore life, is really all about. Meditation on death awareness is one of the oldest practices in Buddhist traditions. In the words of the Buddha, 'of all the footprints, that of the elephant is supreme. Similarly, of all mindfulness meditation, that on death is supreme.' Fifteen years ago, Peter, a Buddhist friend, taught me a simple yet powerful meditation on death. He guided me through a brief technique (he also taught me a longer, more detailed version), and I've practiced it on a regular basis ever since. Peter's instructions were straightforward. As he guided, I sat on a chair in his front room, with my shoes off and my feet on the carpet.

'Focus on your breathing for the next five minutes, and allow any thoughts to come and go as they please. Maintain your awareness on your breath and nothing else for five minutes, when I will guide you further.'

After five minutes, he continued,

'Visualise members of your family, one by one, for about a minute each, in your heart and send them loving kindness. Focus all your awareness on your family members and on these feelings of loving kindness.'

'When you have done this, visualise your friends, one by one, for about a minute each, in your heart and send them loving kindness. Focus all your awareness on your friends and on these feelings of loving kindness.'

'Then, visualise anyone who you have any unkind thoughts towards, one by one, for about a minute each, in your heart and send them loving kindness. Focus all your awareness on these special souls and on these feelings of loving kindness.'

'After you have done this, maintain all your awareness in your heart and stay here for another fifteen minutes, or as long as you wish. Thereafter, in your own time, consider the reality of physical 'death' and, visualise the body slowly, and gently dissolving into the oneness until nothing remains.'

'Stay in this place of peace and love for as long as you wish.'

As stated above, whilst my initial emotional reaction to this meditation was very upsetting, after several weeks of practice, it gradually gave way to a sense of calmness and peace within me. This oneness is perceived as my body and ego disintegrating into a consciousness of unconditional love that permeates the universe.

I've found several benefits from meditating on death. It:

- Encourages me to live in the present moment, with a much greater sense of gratitude for the opportunity of life and health.
- Helps me feel a deeper sense of connection and compassion for mankind.
- Brings to the forefront who the most important people in my life truly are, and whether I openly express how much I love and value them.
- Helps me to recognise how yearning for power, fame, and money, do not bring peace of mind.

When I feel anger or resentment towards others, it reminds myself of the reality of death, and helps me to find a much healthier perspective on life. As the mind becomes still, I intuitively sense I am a spiritual being, beyond the reality of body consciousness. There is an eternal quality to this realisation. Whilst I find this meditation is empowering in my daily life, if the PTSD has been triggered, I am often very depressed and sometimes have suicidal thoughts, so this particular meditation can be counterproductive. At these times, I focus on concentration techniques to help me stay present, and hopefully stop me from disassociating. I often find meditation impossible as my body is so tense and so emotionally charged I can't relax and breathe normally. My mind is hyper vigilant, so the last thing I want to do is to try and 'go within'. Some time after this, meditation can often be helpful. Peter also developed his spiritual awareness of death by regularly walking in a graveyard near to his home. This practice might seem macabre and depressing, but, for Peter, it served as a powerful reminder of the transitory nature of everything and helped focus his mind on what is really important in life. He was one of the most peaceful men I have ever met – so something was working for him!

In 2013, a fascinating study was undertaken by Bronnie Ware, a nurse in a terminal palliative care unit. She listened to her patients during their last days, and heard their regrets, and decided their wisdom would be helpful to others. She compiled a list of the five principal regrets, which are a great guide to how we might approach our own lives. She listed the top five regrets of her patients:

- I wish I'd had the courage to live a life true to myself, not the life others expected of me.

- I wish I hadn't worked so hard.
- I wish I'd had the courage to express my feelings.
- I wish I had stayed in touch with my friends.
- I wish I had let myself be happier. [41]

Watching the funeral pyres being set alight on the temple riverbank, in Kathmandu, I was not prepared for the smell of the cremated bodies. I had braced myself for the smell of decaying flesh, but instead there was a very pleasant aroma of the different spices the Sadhus used to treat the bodies. It was rather like the variety of aromas one is aware of when wandering around a shop that sells scented candles or incense. It was here, as I watched the pyres burning fiercely and then gradually reduced to a gentle smouldering, that I met Milk Baba, a yogi who was reported to be well over eighty years old. My guide told me he lived on the riverbank, opposite the temple, and had survived on a glass of milk, a few beans, and yoga each day for over fifty years. I watched him, from a distance, for twenty minutes and his skin did have a rather effervescent glow about it which was remarkable, considering his diet and the fact he lived outdoors. I walked over and introduced myself. He looked at me intently, smiled, and then invited me to sit with him and meditate for a short while. His aura emanated a very peaceful energy. Unlike several of the other Sadhus nearby, who looked 'high' and may have been taking drugs, he was fully in the present moment; he was not stoned.

For some bizarre reason I suddenly thought about the famous scene in the 1989 comedy *When Harry met Sally*. Meg Ryan (Sally) performs a very loud 'faked orgasm' in a crowded restaurant as Billy Crystal (Harry) looks on with increasing embarrassment. The scene's punchline is delivered by an older woman seated nearby, when she says to the waiter, 'I'll have what she's having'. I know it must seem a strange mental association to have, but Milk Baba had clearly connected to something very special through his yoga. I wanted to hold on to the peacefulness that was being generated from within him. I wanted what he had! After thirty minutes of meditation, I thanked him, and made my way back to my hotel. I hadn't attended an AA meeting

---

[41] The original article was expanded into a bestselling book by Bronnie Ware: *The Top Five Regrets of the Dying,* (2012). Hay House, INC., Carlsbad, CA.

for a few weeks and knew I needed to touch base; I find that if I drop the number of meetings I go to, after a while my perspective on life somehow changes and I can become irritable, so regular meetings are the bedrock of my recovery to this day.

There is also something incredibly special about attending a meeting when you are in a foreign country, especially when it is a country that is so exotic and culturally different from your own such as India and Nepal. You are welcomed as a long-lost friend by a room of total strangers.

The evening the meeting was held coincided with Nepali New Year, and after dinner, I took a pedal rickshaw from my hotel through the city centre to the main hospital, seven kilometres away, where the meeting was located. The meeting was in Nepali, so there was an immediate language barrier as none of the other three men who were attending the meeting spoke English. But it was still very moving for me nonetheless, as one of men was shaking so much from alcohol withdrawal, he was obviously a newcomer and desperately in need of support. This is why one alcoholic working with another is such a powerful experience as we have an understanding of the living hell of active alcoholism, and the psychological, emotional and physical challenges alcoholics go through, during drinking and in recovery.

I'm so grateful that the AA 12 Step programme encourages me to explore my spiritual life, and to find what works for me.

Despite my reservations with organised religion, there is much about religious practice, (communal singing and prayers in the Christian church, and taking part in the Hindu ceremonies of puja and arti), that I have enjoyed, both in India, Nepal, and back home in the U.K. Whether it is Christmas services, prayers for those in distress, or specific religious rituals, these are all mechanisms to help connect with the divine presence within each one of us, as far as I am concerned.

Puja is the act of showing reverence to a god, a spirit, or another aspect of the divine through prayers, songs, and rituals. Most often that contact is facilitated through an object which might be a sculpture, a vessel, a painting, or a print. The object used is not the deity itself, but rather it is believed to be filled with the deity's cosmic energy. Often called the 'ceremony of light', arti involves a priest waving lighted wicks before the sacred images to infuse the flames with the deity's love, energy and blessings, which the devotee is blessed to receive. Other auspicious articles offered during the ceremony include incense, water, and flowers.

There are no such rituals or symbolism in AA, and the issue of faith is a strictly personal one. AA meetings all over the world will broadly follow a very similar structure, and are a means for practice what we refer to as 'our primary purpose is to stay sober, and help other alcoholics to achieve sobriety.'

Back in Kathmandu, as the AA meeting at the hospital finished, we heard what sounded like gunfire outside, and whilst it was Nepali New Year and might have been firecrackers, we weren't entirely sure it wasn't something more sinister. My AA friends advised me (with the help of a hospital worker who translated Nepali into English) to be very careful and to return to my hotel straight away. In the event, the curfew was just coming into force and within half an hour or so the streets were empty of rickshaws and people. I had a very nerve-wracking walk through the deserted streets and alleyways of central Kathmandu to my hotel, narrowly avoiding the Nepali army patrols on a number of occasions by ducking into doorways, and praying not to be noticed. My hotel was also quite close to the Royal Palace where the army had, for obvious reasons, a heavy presence, but thankfully I got through unscathed.

I knew there were huge risks with what I was doing; the media had reported the army recently detaining and beating journalists, and the British Embassy had clearly warned me they were powerless to help if I ignored the curfew and got caught. Perhaps there's an innate arrogance inside me, but I loved the buzz I felt; it was similar in a way to the effect alcohol had on me when it 'worked'; I had a very conceited, devil-may-care attitude, and I didn't believe for a minute I'd be caught. My ego also loved the idea of telling the tale, if I'm really honest. Whether the army saw me, and couldn't be bothered to do anything, I don't know, but I was relieved to finally get back to the safety of my hotel. The front door was locked, but after a few solid bangs was quickly opened. The staff told me how worried they had been for my safety. One of them then handed me a handwritten message instructing me to contact the British Embassy immediately.

Dear Mr Carey,

Sir, please contact the British Embassy as soon as you receive this communication. We have received information, from a trusted source, that

A Revolution In My Head

flights between Nepal and India will be forced to stop within the next 24hrs - 36hrs. Please contact the embassy using the telephone number listed above immediately, as a matter of urgency. Yours sincerely

I telephoned straight away, and the consulate staff told me they had been advised the Maoists were pressurising the airline companies to join the general strike, and that this was inevitable sooner rather than later. I was instructed to make plans to leave Kathmandu within the next 24 hours, and once I had booked my ticket to inform the embassy accordingly. My options were limited; I needed a flight to India or I would have to walk over the Himalayas! By the time I'd got through to the airline companies, there were only a few seats available on any flights out of Kathmandu, but I managed to book a flight for the following morning to a small Nepalese airport forty kilometres or so from the Indian border. After we landed, I found a bike rickshaw outside and asked to be taken to the Indian border. It felt sad to be leaving Nepal under these circumstances; the Nepali people had been so wonderfully gentle and helpful. They had gone out of their way to welcome me, despite the dreadful political uncertainty and day to day challenges (food, water, security) they were facing.

As we travelled to the Indian border, a few kilometres from the airport, we came across a very tense demonstration with several hundred men marching along the main road through a small town; they were shouting and some were carrying burning torches above their heads. There was only the main road where the march was taking place, and several dirt tracks leading off it on either side, with perhaps a dozen or so one storey dilapidated buildings which looked to be a mixture of homes and small shops. I presumed the march had been attracting more demonstrators through each town and village it had been through, (I could see several men joining it ahead of me), which concerned me as it was inevitable the army would now have more time to react if it had been growing in strength over a period of time. Above us there was a helicopter and my immediate fear was whether the army was anywhere nearby, as their reputation in recent months was to crack down ruthlessly on any protests. I'm sure the demonstrators felt this way as well, as a number of them kept looking at the helicopter.

In these circumstances, I was very concerned for my welfare for the first time since entering Nepal. I'd felt excitement and fear avoiding the army patrols after the AA meeting in Kathmandu, the previous evening, but now I felt raw, visceral fear, which triggered the hyper-vigilance and panic in my mind and body. I could feel my heart pounding fast and hard, and I feared the worst of the PTSD might be triggered. There was good cause for concern; I'd read a number of media reports online, and remembered the Embassy's warning to avoid any political demonstrations at all costs. But here I was, whether I liked it or not, in the middle of one. There was a palpable tension in the air; and the demonstrators were, I was in no doubt, ready and prepared for a confrontation with the army, such was their number and their obvious anger. I'd no idea what they were shouting so I asked my rickshaw man, who told me,

'They are demanding democracy and jobs'. He then told me, in broken English, but good enough for me to understand, 'Almost every Nepali hates the Maoists, but we also resent the Royal Family, and the army, who have not helped us. Most of the men you see have had no work for weeks and, at home, are struggling to provide food for their families.'

Despite the angry demeanour of the men, and the tension I felt, I reminded myself that the Nepali are, by nature, a remarkably gentle people. I decided to trust the judgement of my rickshaw man as he started to move slowly forward through the demonstration, which was marching in front of me as far as the eye could see. We tentatively approached the back group of the protesters. I didn't want to ignore their protest by trying to overtake them, not least because I feared they might turn on me; the atmosphere was, after all, intimidating, but I also wanted to respect that they were, as I understood it, protesting for democracy, for their livelihoods and for their families. Over the course of a mile or so, we moved very slowly and weaved our way from the back, and through the middle of the protest. We deliberately did not overtake them, as I sensed this would look disrespectful to their cause, so we maintained the same speed as the walking protesters; and as the men in front of us looked behind and saw we were there, so often they would stop shouting and chanting, and suddenly smile and say 'Namaste'. It was a remarkable experience. They were taking huge risks to publicly demonstrate in this way: risks of the inevitable beatings and imprisonment if the army found them, but despite their circumstances they had control of their emotions, and offered me their friendship. It was truly humbling.

After a couple of miles 'joining' the protest we finally turned off the route they were following, and continued our journey to the Indian border. I later felt a huge relief as I walked across the border into India. I waited in Sunauli for an hour for a bus to take me to Gorakhpur, from where I caught a train to Old Delhi railway station. On the train, the reality of the situation started to dawn on me, and I realised how fortunate I had been to come through both the curfew and the illegal demonstrations unscathed. It could have been a very different outcome. As I relaxed on the train to Delhi, I asked myself why I hadn't waited for the protest to pass and then to follow, at a distance, in their wake, but something inside of me had just gone with the experience as it unfolded around me. I also wondered whether a tourist, suddenly finding himself in similar circumstances in the UK, (in the middle of a tense, angry demonstration) would have been treated the same way? Sadly, I very much doubt it.

Whilst I love exploring new places, there are some I have an irresistible urge to return to whenever I can. Tiruvannamalai, in South India, is always top of my list; I regard it as my spiritual home. There is a sacredness to the holy Mount Arunachala which draws me back time and time again. I am more aware of a powerful spiritual presence here than anywhere else in the world, and consequently, it is here that I feel more peaceful and connected to my higher self.

After enjoying a month in Auroville during February 2014, which had helped me to re-connect to my spiritual path after the mental trauma of the previous twelve months, I decided to return to Arunachala for the Hindu festival of Mahashivartri. My previous visits had been among the most important of my spiritual journey. Twenty years ago, during an audience with Sri Lakshmana Swamy, I first experienced living proof of an ascended master who had transcended the ego and become 'enlightened'. I had no doubt Sri Lakshmana was fully connected to absolute reality. During my teens and early twenties I would have openly and contemptuously ridiculed such a statement, had I heard or read it somewhere. (In the west we are quick to reject the possibility of enlightenment. When we hear about Indian gurus, we are often reminded of fleets of Rolls Royces, and have fears of being conned out of our hard earned money. There are the frauds for sure; of course one should not accept everything on face value).

Our western religious traditions do not readily accept the possibility that spiritually advanced souls, let alone genuinely enlightened beings, might exist today, especially teachers who are not recognised within the established church. The books of the most popular modern day spiritual masters, such as Dr Wayne W Dyer, Deepak Chopra, and Neale Donald Walsh, are to be found on the self-help shelves, not the religious ones.

I've been drawn by the similarities in the spiritual writings and the experiences of Dyer, Chopra and Walsh, with Christian mystics such as Thomas Merton, Johannes Tauler, St. Augustine, and the teachings of, as previously described, Sri Ramana Maharshi, Sri Sathya Sai Baba, and Sri Lakshmana Swamy. They are all surely describing the same thing; the benefits of meditation, and of following a spiritual path. Somewhere along the line the core spiritual truths have been confused and corrupted, and another religion with endless rituals has been created. Regardless of the label we use, they all agree that our spiritual truth, our divinity, lies within us.

The utter simplicity and obviousness of the infused light which contemplation pours into our soul suddenly awakens us to a new level of awareness. We enter a region which we had never even suspected, and yet it is this new world which seems familiar and obvious... You feel as if you were at last fully born.[42] Thomas Merton (1915 - 1969)

The soul has a hidden abyss, untouched by time and space, which is far superior to anything that gives life and movement to the body. Into this noble and wondrous ground, this secret realm, there descends that bliss of which we have spoken.[43] Johannes Tauler (1300 - 1361)

I return to India as often as money and work permits, as I have always found it easier here to connect within myself to a spiritual truth that works for me. Back home, in England, I feel a resistance within our society to discussing spiritual philosophy, and to having an open, relaxed, non-

---

[42] Thomas Merton, *New Seeds of Contemplation* (New Directions, 2007)
[43] Maria Shrady, trans., *Johannes Tauler: Sermons, 89-90* (New York: Paulist Press, 1985)

confrontational conversation about our approach to, and our issues with, 'God', whatever that word or reality might possibly mean to us. This is unfortunate, as my experience is that the spiritual journey has been instrumental to my healing, and hence, why I returned to India in 2014.

As a society, at the hectic pace of life we live, and with the influence of social media constantly invading the quiet of our minds, we often set a ceiling on our spiritual journey and deny ourselves the genuine opportunity to develop a greater spiritual awareness. Perhaps this is because, at least in the west, we do not consider ourselves to be inherently divine, and consequently look outside of ourselves for peace and happiness in our careers, possessions, and relationships.

When I met Sri Lakshmana Swamy in February 1996, I knew there was no individual spiritual entity separate from the wholeness of creation inhabiting the physical body I saw before me that day. I wrote in my diary later that evening, 'this amazing being is truly and wholly connected to the spirit of the universe. I now know, without any doubt, that it is really possible to destroy the ego, to be fully awake, and know a peace that passeth all understanding.'

The experience of meeting spiritual masters such as Sri Lakshmana Swamy, Sri Sathya Sai Baba, and Yogi Ram Surat Kumar (a beautiful soul known as the beggar saint of Tiruvannamalai, who I met a number of times on previous visits), opened my awareness to the certainty that there are indeed higher levels of consciousness within us. Becoming aware of these higher levels of consciousness, I have come to know, is our spiritual destiny.

My last visit to Tiruvannamalai, in February 2006, had been with an American friend, Marcus, and my spiritual learning continued. I had travelled south, from New Delhi to Cochin in the state of Kerala, to meet him. Marcus is an old friend who had joined the meditation group I ran. He was a self employed architect, and decided to take twelve months from work to go travelling. By the time we met in Cochin, he had already been on the road for several months, visiting Thailand, Cambodia, and Chile. Marcus was short, fairly chubby, red-faced, and grizzly bearded; he looked like a younger, slightly smaller version of the actor Brian Blessed. He even had Blessed's distinctive laugh. He'd have made an excellent pirate in Peter Pan.

After a few days relaxing at an Ayurvedic resort on the Indian Ocean, we travelled by train to Tiruvannamalai, a 480 kilometre overnight journey north. Along the route, we were joined by many thousands of fellow pilgrims on the same train who were also making their way to Arunachala for Mahashivartri. The atmosphere and energy was welcoming and exciting; the singing, chanting and sharing of food between strangers felt so special. When we finally arrived, we saw the narrow streets and alleyways around the temple were heaving with pilgrims looking to settle down for the night, using their bags as pillows and newspapers for mats. Our hotel foyer was much the same as the busy streets outside as we carefully stepped over numerous sleeping bodies and made our way to our third floor bedroom. It was the only room we could find; no air conditioning, no working fan, a broken window in the bathroom, and a very small, somewhat shaky verandah with a family of monkeys, somewhat curious at our late arrival, holding fort. In the humidity of the night, with the mischievous monkeys outside, and our fellow pilgrims snoring in the corridor, neither of us slept a wink that night.

When traveling with a friend you really get to know them. Sharing a room with someone else, there's nowhere to hide. I listened to Marcus' hopes, dreams, regrets and fears. Underneath his good humour and bonhomie, I saw a very sensitive man. We both meditated at the ashram the following afternoon, and had dinner in the early evening at a restaurant nearby. As we sat waiting to order, Marcus slowly opened up about the emotional issues that had been upsetting him. He spoke of his childhood and the difficult relationship with his parents, and with his father in particular.

'My father and I always felt very awkward in each other's company. We never really saw eye to eye, we never got on....we had so little to talk about. It was strained until the day he died. I tried to get to know him. I guess I never felt he.... I never felt he accepted for who I am. That made it very difficult for me; I saw the shame in his eyes, and I... I felt I'd let him down.'

'How do you let him down, Marcus?', I asked.

'Well, you know. We live in a different time, now. People are, umm, well people tend to be more open to umm, you know to being gay. My father's generation.... My father was a man's man; he wanted me to drink beer with him and hang out with the guys, you know, but that wasn't me.'

As he spoke, there were frequent pauses when he stared into the distance, or looked down at his feet. When he looked down, he suddenly looked much smaller; his body language was like that of a little, lost boy.

A Revolution In My Head

During those moments he was rarely able to look at me. It was so obvious he was struggling with the intensity of emotions he was feeling, and which he had presumably bottled up for many years. Whilst his body looked smaller, on those few occasions he did look at me, his face suddenly looked so old and tired; it was racked with raw emotion.

I said to him, 'You've been holding onto this for so long, Marcus. It's time to let it out, allow yourself to cry. You've held onto all this pain for so long; it's time to get rid of it; let it go, my friend.'

He nodded and continued speaking through his tears,

'He couldn't tell me he loved me. He wouldn't accept I was, well you know, that I was a gay man. He kept waiting for me to find a gal, bring her home...I don't know if he ever really accepted or loved me....' He started to weep quietly, I could see he was trying to suppress his tears. He continued, 'He never told that he loved me, I felt his disapproval all my life.'

I listened to him as he gradually became more upset. I suddenly noticed the presence of three spiritual beings. They were twelve foot above us, to my left, and slightly behind Marcus. To see them properly I had to turn my head a bit to the left. Visually, I saw them from the waist to the top of their heads. They were next to each other, as three distinct personalities, but there was no gap between them. I started to describe what I could see to Marcus. Thankfully he had been open to healing and spirituality for many years, so he was able to accept what was happening.

'As you were just talking then, Marcus, my attention was drawn to three beautiful spiritual beings who are with us. They have so much love for you; I can feel a powerful healing energy coming from them, and my role is to try and channel it to you.'

He replied, 'I'm aware of a very loving presence right here (he pointed to his heart), I know we're not alone. I don't see anything but I can feel, I can definitely feel something, kinda.... around me.'

As Marcus continued speaking, I looked directly at the spiritual beings and felt the extraordinary love emanating from them for him. It was a truly beautiful feeling of unconditional love. I sensed they were always with him, that in some way they were inextricably connected, and that they could never be separated from him. It was as if Marcus and these three beings were the same soul expressing itself as four different entities for this game of consciousness.

'They are telling me they are always with you, although you are not usually aware of it. You have moments of sensing their presence, but then your mind doubts the experience, and you close down. They are always, and they are stressing ALWAYS with you. They can never be separate from being you. Marcus, they have so much love for you.'

Marcus nodded and said with considerable emotion, 'I want to see them. I can feel the energy, but I can't see them.'

I replied, 'I very rarely see anything. I am now, and it feels so special. They are intrinsically connected to you, it's as if you are one soul.'

A few moments later, when Marcus cried, their compassion was immediate and immense as evidenced in their expressions. As I looked up at the spiritual guides I could see compassion on their faces, and could feel compassion in my heart; as fond as I was of Marcus, the intensity of this emotion I felt came from them. It did not originate from within me. When, twenty minutes or so later, he felt more jovial, their unalloyed joy and happiness for him was beautiful to see and feel. Again, I could see the joy on their faces; their animated reactions between each other were so real to me, and the feeling of joy in my heart was blissful and full of so much energy. I did my very best to describe everything I was experiencing to Marcus. It was as if their role was to guide and help him and in that particular moment, I was the channel to communicate everything I was experiencing to him. So my role was to describe what I saw, and transmit as best I could the love they had for him. I was aware of their presence for perhaps an hour, during which Marcus told me much of his life story – his hopes and dreams, his fears and regrets. The healing presence emanating from the spiritual beings was very powerful, as Marcus confirmed that whilst he could not see them, he physically felt healing energy around him which he described, at times, as 'very comforting' and 'uplifting'. I have occasionally seen clairvoyantly before, but this was by far the most powerful in terms of the length of time it lasted, and the clarity of what I had seen, and the connection I had felt. I am in no doubt that the meditation earlier that day had 'opened' me up to a higher consciousness, and this had enabled me to 'see' the spiritual guides.

It seems so clear to me now that our sole purpose, over many lifetimes and much karma, is to fully realise the highest level, that of Christ consciousness, and I believe that this is the consciousness that Jesus realised when he said 'I am and my Father are one', and perhaps this is what is really meant as the eternal life. It has always seemed illogical and arrogant to assume that in this vast universe of which we know so little, the human race are the only spiritual beings in existence. Even if we are the only physical beings to exist (which is highly improbable to me), I know from my personal experiences of clairvoyance that non-physical spiritual entities are able to interact with us from the higher levels of consciousness.

Whilst the clairvoyance I've experienced has been few and far between, it has given me huge comfort to know that there is so much more (which is benevolent and loving) going on beyond our understanding of the physical universe.

My time in Tiruvannamalai during March 2014 had been enlightening for different reasons. I wanted to spend a few days on my own meditating at the Sri Ramana Maharshi ashram before meeting up with a couple of friends, Marjut and Danielle, who I'd met in Auroville. They arrived a few days prior to Mahashivatri, and we had time before the huge crowds of pilgrims descended upon the town to meditate at Sri Ramana's ashram and in the caves on Arunachala. Whilst I'd love to say I felt the powerful magnetism of the holy mountain and consequently a profound sense of peace deep within my soul, as happened twenty years earlier, unfortunately most of the time I was much more aware of a profound sense of pain in my bottom from sitting on the rock floor than any notion of impending enlightenment!

Marjut was far better suited to these austerities than myself. She coped with the hard, rock floor far more easily than I did. She never complained, nor shifted around trying to find a way to feel more comfortable, like I did. We spoke of her granite-like arse quite frequently after this. I longed for a nice, comfy cushion. I grew up watching *Monty Python*, and during this particular meditation, the thought of a comfy cushion prompted me to think about the 'Spanish Inquisition' sketch, which brought on a giggle fit. The ultra-menacing Terry Gilliam, all dressed up in catholic attire, threatens a terrified Eric Idle with the line; 'Biggles, fetch the comfy chair.'

Every day many thousands more devout Hindus arrived on foot, and by coach, car and train from all over Southern India for the festival. It was an incredible sight to see hundreds of sadhus in their ochre robes gathering around the foot of Arunachala, playing musical instruments and singing bhajans (hymns) throughout the day, and then, in the late afternoon, as dusk approached, the huge crowds would start the twelve kilometre pilgrimage. It was a really enjoyable experience to soak up the positive energy, and to share such an auspicious occasion with Marjut and Danielle. We went our separate ways after this, but stayed in touch via email. and eventually met up at another ashram a few weeks later.

I hadn't been to an AA meeting for a while, so I went online and emailed an AA contact, and we arranged to meet the following day for lunch, and then go to an AA meeting together. Arun arrived at my guest house with four other members, on their motorbikes, and I was received like a long lost brother. Every afternoon, for the next two weeks, they would pick me up on their motorbikes and we would whizz through the chaotic streets of the town to a meeting. The meetings were sometimes held on a verandah of an old house in the middle of the forest, and other times in a school classroom, and we would try and squeeze ourselves behind desks more suited for eight-year-olds. Typically, after a meeting a half a dozen of us would take off on the motorbikes again, and explore the Indian countryside, under the moonlight, around the foothills of Arunachala, and have some chai (tea) at one of the roadside stalls. We would talk about life, relationships, work, AA, and, of course, cricket, as the Indian Premier League (IPL), the professional Twenty20 cricket league was in full flow. I felt so grateful to be alive, sober and enjoying their hospitality. It is at times like this that I pinch myself for my good fortune to have found AA so young and to have remained sober. You really do meet the most extraordinarily kind, generous people in AA.

On my final day in Tiruvannamalai, my AA friends surprised me by turning up en masse at the bus station for a final cup of chai together, and to see me on my journey to Bengaluru. I then flew to New Delhi in good spirits, and after a few more months travelling around India, I flew back home to the UK, looking forward to the next stage of my journey; whatever that might bring.

13

LONDON CALLING

*Everything comes to us that belongs to us
if we create the capacity to receive it.*[44]
Rabindranath Tagore (1861-1941)

After five months in India, staying at a number of ashrams and trekking once again in the Himalayas, I returned to the UK in time for my father's eightieth birthday at the end of June 2013.

My father was born and grew up in North Wales, and my mother, although born in London, was evacuated to North Wales at the outbreak of the Second World War. My maternal grandmother had also lived here in North Wales for many years and so we had many family holidays in this area with her, my aunt and uncle, and cousins. Though my memories of these holidays are vague, I know I really enjoyed them. I sense only positive and fun associations with North Wales so to return is always a pleasure. With my parents' strong links to the area, it was only natural therefore for the extended family to congregate once again in North Wales for my father's 80th birthday. There were ten of us living together for a wonderful week in a large country house, with plenty of garden for the children, and us oldies, to play in. The main celebration took place in a beautiful country house hotel with eighty family members and friends for a three course lunch and speeches

---

[44] Rabindranath Tagore's *Sadhana* (A Word To The Wise, 2013)

from my father and myself, on behalf of the family.

I was really grateful for the opportunity to pay tribute to Dad at his party, and talk about his life; his childhood in North Wales, his university years in London where he studied Law at University College; National Service in Hong Kong; and, of course meeting, and then marrying Mum in May 1961. Both he and Mum worked really hard to provide everything my brother, sister and I needed as we were growing up, and so it was so good to have the opportunity to honour them both during my speech. I felt proud to describe him as I saw him.

'Everyone who knows Dad will, I am sure, attest to the fact that he is a gentleman, in the truest sense of the word. He is a very decent, honest man, and of the utmost integrity.'

I also enjoyed gently teasing him about his foibles.

'One of Dad's hobbies in to sit at the organ, in the hall at home, and play the hymn, 'Thine Be The Glory', very slowly and so dreadfully out of tune, it is almost unrecognisable. It's rather like a demented cat desperately chasing a mouse over a piano keyboard several times. His commitment to self-improvement is truly inspiring, but sometimes, Dad, admitting defeat is far less painful. I think he found his inspiration from the Les Dawson piano sketches on television!' (In the 70s and early 80s, comedian Dawson, who was an excellent concert pianist, was well known for deliberately ruining classic piano solos, such as Beethoven's *Moonlight Sonata*, for comic effect, on his BBC TV shows.)

'Dad also has some rather eclectic interests, from a childlike fascination with baby elephants, steam trains and model railways, to smelly French cheese, old milestones and toll houses. During my childhood, it was not uncommon for him to suddenly stop the car at a roadside, in the middle of nowhere, disappear into a hedge with his camera, and return triumphantly, and somewhat dishevelled, five minutes later with a photograph of a one hundred year old milestone!'

It felt very poignant to make the speech, as throughout my drinking and into my early twenties, I had harboured deep-seated resentments towards him and my brother. I unfairly blamed them for having not protected me, and for not preventing the abuse from taking place. I noticed that whenever I watched a violent scene in a film, I would think of my father or my brother, and imagine it was one of them being attacked in the scene I was watching. I was not consciously aware of these resentments until I had worked Step 4 of the AA programme, when I was eighteen months sober. (In Step 4, our sponsor helps us to list our resentments, and we recognise how important it is to maintain our sobriety and spiritual development to identify and to let them go). It was really upsetting to acknowledge the resentments, as I have always loved both my father and my brother, and neither of them were responsible, in any sense whatsoever, for the abuse. It is a perverse credit to my skills as an actor that I managed to hide the truth about what happened from absolutely everyone; so how could they, or anyone else for that matter, have stopped it?

However, it was easier, at that time in my life, to focus my rage and blame on them. At some level of my psyche, I was too scared to acknowledge the guilt and shame I felt for what I had done during the abuse. The resentments were diversions from the truth. The reality was that I detested the small boy for being so weak and pathetic that he wasn't able to stop the abuse. Later, my subconscious mind became my teacher. It was showing me that I needed to go within and deal with the anger I was suppressing.

In my early twenties, I found these family holidays really tough. I was single and had no children; I felt so different from everyone else. Over the years I've settled much more, and learnt to be grateful for what I do have, than regret what I don't, and consequently I've really enjoyed these occasions for the special times they are. AA encourages me to write a daily gratitude list, and this really helps me to keep a healthier perspective on my life, and to recognise that I choose how I deal with my feelings and thoughts, and not the other way around. In light of this, it was therefore a very special occasion to share the 'stage' with Dad.

The rest of the week was spent catching up with everyone, going for walks in the countryside, taking the kids on the Llangollen steam railway, playing football with them in the garden, going out for a few meals, and to rest and read. As a family, for the past twenty years we've celebrated Christmas together either at Mum and Dad's, or my brother's or sister's homes for the week between Christmas and New Year. Every few years, usually coinciding with one of my parents' special birthdays or their wedding anniversary, we get together and lease a country house for a week.

After returning home from North Wales, I needed to find a job. Whilst in India I had met a young man named Graham at an AA meeting in Auroville. During conversation he mentioned a national charity he'd been working for, which created opportunities for young people to develop self esteem, self confidence, and trust, and encouraged them to be involved with their local community. After the AA meeting in Auroville, he asked me, 'Have you got any work lined up when you get back to the UK?'

'No, not yet', I replied. 'At some point I really need to start looking online, and sort something out. My money will only last for a few months when I'm back to the UK.'

'I've just had confirmed a short term contract with a charity working with teenagers in the summer. I did it last year; the money's quite good, and the job is great fun'.

'Sounds interesting, Is it some kind of outreach project?' I asked.

'Yes, I suppose it is... I think you'd love it,' Luke replied, with real enthusiasm in his eyes.

'There's seven adults looking after fifty to sixty 16-17 year olds; the first week is outdoors in the country somewhere, abseiling, trekking, rock climbing, you know, that sort of thing, and then two weeks in London with various workshops, and volunteering in the local community. Go online and check it out. You'd be a great Project Lead, I'm sure.'

A few months later, whilst staying at an ashram in Rishikesh, North India, I had started the online application for the position of Project Manager, and needed to email Graham with a few questions. I went looking for an Internet café, and stopped for a coffee on the way. I ordered my coffee, sat down, and as soon as I looked outside, I saw Graham walking past! I had no idea he was in Rishikesh. The last time I had seen him was several weeks earlier, in Auroville, over 2500 kilometres away! I rushed outside and shouted after him,

'Graham! Graham! I didn't know you were here! How long have you been here?'

'Hey, how are you doing? I'm here for a few days, and then plan to get to Srinagar, in Kashmir, if I can.'

We had a coffee and I asked him my questions. Everything regarding the job application fell into place really quickly. A week after returning to the UK I was offered an interview, and a few days after the interview, I was offered the job. As Graham had described to me over coffee in Rishikesh, the three week programme included a range of physical challenges, including trekking, abseiling, canoeing, and rock climbing, at a rural outdoors residential centre in Cumbria; a week of creative sessions when we all stayed at a halls of residence in London to encourage the young people to live more independently; and then the final few days, when they travelled in from home, to promote awareness and raise funds for a local charity within their community. The creative sessions included an excellent workshop, hosted by the Speakers Trust, which taught the young people how to improve their communication skills and develop the confidence to speak in public with confidence and clarity. It seemed to me to be a great idea to introduce this into all secondary schools, to support young people with presentations and interviews. Their response, and the immediate benefits, were so positive.

I am sure that a similar programme of activities for survivors of sexual abuse (which incorporated Equine Assisted Therapy, as discussed later in this chapter), would be beneficial, as it offers the opportunity to learn trust, acceptance, develop confidence and to confront fears. Whilst I ran the programme, my participation in a number of these activities (particularly abseiling, as I still hate heights) helped me let go and trust my team to look after me.

Over the next eight months, until the Autumn of 2014, I enjoyed a number of short-term contracts with the charity, whilst I continued to look for a full-time job. Browsing the Guardian website one morning, I noticed an advertisement for my 'dream' job working as a Project Manager in a large events organisation. I went through a rigorous interview process both sides of the Christmas holidays, which whetted my appetite for the position even more, and in January 2015, I was delighted to be offered the position on a permanent contract. The new role gave me the opportunity to develop a key sector of the overall business which had built up very successfully over several years but had since outgrown its old-fashioned systems and procedures, and was struggling to support the day- to- day operation. It had become a victim of its own success, and the delivery of high quality customer care from first contact with the customer was being compromised, despite the staff's efforts to the contrary.

Over the course of the next twelve months, working with the in-house IT team, I introduced a bespoke online booking system, which was designed to incorporate the systems of several external partners over the course of the next six months; I oversaw the revamping of the marketing operation to maximise both traditional and social media channels; and I devised a three-year business plan which projected a considerable year on year increase in profitability. By the end of first year, the net income was up over twenty percent on budget, not least due to the massive increase in online bookings boosted by social media promotions. The ultimate goal was to develop the business to such an extent that our parent organisation would commit to a multi million pound capital investment, which was being discussed as a possible strategic objective within the next five years.

Whilst I was enjoying working with colleagues and developing the business strategy, I found it increasingly difficult to manage a work colleague, named Alistair, He was a difficult character to manage in the best of times, and our working relationship coincided with two other very strong triggers. Alistair triggered the PTSD which manifested in such an aggressive way it eventually floored me completely. There was so much about him physically which reminded me of the paedophile who had pulled the scissors on me and threatened to kill me; his physical build, his bulging eyes, his stare, even his smell. His behaviour was also a trigger; he was a passive / aggressive type who would mix a false charm with frequent undermining and bullying behaviour. When Alistair was angry that he hadn't got his way, he would often grunt or completely ignore me. This pre-occupation was also a trigger, as I remember the men abusing me, and not being 'present', in the sense that I had detached and disassociated from the experience. It became clear to me that he was a control freak. When Alistair disagreed with a decision he would passively and cleverly work to either limit or negate any opportunity for success, to prove himself correct. When I tried to find a solution to a problem, the problem would change, and I found myself going round and round in circles.

If we discussed an issue which had since been resolved, having originally trashed it, he would insinuate that it was his idea or that he had made the crucial contribution to make it a success – he had to believe he was correct. It also seemed to me that he often assumed a position of being the victim of an oppressive regime; that he was overworked, was owed huge amounts of overtime, and rarely, if ever, able to take any holiday. Alistair would, for instance, complain that he was constantly required to work much longer hours than he was contracted for, in order to get the job done and so, as his line manager, I had a responsibility to look into his concerns and find resolution. It had surprised me that the new IT system I had introduced, which had brought about a significant decrease in both emails and telephone calls, had not alleviated some of these time management issues. Our customers found it much easier to book online, and I was working with IT to improve our e-commerce with external partners still further, which would reduce office administration even more. This was not a prelude for any redundancies, a suggestion Alistair raised during a staff meeting.

I said categorically, 'There is absolutely no intention of making anyone redundant. This has not been suggested by anyone within the organisation. It is about streamlining our administration, improving the quality of our public offer, and increasing our income, so we can then focus on other areas of the business that have been neglected in the past.'

And this was true; it was never about cutting back on staff. The plan was to maximise the benefits of the new IT operation we had introduced, and to then re-allocate some of our resources to develop other areas of the business.

I then asked Alistair to keep a record of his typical week, broken down into each day, so we could discuss how he was spending his time, what took up most of his time, how work was prioritised, what could be practically delegated to someone else, and what might not be necessary to do any more. I hoped I could see where changes could be made to improve the situation. When I said this to him, he looked back to me in disbelief, shaking his head angrily, and said 'You are not listening to me,' he bluntly told me. 'I don't have the time to do this.'

Hearing these words, my heart sank, and I suspected he had no genuine interest in changing the situation, but was, in some perverse way, getting satisfaction from the attention and games (I thought) he was probably playing. Nonetheless, on the surface, I stayed calm, tried to remain open-minded, and told him that we needed to work through this document so we could find a solution to the concerns he had raised. He often used the word 'exhausted' when telling a colleague how he felt, and this would be discreetly brought to my attention. In conversation, shortly after being told this, I asked him how he was,

'You know how I am. I am being taken for granted. I haven't had a holiday for months, I am owed so much overtime.'

He looked at me angrily, and pulled out a crumbled piece of paper with dates and figures on it. He pointed at a figure at the bottom of the page,

'I worked out how much overtime I've done since the beginning of the year. It's over 230 hours, and we're only in October.'

'Okay, that works out at an hour, perhaps an hour and a half each working day, which is a concern. When we discussed these hours with HR last week, I asked you to put together a brief record of your day to day work, so we can look at what changes can be made to reduce these hours. Have you done that yet?'

'No. I've been too busy,' he said defiantly.

I felt exasperated, and replied, 'I've also said, on several occasions, that I was relaxed about you taking time off in lieu, but you have not done this either. For instance, we are very quiet at the moment. Is there any work reason, anything I am not aware of, that needs doing next week, which could, in theory, preclude you from every afternoon off, or taking the week off?'

'And my holiday...? I am owed practically all my holiday' he said, somewhat aggressively.

'Why don't you take next week off? Or, if you need more time to plan what you do, take a week off at the beginning of next month? Why not? We have been over this, the overtime and the holiday, so many times now. It is your responsibility to give me the dates you want to take for holiday. I've never had to say 'no' to anyone's request for holiday, since I've been here. But you haven't given me any dates, despite my asking you on several occasions during the last few months..... Why don't you take a week off at the beginning of next month?'

'What would I do?' he immediately added. His answer went to the core of what I was convinced this issue was really all about. He was using work to run away from himself, something I had done myself several times in the past. I studied his patterns and the content of his work, and, as far as I could see, there were no work-related reasons why he worked so many hours, particularly after the new IT system was introduced. It was, of course, sometimes necessary to stay on after 5.30pm; I did this myself numerous times, but even then certain responsibilities such as locking up or passing last minute information to colleagues, could be delegated, and shared amongst the team.

I needed to find some distraction from these issues at work. I needed to feel I could accomplish something, to get some self esteem, some approval; I desperately needed something to lift the thoughts of depression, with the onset of the PTSD, so I decided to fulfil another lifelong ambition and run the London Marathon. Training took place in Regents Park and on Hampstead Heath in earnest three times a week in the evenings after work, during September and October, 2014. As soon as it got colder in mid-November I started to miss a few sessions. It was so difficult to get back into the routine, and whilst I ran a few miles most weekends until the New Year, in all truth I knew I would be in no shape to run the marathon in April 2015. Training also brought up issues about my physicality. I felt really self-conscious wearing shorts at first; I felt uncomfortable with the possibility of anyone noticing me effectively half-naked but I soon relaxed and accepted that no-one else, particularly in a big city like London, really cared one iota what I was doing or what I looked like. Besides, there were always plenty of other runners doing their training at the same time. As ever, it was my relationship with me; it had nothing to do with anyone else.

An AA friend encouraged me to run a 10,000m race in Regents Park in early March 2014 as a trial, and I somehow ran under 45 minutes, a time that really surprised me. I knew that I needed a miracle to complete the 26.4 miles in one piece and survive without injury six weeks later! The closer I got to the date of the marathon, the less training I did. I knew psychologically that if I realised how physically unprepared I was, I would panic and pull out. But I was too proud to throw the towel in, especially as I was running for a small charity and had a financial commitment to meet. My reaction to training was similar to my behaviour as a teenager; if I didn't think I could win or be very good at something, I didn't want to do it, and with the PTSD being triggered most days, my emotional reactions were certainly childlike at times.

I would look on Facebook and see the training distances and times posted of my friends and others who were planning to run the Marathon, and think to myself, 'Oh my God, what the hell am I doing?' A good friend of mine, Fiona, was obviously training really hard, and she kept asking me how mine was going. I would reply, 'It's okay, but I know I need to do more.' And Fiona would reply 'yep, don't we all', and I'd think to myself, 'oh, Fiona, you haven't got a clue....!'

When the day itself came, I had had the experience of a 'long run' run over twelve miles on one occasion, which was in February, but during the previous six weeks had gone for light runs of only a few miles each. I spoke to a para-athlete friend who, whilst concerned about my lack of training, told me to run my own race, no one else's, to focus on getting a steady rhythm and to enjoying the occasion. 'Let the atmosphere carry you along.' Very wise words, which really helped me. So I had a last minute, simple strategy;

1. To run my own race, which meant accepting other runners, probably a lot of them, would overtake me!
2. To accept much older runners were fitter than me, and that was okay. I'll never forgot a lady, probably in her early seventies, overtaking me at one point during the last few miles and asking 'Are you okay?' I replied 'Yes, thank you. I'm fine,' to which she gently replied, 'Are you absolutely sure?'.
3. To take a toilet break whenever possible, even when I didn't need it, so I could recharge my batteries as often as possible. Other than that, to keep moving forward regardless; unless, of course, I had damaged myself.
4. To enjoy the atmosphere of my fellow runners and to soak up the energy of the crowd.

My Mum had her own strategy all planned out, and probably went into much more detail that I did. She had studied the route against the map of the Underground, and realised she could see me at four different locations if she, in her late seventies, could move quickly enough to do it. There were times during the marathon I am convinced that she, and the rest of my family who were with her, were moving much more quickly than I was!

As I lined up with tens of thousands of other runners in Greenwich, I reminded myself I had decided I was going to finish it, so I would do everything in my power to make sure I did. As long as my body held out, I knew I would be fine. I prayed to a Higher Power, saying 'Over to you, I hand whatever happens in the next eight hours, or whatever, entirely over to you!'

The crowds were raucous and supportive all along the route. They would offer sweets, water, fruit, even vanilla ice cream to help runners keep going. I decided to run alongside the crowd to take full advantage of their generosity, and stuffed myself so full of food during the race, I was surprised I didn't actually put on weight. The banter between the runners was also really special as we automatically bonded together. There were occasional, knowing looks of gentle desperation between a few of us as our minds and bodies entered a debate as to what the hell did he (me, that is) think he was doing, how utterly mad was he (me, again), even thinking of doing this. I hit the proverbial wall at eighteen miles, and then it was a case of jogging twenty metres, and then walking one hundred metres until the finish; but I did not care, as I knew I would finish it and that, with my health intact, was all that mattered. Mind over matter helps enormously in these circumstances, and I think it was sheer bloody mindedness, absolute stubbornness that got me across the line.

In the event I somehow completed the marathon in 4hrs and 43 Minutes, which I was delighted with. I have my medal, and a goodie bag to prove it! I'd also raised £1750 (or thereabouts) for charity, the knowledge of which, when it got tough, was a spur to making sure I finished the race. Somehow I managed to finish only two minutes after Fiona, who never knew how little training I had done compared to her. I could never tell her; she was rightly really proud of her time, and I felt I had got away with it. (Author's note: her name has been changed, so she'll never know!)

As a postscript to the marathon, I do not recommend my training approach to anyone, particularly when I read a story online last year of a member of the Armed Forces collapsing and dying on the route. I consider myself to have been extremely fortunate, but will never do this again without proper training.

Back at work, the PTSD was so savage that I soon began to feel subservient; I felt weak in Alistair's presence, and intimidated by his physicality. At a deeper level I felt he hated me. I knew I was transferring my feelings about the paedophiles, but nevertheless my thoughts and emotional reactions were increasingly unstable, with regular flashbacks, panic attacks, and physical tension throughout my body along with mental anxiety, and depression. Previous to this, when I moved to London in June 2014, I had started swimming each week, for the first time in years, and had relaxed enough to enjoy it. Now, the idea of being half naked around men (and women) was too frightening; whilst I knew I was paranoid, I felt scared I might be cornered in the changing room and attacked, so I abruptly stopped swimming.

The reality of this fear came to a head when, in April 2015, I was invited to my nine-year-old nephew's swimming party. The idea of being around children at a swimming party who were the same age as I was, when I was being abused, felt excruciating, and so I created an excuse and avoided going. It brought everything much closer to me, and I was eating very little each day, and had several weeks of little sleep as I moved between the bed and sofa trying to get some rest from the flashbacks and mental torment. As the exhaustion overwhelmed me, I absolutely dreaded my morning walk into work. Feeling nauseous and dirty under my skin I tried to psyche myself up, but as the rage boiled up within me I felt like taking a baseball bat to Alistair and smashing his skull into pieces. Thankfully, I had enough awareness, despite the pain, to know he was a trigger, not the protagonist. I am also so grateful that I am not a violent person. I abhor violence, and know that had I been an aggressive person by nature, I would have had a very different life. I have one of two acquaintances who have 'enjoyed' acting out through violence, in the same way it seems as I used to enjoy the initial buzz from an alcoholic drink. I am in no doubt that had I allowed my rage to get the better of me, this would have met with serious consequences.

Put it this way; I genuinely wonder how many lifers have PTSD, or another mental health issue, as a direct result of some form of physical, emotional or sexual abuse from their childhood, and which might not have been diagnosed? It doesn't excuse their actions, but I hope they have adequate access to the psychological help they need.

I knew that my aggressive mental and physical reactions to Alistair were because he reminded me of a specific incident and an horrific period of my life. He clearly had (by his own admission) his own mental health issues, so I could feel some compassion. Even during these experiences with him, I shared in AA meetings that I knew intuitively I needed him to be exactly the person he was, and I also knew that only a powerful present-day catalyst could trigger my deepest traumatic memories to be revealed. We did not share the same reality on so many of issues, and the constant mind games, to be blunt, took me back to the abuse whenever I saw him. Despite working with my line manager and the Human Resources department to find some resolution, it got to the stage that, for the first time in my career, I walked out of the job one afternoon.

There were two other significant events during this period of my life which were vital triggers that enabled my memories to be released in more detail. Over the years, the challenge with PTSD is that I would get flashes or fragments of a number of memories and an overwhelming emotional reaction which put my body and mind into a state of shock – in my case when this eventually passed I felt immense relief and exhaustion but with nothing substantive in my memory to talk through, and to therefore try and heal.

In November 2014 a friend had a spare ticket for a performance of *John* by DV8 at the Royal National Theatre, but its themes of violence, addiction, loneliness, and silent, predatory sexual activity, and being starved of love triggered me in the theatre, and during the following week I was depressed and self-absorbed with emotional flashbacks. I kept getting lost on the Underground and losing things. I retreated into my flat, locked the door and hid away until I had enough energy to psyche myself up to attend an AA meeting and release some of the pain.

Then a few weeks later, in the lead up to Christmas, I was walking through Selfridges and as part of a meditation to help heal my fears of sexual intimacy I was visualising myself enjoying making love and having sex with a woman who loved me. For several years I had created this vision in my mind's eye to counter the painful memories of the abuse, and to help me gradually feel more comfortable with the idea of intimacy, of feeling someone touching me, of bodily fluids being smelt and touching my skin.

As I walked through Selfridges, I felt the PTSD symptoms building up within me and suddenly noticed the visualisation was 'interrupted'. During the actual act of sexual intercourse, when I penetrated the lady and at the moment of ejaculation, my erect penis suddenly broke in two underneath my skin. This realisation really shocked and upset me, and then it hit me that this had always happened. Whenever I had imagined this vision during the previous seven years, the same thing had happened, and yet it was only now I had noticed it. I hadn't been able to consciously acknowledge it before; it had been too overwhelming. It was as if my subconscious mind was interrupting my conscious mind with information from my childhood. I asked my subconscious mind what this meant. Why did this happen in my visualisation? Why had I not been aware of something so graphic and disturbing before? During the following week, this main flashback memory that was replayed in my mind whenever the PTSD was triggered came back to me in more detail.

The paedophile that Alistair so vividly reminded me of is standing over me, telling me 'we know where you live, we know who your father is. If you tell anyone what has happened, we will find you, and we will kill you.' I have had this memory of him standing over me since my late teens, and the specific words of the verbal threat came back to me whilst watching the film *Taken* fours years ago. Now, I could vividly remember the man pulling out a pair of scissors, gesturing to my penis, and threatening to cut it off. I realised at a much deeper level why I was so terrified of physical intimacy; why a psychologist had once told me in my early 20s 'you almost have a phobia of relationships, almost'. It no longer felt so irrational; I could finally understand why the idea of sex and physical intimacy was so crippling to me.

As I write this, I feel energy rushing through my body, my legs have automatically closed to 'protect' my penis, and my awareness is heightened. I am hyper vigilant and fear I might be attacked, even though I am on my own. My mind projects the possibility of men breaking down my front door, and so I plan my escape route etc.. I touch the table in front of me, to help me stay present and to stop dissociating. I focus on my breathing, and in my mind with each in-breath I try to release the tension I feel inside my body. I know these fears are irrational; but my mind and body reacts as if they are inevitable. I then feel the tears welling up within me for the young boy who experienced such horror. The developed memory has become a benchmark for me. Although I still have more to be revealed about the memory with the bed and the camera, I have decided that nothing can be worse than what I already know.

From this point, I realised I could now go forward. I didn't need to continue searching any longer for more memories - I now remembered everything I needed to know to make more sense of my life and to be able to heal. There was no longer any need to look back and search for more pain. The experience in Selfridges (when I first noticed my penis 'breaking' in half in the vision), was the catalyst to seek professional help once again. I knew I had to talk at a deeper level about these events. I was determined to finally work through everything I could remember, to find peace.

My employer was very supportive and through their health insurance policy I found an accredited psychotherapist who specialised in everything I needed. Sarah Paton Briggs has extensive experience counselling clients with PTSD, sexual abuse survivors, and those with addiction problems. Her calm, friendly nature and her professional expertise were just what I needed to finally talk openly and in-depth about everything I could now remember about the abuse. Her sense of humour helped a lot as well! Over the next five months of trauma therapy she gently encouraged me to write down everything I could remember. It took half a dozen sessions with Sarah until I started this painful process and it was remarkable how much came up, once I had managed to open the 'disgusting, rusty tin', as I saw it, in which I had buried all the memories. When I was with Sarah talking about my memories of the abuse, almost always I was out of my body looking down on the event. The memory is therefore split between a physical dissociation (so that my 'spirit' effectively separates from my body and my mind goes into shock and to some extent shuts down), but I can still feel the emotional trauma taking place. On one occasion in therapy, in particular, the recall was very different.

I was back 'in there', in the sense that there was no 'looking down', but rather I was fully in my body recalling the event as if it was happening again. There was no visual memory at this point, rather a blankness. I was in shock, I felt numb and completely bewildered. I felt I had been energetically split in two pieces, so that my mind, and heart/body, were two separate entities. I suspect this is how PTSD develops; often I am triggered off and have flashbacks and 'see' the abuse from above; I feel the physical trauma in my body, but the full force of the emotional trauma is delayed, and is suddenly felt a few hours later.

Sarah's understanding of the 12 Step programme and her holistic, spiritual approach to my recovery were crucial for me to be able to work through the trauma. After several weeks of therapy with Sarah, I had psychiatric assessments with two experienced psychiatrists who both independently diagnosed me with Complex PTSD, and recommended further trauma therapy and anti-depressants to help me cope with the worsening symptoms of the PTSD. I decided not to take the anti-depressants, although there were often times when I was so overwhelmed with rage, shame and suicidal thoughts it would have been helpful for something to have taken the edge of the mental pain. I attended AA meetings every day for these several months during the trauma therapy, and this definitely helped me with my emotional sobriety. My fellow AA members provided amazing support to me, as I knew they would. In the meetings I felt the love, strength and compassion of fellows members.

'My name's Matt, and I'm an alcoholic'.

'Hi Matt.'

'I'm trying to work through some really traumatic stuff at the moment, for which I'm getting outside help. I don't want to drink, but this mental / emotional crap is affecting my sleep, my eating... I'm exhausted a lot of the time, which doesn't help my mental state one bit. It makes me more paranoid, I'm scared I'm going to be attacked.... At some level I know this isn't going to happen, but my mind and body are anticipating something dreadful, and I start isolating to keep myself safe.... it's so fucked up sometimes. But it's good to get to a meeting. The support of the fellowship has been amazing; friends in AA have texted me, called me, invited me for coffee. I've been here before; I know it will pass. Thanks for listening.'

By talking I felt more connected to the group, and the friendly smiles of understanding and encouragement from AA members helped me to hang in there, when it's got tough. It's also inspiring to hear how other people deal with their challenges in recovery, and the wisdom, they often share which I can so easily forget. It helps me to know that I am not alone, and to try and help others as much as I can. I love the simplicity of the AA programme, especially the statement I heard so many times in my early meetings:

'No matter what happens, we just do not drink.'

I applied this approach to my situation as I decided that, no matter what I was feeling, no matter what I could now remember, I would not drink and I would not hurt myself or anyone else. My many years of recovery in AA played a huge role in my being strong enough to work through the emotional and psychological trauma I was experiencing on a daily basis. I know the AA 12 Step programme works under all circumstances; I've seen too many miracles, including those I've personally experienced, to doubt it. When I felt really rough, I used my anger to help me. I allowed my stubbornness to get me through each day as I was struggling to keep safe and sane. I would tell myself 'there's no way I'm going to let sick, fucked up bastards like Savile beat me, no way.' That focused my mind to simply survive.

I reminded myself of the spiritual experiences I'd had; meeting with the paedophile in McDonalds during the first year of my recovery; the profound spiritual experience I'd had in the presence of Sri Sathya Sai Baba; the enlightened teacher, Sri Lakshmana Swamy, in Tiruvannamalai who had spoken to me telepathically; the drunk at Clapham Junction who encouraged me to stay sober; the vision of the beautiful angel in my lounge, and so many remarkable people I had met along my journey who had taught and inspired me. Along with the daily AA meetings, my weekly sessions with Sarah became something I started looking forward to, and even though most sessions were very challenging, we did manage to have a few laughs along the way. I knew I could trust her professional guidance and she has a genuine empathy which was healing in itself. Like the wonderfully inspiring Dr Ron Hutchinson over twenty years earlier, I know Sarah was bought into my life to enable me to move forward through this process. During the trauma therapy sessions, I described the panic attacks and the feeling I often got of my consciousness leaving my body very suddenly and Sarah would teach me techniques to help me stay in the body and stop me from disassociating.

These simple, practical techniques would get me from a therapy session to an AA meeting, then home safely. Obsessive fantasies about how I'd commit suicide, though, were often and real. I would feel tension throughout my body near certain men, paranoia in my mind, and shame in my genitals. I did not trust myself on the Underground and on the few occasions I used it during this period of my life I'd stand with my back touching the wall as the train entered the station. The urge to be reckless and say 'fuck it', close my eyes, and jump was there many times.

Similarly, when the flashbacks came on and my mind was savage I would fantasise about either slashing my wrists in the bath or taking a rope and hanging myself on Hampstead Heath. I would sometimes imagine what it would feel like with my legs jerking as the life force left me. The adult wanted to live but the child, so traumatised, wanted the pain to go, and wanted to die. I thought of my family, especially my mother, and knew how it would destroy them if I acted out these fantasises, but at times I felt I just could not go on. Thinking of their pain helped me to cry, and when I started to eventually cry, I could not stop. I also felt encouraged after a few weeks of counselling with Sarah to speak in more depth with my family and closest friends about the abuse. Even though I chose not to tell them everything I could at least explain about the recent Complex PTSD diagnosis, and what this meant practically. It has helped destroy the false belief I have carried subconsciously for many years about my family not loving me if they knew all about me. As a child, I was scared I might be put up for adoption if they knew what (I believed) I had done, such was the crippling shame the paedophiles had convinced me of.

Talking with Sarah had helped me to recognise and release a lot of the shame I had been carrying for so many years. I've found shame to be the hardest, most elusive and corrosive emotion to deal with; it affects every other emotion I have, and cripples my ability to connect to myself and to other people, and for so long I didn't realise I felt shame. The shame came from the small boy being told by the paedophiles that he was responsible for everything that was happening. That his actions and behaviour had opened a 'Pandora's Box' of actions which had to now take place, and it was all his fault. I had believed this as a truth, buried it as deeply as possible, and it had affected me for much of my adult life. It was the filter through which I had viewed my relationships, my career, my hopes and dreams, and myself for over thirty years.

Children are by nature trusting of adults, and are conditioned to respect and obey them. Evilly, paedophiles take advantage of this for their own twisted and perverted purposes. Long before the internet and Facebook, men were grooming boys – manipulating, threatening, blackmailing – to carry out sexual abuse. The manipulation was also the main reason I had not allowed my loving family into the depth of my pain. I was scared they would judge and condemn me. That is what shame does, and it contrasts with what my actual experience with my family had always been, namely one of support and love. Shame, and creating a feeling of complicity, are the ultimate weapons for the predatory, narcissistic paedophile to use to ensure a survivors silence, and have control.

After several weeks of therapy, I remember one occasion when I managed to cry so much the tears stopped flowing but the motion of crying continued for another forty minutes. I felt my breathing effectively expelling energy from within the organs of my body in some way. Some internal energetic shift seemed to be taking place, and after I awoke from a very deep sleep the next day, I felt a much deeper level of calmness within me. The suicidal thoughts had always precipitated my breaking down in tears, which for many years I had found so desperately difficult to do. I began to recognise a pattern, though, which helped me deal with the experiences. I would feel the tension and shame building up within my body, starting in the genitals, and when my body felt clumped with shame I would feel suicidal. As these emotions built further, eventually I would break down in tears which would continue for an hour or so, after which I would feel exhausted, but 'clean' in a way.

Sarah helped me develop a relationship with my inner child, something I ridiculed when this was suggested to me in my early twenties. After one meeting with her, I visited my parents and looked through the family photo album and asked Dad to scan and send me a dozen or so photos of me as a child, taken before, during and after the times when I had been abused. Later on, I brought three of these photos to the trauma therapy to show Sarah. I had wanted to punch the face of the younger me I saw in the photos, or burn them, as I still felt so angry with him that he hadn't got away, that he hadn't escaped. Over the next few months of intensive therapy, as I spoke in detail about what 'he' had experienced, I started to acknowledge what a truly remarkable, incredibly resilient and brave child 'he' was, to have survived such horrific experiences and to have grown into a decent, kind man.

I chose the three photos I'd shown Sarah to have next to my bed, and each night I would talk to the younger me, and send myself love and admiration for what I could now see that 'I' had achieved. There is one photo in particular I have changed my view of completely as a result of this process. I am wearing my prep school uniform with my red cap, and my eyes tell a thousand stories of the pain I was feeling at that time, and for years I would flinch whenever I saw it. This was the photo I would deliberately speak to each night before going to bed. I would acknowledge the trauma the child had suffered; that he had been too scared and ashamed to share with anyone. I often told him he was incredibly strong and courageous to have survived; and that I am so proud of him; that I love him so much. It felt rather like a father might talk to his son, in a very intimate, emotional moment in their lives. I spoke with tears streaming down my face, and a genuine sense of admiration for the young boy I once was.

'You are such an amazing little boy. I want you to know how much I love and admire you. You were so unbelievably brave to have gone through what happened to you. What you went through was horrendous, what you were forced to do was so dreadful.... How you survived all of that is truly incredible. It is unbelievable. I am so proud of you. You're amazing...so amazing.'

    I didn't always feel I was talking to my younger self, but rather I was gradually reaching out to a very scared, small boy who needed love and gentle encouragement. As the inner child has healed, the adult has become more at peace.

    I also often shared with Sarah, when my PTSD had been triggered, my fear of being attacked by men. Under normal circumstances, this is not my reality, and only when I have been triggered does it become an all but certainty in my mind. The physicality of certain men scared me, even if they were behaving in a calm, friendly way, and I felt hyper-vigilant around them. Only after therapy was I able to process these fears more easily. Sarah suggested I try Equine Assisted Therapy (EAP). I have always been scared of horses; it is their immense physicality compared to me which at some level reminds me of the men who abused me. I have also always anticipated a horse will attack me, even though I have never had any negative experience with them previously. In recent years, horses have been recognised as playing an increasingly important role in supporting the healing of war veterans, sexual abuse survivors, and others who have PTSD. EAP, both here in the UK and in the United States, has been very helpful with clients who suffer from the nightmares, anxiety, depression, anger, irritability and other debilitating effects of PTSD.

    The thinking behind EAP is that horses are prey animals, and, like those who have been to war or have suffered great trauma, they rely on their heightened senses for survival. They react to and mirror the emotions of visitors directly, without words, so they respond negatively to negative emotions. Correspondingly they respond positively to positive emotions, and they have no ulterior motives. I had a session with Sarah and her two horses at a farm outside Cheltenham. We sat next to each other in the thirty- by twenty- metre pen as the two horses were free to walk around as they pleased. I felt tension throughout my body, particularly in my genitals, stomach and lower back.

They were huge mares; Jazz was 16 hands 3", and Tia, 17 hands 1". Their immense physicality triggered me in a profound way; it's hard to describe quite how, but it felt as if the men were physically closer to me than they ever have been since the abuse took place. Something very visceral was being released as the horses wandered around the paddock. It took over an hour for me to be willing to touch one of them, and then it was only a tentative touch as I leaned forward whilst sitting in a chair. After ninety minutes I finally was able to walk close to one of them and gently stroke its mane. Sarah knew my primary fear was being suddenly attacked by the horse, kicking me from behind, but I followed her lead and was soon massaging the horses' bum, either side of its tail.

The horse responded by looking back at me, and then gently lifting its tail in appreciation. This was a huge achievement; I knew full well that it symbolised so much more than just stroking a horse. I never knew massaging a horse's arse could be so rewarding! (We've all got to find some humour to life, and even black humour helps). During the afternoon session, I had the task of leading a horse through an 'assault course' which was to be symbolic of my fears or concerns, to see where I was with each of them. The course was very simple; we arranged a few poles and cones to form three slightly different obstacles to lead the horse through. I decided to focus on three main fears;

1. Writing the book, and therefore dealing with all painful memories that would inevitably come up.
2. Hangups about being sexually intimate with a woman.
3. Being compelled to work full-time before I was ready.

Before approaching each obstacle, I held the horse's lead, thought of the fear in detail, and then verbally commanded the horse to walk with me. It was incredibly striking how the horses instinctively reacted when I focussed on each issue in turn. I had the least concern of the three about writing the book – I had made the decision to do it and that was that, regardless of how difficult I knew it would be at times. Working full time was another one of those issues that I knew I would be able to go back to at some point; I knew I was not ready yet, but I would be in time. The horse obeyed my direction, without hesitation, on the first two commands.

However, with the intimacy issue, which has always been 'the abyss' in my mind, the horse would not move however I tried to pull or cajole it. Its intuitive understanding of my fear somehow helped me acknowledge the truth of this fear in a weird way.

With Sarah's encouragement I also decided I needed to join a support group for survivors; something I had often thought about but dismissed for years. I went online and quickly found SoSAA, a new 12 Step-based charity for survivors of sexual abuse, which had started a weekly meeting in South London. The group was warm, friendly and well organised. There were originally six regular members, which was just about as much as I could handle initially, and the meeting was predominantly female which really helped. (For the first few weeks, I didn't feel comfortable speaking openly about my experiences in front of any men.)

The SoSAA programme has been adapted from the AA 12 Steps, and group members support each other as they work through the programme of recovery each week. My group was informal in the sense that there was no pressure to talk or to work the steps until a member felt they were ready; but most importantly its members were all survivors, and the support, compassion and understanding came from a genuine place; we all knew exactly what it felt like to be a survivor of sexual abuse. We could all relate to the emotional, physical and psychological challenges of recovery, and this, in itself, created an extraordinary opportunity for profound healing to take place, over time. I have met the most extraordinarily courageous, decent and kind people in SoSAA. I find their strength truly inspirational as we learn to share honestly about what we experienced, and despite the anger, fear and challenges we all face, how we each have found a way to gradually learn to live our lives through working a spiritual programme with acceptance, peace and love. Joining the SoSAA group and attending weekly meetings enabled me to be more open with my family, which was very painful for all of us but hugely rewarding. Their love and support has been crucial. My long term sobriety in AA encouraged me to be as honest as I could be from the first meeting.

I felt physically sick to the stomach before I opened my mouth and introduced myself to the group. I went into shock and dissociated as I started to speak;

'My name is Matt...... I'm a survivor. I was abused....raped... whatever you want to call it, many times as a child. It went on for about eighteen months. I was eight when it started.... I didn't tell anyone about it. I was too scared, I went into shock and felt so confused about everything... It's taken years to be able to deal with it. The worst of the memories were buried so deeply they've only recently come up... in enough detail to talk about them. I've had counselling on and off since I was twenty, when I got sober in AA. As painful as it has been, talking about it one on one has helped me, but it's taken me years to find the courage and talk about in a group with other survivors. I've put it off so many times. But I know I need this... I wasn't ready. It's good to be here.'

I listened to a few other members who were courageous enough to share in detail what had happened to them, so I decided to be more open as well.

'It happened so many times, it's only dawned on me recently how often, and I sometimes question how the hell I hid it so well from my family. In the last year, more memories have come back, and I can remember a lot more detail as well. There were at least a dozen different locations, public toilets in parks and on the sea front, and almost always I remember there were three men. Each one would make me 'perform' on them, or them with me, in turn..... it happened so many fucking times, I used to feel like a child prostitute. That's enough for now.... Thanks for listening.'

During my weekly SoSAA meeting and attending trauma therapy with Sarah, I decided to write down everything I could now remember from the abuse. After several weeks of putting this off, I finally committed pen to paper. It is shocking how much more you can actually remember when you start to write. It took on a life of itself after a while; I just had the pen and it flowed most of the time and then, when writing about the abuse, I would hit a wall; I would feel the physical tension in the groin, stomach and often in my lower back, and would have very vague memories come up, or rather fragments of memories, but enough to see myself in different locations being abused. I would see the men standing around me in a cubicle, which would throw me. I'd take a deep breath, and think to myself, 'another fucking memory. How many fucking times did it happen?'

I would ask myself, 'What happened in there? What did they say? What did they then do?' It was sometimes a day or so later that the memory, with all the accompanying shock, rage, and fear, would finally come up, and then after a short while the adult in me would feel so much compassion for the small boy who had somehow survived it. Often I would first recall odd things, like the leaves behind the toilet, the crispness of the toilet paper, the rusty cistern above me, the whitish brown pebble dash walls, the broken tiles. The brokenness of everything. Eventually so much more came up, and I felt shock, tears and relief as well. I had waited over thirty years for these memories to be revealed – I knew this was a turning point in my life.

The memories have been there, deep down, and have always been affecting me in one way or another so I wrote with the hope and intention that bringing it into the light would take the energy out of it, and I could heal. Just focussing on the abuse, though, lacked perspective. I realised I needed to put it into the perspective of everything else in my life; my family and close friends, my hobbies, my theatre career, and my spiritual journey. Only then could I really move on and let go. I am so grateful that a healing has taken place within me emotionally, physically, psychologically and spiritually.

One of The Promises in AA states 'we are going to know a new freedom and a new happiness. We will not regret the past nor wish to shut the door on it.' I can now fully relate to this Promise, having experienced it coming true in this area of my life. It is what it is, and with my healing, I hope what I write and say will help others to heal.

It was at my very worst time, the darkest point in my life, two months after starting therapy with Sarah, and a few weeks after joining SoSAA, that suicide seemed the only way out of this seemingly never-ending hell of the flashbacks to the abuse. Then my loving power created another improbable miracle to help me. It had started twelve years earlier with a remarkable chain of 'coincidences'. I said hello to an Indian girl called Prisha (which means Beloved, or God's Gift) in an AA meeting in Birmingham. She was receiving treatment in a rehabilitation centre outside the city for her alcoholism.

Six months after the meeting in Birmingham, and over eight thousand kilometres away, I was in Bangalore, India looking for an AA meeting near St Mark's Cathedral. I noticed an Indian girl standing in the doorway of a hall. She looked very familiar to me, but I quickly rubbished this thought in my mind as India has a population over one billion, and I rationalised the chance of bumping into someone I knew were so remote as to be impossible. Nonetheless, thinking this was the location for the meeting, I walked over and introduced myself;

'Hi, my name's Matt, I'm looking for the AA meeting.'

'Welcome. You've found us', she replied, with a warm smile.

'I know this sounds really bizarre, but you look really familiar. Have you ever lived in England?', I asked her, hoping it might be one of those magical moments of synchronicity that sometimes happens in life.

'Yes', she replied, with a look of surprise of her face, 'I.... I went to a treatment centre in England.'

I then remembered how we had met. 'My God! I thought I recognised you! We met very briefly at a meeting in Birmingham, on a Saturday evening earlier this year. In the kitchen!' I said. She looked at me intently for a few seconds, and after a brief pause, she replied with a huge smile of recognition,

'Yes, we did. Wow! This is really crazy....How are you?'

The story now becomes even stranger! Six weeks later I was in New Delhi, a city over two thousand kilometres north of Bangalore, with a population of 18.6 million people, and as I walked through Rajiv Chowk (a very busy market in the centre of city, also known as Connaught Place), I accidentally knocked into someone as I went to walk past them. I stopped and turned to apologise, and I realized to my utter amazement it was Prisha! She was as shocked as I was and I was speechless. Then she told me she had not been to an AA meeting since we met in Bangalore and desperately needed one.

She added,'It's so crazy to see you. This is meant to happen. I really need a meeting. I haven't been to one since the one in Bangalore, and my head's not right. I feel really unsettled inside, just not centred at all... You know when you really need a meeting?'

'Yes, I know exactly what you mean. Its just so completely bonkers that we've bumped into each other in middle of Delhi, in probably the busiest market in India, just as you are feeling vulnerable and need a meeting... You are definitely being looked after.'

Prisha then told me that she had been praying to her Higher Power for the strength to stay sober, just at the moment as we bumped into each other. As we spoke in the midst of the hustle and bustle of the market, the 'Love addict' in me immediately wondered if there was something more romantic in this incredible run of events; that this might be a blindingly obvious sign from above! We spent the next forty-eight hours sightseeing, getting to know each other, and I realised I wasn't attracted to her romantically at all. We clearly enjoyed each other's company, but there was no chemistry for me. I felt really uncomfortable broaching the subject, but I wondered whether she felt attracted to me. Over lunch, the following day I said,

'Do you know, when we bumped into each other yesterday, it occurred to me what a bizarre series of coincidences had brought us together again.'

'Yes, I still can't get over it. I phoned my sister last night, and she's called me back at least three times to say she's still in shock about it all!'

'I must admit, I did wonder whether this was some incredible sign from the powers that be.. you know, in a kind of um.. you know romantic way. But I don't... I don't feel it is...?' I said, feeling nervous that she might be really upset.

'I thought that as well. It is so weird. My sister is convinced it is a sign, and told me to be patient. Ha! I don't feel it is either to be honest with you. I think we're here to be friends, to support each other like two AA's do.'

I felt relief, and even though I didn't find her physically attractive, I was slightly upset she didn't find me attractive at the same time. The initial reason for our paths crossing yet again became evident the following day. On our final afternoon, we visited the Masjid-i Jahān-Numā (also known as the Jama Masjid), one of the largest mosques in India. After meditation, we decided to climb one of the two forty metres tall Minarets which, having a fear of heights, terrified me. (Minarets are traditionally used for the Muslim call to prayer.)

As soon as we reached the top we sat down on the stone floor and Prisha suddenly told me she needed to tell me her Step 5, which in the AA programme is when we admit 'to God, to ourselves and to another human bring the exact nature of our wrongs'. The wording might sound heavy and overbearing, but it's a vitally important step in the 12 Step programme as it allows us to release the guilt and shame we've been carrying for so many years, and empowers us to change our attitudes and behaviours. The power of this step is also in the fact that it helps us to recognise how we have often contributed to the pain and chaos in our lives, and so we can learn from our past. Prisha looked very nervous as she sat down opposite me, about three foot away, took a pad of paper out of her handbag, and took a deep breath.

'Please, I'd rather you didn't say anything until I've finished reading everything I've written down. I just want to get it all out. I need to get rid of this horrible feeling in my stomach, I've felt sick with worry about doing this.. But this is the time to do it, I know.'

'I understand, just take your time. I'm sure there's nothing you will say which will shock me. I've heard many Step 4 and 5's before, and some really hardcore stuff..... I'll say nothing. I'll just listen.'

Prisha looked down at her writing, and started to read it to herself. She said nothing for a couple of minutes, and looked more and more uncomfortable the longer she waited. In the end I felt I needed to say something,

I gently said, 'We all hate doing this; everything in us tells us to keep it all in, don't let anyone ever know our secrets, they're too dreadful, and we are convinced we'll be judged and condemned. It doesn't happen, but the bullshit in our heads tells us it definitely will. I've found it best to take a deep breath, say 'fuck it' and just get the crap out.'

She looked up, nodded through her tears, and started to read her notes. As promised, I sat in silence and carefully listened to her, making a few mental notes as we went along. Both painful and truly rewarding, the fifth step is simply an honest admittance of personal wrongdoings. It was both humbling and a privilege to listen to Prisha, and to know that her courage and honesty would make such a difference to her quality of life, and her ongoing sobriety.

Afterwards, we climbed down and went for a Chinese meal. Except for a few emails in the following few weeks, neither of us contacted the other until..

Ten years later, it was a Monday morning in 2016 and I had been recently diagnosed with Complex PTSD. It was really on me, and I felt mentally and physically exhausted from the emotional flashbacks; the pain triggered by the psychotherapy had overwhelmed me, and I was scared to catch the Underground in case I felt genuinely tempted to throw myself under a train. I didn't want to drink alcohol to kill myself, as I knew it wouldn't work quickly enough, so I was psyching myself up to either hang myself from a tree on Clapham Common or to slit my wrists in the bath. I had been raging and crying for a couple of hours thinking of my Mum and my family, fully aware of the pain it would cause them, but knowing I couldn't live like this anymore. I couldn't see any other way out.

At that moment, my mobile phone beeped, and after a few minutes I grabbed it. The Higher Power had dealt one of the magic cards! Out of the blue, at the darkest moment in my life, Prisha emailed me. As soon as I saw it was Prisha I felt a powerful connectedness to my Higher Power and a deep feeling of peacefulness within me. My body relaxed, my mind became still and I intuitively knew that 'everything will be okay'.

The healing I felt was nothing to do with the contents of her message. It was the fact that it was Prisha who had emailed reminded of the divine synchronicity of our previous encounters and my memory immediately flashed back to the spiritual awakening I'd had in 1993 when I had met a paedophile in McDonalds after an AA meeting. That night I had stood in my parent's back garden and heard a beautiful voice say to me;

'Everything will be okay. EVERYTHING will be okay.'

As I lay in the bath reading Prisha's email the same message of encouragement was repeated again and again in my mind. I knew in my heart that everything would be okay. The timing was unbelievable, exquisite, miraculous. Perhaps a mathematician could work out the probability of two people meeting in Birmingham, and then;

- six months later and eight thousand kilometres away, meeting in Bangalore, a city of 8 million people;
- six weeks later in New Delhi, over two thousand kilometres from Bangalore, in a city of 18.6 million people;
- ten years later, at the precise moment when I desperately needed help, I receive an email from her

I felt a beautiful sense of divine synchronicity. It reminded me of the play of consciousness that is life, and how the play is sometimes desperately painful, and yet, at other times is beautiful.

Now is the time.
Now is the time to know
That all that you do is sacred.
Now, why not consider
A lasting truce with yourself and God?

Now is the time to understand
That all your ideas of right and wrong
Were just a child's training wheels
To be laid aside
When you can finally live
with veracity and love.

Now is the time for the world to know
That every thought and action is sacred.
That this is the time
For you to compute the impossibility
That there is anything
But Grace.

Now is the season to know
That everything you do
Is Sacred.[45]

Hafiz of Shiraz

---

[45] From *The Gift* by Daniel Ladinsky, copyright 1999, used with permission.

14

THE LAST FIRST

*And so rock bottom became the solid foundation
on which I rebuilt my life.*[46]
J.K. Rowling

My sincere hope is that the story of my journey will offer strength and encouragement to others who may have suffered in the same way as I have done, and that they may find inner peace and self-love in their lives. I appreciate that my beliefs in karma, reincarnation and my interpretation of Christian teachings might, for some readers, not sit comfortably. I'm not suggesting I have found all the answers, and encourage the reader to follow a saying I have often heard in AA, which is, "take away everything that helps, and leave the rest behind." The greatest challenges I have had to face, as a survivor of CSA, were to:

- Admit to myself the full horror of what had happened during the abuse, and the impact it has had throughout my life
- Find the strength to speak with family and a few close friends about what happened
- Seek professional therapy, and start the process of releasing the deep-

---

[46] J.K.Rowling, *Very Good Lives: The Fringe Benefits of Failure, and the Importance of Imagination*. The quote is taken from a speech J.K.Rowling gave to the Harvard Alumni Association on June 5, 2008 when she accepted her honorary degree.

seated feelings of shame, guilt and responsibility I had been suppressing for so many years.

This chapter focusses on how best family, friends and government (including the relevant agencies and organisations in the public and voluntary sectors) might offer support to survivors of sexual abuse, and also how others can be supported, by those of us who have suffered abuse, in understanding the long-term effects of the abuse. Alongside the trauma the survivor faces, it is easy to overlook how painful it is for family members, in particular, to come to terms with the abuse, especially if the abuser is known to them. Within this context I also attempt to address the many issues surrounding the epidemic of child sexual abuse which is being unearthed in the UK, and my concerns with delays and barriers as government struggles to understand the impact (psychologically, emotionally and financially) CSA has upon society as a whole. In my opinion (based on my personal experience and what I have learnt supporting fellow survivors over the last two decades), government needs to acknowledge the serious mental health crisis that continues to grow before us. From the data I have gathered and the academic reports I have read, my view is that the government is, whether wilfully or not, negligent in its responsibilities in providing trauma-informed support to an ever-growing community of deeply traumatised children and adults among us.

In simple terms, with the ongoing crisis facing mental health services within the NHS and the cost of professional counselling sessions (often starting from £60 for a fifty minute session), those without financial resources will find it very difficult to secure the professional support, both short and long term, they so desperately need. This creates an even greater pressure on the NHS, and charities such as One in Four (who are referenced within this chapter), which has a waiting list of at least four months. If this book serves any purpose, beyond my personal healing, it is to raise awareness of the chronic lack of accessible and affordable professional therapy for so many survivors.

The next chapter, *Soulful space: reflections on my therapy work with Matt*, has been written by my trauma therapist Sarah Paton Briggs. I am so grateful Sarah agreed to write an account of our counselling sessions from her professional perspective. I have given Sarah permission to use these sessions, her notes, and our subsequent conversations as she sees fit. For many survivors, the idea of talking about the abuse they experienced to anyone is an horrific prospect. It can take years before a survivor is prepared to even consider talking about what happened. My hope is that Sarah's chapter will offer a detailed explanation (both from our sessions and from her considerable expertise working with survivors of CSA), of the varied therapeutic processes that can help a survivor to heal, which in turn will offer them encouragement to seek the help they need.

For many survivors like myself, the sordid revelations that the TV personality and charity fundraiser, Savile, had been systematically sexually abusing so many people for decades was a watershed in their recovery. I have met survivors, in AA, SLAA and SoSAA, who experienced the news of his crimes triggering off hellish memories of their own sexual abuse, and for some this was the catalyst for them to speak out for the first time. Behind the mask of charm and charity, Savile was a vile, predatory destroyer of lives... but he was only one of many, as NSPCC and other respected charities have verified. I never met Savile, but he became the epitome of all the men who had abused me. As soon as the revelations of the shocking depravity of his crimes became public knowledge in the autumn of 2011 and, even though he had died earlier that year, every time I saw Savile's smug, smiling face on the news, I began fantasising hunting him down and killing him. His photo brought up the venom that had been locked up in the PTSD, and with it came an undercurrent of rage within me that went on for months and which terrified me. It was a significant event in my life, as well as triggering the immense, deep-seated feelings of rage and shame, so too were released the most traumatic memories of the abuse that I'd buried deep within me. I had a breakdown, which eventually led to a breakthrough in my healing.

I unfortunately met several men like Savile when I was a child. Through their sick actions, verbal threats and coercion they did their best to silence me, to destroy my innocence, my hopes and dreams, my identity, and my sanity. In spite of the challenges I have since faced, ultimately they failed miserably. However, the pain has had a healing purpose. It has served as the crucial motivator for my spiritual journey, which has brought about over the years an immense and deeply rewarding emotional and psychological healing. It is therefore ironic that Savile, possibly one of the UK's most prolific predatory paedophiles, helped me to heal. Savile died on 29 October 2011 and, at least in worldly terms, escaped justice. However, the Law of Karma teaches me that he will experience what I understand to be the true meaning of 'as you sow so will you reap' (Galatians, v.7) and 'an eye for an eye and a tooth for a tooth' (Mathew v.5: 38) in further lives on earth, and will live through the pain and agony he created in the lives of so many people.

It makes logical sense to me that we are ultimately responsible for all our actions, both positive and negative. We are given life and 'free will' to play a game of consciousness, and during each lifetime we have an opportunity to experience the consequences of the previous Karma deliberately done, in many past lives, as well as in present life. We cannot be 'saved' or enlightened until and unless we have each neutralised all effects of past and present Karma, and bringing the Karmic balance to nil. It is perhaps this spiritual teaching, more than any other, that has helped me to forgive the abusers and to allow spiritual justice to be dispensed accordingly.

During the early stages of the investigation into Savile's crimes, BBC *Newsnight* aired an archive interview from a 1995 documentary called Westminster's Secret Service. Former senior Tory MP Tim Fortescue revealed how the Whip's office in Parliament would try to 'get a chap out of trouble' in return for loyalty. (The Whips are MPs or Members of the House of Lords appointed by each political party to help organise their party's contribution to parliamentary business. One of their key responsibilities is making sure the maximum number of their party members vote, and vote the way their party wants.) It is somewhat ironic that it is called the Whip's office as a whip is used as a means to control, punish, and humiliate by both politicians and sadists alike.

Mr Fortescue said: 'Anyone with any sense, who was in trouble, would come to the Whips and tell them the truth and say, 'I'm in a jam, can you help?'.

'It might be debt, it might be... a scandal involving small boys, or any kind of scandal in which... a member seemed likely to be mixed up in, they'd come and ask if we could help and if we could, we did.

'And we would do everything we could because we would store up brownie points... and if I mean, that sounds a pretty, pretty nasty reason, but it's one of the reasons because if we could get a chap out of trouble then, he will do as we ask forevermore.' [47]

The offhand, nonchalant way in which he said this was shocking. It showed no concern whatsoever for the welfare of the abused children, nor indeed for the rule of law. At the very heart of government was a systematic attempt to pervert the course of justice. Labour MP Lisa Nandy said Mr Fortescue's interview was 'just one powerful example of how personal and political interests can conspire to prevent justice from happening'. She added: 'If those systems are found to exist today, [they must] be overturned, whether that makes life uncomfortable for political parties, whether it makes life uncomfortable for Parliament, or whether it makes life uncomfortable for the Government itself.'

Although the high profile convictions of several media personalities in the UK, as noted earlier in the cases of Rolf Harris and Stuart Hall, have brought the issue of sexual abuse to the forefront of national consciousness, government cuts across the board - in healthcare, education, social care, welfare and Legal Aid - have increased the financial burden on survivors, who feel even more shame and blame if they speak out, as often the expert support they desperately need is not available to them. The lack of support can further shame survivors into feeling their voices do not warrant or deserve to be heard; the implicit message is that they are not considered worthy of help. When the survivor is ready to talk - which can take many years - the help must be there.

Whilst society is starting to wake up and recognise a situation of what many would argue has been years of criminal negligence and denial from both church and government (both locally and nationally), we are now starting to acknowledge the shocking reality that epidemic levels of sexual abuse have been, and still are, taking place in this country. There now needs to be a massive change in the provision of support for survivors. The National Society for the Prevention of Cruelty to Children (NSPCC) is the leading children's charity fighting to end child abuse in the UK, Channel Islands and Isle of Man. The charity helps children who have been abused to rebuild their lives, protect those at risk, and find the best ways of preventing

---

[47] Matt Chorley, MailOnline Political Editor, *Westminster's dirt book: How Government whips covered-up MPs' 'scandals involving small boys' in exchange for loyalty,* from www.dailymail.co.uk published on 8 July 2014.

abuse from ever happening. There is a wealth of information on their website about the work they do, and the support they can offer.

Abuse robs children of their childhood. Without help, the scars of abuse can last a lifetime. And as devastating as it can be for the child, society pays a heavy price too.
Reference: www.nspcc.org.uk

The NSPCC defines two different types of child sexual abuse, which are contact abuse and non-contact abuse. Contact involves touching activities where an abuser makes physical contact with a child, including penetration. It includes:

- sexual touching of any part of the body, whether the child's wearing clothes or not
- rape or penetration by putting an object or body part inside a child's mouth, vagina or anus
- forcing or encouraging a child to take part in sexual activity
- making a child take his or her clothes off, touching someone else's genitals, or masturbation.

Non-contact involves non-touching activities, such as grooming, exploitation, persuading children to perform sexual acts over the internet, and flashing. It includes:

- encouraging a child to watch or hear sexual acts
- not taking proper measures to prevent a child being exposed to sexual activities by others
- meeting a child following sexual grooming with the intent of abusing them
- online abuse including making, viewing or distributing child abuse images
- allowing someone else to make, view or distribute child abuse images
- showing pornography to a child
- sexually exploiting a child for money, power or status (child exploitation).

I believe the word 'epidemic' is wholly appropriate when one consider these statistics:

- There was a 60% increase in recorded cases of CSA between 2011 - 2014. (Alan Travis, Reported child sexual abuse has risen 60% in last four years from The Guardian on Thursday 9 April 2015).
- Over 54,000 sexual offences against children were recorded by the police in the UK in 2015/16. (Bentley, H. et al (2017), *How safe are our children? The most comprehensive overview of child protection in the UK 2017)*.
- There was a 31% increase in reported cases of CSA during 2016/17. (Matthew Weaver, *Cases of UK child sexual abuse up 31%, says NSPCC* from The Guardian on Monday 18 December 2017).
- Since 2014, there has been a 700% increase in the number of suspected incidents of online child sexual abuse referred to the Metropolitan police.[48] (Owen Boycott, Online child sex abuse referred to Met increased by 700% since 2014 from The Guardian on Monday 22 January 2018)
- There are 29,837 offenders on the Violent and Sex Offenders Register (ViSOR) Dangerous Persons Database with convictions against children (aged under 18) (from House of Commons Hansard Written Answers for 13 December 2012

A 2015 report from the Children's Commissioner for England estimated that approximately 1.3 million children currently living in England will have been a victim of contact sexual abuse by the time they reach 18 [49],

---

[48] The US-based National Centre for Missing and Exploited Children identified 30,661 suspects with IP addresses in the UK in 2016. In 2009, the comparable figure had been only 1,591.

[49] Office of the Children's Commissioner (2015), *Protecting children from harm: a critical assessment of child sexual abuse in the family network in England and priorities for action.*

whilst a U.S research paper [50] reports that more than 80% of survivors of CSA are reported to experience some symptoms of PTSD. (such as sudden, aggressive flashbacks to the sexual abuse, depression and anxiety, or addictions, self-harming, eating disorders, and recurrent suicidal thoughts).

Alarmed by these statistics, I decided to do more research into the provision of counselling specifically for children and young people who might be survivors of CSA, and who have shown the enormous courage to come forward and ask for help at such a young age.

One of the shocking things I learned from the 2016 NSPCC report *How Safe are our Children* was the fact that there has been an 80% rise in reported sexual offences against under 18 year olds in England over the last 4 years. Despite this dramatic increase, research by YoungMinds [51] revealed that 64% of the 199 Clinical Commissioning Groups diverted some or all of the new funding received for children's mental health to other priorities in 2015-16.

The devastating knock-on effect for the children needing professional support is clear to be seen. More recently the office of the children's commissioner estimated that as few as a quarter or a fifth of children with mental health problems received the help they needed last year, with, in some areas, children with severe mental health needs waiting as long as 18 months for an appointment [52].

Tragically, the article also reported that some children are resorting to suicide attempts, in a desperate attempt to ensure that they are seen by Child and Adolescent Mental Health Services professionals. It beggars belief that half of all the CCGs are not planning on spending more on mental health services this financial year (2018), despite the continued huge increase in demand for these services. [53]

---

[50] McLeer, S.V., Deblinger, E.B., Esther, B., et al. *Sexually abused children at high risk for post-traumatic stress disorder.* Journal of the American Academy of Child and Adolescent Psychiatry (1992) 31:875-79.

[51] YoungMinds, *Children's mental health funding not going where it should be*, from www.youngminds.org.uk

[52] Adi Bloom, *Need to know: Pupil mental health*, from www.tes.com on January 29 2018.

[53] Bettina Friedrich, *Raising awareness of mental health issues is not enough*, from The Conversation on January 31 2018.

I then considered what the response of the professional community was to the standard of mental health provision for children and young people under the NHS.

The Royal College of Paediatrics and Child Health (RCPCH) said there had been "destructive" reductions in preventive services with England falling further behind the rest of the UK when it concerned policies aimed at improving child health. They continued, "Children deserve better. It is they who are disadvantaged most by inefficient health services, cuts to public health and the rising tide of poverty." [54]

Perhaps the following quote from Peter Hindley (the former chair of the Royal College of Psychiatrists faculty of child and adolescent psychiatry) sums up the role the government has played to worsen this mental health crisis, and indeed its lamentable record offering protection and care for vulnerable children.

> *Cuts in recent years to early intervention services provided by the NHS and local councils meant children's mental health problems worsened because they were not detected or treated quickly enough, often leaving schools to pick up the pieces.* [55]

There is a wider context that also needs to be considered. Whilst I've been fortunate to have worked full time for almost all of the last twenty-four years, I've had periods when I've needed to have extended professional therapy (at least 12 weeks) to help me deal with flashbacks and the PTSD. I've always been in a position to pay for this therapy myself, but this is often not the case for many survivors. More recently the consequences to my mental health of living with Complex PTSD had become so severe that I felt compelled to walk out of my last job. But for the support of my family, I would have been at the mercy of the welfare state, which has undergone drastic cuts and which, as widely reported in the media, have particularly impacted upon many people with physical and / or mental health issues.

---

[54] Paul Gallagher, *Children 'hit hardest' by public health cuts, doctors warn*, from i News on January 23 2018.
[55] Denis Campbell, *NHS mental health services failing young people, say psychiatrists* from The Guardian on Mon 26 Dec 2016

An online survey of nearly 400 adult survivors of CSA took place in 2016.[56] The survey explored their experiences of abuse, satisfaction with different types of service and the availability of information about services. It's key outcomes were particularly revealing and reflect the complex nature of dealing with the trauma of CSA:

- The average duration of CSA was 7 years.
- Over 50% were abused by more than one person.
- 70% of cases were not reported to the police. Almost 90% of survivors have not seen their abusers brought to justice.
- 42% did not receive any support until, on average, 12 years after they had first disclosed they had been abused as children, with 50% waiting at least 9 years.
- 25% used services specifically because of their abuse before ever disclosing.

Sometimes the fear and the shame is too great to be able to say anything no matter how long ago it happened.
Adult CSA survivor, Focus on Survivors survey respondent

Professor Noel Smith commented: 'They highlight both the sustained duration over which children are typically sexually abused and the lifelong impact of that abuse. As a society we clearly need to be more strategic in tackling sexual abuse and we are not doing enough to support survivors of abuse'.

Beyond my immediate concern, which is of course for the welfare of survivors, it is important to recognise that there is a significant cost to society, which could be mitigated with an investment in prevention and early identification of CSA as the underlying trauma in mental health services. Many survivors will end up in the criminal justice system mainly through the misuse of alcohol and drugs, whilst others might be regularly admitted to hospitals through other forms of self-harming. The financial costs of failing

---

[56] Smith, N., Dogaru, C.M, and Ellis, F. (2015) *Focus on Survivors: Identifying barriers to accessing support for those who have experienced childhood sexual abuse.* University Campus Suffolk and Survivors in Transition. www.uos.ac.uk

to treat survivors of sexual abuse is significant – it is estimated to cost £40,000 to keep a person in prison per year.

This cost could surely be reduced through better diagnosis and the wider availability of treatment for survivors of CSA.

The NSPCC estimates CSA costs £3.2 billion per annum [57], an estimated cost for 2012 which is based on costs for health, criminal justice services, services for children, and loss of productivity to society.

Beyond statistics, the human story....

Sarah once asked me, when I was feeling very angry during a therapy session during the summer of 2016, what I thought the sentence ought to be for paedophiles who were guilty of abusing children. I thought about it, and I remember replying; 'You offer them life in prison, until they die, or the firing squad.'

In that moment, I would have gladly volunteered for a firing squad to execute paedophiles. Now, I feel truer to my real self and see that such an action, though understandable, would have compromised who I really am. My belief in the Law of Karma has helped me forgive the paedophiles (and I feel at peace in the knowledge that justice will be ultimately served), but it also guides me to keep in control of my actions so that I do not create any negative consequences for myself, however justified my anger might feel at times. Despite the rage I feel when the PTSD is triggered, I am not a vigilante, and do not condone violence against paedophiles. To condone violence would show that I had not let go or forgiven the men who abused me after all, and that would have prevented me from connecting to a deeper peace within myself, which has allowed me to heal.

A friend of mine works in a prison which has a sex offenders wing, and his experience has helped me to understand the consequences convicted paedophiles face in prison. It's called E Wing, with A to D wings at the older end of the prison (a wing is an extension out from the main part of the prison, which holds the admin offices and the 'Seg'; the segregation unit for misbehaving prisoners.) E Wing has two spurs (smaller extensions), each

---

[57] Sailed-Tessier, A. 2014, *Estimating the costs of child sexual abuse in the UK*

with two levels, and both levels have around thirty individual cells arranged in a horseshoe shape. Sex offenders are separated from the rest of the prison for their own safety, and they spend much of their time in their cells. Once when my friend visited the wing, an officer was seated outside one of the cells on suicide watch; she was seated on a high chair looking through a small rectangular opening in the metal door of the cell at the prisoner inside. The officer was on a five hour shift; there was food on an elevated tray next to her chair. Much of her time was spent watching a man sleeping. The most famous resident of E Wing was Rolf Harris, who was convicted in 2014 of abusing four young girls. He spent his time on the wing making sketches of fellow prisoners and, when they came for visits, their families. However, he had to be transferred to another prison for his own safety, after being threatened and spat upon by other prisoners. The responses of these two groups of prisoners highlight the bizarre relationship between celebrity culture and paedophilia.

How do I feel when I read about paedophiles in prison? Mostly I feel nothing. I prefer not to have any connection at all with them. I want them caught, incarcerated and rarely, if ever, released. I believe their actions are so vile, and cause so much damage, that they have negated any right to freedom.

As part of my research for this book I read several academic papers, watched various documentaries and fact-based films, and my anger at the injustice became very real to me. One of the most upsetting was the Academy Award-winning 2015 film *Spotlight*, starring Mark Ruffalo and Michael Keaton, about the newspaper team which exposed the Catholic Church's systematic cover up of paedophile priests who were abusing dozens of children in the Boston area for decades. It has since become common knowledge that this practice of cover up had taken place in many other dioceses across the US, and elsewhere in the world, for a very long time. The deliberate cover-up of these crimes, and the failure by the church to inform the police (which enabled the abusers to continue molesting and raping children) is in some ways worse than the original crime itself. I accept that paedophiles are sick people; that doesn't justify, lessen or condone their crimes. Their crimes are consciously done, and the cover-up is another conscious evil, and any organisation that systematically denies the truth of these acts, thereby preventing justice being served and allowing the abuse to continue, is as far removed from the love and teachings of Jesus as it can be. The cover up was motivated by religious politics and to protect the church's reputation, at the expense of children.

> *When paedophiles say to their victims, as they all do in one form or another, "If you ever speak about this, unimaginably bad things will happen to you," what they are doing is perhaps on one level even worse than the physical act of abuse itself. They are manipulating their victims into being complicit in the abuse.*[58]
> James Rhodes, internationally acclaimed musician
> and author of Instrumental

This brings to light the teaching of original sin in the Catholic faith, which I have seen bring much misery to many survivors as they consider whether the abuse they experienced was 'God's will'. I reject the idea of it being God's will, as I do the notion that an atheist (or any non-Christian, for that matter, like myself) who has been abused is eternally damned, whilst the priest who is the abuser, who allegedly repents, and who is 'absolved' of his sins, finds eternal peace in heaven. This is a truly vile, reprehensible teaching.

Advaita Vedanta has really helped me understand this better. The meaning of the 'fall' is surely symbolic of the movement from the highest consciousness (which Jesus described as 'I and my Father are one', and what advaita vedanta refers to as absolute reality) to individual reality, the illusion of duality and birth of ego. This is no sin, but merely a play of consciousness that is, essentially, the 'reverse' of enlightenment. For the play to commence, Adam became aware of Eve in a physical sense, rather than purely in a spiritual sense, and the play of human life began. It follows, therefore, that perhaps the meaning of life is to 'reverse' this process, and recognise our inner divinity. In my opinion Jesus, and other spiritual teachers, knew this and showed us the way.

There is obviously anger within me, but it no longer consumes or

---

[58] From the Foreward to *Survivors' Voices: Breaking the silence on living with the impact of child sexual abuse in the family environment* (Published by One in Four, 2015). www.oneinfour.org.uk

controls me anymore. I do not feel shame expressing it either. Now, that is a miracle!

Supporting the survivor of sexual abuse

The NSPCC states on their website, 'the problem is much bigger than shown in official statistics, as most crimes are not disclosed and/or reported. Most sexual abuse isn't reported, detected or prosecuted. Most children don't tell anyone that they're being sexually abused. It's a crime that is usually only witnessed by the abuser and the victim.'

The consequences of sexual abuse can manifest as long-term health conditions such as post-traumatic stress disorder, dissociation, mental health problems including depression, anxiety disorders including OCD, addictions, eating disorders, self-harm, suicidal behaviour or thoughts, and challenges with intimate relationships, trust issues and a damaged sense of self. It is estimated that 90% of children were abused by someone they knew.[59] Very few of these cases ever come to the attention of the authorities; this is due to many of the reasons I have outlined already, but it is mainly because of the stigma and shame, and the complexity of prosecuting a family member. Most survivors remain silent. Regardless of the context of the abuse, the devastating consequences are invariably the same for most if not all survivors. The following observations are based on my personal experiences, along with those of fellow survivors who have been kind and courageous enough to share their stories with me.

I am also indebted to my good friend Clarinda Cuppage for allowing me to reference an excellent report from 2015 called *Survivors' Voices: Breaking the silence of living with the impact of child sexual abuse in the family environment*, which she conceived and developed with the UK charity One in Four.

Being heard, believed and listened to is vital at the very beginning of the healing process. Most survivors fear their experiences will not be believed, particularly if the abuser is known to the family. Disclosure is often met with shock and disbelief, and as a society there needs to be more education as to

---

[59] Radford, L. et al (2011) *Child abuse and neglect in the UK today.*

how to approach this issue in the most appropriate way. I talked myself out of disclosing what happened to me many, many times before I eventually found the courage to get it out. I would pysche myself up each time as I tried desperately to block out all the inner voices trying their best to destroy me. My fear went beyond the fear of not being believed; it opened up an overwhelming feeling of shame, self-hatred, and a fear of being judged and humiliated. In the end, however, the pain of silence was too much, and I was desperate to be heard.

I chose very carefully the friends I would disclose to. They went through a painstaking vetting process the CIA would have been proud of, as I obsessively analysed their attitudes and behaviours to work out their likely response, before I forced myself to open up. I had to know before I spoke that I was safe, and that they would not reject my story. I chose well. After I stopped drinking alcohol and joined AA, this decision was the most important one I've ever made in my life. The handful of friends I initially spoke to were honest enough to say, with kindness, 'I'm so sorry you went through that. I just don't know what to say. I can't imagine how you must feel.' Each one of them was patient with me, allowing time for my hesitancy and shame to fade, and for the story to slowly come out, and what they said actually helped me. It is often not what people say, but how they say it. Friends can feel scared they might say something 'wrong', and that I'd break down in front of them (which never actually happened).. but as long as they speak with sincerity and kindness, that's all that has really mattered to me. It's similar to speaking to someone who is grieving. We can feel their pain and might feel slightly intimidated by the situation. We know there's nothing we can say that will change what's happened, so the kindness behind the words is what matters most, it seems to me.

In January 2017, BBC Three published a short film called *Things not to say to someone who's been sexually assaulted*. It features eight incredibly brave interviewees talking frankly about their experiences of opening up to family and friends about the abuse they went through, and the questions they faced. It serves as a really useful guide as to what questions to avoid; some of which are probably quite obvious, and no doubt asked in the shock of the moment.

'Oh God. What were you wearing?'

'You're such an attention seeker.'
'Were you drunk?'
'Men can't be sexually assaulted.'
'Why didn't you fight back?'
'Why didn't you report it?'
'But did you enjoy it at all?'

Friends or family will feel shocked and horrified at what has been disclosed, and sometimes respond instinctively and without realising the consequences of their questions, however well intentioned they might be. It is crucially important that the survivor not feel judged, or responsible for what happened, or under any pressure to say more than they are ready to say. The fact the survivor has disclosed has taken enormous courage. My personal experience was that I needed a friend to listen and just be there more than anything else. Therefore, questions about 'suggestive' clothing, whether the victim was drunk, why he or she didn't fight back or report it will, more often than not, trigger feelings of shame and suggest to the survivor that they were responsible in some way. He or she might then shut down and refuse to speak further, when actually they are desperate to say more... but are held back by the fear and shame they feel.

Perhaps a surprising question, and one to be very sensitive about when asking a survivor, is 'Do I know who did it?' or 'Can you tell me who did this?' There are, of course, circumstances when it would be considered irresponsible (and perhaps against a safeguarding policy) NOT to ask, as it might prevent other children (or adults) from being abused. My suggestion is to be mindful that when approaching this specific issue; one ought to be fully aware that it places an enormous burden on the survivor, which he or she might well be unable to deal with at that time. There is only so much that any survivor is able to disclose in the first instance, and saying the name of the abuser opens up so much more pain. If the family member or friend knows the abuser, the survivor will often fear they will not be believed, and worse still, might be forced to confront their abuser. Once again, placing the survivor under pressure to name or identify their abuser/s might force them to shut down from saying any more until they feel safe enough to do so, which might be months or even years later. The specific fears I can remember as a child were that; I was scared that;

- if I identified the abusers they might find me and kill me
- I was responsible for everything that had happened, and would get into even more trouble
- I would not be believed if I told someone

Denial is often the initial reaction within many families when the survivor finds the courage to talk about abuse. Regardless of whether the abuser was a family member, known to the family, or strangers (as in my case), family members can struggle to come to terms with the abuse for a number of reasons. I was fortunate that, from the start, my family, whilst very upset at what had happened, were very supportive, even though I told them only a little. If the abuser is a family member there is the possibility, of course, that other members were also abused, and haven't been able to talk about it. Their silence is a form of self-protection; they feel so deeply traumatised and it's an area of their lives they cannot admit, let alone talk about. The disclosure might be the catalyst for their healing, of course, but many are too devastated to disclose. If other family members were not abused, hearing that a sibling was abused challenges the dynamics of core, established relationships with someone family members love, and often denial is the immediate response to protect this reality. They cannot imagine a father, brother or uncle committing such dreadful crimes. It also challenges their memories of what may have been, for them, a happy childhood.

If the abuser is not a family member, there is still often denial, as parents and siblings can feel responsible for what happened, and have immense guilt for having not protected their child or sibling, for having not noticed. This denial by those not directly affected makes it even harder for survivors - who need support and empathy, not judgement and fear. When the disclosure is denied or ignored, the abuse sometimes continues and the survivor feels further betrayed. And even if the abuse has ended, the impact of the disclosure being ignored can have negative consequences. The survivor must, as far as possible, choose carefully who to talk to, but sometimes their options are very limited.

Support from family, including siblings, is so important for the healing process, but some survivors realise they need to sever all contact with family members, if their experiences are denied and rejected, as the survivor can become the target of anger and blame when the family 'sides' with the abuser. This is where access to information is vital; at the point of initial contact, the survivor needs to know they are not alone and that recovery is possible, regardless of financial constraints and family rejection.

Many survivors need long-term therapeutic support from counsellors with psychological training and expertise of working with survivors of CSA, and who are willing to reach out and accept the survivor. These professionals need experience of working with trauma symptoms, and be able to work with the whole family if necessary. I have found the support of others who have trod the path of counseling and group support to be a vital component in my own healing. The presence of role models, and personal accounts written by other survivors, create a sense of belonging, and offer hope from those who have lived through and healed from very similar experiences.

There are also a range of other therapeutic interventions which can be considered, such as addiction therapy, rehabilitation and, of course, the twelve-step programme. Alongside group therapy, some survivors have also found the following to be helpful: acupuncture, physiotherapy, bodywork, reiki, homeopathy, reflexology, and shamanic healing. In addition to the above-named and exotic-sounding therapies, there are some more familiar-sounding ones worth noting. These include grounding or concentration techniques, meditation, re-association to the body, regular exercise, forgiveness, reading about abuse, self-help books, personal development workshops, and having a creative outlet through art and performance, especially music or singing. Most of these healing strategies underline the importance of connecting with and developing friendships and building a support network with others, including other survivors, to break the silence and alleviate the sense of shame. Any healing strategy which is used to encourage the survivor to speak about the abuse may seem genuinely terrifying at the beginning of their healing journey; but they need not be discouraged, as every survivor I have met will identify with this sense of horror and hopelessness when they first started.

Due to this specialist support for childhood sexual abuse I am a success story, transformed. My abilities are unleashed, my sexuality is far less

A Small Boy Smiling

hindered, my quality of life is coming under control.
Steve (Survivors' Voices, One in Four)

It is remarkable how survivors of sexual abuse can often start the long journey of healing after meeting fellow survivors who have released so much of their pain. One of the key outcomes of *Survivors' Voices* project by One in Four was that the participants (who wrote their accounts of how child sexual abuse impacted on their lives) found much healing from being seen, heard, and understood by professionals who had the specialist skills to work with survivors of CSA.

Survivors of CSA need support early in their lives after disclosure. As my story has shown, the impact of CSA and the avoidance coping strategies (such as drinking alcohol excessively, using other drugs, and self-harming) often starts in teenage years, so young people need to know that if they have had experiences of CSA they can get help. The distress can also manifest through challenging behaviour – becoming aggressive or withdrawn, stealing, failing in school – and these warning signs are often judged as being 'bad' behaviour, rather than signs of a much deeper crisis. Because CSA is often undiagnosed as an underlying cause of traumatic behaviour such as self-harming, alcoholism, and depression, survivors rarely receive the most appropriate treatment for these conditions. Many survivors often make multiple attempts to get help for their symptoms, and when the link to the underlying cause is established early and appropriate interventions are given, healthy post-traumatic growth is possible.

This also raises the issue of how best to provide professional support for survivors. AA has a saying, *First Things First*, and in my experience the initial focus must be solely on recovery and the management of the symptoms of trauma, e.g anxiety, PTSD etc. It is, of course, a personal decision each survivor must make for themselves, but ideally issues of prosecution ought to be kept separate from the healing process, particularly in the early stages of healing. The legal process can be traumatising at the best of times, but this is true especially for survivors, whose trauma will be ruthlessly questioned, challenged and doubted by the defendant's legal counsel. Nevertheless, I have known several survivors who have found immense healing through the criminal justice system. Any decision, however, needs to be in the context of the therapeutic process. With this in mind, perhaps specialist counselling is best provided outside the provision of the State, so the survivor feels they have control at all times.

Survivors need long term counselling – for instance One in Four offer two years - to feel safe enough to start to look at what happened to them. It's common that many sessions are spent building a sense of trust between the counsellor and the survivor, thereby creating a safe environment in which the survivor feels more able to talk about the abuse. These early sessions will usually introduce trauma management skills which provide practical support for the survivor, which is necessary when they go into such dark and terrible memories. The survivor therefore needs to be in a comfortable environment and not perhaps in a clinical setting where a much shorter period of therapy is offered, due to the huge demand and budgetary restraints. I've been very fortunate in that when I've needed counselling I've been able to afford it, either through health insurance or by dipping in to my savings. Finance is often a huge problem for many survivors, and there are obvious financial challenges for those with long-term mental health issues who struggle to maintain regular, or perhaps any, employment due to their ongoing trauma.

> *Sexual abuse is not just something that happened in a person's childhood. It can remain alive inside them and their families, sustained by secrecy and silence to protect the abuser and other relatives. Trust is often distorted and ultimately destroyed, and it is vital that health professionals understand this process so they can treat survivors and help them to ultimately escape from their past.*[60]

Christiane Sanderson, Senior lecturer in Psychology at the University of Roehampton with over 25 years' experience working with CSA survivors.

After years of austerity, it is clear from statistics that demand for mental health services far exceeds supply. Despite the widespread media coverage of several high profile cases such as Rolf Harris, Stuart Hall and the ongoing *Independent Inquiry into Child Sexual Abuse* (led by Prof. Alexis Jay), the reality is that many survivors (particularly those with long term mental health

---

[60] *Survivors' Voices: Breaking the silence on living with the impact of child sexual abuse in the family environment* (Published by One in Four, 2015). www.oneinfour.org.uk

issues) on low incomes cannot afford to pay for the professional therapy they need. They are forced to rely on the NHS, or support from charities - which might not have the capacity to provide the clinical expertise or the longer term support they need.

But there is a far greater human cost. When one considers the changes already made in recent years to healthcare, education, social care, welfare and Legal Aid, and the detrimental effect, as widely reported, that these have had on the most vulnerable in our society, I have a plea to government to listen to the NSPCC, MIND, One in Four, YoungMinds and other respected charities and organisations, and to act positively and decisively on their advice and recommendations. The experts working at these charities are much closer to the often tragic reality of the unnecessary pain and suffering that these cuts have created in the lives of so many people with mental health issues.

Former Conservative Prime Minister Margaret Thatcher once famously said, 'There is no such thing as society'. If she meant that we have personal responsibility for our lives then I would, in essence, agree with her. But only so far. The reality is that there are many people with physical and / or mental health issues, children included, who need much greater support than the State presently offers. A much larger proportion of the revenue from our taxes ought to be more fairly distributed to the most vulnerable for the benefit of all society.

My view of my childhood has changed so much during the last twelve months. The turning point came when I walked out of my last job and found the courage to seek help again. A week or so later, in early February 2016, I met my psychotherapist Sarah Paton Briggs and with her expert guidance I was finally able to process so many memories which had been buried in what felt like a 'disgusting, rusty tin' in the depths of my mind. These were the shameful, dirty secrets I'd once decided never to tell anyone about. I'd take them to the grave. For most of my adult life I felt that, for the eighteen months I was abused, I was a childhood prostitute, and these paedophiles were the pimps, sharing me amongst themselves.

I can remember almost everything now, and I no longer see a child prostitute, but rather an amazing young boy who had the strength to survive. The shame and guilt has now been released and I feel a much deeper feeling of peace and love within me.

The Last First

Sarah created a safe, non-judgemental space in which I finally allowed the eight year old boy to have a voice, and for his thoughts and emotions to be heard, and validated. It has also helped me so much to remember how I used to be before the abuse; the loving, enthusiastic, impetuous, carefree boy....who LOVED life. I now remember who I AM ... and I like what I see.

The abuse is not my whole story. It never was. It just felt like it for many years.

But many who are first will be last, and the last first.
Gospel of St.Matthew, 19:30

And indeed there are last who will be first, and there are first who will be last.
Gospel of St.Luke, 13:30

15

This chapter is written at the request of the author of this book. Following a discussion with Matt regarding the implications of releasing this confidential material, he made an informed decision giving consent for my disclosure of material from his therapy sessions - which would ordinarily be prevented by my adherence to ethical codes of conduct as his therapist. The chapter below is provided within professional ethical guidelines regarding confidentiality, in that he has given his written permission for it to be published. A copy of that written permission has been lodged with the publisher of this book.

Soulful space: reflections on my therapy work with Matt

Introduction
Ordinarily, the workings of therapy are conducted in the private and sacred space provided by the counselling room. This is a rare opportunity to publish a commentary on therapy that has evolved with a client. It is even rarer that the client's commentary is published alongside that of the therapist.

I was privileged to work with this brave and dedicated client, as well as being humbled by his own healing talents and creativity.

I'm offering this commentary at his request, in the hope that it may encourage others – whether survivors or clients or therapists – with any struggle related to the topics described by him. There is hope after hopelessness; there are ways of transcending unspeakable horror.

What this is and what it's not

This is a commentary, a description from my own subjective stance, to sit alongside the client's written account of his experiences which included therapy along the way. It's intended to bear witness to his bravery and poignant processing of his life experience. This chapter is not a text book; it's not a training manual for therapists. Neither is it intended as a template for use with other clients, as the approach for each client' is tailored according to their individual needs and preferences in therapy. Nor is it a literature review or an academic essay. It's not an exposition of aggregated research data gathered from a double-blind randomised controlled trial. It is absolutely not a diagnostic model including a recommendation of particular treatment approaches; nor is this an exemplar of trauma treatment protocols. Matt's journey is unique and highly personal. He had undertaken years of personal development work before his first appointment with me. All of these factors should be taken into consideration when reading this commentary.

After reading an initial draft of this chapter, Matt said he found it massively validating and healing. That's the outcome, as far as I'm concerned. Yet if this chapter provides guidance or support or reassurance for anyone else in addition, I am honoured. When Matt shared a draft of my chapter with another survivor of childhood sexual abuse, this was the feedback received:

> *Sarah comes across as very skilful and compassionate. And I think her chapter is so important for other survivors to read as I think the counselling process can be confusing and hearing an account from a professional is very valuable. It works very well especially as you have done all the disclosures, so you keep your voice.*

After I sent him the first draft, Matt himself commented to me that the therapy lifted a huge amount of shame he'd previously felt about the abuse. He stated to me that he now feels very differently about that period of his life; the shift in energy enabled him to write this book. This chapter is a description of therapy that worked, which is why it's worth sharing.

Matt's initial enquiry about starting therapy with me
I remember his first email contact with me, early in 2016:

> My work has given me paid leave of absence to help me address a number of issues I am presently experiencing. I was sexually abused many times as a child, and was diagnosed with PTSD when I was 20 years old. I am now 43 years old, and have had counselling on and off throughout my adult life to help me deal with the abuse, and how it can affect me emotionally and in my relationships. I am also a recovering alcoholic and been sober since I was 20 years old.
> I recognise I need to attend counselling again to talk through issues that has arisen during recent months. Through my work's health insurance policy, payment would be made by Bupa.
> I look forward to hearing from you at your earliest convenience. Thank you.

In responding to this his enquiry, I was confident that I would be able to offer support. We met within a few days. I liked him immediately and was humbled at the prospect of working with him. At that initial stage, there was no guarantee that he would take such huge strides in reclaiming his life by turning his dreadful experiences into a force for good.

There were undoubtedly profound moments of huge pain and distress when he told me about the repeated suffering he endured in the organised and brutal sexual abuse perpetrated by a group of men who predated upon him and other boys during a particular period in his pre-pubescent childhood. Yet the impact of those times stretched cross the entirety of his life thereafter; robbing him for many years of seemingly natural things that might otherwise be taken for granted: dating, marrying, having a family of his own.

Most journeys through life are never a straight line from an intentional known point of origin to a predetermined destination. This is certainly true of his therapy. Although the direction varied and the terrain was rough at times, I had an unswerving faith that he would pull through, all the more so if I could offer him soulful space to talk where he felt safe and could trust the process he was following intuitively.

So, what happened during his therapy conversations with me? His own account of this is contained in the chapter titled *London Calling*. I uphold that narrative as his own authentic experience of his therapy process. Additionally, I would like to offer a commentary from the perspective of his therapist, in the hope of inspiring other survivors to embark upon or continue their own therapeutic journey of speaking their truth. Writing this chapter is a markedly rare opportunity to describe what happens in counselling for survivors of sexual abuse. My way of working is tailored uniquely to each individual client or couple. There is no standard format, so anyone else's therapy with me would in its very essence be different. Yet I sincerely hope there is value for others in shining a light into the otherwise hidden process in the counselling room.

My approach here is to highlight aspects of his therapy that can be commonly experienced by survivors of sexual trauma, as well as providing signposts to sources of support.

Listening and presence

A primary task for the therapist is to listen, to be able to hear the client in starting to form the words to describe what has happened to them. By being a consistent and constant ally, the counsellor can create a working relationship with the client to encourage the expression of what needs to be said. My stance is that if the client has endured such experiences, my role is to bear witness and be able to hear their history. By being present and attentive, I strived to create an environment where he could bring his inner world to be explored with the aim of validation and confirmation. Even though at times he showed distress and torment, he also showed courage to bring the hideous aspects out into the open. That said, he also brought much humour and humanity into the conversations too.

Dissociation

Dissociation can be defined as detaching from an intrusive experience, which can be viewed as a psychological defence as a coping mechanism. Unsurprisingly, dissociation is commonly reported by survivors of sexual abuse. As this client describes in the chapter titled *The Disgusting Rusty Tin*, he dissociated by viewing the abuse as if from above rather than through the more intense associated imagery from the viewpoint of his own eyes (dissociation is the mind's attempt to limit the severity of the imagery).

Many survivors of sexual abuse in my practice have also mentioned looking at a spot on the wall to distract themselves while abuse is occurring, as a method of separating their awareness from what's happening to their body.

When someone dissociates, many useful activities of the brain shut down their effect, such as reducing ability to think clearly, to make proportionate assessments of a situation, plus either numbing or becoming chaotic in reaction to perceived danger or threat.

Ultimately, part of trauma recovery is concerned with developing ways for the client to be able to live in a way where mental images and bodily experiences are associated in a more connected way. But before that is attempted there are two other treatment stages required: stabilising the client so that dissociation reduces; before processing the traumatic memories.

There are evidence-based ways to address dissociation, so that the client can develop increased skills in emotional regulation – hence avoiding the tendency to dissociate. Useful approaches are psychoeducation to understand trauma responses; techniques to increase a sense of safety, containment and stabilisation of symptoms. Grounding techniques are helpful at this stage, such as mindful breathing and focusing on the here and now in the environment.

Shame
Incorporation of shame is a poisonous effect of childhood sexual abuse – that the survivor is left with a sense of shame and responsibility (which, in my opinion, belongs solely to the abuser). In psychoanalytic terminology, this would be a projection by the abuser of an unacknowledged part of self (the shame) into the target victim: the child who is being abused.

So, the therapeutic aim is the reduction of shame, rather than its cultivation. The client may feel a huge mass of confusion and shame. The therapist's main job is to bear witness and validate the client's experience so that the client can rely on the integrity of their own mind.

It is an understandable wish of survivors of sexual abuse to wish that they could forget the abuse by erasing the memories. My response is that those abuse events are part of the survivor's history but do not need to be the story for the future. The events themselves cannot be changed, however, the survivor can change the way they think and feel about those events. It's here that concepts come into play such as acceptance, understanding, compassion for their childhood self. Timing is a big part of this process, which can happen only when that person has reached a place in their recovery journey when they are able to look compassionately at what has occurred.

In this case, I share his sense that we were aligned to work together. I also share an impression that the success of his therapy consisted in a combination of cognitive approaches (information about how therapy works, as well as descriptions of how the mind adapts to the trauma of abuse), managing emotional and bodily reactions (mindfulness and anxiety management techniques), along with acknowledging the role of spirituality in healing the psyche.

Information-giving

Psychoeducation is another important facet of facilitating therapy for trauma recovery. I hope that by adopting a nuanced and sensitive approach, I offered these nuggets of information to the client when he was ready to absorb how these ideas could help him understand there were good reasons for the ways he had reacted during the abuse, then developed through his teens and adulthood.

I remember talking with Matt about the neuroscience of trauma: this relates to the three-part structure of the triune brain[61]: 1) the reptilian brain regulates basic functions such as breathing, heart rate, body temperature, digestion; 2) the limbic brain, which developed in mammals, is the relational and emotional area for connection with others, including memory functions; 3) the frontal cortex where logical, conceptual, planning thought takes place.

It's usually helpful for abuse survivors to understand what happens in the mind and body when they feel frightened; how the mind and body react when perceiving that a life-threatening situation is occurring. Many people have heard of the "fight or flight" response. In my trauma work, I describe five key-words beginning with 'f' that describe the range of options which the limbic brain automatically chooses from as an unconscious reaction to a perceived threat: fight, flight, freeze, flop, friend.

This client tended to go to flop or friend when under duress to perform

---

[61] Paul D. MacLean (1990), *The triune brain in evolution: role in paleocerebral functions* (New York: Plenum Press)

in the way they were coercing him to do. The threat level was high: there were menacing threats to cut his penis, report him to his father or headmaster, sell him to even worse abusers. This client was manipulated so that he was acting through fear rather than acting through informed choice.

In his book, *The Other 90%*, Dr. Robert Cooper, a neuroscience pioneer and leadership advisor, states that intelligence is distributed throughout the body and that the mind cannot be separated from the body (both are connected by the cybernetic neurological system). He urges humans to harness the art and science of this powerful potential.

In another book, *Mindsight*, Dan Siegel encourages vertical integration of mind, heart (emotion) and body sensation (gut-feel) for an all-powerful alliance of information sources within us; as well as horizontal integration of right-brain assets such as creativity, alongside left-brain features such as strategic planning.

This information was intended to resource the client in generating a healthier relationship with his own body as a source of comfort and intelligence. My input was intended as a counter-balance to the disgust and distance that the client demonstrated towards his body.

Common emotions that linger after a trauma are shame, disgust, guilt, anger, sadness. In striving to normalize this for Matt, I found it reassuring to see the times when he began to manage the impact of these emotions more effectively.

Internalisation of responsibility for the abuse

I am resolutely clear with any client who has been sexually abused as a child, that total responsibility rests with the adult(s) involved. I cannot be more definitive on this point. Allocation of responsibility can be a source of great internal conflict or confusion for the survivor, especially if the abuser(s) have instilled a belief that the child has somehow led them astray or has teased them or incited them to the sexual contact. There can be even greater complexity for the survivor if they remember any sexual curiosity or even pleasure at physical touch during the abuse. Regardless, the full responsibility remains with the abuser who as the adult carries moral and legal responsibility for their actions.

Part of Matt's healing journey has been to reclaim his childhood in a more balanced and integrated narrative. Notwithstanding the horrendous abuse that he endured, he is now able to put those episodes in context of being a talented at sports, coming from a loving family, showing his evident acting ability. This boy excelled – he became head boy of his prep school and captain of the first team at cricket. A light that shines so brightly can attract the darkest shadows – perhaps the abusers saw his sporting prowess and attractiveness, which they found too appealing to resist.

To my mind, it stands to reason that a boy with such talent, energy, spirit, and ability could be a channel for spiritual healing. This sensitivity and attunement maybe created an energy which the abusers sought to channel for their own degrading gratification. This man's talents found solace and satisfaction in adulthood, there was a huge tariff exacted through his traumatic abuse. Bright light can cast a deep shadow. Matt is now living more consciously in the light for more of the time.

Aversion from intimacy caused by emotional wounding

It is common for survivors of childhood sexual abuse to describe difficulties not only with their own body but also others', consisting in an aversion to emotional closeness or physical intimacy with other people. My client certainly was affected by this symptom. Therefore, it is remarkable that he had the capability to conduct the healing sessions and lead the meditation group during his recovery process. The proximity of other people in a room – which constituted an emotionally intimate space – was troubling for him and yet he persevered, doing much good for himself and for others in the process. The light of his powerful being still shone even through difficulty.

Avoidance is a common symptom experienced by survivors of sexual abuse: avoidance of people, places, objects or situations that might remind them of the traumatic incidents – leading to re-experiencing such as flashbacks. Thankfully, avoidance can be overcome by gradual supported behavioural experiments so that the individual builds a new set of experiences offering proof that they can indeed cope with situations that were being avoided.

The aversion from intimacy can take another form, not manifested by this client, as being able to be sexual often and with lots of different people. So much so that other clients have described being overtly sexual while dissociating or using substances like drugs or alcohol to create a dissociating effect before they are able to go into a sexual encounter. This client talked about sexual anorexia, how he refrained from sex. Other clients can become more sexually provocative or highly sexually active as an echo of the way that sexualisation was encouraged by their abusers: this can leave a sense of being hugely valued for their sexual potential, outweighed by other valuable aspects of their selfhood.

I'd like to offer a commentary on some common behavioural effects of early sexualisation of children. The abusers probably brought forward the age at which this boy became aware of embodied sexuality. The author gives no commentary of being aware of sex or attraction to others before the abuse started. During therapy conversations together, we discussed how the abusers had robbed him of a more normative development of sexual awareness or crushes or attraction to girls. In the chapter about his childhood, he describes flashing his penis at the girls in his primary school at the segregated changing rooms after sports lessons. He writes that he's curious about whether this was a cry for help and wonders what a psychologist would make of this.

My offering here is that children who have been abusively targeted by sexual predators can internalise hyper-sexualisation which leads them to act out this sexualisation manifested through inappropriate sexualised behaviour (such as a boy who may flash his penis). Children who have been exposed before puberty to sexual imagery or unwanted sexual experiences with adults can lack the emotional maturity to contextualise those events; they can exhibit with sexual behaviour that is inappropriate to their age and to the social situation. I'd encourage any adult in a position of responsibility to be aware of this and to consider that any child who is acting out sexually could have experienced some abuse or could have been exposed to inappropriate sexual material such as pornography too early to be able to process it with emotional maturity. Sadly, given the prevalence of online pornography, many adults in my practice have reported seeing pornographic images or videos as young children. They usually say that in hindsight this distorted their view of sex such that it impeded their ability to develop healthy sexual relationships in adulthood; or this imagery led them to experiment with behaviours such as paid-for sexual services because their expectations of sex had been shaped largely by hyper-stimulation by pornography.

Compassion for his inner child

He writes about revising his concept of his boyhood. This was a massive shift from blanking out his childhood memories. Later he could see that the boy, only eight years old, had survived horrendous experiences. He became a caring and compassionate adult who could metaphorically hug and encourage the boy to be seen and heard with compassion. This is a true aspect of the healing journey: to accept and act collaboratively with a part of his being that had suffered for decades without being witnessed.

Survivors of sexual abuse can find it incredibly challenging to acknowledge their inner child. Assessing this damage and being in contact with than emotional pain can be monumentally difficult. However, over time, there can be huge benefit in doing so when the client feels ready.

A result of the inner child discourse was that this client began to see that the 9-year-old little boy was a brave survivor, who had endured things that were almost unbearable and that as an adult he could embrace that marginalised and isolated little boy and keep him safe as an adult. Just as he had pledged that he would never, ever, let anyone hurt him again.

The downside of this pledge was that he created relational boundaries that were too strong and too big for any intimate couple relationship to be sustained in his teenage years and early adulthood, as a tragic effect of the abuse. He describes the perversity of craving female attention, then, if he received it, feeling repulsive; this is a reaction to trauma which resulted in self-sabotage of a natural desire for mutual attraction or affection. These strong boundaries and self-sabotage led to the sexual anorexia he describes. Part of the therapy work with me was a discussion on how he could manage dating or a couple relationship in a way that built slowly, so he could manage the process with enough safety to allow himself to stay involved in it.

Stabilisation through mind-body techniques

During the therapy, I facilitated some mindfulness techniques with him to overcome the shame and terror he described regarding his relationship with his body. His body had been the location of hugely distressing experiences during the sexual abuse in childhood. However, at its best, the body is the receptacle where the spirit is incarnated. The body is a fount of wisdom and information. Mindfulness techniques can help to reunite the mind and body, with the aim of the client becoming more trusting that the body is the safe place it's meant to be as a dwelling place for that person to inhabit.

Mindfulness techniques often involve breathing exercises as methods of emotional regulation. Care is needed to ensure that clients are not re-traumatised because of greater attention to mind-body connection. Yet it can be of great use for clients to become more aware of their emotional state, such as rating their level of emotional arousal on a scale of 0-10. This awareness fosters emotional intelligence which is most often useful in tracking their triggers and responses. Over time, if stabilisation and relaxation techniques are practised regularly, the client gains confidence and a greater sense of calm control. Otherwise, triggered arousal states can feel uncontrollable, leading to isolation and hopelessness or distinctly uncomfortable symptoms such as panic attacks.

Other grounding techniques include focused attention on the current moment and current environment, such as touching objects in the room, or gently throwing and catching a pillow or soft ball, or counting the number of particular objects like windows or cushions which are visible in that place. The purpose is to instil in the survivor a sense of their own agency and their ability to manage their emotional state. This overcomes the common thought that flashbacks and uncomfortably bodily symptoms are uncontrollable.

The stabilisation phase in trauma therapy is, in itself, a major topic. For the purposes of this chapter, it's worth recognising that the client had already covered a lot of this ground in his meditation and mindfulness practice over the years. Although he did report instances of being triggered in recent history, he also developed a greater ability to experience his emotions and make meaning of it.

The first phase comprises safety, containment and stabilisation, so that the client can gain greater control over managing the intrusive trauma symptoms such as flashbacks or panic attacks or dissociation. Briefly put, stabilisation methods can include relaxation techniques and/or diaphragmatic breathing techniques where deep breathing reduces sensations of anxiety or panic. Another aspect of stabilisation is psychoeducation regarding definition and symptoms of trauma, including information on how the brain processes traumatic experiences differently from everyday life, plus emphasis that trauma symptoms and accompanying distress can be treated through focused therapy which resets the functioning of the brain more tolerably.

Trauma processing
Trauma processing is the second phase. A variety of treatment approaches exists, some of which are more relevant to single-incident trauma, whereas other approaches are more effective for repeated complex trauma. The kinds of therapeutic approach may involve any of the following kinds of therapy. Choice of approach very much depends on the evidence base, the training taken by the therapist to inform their scope of practice, as well as involvement and agreement by the client. This is by no means an exhaustive list. These are the approaches where validation by research is in place, or the evidence base is being developed:

TF-CBT (Trauma-Focused Cognitive Behavioural Therapy)
CPT (Cognitive Processing Therapy)
EMDR (Eye Movement Desensitisation Reprocessing)
NET (Narrative Exposure Therapy)
PE (Prolonged Exposure)
IRRT (Imagery Rescripting Reprocessing Therapy)
EFT (Equine Facilitated Therapy)

The greater part of processing the trauma with this client was achieved through creating a coherent narrative of his life experiences. The client is encouraged to talk through the troubling events, having their experiences validated and their responses upheld by the therapist – as well as updating any resident beliefs which might have been an obstruction to recovery.

A valuable part of the therapy was described by the client as gaining a greater sense of empowerment in relation to the memories and images associated with the abuse. This approach enables the client to direct and control an alternative view or version of events, so that the current adult power is brought into effect. This resonates with the author's narrative of originally being locked into the trauma, but then through therapy being able to change his relationship with the trauma imagery so that he could view those trauma memories with the awareness that he was a child being manipulated by powerful adults. It is a key step in trauma recovery when the individual realises that now as an adult they are better equipped than ever to support their inner wounded child – which they were probably not resourced to do when they were a frightened child being predated upon.

On the upside, it's worth remembering that whenever a trauma client comes to therapy, the awful event(s) have already happened; the client has survived; the events are in the past. On a cognitive level, this is true. However, those suffering from emotional or visual flashbacks often feel hostage to memories that may intrude at any time: unwanted imagery and emotions with accompanying body sensations which are not being summoned consciously. When the embodied discomfort or distressing imagery of the trauma persist in the present, the survivor can feel afraid of being afraid; if they lack conscious means of managing unconscious processes. Part of my role with this client was to explain how those intrusive memories are triggered and experienced in the present, so that he had greater understanding so that he could develop ways to manage the symptoms when they are evoked.

I would add that proper assessment and diagnosis of trauma / PTSD / Complex PTSD is essential, to ensure that a full history is taken and that a well-founded understanding of the client's presentation has been reached before any trauma processing takes place. In Matt's case, he undertook a psychiatric assessment, which resulted in a diagnosis of complex PTSD.

Reclamation and reintegration
The third phase of trauma therapy is to do with making sense of the past in a way that enables the client to move forward with greater solidity and certainty.

When he felt strong enough to do so, Matt reclaimed more of his sense of self. This identity reconstruction is an important part of trauma recovery: to acknowledge the good things about himself and to uphold his talents along with his accomplishments. He describes how that victory is achieved by directing energy away from destructive revenge fantasies involving his abusers. Instead, he found it more healing to channel energy toward accepting, embracing, and supporting his wounded inner child. This process of integration has rendered him more whole and more accepting of himself. That reclaiming of his soul and identity is, in my view, the triumph over adversity.

Trauma therapy, specifically in this case regarding childhood sexual abuse, is a tender process of containing the patient's struggle to come to a personal resolution, by supporting the client in sorting through confusing, often contradictory images of self in relation to the way that child was viewed by others (principally the abusers). The outcome of trauma can leave an imprinted distortion of the survivor's sense of self: that the survivor is somehow at fault or damaged. This therapeutic process of making a coherent meaning of the abuse events also encourages greater discernment that the way the abusers viewed and dealt with the abused was a harmful projection onto the abused child of the abusers' subjective yet distorted reality, usually involving all sorts of unhealthy beliefs and projections.

It's the realm of trauma-informed psychotherapy – involving validation and education - to explore the client's experience in seeking internal resolution.

Pivotally, this requires trust – the very thing that the survivor has lost through the abuse.

The therapeutic response to client disclosure needs to be clear and supporting: an acknowledgement of what has been heard; expression of regret that it occurred; the statement that the abuse was wrong; that nobody has the right to initiate sexually without consent; that it was not the survivor's fault.

Developing healthier boundaries

I strived to preserve at all times the ethical principle of informed choice, whereby the client's autonomy is respectfully upheld. Any topics or techniques suggested during the therapy were offered as an option. This maintained a position of choice for the client (especially important since the abusers ignored his autonomy). Psychological education lays a foundation for the client to develop healthier boundaries by becoming more aware of the processes in operation within their mind and body.

As the client's physical and sexual boundaries had been violated by the perpetrators of the abuse, it was fundamental for me to respect his boundaries and to support him in being able to set healthier boundaries – especially when the therapy conversation turned to the potential for him to be involved in dating or couple relationships in future. Hence, I was careful in making agreements with the client regarding appointment-setting and confidentiality: this is described in therapy as attention to contracting and boundaries. He began to contemplate how he might go about romantic relationships and he also began to imagine that physical touch or sexual contact with a woman might be possible in future – if he were better equipped to manage such situations by starting with what's comfortable then making controlled progress thereafter.

Help from horses

Matt writes about the equine-facilitated therapy sessions that he attended with my horses. (I prefer the philosophy of the term 'equine-facilitated' rather than 'equine-assisted' because the former views the horse as owning the wisdom for the session where the human therapist holds the sacred space of possibility[62] for the work to evolve, whereas 'equine-assisted' can have the connotation of the horse being the assistant to the human therapist.)

Because horses are prey animals with a large limbic brain who in the wild live as part of a herd with complex social interactions, they can detect the emotional and bodily state of humans interacting with them, just as they are able to scan the horizon for predators or assess the behaviour of other horses in their social group. This means that horses can give powerful feedback to human clients, in a non-verbal way which can resonate deeply with human clients through emotions and body sensations. This emotionally-embodied learning can have a lasting effect which is transferable from the equine session to other aspects of life and other human relationships.

In this case, the client's first impression of the horses was that they were very large and powerful beings who had the potential of violence and harm. It was noticeable that even after the mind-body exercises and safety briefing from me before he entered the arena with the horses, he felt a strong trigger effect of fear. It can be very evocative for human clients to go into the unfamiliar space of being with horses. The anxieties or beliefs ruling clients' lives can be brought to the surface very quickly in equine-facilitated sessions

---

[62] The concept of the "sacred space of possibility" was created by Kathleen Barry Ingram, one of the original grandmothers of equine-facilitated therapy. Being taught by Kathleen at Sun Tui's IFEAL training centre has been one of my formative experiences as a facilitator of therapeutic work guided by horses.

and with great strength. In this case, he felt a trigger about being harmed by beings larger than him (a flashback to the sexual abuse scenarios when men much larger than an eight-year-old boy were dominant, abusive, and tyrannical).

After an hour of sitting at the side of the arena, talking gently, watching the horses, he acknowledged that his fears were based on historical experience with his abusers were not related to the current experience with the two gentle female horses (called mares). This session seemed a valuable way for Matt to absorb an emotionally-corrective experience: that it was possible to see the horses as beings who were separate from his own history of abuse.

Towards the end of that session, he managed to approach them and said he felt their gentle acceptance of his presence. To his credit, through the generosity of spirit from the horses, he found it within him to approach them and touch them. It is notable that he could approach and touch the adult female horses, by contrast to his post-abuse aversion from women. He experienced pleasurable yet appropriate touch with the horse, although interestingly Jazz appeared to invite him to scratch her hindquarters especially around her tail (near her genitals and anal area).

When he first went into the arena with the horses, the client became hyper-activated emotionally because of a sense of danger evoked by the threat sensor in his brain (amygdala). He used emotional regulation techniques to calm himself, stretching his window of tolerance. This started to repair his hyper-sensitivity with a more balanced emotional response to the stimulus of being with the horses.

Time after time I have seen horses in equine-facilitated therapy show their unfailingly intuitive grasp of where the client's difficulties are located both in the mind and in the body. The experience of touching the horses in the first session, then in the second session interacting with the symbolic obstacle course, the horse elicited the nugget of learning for the client. Just as Matt has written about key moments of the room-based trauma therapy, he is also able to recall in clear detail the crystals of wisdom that he carries from the horses to this day.

Seeking support

This client had received a formal diagnosis of CPTSD (Complex Post-Traumatic Stress Disorder) from a psychiatrist. I broadly followed the tri-phasic trauma treatment model: stabilisation, trauma processing, reintegration with life. This phase-based model is recommended by **UKPTS** (UK Psychological Trauma Society)[63] and Royal College of Psychiatrists.[64] **UKPTS** also recognises that effective trauma treatment takes place in all three of the essential domains: cognitive, emotional, embodied experience.

Still, it takes courage to embark on therapy even with such a diagnosis.

I believe it's part of the beauty of human potential that even people who have been severely traumatised by sexual abuse can retain openness to new possibility for the future. This client was courageous in seeking help: therapy with the psychologist; sessions with Dr. Ron Hutchinson; joining AA; his spiritual experiences in India and with John of God; enquiring about therapy with me; joining SoSAA. I surely believe that the light that shines from this client will be seen and honoured in future by many others, just as I have seen and honoured it.

Many clients have said to me that it's taken years, if not a decade or more, before they have felt the time has come to enter therapy or seek support. My hope is that this book may play some part in limiting the suffering for others who have experienced the distress and after-effects of childhood sexual abuse (or indeed any other trauma).

The good news is that although sexual abuse can leave long-lasting trauma imprints on the brain (and therefore the body) of the survivor, these effects can be overcome. However, sexual abuse, trauma, PTSD can be treated with a tailored therapeutic approach. The uncomfortable body sensations and emotional reactions can be soothed so that life becomes more manageable. There is hope for anyone suffering the ongoing distress of trauma or abuse.

---

[63] UK Psychological Trauma Society, *Guideline for the treatment and planning of services for complex post-traumatic stress disorder* (CPTSD) 2016. Draft document.
[64] Royal College of Psychiatrists: *Post Traumatic Stress Disorder*

Soulful Space: reflections on my therapy work with Matt

Overcoming the past

I am deeply touched by my work with this client. Even more so that he invited me to contribute to this amazing book about his journey through life. He is an astoundingly kind and generous person who has truly transcended the horrendous abuse in his childhood. Heroic stories abound in every culture[65] where the main character is called to accomplish a hugely challenging feat; an epic journey where demons must be faced, difficulties need to be endured; mentors and guides are found as support along the rocky path before success is achieved at great cost. I believe that good will triumph over evil. His story is but one example of human spirit transcending searing pain with sufficient goodness remaining to share for the benefit of others. I sincerely hope that he continues his journey through life reinforced by all that he has transcended. His is a joyful victory over adversity, with extra hope that is inspired for others.

I offer trauma-informed therapy in the belief that it is a force for good in a world that is uncertain, challenging, and at times violent. It can truly change lives as a force for good when evil and hardship are all too common. It's a vivid demonstration that human collaboration, as well as tuning into the power of the natural world and the spiritual dimension beyond human understanding, can create possibility hitherto unimagined. If anyone in need is reading this book, I wholeheartedly hope that it may propel them towards seeking support in one of the many ways that he has written about. The force for recovery and healing will come when needed and when it is called in at the appropriate time.

When this process works, it really works. It goes beyond counselling and into a soulful journey of recovery and identity reclamation which makes coherent sense of the past. Even better, it gives a whole new lease of life for the future. That's why I do this work.

---

[65] Joseph Campbell's book "*The Hero with a Thousand Faces*" documents that every culture has sagas or myths denoting how a hero or heroine will be called reluctantly to a taxing task where they will be tested by demons and will ultimately return in a changed state after completing a seemingly impossible mission. This narrative structure is markedly similar in every culture and across millennia.

REFERENCES

- Van der Hart, O., Brown, P., & Van der Kolk, B.A. (1989) tri-phasic model (1) containment, stabilization, and symptom reduction; (2) modification of traumatic memories; and (3) personality integration and rehabilitation
- Van der Hart, O., Brown, P., & Van der Kolk, B.A. (1989). Pierre Janet's treatment of post-traumatic stress. Journal of Traumatic Stress, 2 (4), 379-395.
- UK Psychological Trauma Society, Guideline for the treatment and planning of services for complex post-traumatic stress disorder (CPTSD) 2017.
- Royal College of Psychiatrists: Post Traumatic Stress Disorder (information sheet).
- Siegel, Dan, Mindsight.
- Cooper, Dr. Robert, The Other 90%.

RECOMMENDED READING

These books go into much more practical and scientific detail than my overview allows. Many clients have said that they found these books really useful in validating and explaining their symptoms. Importantly, these resources provide ways forward to treat and heal. These authors and techniques show how to regain a sense of self, take ownership of the future, develop a connected way of living, while reducing the level of distress caused by trauma symptoms.

- Rothschild, Babette: 8 keys to safe trauma recovery.
  W. W. Norton & Company, 2010. ISBN-13: 978-0393706055
- Walker, Pete. Complex PTSD: From Surviving to Thriving.
  An Azure Coyote Book, 2013. ISBN 9-781492-871842
- Van de Kolk, Bessel: The Body Keeps the Score.
  Penguin Books, 2015. ISBN-10: 0143127748
- Siegel, Daniel. Mindsight: Transform your brain with the new science of kindness. Oneworld Publications, 2010. ISBN 978-1-85168-793-0
- Salter, Dr Anna C. Transforming Trauma: A Guide to Understanding and Treating Adult Survivors of Child Sexual Abuse. Sage Publications, Inc, 1995. ISBN-13: 978-0803955097

- Davies, J & M. Fawley. Treating The Adult Survivor Of Childhood Sexual Abuse. Basic Books, 1994. ISBN-13: 978-0465066339

TO CONTACT SARAH

Sarah Paton Briggs holds multiple accreditations as a psychotherapist, sex/relationship therapist, drug and alcohol counsellor, and clinical supervisor. She has taken specialist training in working with childhood sexual abuse and in trauma therapy approaches. She also holds double certification by IFEAL and by LEAP as an equine-facilitated therapy practitioner. Sarah is experienced in working with individual and couple clients, especially those who have suffered neglect or who have survived sexual trauma.

Sarah has worked with serving armed forces personnel on a private basis, as well as military veterans through Walking With The Wounded (Head Start Programme), Help for Heroes, and Dare To Live Trust (equine-facilitated programme). In private assignments or through employee assistance programmes, she has worked with clients from Wiltshire Council, as well as with emergency services staff from Wiltshire Police, Gloucestershire Constabulary, Wiltshire Fire and Rescue Service, and the Metropolitan Police Service.

She offers trauma-informed therapy in London W1 at The Grove Practice, alongside her private practice in Malmesbury, Wiltshire, where equine-facilitated sessions are also available. Sarah welcomes clients who are able to self-fund or who can access provision through private health insurance (she is recognised by most private health insurance companies). Anyone seeking or considering therapy is welcome to contact Sarah for further information or guidance on a confidential basis.

CONTACT DETAILS

www.thegrovepractice.com or email sarah@thegrovepractice.com
www.ashlar-evolution.com or email sarah@ashlar-evolution.com

For Sarah's training and accreditations please see the Appendix.

16

TRYING TO MAKE SENSE OF IT ALL

I wish I could show you when you are lonely or in darkness the astonishing light of your own being.[66]
Hafiz of Shiraz

There is so much in my life today that I am grateful for. When I first heard people like Grateful Dave, Peter Rabbit and Flat Cap Bill speak of their gratitude in AA meetings, shortly after I got sober, I just didn't understand what the hell they were talking about. I thought they were either completely deluded or lying. Thankfully, I stayed, listened, and gradually learned how to change my thinking. The people in AA make AA what it is, and I have been blessed throughout my recovery to have shared my journey with so many truly inspirational members. When you meet and listen to people, week in and week out who have walked the path before you, and hear how they have changed from a state of utter despair and hopelessness. To know that they have come back from the very brink to lives with love, kindness, humour and integrity; it not only offered me hope, but also showed me how to change.

AA has been the foundation to my life, and the 12 Step programme has

---

[66] Excerpt from the poem, *"My Beautiful Image"* from *I Heard God Laughing: Poems of Hope and Joy* by Daniel Ladinsky, copyright 1996, 2006, used with permission.

gifted me so much more than my physical sobriety; it has given me the strength and hope to go within and release the psychological and emotional pain I suppressed for many years, and to find a deeper peace within myself. I am grateful for a programme which has enabled me to stay sober on a daily basis for over twenty-five years, and has consequently;

- Improved my physical, psychological and emotional health
- Encouraged me to develop a relationship with a loving Higher Power
- Helped me develop an intimate, loving relationship with my family
- Guided me towards a greater purpose in life, which is to live in love and peace with myself and others
- Enabled me to enjoy genuine, lasting, and trusting friendships, both in and outside the programme
- Led me to find success through a career in the professional theatre which has given me lifelong friendships and memories of so many great occasions
- Inspired within me the love of and the opportunity to travel

Recovery from the psychological, emotional and often the physical impact of (child) sexual abuse, alcoholism, and sexual anorexia is a long journey. Put bluntly, and please excuse the word, it has many times felt like a hard, fucking slog, especially when living with Complex PTSD. There are moments of grace, though, when you come across a book, magazine article or overhear a snippet of a conversation which brings an awakening in your consciousness, and healing takes place. I've experienced this several times in life, one of the most profound being when I read M Scott Peck's bestselling book, *The Road Less Travelled* many years ago; I bought it on the sole basis of its opening line;

Life is difficult. This is a great truth, one of the greatest truths. It is a great truth because once we truly see this truth, we transcend it. Once we truly know that life is difficult -- once we truly understand and accept it-- then life is no longer difficult. Because once it is accepted, the fact that life is difficult no longer matters. [67]

---

[67] M Scott Peck, *The Road Less Traveled: A New Psychology of Love, Traditional Values and Spiritual Growth* (Simon & Schuster, 2002)

When I had therapy with Dr. Ron Hutchinson at twenty years old, he showed me he had a similar, direct approach to life, and I am hugely grateful that he did so. He refused to allow me to feel sorry for myself (my default position was to blame everyone), so when he confronted me during a session with, 'Matt, sooner or later you really must grow up' it truly shocked me. It was a statement of truth, and I needed someone to tell me exactly what I needed to do to heal. I also had to take responsibility for my healing. His considerable expertise and immense generosity of time and spirit became the catalyst for everything that has since happened in my life. He brought out the first memories of the abuse and created a safe place for me to speak; he gave me the concentration exercises needed to bring me into present time when the PTSD had been triggered; he introduced me to meditation; he guided me spiritually; and he encouraged me to attend AA. I owe he and his wife, Esther, a huge debt of gratitude.

I have come to a place of acceptance within myself and feel much more peaceful. Whilst the wounds have not wholly healed, I accept it is an ongoing journey and an opportunity to learn and grow as I move forward. From how I feel about my life now, with hindsight I can see how my healing was held back by;

- my inability to cry about the abuse
- the shame I felt about my active involvement during the abuse
- the aggressiveness of the PTSD flashbacks which did not lessen in their intensity for many years
- the fact I couldn't remember the most traumatic events until five years ago (2013)
- the fear, shame and confusion which limited my desire to talk openly with my family

I would not allow myself to cry. I feared once I opened up the floodgates I would be overwhelmed by the force of the suppressed energy within me, and become a nervous wreck. The idea of the emptiness inside of me after the tears, of feeling 'weak and vulnerable', really scared me, yet to hold on would keep me in so much pain for much longer. Linked to this fear of emptiness was the crippling shame about my role in the abuse; I felt more ashamed at what I had done during the abuse than what the paedophiles had done. To cry also meant I would be a step closer to talking about the shame and rage I felt, after acknowledging this was a no go area for most of my adult life.

I was terrified I'd be judged and condemned in the same way I had been subconsciously judging and condemning myself for years. Whilst it was, for the most part, buried deep in my subconscious, the corrosive, destructive power of shame still crippled my ability to communicate with myself, let alone with the people who loved me. Yet I could break down and cry uncontrollably at certain films, such as *The Killing Fields*. When the lead character Dith Pran, having trekked for several months through the Cambodian jungle to escape from the Khmer Rouge, finally sees the Red Cross buildings in the valley below and knows he has survived, I sobbed deeply. The film then cuts to a scene in the press office of the New York Times when his journalist friend, Sydney Shamberg, telephones Pran's family to let them know he has survived, and I was by now emotionally in bits. I felt a variety of emotions, from anger and revulsion, to deep sadness, watching Steven Spielberg's *Schindler's List*, but it is the scene at the end of the film (outside the factory on the first morning after the German surrender, when the Jews give Schindler a gold ring as a gesture of their thanks for his saving their lives) that led me to break down and cry.

There is a scene in ITV's *Prime Suspect*, starring Helen Mirren, when one of the police officers, investigating the abduction of a child, breaks down, admitting he had been sexually abused as a child. I have watched this scene several times over the years, and have always sobbed. I felt a sense of understanding and solidarity with the characters on the screen. On those very few occasions when I cry now, I still cry alone. I can't remember the last time I allowed myself to cry in front of someone else. I fear feeling so vulnerable and exposed with other people. After each PTSD episode in my twenties I felt an immediate and huge sense of relief that it had passed, but I knew that the venom in the PTSD would automatically return to an imaginary 'dirty, rusty box' deep in my psyche without any change in its ferocity. Every time I was triggered, the flashbacks would be just as aggressive, so there was no sense of healing or moving forward for many years.

I even questioned for a while whether the paedophiles had used some form of witchcraft or hypnosis during the abuse, as the memories of the worst times of the abuse were so deeply buried and enmeshed within the PTSD I couldn't remember them until I was in my late thirties; and yet I always knew there was so much more there. Even though I visually remembered so little for years, the emotional baggage that exploded when the PTSD was triggered came with its full force every time.

The emotional pain of Becky's rejection, the lady I had convinced myself was the love of my life, and the trauma of the suicidal girl on the railway bridge, were the crucial catalysts I needed for these memories to come up, and in enough detail for me to talk about what had actually happened. (It is strange how such a long-held fantasy for Becky actually played such an important role in my overall healing.) I could remember for the first time, in detail, how I had been threatened and manipulated during the abuse which, in turn, enabled me to start the process of self-forgiveness.

> *Don't turn your head.*
> *Keep looking at the bandaged place.*
> *That's where the light enters you.* [68]
> Jalāl ad-Dīn Muhammad Rūmī

Until then, I had not realised how much rage and shame I had for my own involvement in the abuse; I could now see that I could not have walked away, and I could understand that my active involvement was an instinctive survival mechanism. This meant I could finally let go of the 'child prostitute' label I had felt deep down for many years. I had a tremendous internal resistance to allowing my family to really know what had happened to me during the abuse. So long as I felt shame about my involvement, I could not talk in any detail with them about it. As a child I was also scared I had broken the law and might be punished even more, and so this non-verbal, non-visual sense of immense fear and shame was buried deep down within me. I had to recognise it was there and release it before I could talk openly with my family.

---

[68] From the poem 'Childhood Friends' (Mathnawi, I, 3150-3175, 3192-3227) by Jalāl ad-Dīn Muhammad Rūmī. Coleman Barks, trans., *The Essential Rumi* (HarperSanFrancisco, 1995)

There is a very important point to make here. I have always received plenty of love from my family, both as a child and as an adult. My feelings were not because I didn't receive love, but because I didn't feel worthy of their love due to the shame. It was about my relationship with me; the resistance to talk had nothing to do with my relationship with them. I told them in very brief terms, when I got sober and was in therapy, that I had been sexually abused, but deliberately played it down. I gave no indication how often it happened, nor how horrific it was. I didn't want to admit it to myself at that stage, let alone hear myself say it aloud to people I loved. Besides, there were so many mixed emotions in my early twenties; anger, blame, fear, doubt, shame; I didn't know how I felt about anything. For the most part, I didn't know what the hell was going on.

Over the years, I've referred to it indirectly, usually with my sister when we've spoken about dating and relationships. By virtue of these conversations, she has played a really important role in my being able to gradually open up more about the abuse. When I've had counselling I've told them 'I need to talk through the old crap again'. I was always defensive, though. At some subconscious, non-verbal level, I can see now what I feared: if my family really knew the truth, would they still love me? Would they also feel the feelings of disgust and shame that I felt with myself? Whilst I have intellectually known for years that I am loved, when the PTSD is triggered the intellect more or less shuts down, and my consciousness falls in line with the emotional narrative the paedophiles used to manipulate and threaten me. This is possibly the greatest crime to level at the paedophiles; they made me doubt I was worthy of my family's love. Their words and actions made me hate myself.

I had so few memories of my childhood before the abuse (the PTSD seemed to work as a general anaesthetic, to some extent), because I blanked out as much as possible before I was twelve years old. The production of *Peter Pan* in 1985, which I loved so much, became the watershed between the old and the new versions of me, to some extent. The memories of the abuse had been buried deeply in my subconscious mind. I had yet to reach puberty and the bully from prep school had moved on to another school, so there were no PTSD triggers. I felt an enormous feeling of freedom and excitement about life, which was epitomised by my relishing every single second in rehearsal, and acting on a stage in a professional theatre to full houses during the run of *Peter Pan*. A few months after this production I had reached puberty, and the flashbacks to the abuse began.

The conscious decision to 'go back in' and re-live the memories takes enormous courage for a survivor and, for a while, it dramatically changes one's perception of oneself, others, and life in general. Life feels so savage and overtly threatening when one goes back in. Perhaps the key issue preventing me from talking more openly about the abuse when I became an adult was the state of shock I had when the PTSD was triggered. The energy trapped within the memories is suddenly released, creating a physical reaction which manifests as shock within the mind and body. After each PTSD episode, the last thing I want to do is talk about it again, and especially with my family. I am exhausted. Besides, for many years, due to the vagueness of the memories, I also felt I didn't have the answers to the questions my family might ask.

During the last twelve months so much has changed. It has been the years of working the 12 Step programme, visiting my spiritual home of India, meditation, and professional counselling that has helped me to change the inner narrative so that I am able to, for the most part, replace the negative conditioning of the abuse with more gentle, kinder and loving thoughts. The turning points have been to recognise and release so much of the rage and shame I was carrying, and the memories of the worst experiences coming back have helped me to understand myself much more. It made me realise what an extraordinarily strong, resilient and courageous young boy I was, to have lived through this trauma, and to have survived into adulthood relatively sane.

When I finally opened up to my family in more detail about the abuse they were, of course, very upset, and shocked to hear the extent of what happened. I decided to tell them only some of what took place; I saw no point in going into the depth of it as it would only have created more distress for them. Talking with Mum and Dad, in particular, was profoundly healing for me. It laid to rest the false beliefs I'd been carrying for so long, about not being worthy of their love, and my fear, as a child, of being disowned if they knew the whole truth. It became clear they felt they had let me down by not protecting me, and by not realising what was going on. They both felt very guilty that they hadn't noticed; and then questioned why I had not felt able to say anything at the time. I think this was their most difficult question, and one which many people in this situation struggle to understand. Family members seem to feel that the survivor's silence demonstrates a lack of love they must have felt growing up, but this is not the case (at least, not in my life). I explained to my parents how shame and fear are the tools that paedophiles use to manipulate and control their victims. We spoke at length about my childhood, my hobbies and friends, and I reminded both Mum and Dad that neither my brother nor sister had been through what I had, and yet they had also played in the same park and on the sea front. I even went so far as to say to them on one occasion, when it was clear to me that they still felt guilty for having not noticed what was going on;

'You're not responsible for what happened to me. What could you have done? Locked me in my bedroom all day to stop me from playing in the park? I've come to accept I was in the wrong place at the wrong time. The only people responsible for the abuse are the paedophiles who did it.'

My brother and sister were also very upset to learn I had been abused. They deeply regretted that they had not been there to look after me, and that they hadn't noticed anything. But I didn't tell them; I didn't tell anyone that I was being abused. My sister and I very rarely played together in the park (she is several years older than me), but my brother and I had played cricket there regularly. He, in particular, felt angry when I told him what had happened. It was important for him to know directly from me that he was not responsible; that he could not have changed or stopped it happening, and that he did not know any of the men. Those men were not connected, as far as I knew, to the church, school, cub scouts, or any other organisation, or anyone else we both knew. I found his raw anger at what happened was further evidence, not that I needed it, of his love.

If there is anger in me now to the paedophiles, it is more that their actions have caused distress to my family, than anything to do with me. I know this might seem strange, but I feel I have 'washed my hands of them'; when I think of them, which is very rare, I just let the thoughts go, not wanting to have any association with them, in any way. It is only when the PTSD is triggered than I am consumed with anger, often rage, but I view this now as emotions that have been trapped somehow in my subconscious mind. The desire to hunt them down and have retribution has never returned.

I feel I have lived two extremes in this life. I have been blessed to have experienced, albeit briefly, a cosmic consciousness at Vivekananda's Rock, off the Indian coast in 1996, which convinced me that everything we seek (I.e wisdom, unconditional love, and spiritual truth) is already within us. It really is 'an inside job'. Then, at the other extreme, I've had the challenges of living with Complex PTSD – I received a new diagnosis in August 2016 – with a body and a mind that are sometimes re-traumatised by the memories of the sexual abuse.

For the most part, I live somewhere between the two levels of consciousness. There is an intrinsic relationship between the two; had I not experienced the abuse, become an alcoholic and a sexual anorexic, I doubt I would have developed such an intense yearning for spiritual truth. Once guided to the healing path, the source of my greatest pain created the opening for the teachings I have since received.

Ten years ago, at John of God's healing centre, I had a vivid dream. I could see stars sparkling brightly in the night sky and suddenly they became physically active, darting around everywhere very quickly until eventually transforming their overall shape into that of a bowler, in the game of cricket, running up and bowling a ball. I have always loved cricket, so the dream was very appropriate for me. The message I took from this was that life is a game; it is a game of consciousness; albeit at times a very painful one.

When I returned to the UK from Brazil in 2006, I prayed for a spiritual teacher to come into my life. I had so many questions I needed answers to. A month later, I was introduced at a theatre event to an elderly man called George, and after a few minutes of small talk, our conversation digressed from theatre to spiritual philosophy. George was in his early eighties, small in stature, with thin white hair and a thin, pencil moustache. He always wore a traditional, dark blue jacket with a cravat. Whilst he had begun to slow down physically as he got older, he was mentally as alert and cognisant as I was, despite his advancing years, and he didn't allow his physical challenges to limit his independence. He played regularly with a jazz band and would drive long distances with his lovely partner, Mary, to gigs all over the country. He and Mary were also popular after-dinner speakers, and I would often join them after their engagements, and travel home with them.

George was a fascinating character; he had served in the Royal Air Force during the Second World War, taking part in the D Day landings, and he was an expert diver, an advanced glider pilot, an inventor, a multi-instrumentalist (I often saw him play, to a high standard, sixteen different instruments at a gig. It was a showstopper whenever he did this), and a deeply spiritual man. He became my spiritual teacher, and for many years I would disappear for long weekends and enjoy lengthy discussions with him about Jesus, Carl Jung, Albert Schweitzer, reincarnation and karma.

His next door neighbour was another spiritually enlightened man, called Michael. Michael was one of the most beautiful souls I have ever met. He was in his early seventies when we were introduced. He was a sensitive, emotional man, in the sense that his intuition was remarkably accurate. He was able to connect with people at a level which was profoundly moving to witness; he evidently loved people, and would do whatever he could to help them. There is a saying that the eyes are the windows to the soul; there was a gentle, loving kindness in Michael's eyes. Michael was a remarkable spiritual healer of the highest level. I write this with certainty. Over the course of the ten years I knew him, until his passing, I met at least half a dozen of his former clients (many have since become close friends), and heard their stories firsthand. There were permanent healings of chronic life-limiting illnesses and life-threatening diseases. Michael was a truly beautiful soul, whose love and compassion for his fellow man was so evident when one had the privilege to know him. Michael became my healer mentor.

Michael and I sometimes just sat in each other's company in complete silence – we felt so comfortable we didn't need to talk. The silence was usually broken by his giggling when he thought of a joke, and we'd often cry with laughter after he told one. He had a terrifically daft sense of humour, and the giggles often interrupted our discussions. When he giggled, he often reminded me of Jesus' statement, 'Be ye as little children to enter the kingdom of heaven'. On one occasion, after a period of twenty minutes' silence, I asked Michael what he had been thinking about. He looked up at me, and as he paused, tears came to his eyes and he replied, 'I was thinking about the importance in life of Peace, Love, Gentleness, and Joy'. During my weekends with George and Michael (I referred to these visits as my days away with George-Michael, which raised a few eyebrows!), I learned so much from them about the importance of following a spiritual path, and I remain forever indebted to them for their loving guidance. Michael, in particular, inspired me to consciously practice a more forgiving, loving, and kinder attitude to myself and others.

It was at the healing centre in Brazil that I was able to forgive the paedophiles for what they had done to me. The power of forgiveness was such that during the next six months, I had a number of spiritual awakenings which led to my understanding of consciousness fundamentally changing. These experiences coincided with my tentative forays into spiritual healing, and the timing of both George and Michael coming into my life at this specific time was clearly not coincidental.

I had long accepted intellectually that we lived many lifetimes and therefore experience a wide variety of enjoyable and also deeply painful, challenging circumstances. I also accept that we are governed by the Law of Karma. It seems a ridiculous, illogical notion that we only live one life on this earth and then die. I once struggled with the idea that dictators like Idi Amin, Pol Pot and so many others could seemingly 'get away' with atrocious crimes against humanity without some form of redemptive justice. I couldn't believe, either, that, in Christian belief, these men would be condemned to hell for eternity. There had to be a middle way. The Law of Karma makes absolute, logical sense to me. To know, without any doubt, that the toilet block paedophiles will pay a price for their vile crimes against me has enabled me to move forward with my life. In the context of a loving Higher Power, it seems absolutely fair that 'as we sow so shall we reap', and that until we have paid off our karmic debt, we will physically incarnate many times. Only then will we have 'eternal life' ; that which Jesus spoke about, and which so many other spiritual masters have also taught.

A few months after returning from Brazil in 2006, I had an experience which convinced me of the authenticity of this law. After lunch, one afternoon, I was watching TV when I suddenly felt overwhelmingly tired. It was so immediate and powerful I felt as if someone had anaesthetised me. I dragged myself to the bedroom, collapsing in a heap on the bed thinking 'what the hell is wrong with me?'

I closed my eyes and was immediately aware of a screen in my mind; in fact, all my awareness was on the screen. Oddly enough, it was like the 'Groundhog Day' PTSD flashbacks in the sense there was no 'off' switch; all my attention was on the screen. I 'saw' a short documentary film in which a group of six slaves were being ruthlessly beaten as they desperately struggled to dig a trench. They were evidently exhausted by the physical effort, and by the searing heat. I had a sense this was in Egypt, as behind them in the near distance were large constructions which may have been pyramids or temples. There was a sadist standing over the slaves and viciously attacking them with a large stick. He seemed to have absolute power, and was clearly revelling in the control he had. He showed no mercy. I knew this was me. In the depth of my soul, I knew this was me. The figure on the screen had a different body, of course, but I knew I was being shown myself in a previous life. I was deeply shocked and upset by this realisation. I felt sick to my the stomach, and a huge remorse for my actions. Then, I 'heard' a beautifully soft male voice. There was no judgement, no condemnation; a powerful feeling of unconditional love came over me. The voice said;

'This is the Law of Karma. This is why what happened to you happened. You must let go.'

I knew what it meant. My childhood experiences had not been an accident. One had led to the other. When this voice finished speaking, the documentary film ended, and, within a few seconds, my consciousness was back to normal again.

There is an important caveat to this experience: What happened during my childhood cannot be justified or excused. I am not responsible for the actions of the paedophiles in this lifetime. Neither am I suggesting other survivors' experiences are necessarily karmic. The sick free will of man sadly damages the innocent souls of others. Karma never condones or shifts the responsibility away from the perpetrators for their actions; they will have incurred a huge karmic debt for their crimes. Nevertheless, at some point in my soul's journey over many lifetimes it was necessary for the pain I had done to be revisited upon me. I have come to believe the Law of Karma is a universal law of equality and justice from which no spiritual being is exempt. All actions, good or bad, create their own karmic residues which manifest over a period of time. Self-realisation is regarded as the way out of this endless cycle.

This experience made me consider what might happen after physical death, and during the following three months I 'recalled' experiences from another three past lives which, as far as I am concerned, provided the answer to this question. I will briefly describe one more recall as it has helped me to overcome my fear of physical death, which in itself brought about a shift in my spiritual understanding. As before, I became aware of a screen in my mind, and all my attention was automatically focussed on it.

It is worth explaining that the screen I see during these recalls in not the same experience as I've had with the PTSD flashbacks. During the recalls I am the viewer of a screen which has a magnetic appeal. It is rather like being unexpectedly shown a very special memory you have forgotten for years, and even though it is a very painful and disturbing experience, you *know* its unexpected remembrance is an enormous privilege, and that there is something significant that needs to be fully understood. There is a divine symmetry at play.

Although the PTSD flashbacks have lessened in their horrific nature during the last five years, they are far more aggressive and upsetting than the past life recalls. With PTSD, I am not viewing the memory but re-living the experience as if it is happening again, in real time. I feel it mentally and emotionally consume me; there is no feeling of distance between me and the memory. I am in it.

It was early evening, and I saw 'myself' working on the land in what I recognized as the north of England. I lived in a very simple cottage, with a wife and two children. I could feel my love for my family as I watched them on the screen. The 'film' moved on, and I heard and saw troops marching through a small town, which I intuitively sensed was near to Culloden, in Scotland. I then saw myself fighting and subsequently dying on the field of a bloody battle. At the moment of death, there was no pain; just an immediate sense of peace as my spirit smoothly left my body and rose upwards. I saw beneath me the scars of the battlefield; the countless dead bodies, the moans of the dying, the smoke, and the exhaustion of those still alive – all of this soon disappeared from view, and I was in the astral... which looked like space, and despite my awareness of the vastness around me, it felt very intimate and safe. I sensed I had experienced this process many times before, and that I was in a familiar 'place'.

I travelled further upwards in absolute silence and feeling immense peace, and was met by a spiritual being who looked like a knight (dressed in ceremonial clothing similar to that worn by one of my favourite actors, Basil Rathbone, in the classic 1938 film *The Adventures of Robin Hood*), who warmly welcomed me. We greeted each other as old friends, and I felt that all this had been pre-ordained - it felt like a very familiar experience.

We travelled together through a tunnel of bright light, a vortex of some kind, and as we passed through a portal we entered a beautiful world, a place once again that was so familiar to me. It was physically stunning to behold, and I felt incredibly peaceful. It looked similar to the earth, with trees, mountains, and rivers but there was a refined presence; I felt the consciousness of this 'world' was pure, clean and unsoiled by negativity or ego.

I saw spiritual beings around me, who had the appearance of human form, but their energetic vibration was much finer than I had experienced on earth. As they moved they had a golden glow or aura all around them which gave the impression that their bodies were not as physical as our human bodies are. The experience confirmed whilst at death the physical body obviously dies, the consciousness and personality remain for our onward spiritual journey. As I viewed these spiritual beings, I sensed that the higher the consciousness a spiritual being has realised, the less need for a physical body. Everything I saw was familiar to me, and I knew that I'd been here before, and that it was a case of picking up where I had left off, between lives, once again. After a few moments the recall finished.

I have since come to believe that, between physical incarnations, we need to review our many lives, without any judgement or condemnation, and see what lessons need to be learned. We then play the game of consciousness once again until we are self-realised or enlightened.

These experiences reminded me of my childhood reservations about religion, and in light of my understanding of Advaita Vedanta I began to consider afresh exactly what I believed about my relationship with the higher power. I find the following Swami Vivekananda quote very powerful; 'Christianity considered the human person (Man), to be a sinner... it could not understand the message of potential divinity implied in his (Jesus') saying, 'I and my father are one'.[69]

I reject the idea that I was born a sinner, but I accept I was born into this lifetime with a karmic debt that needed to be addressed. The concept of original sin is, as far as I am concerned, repressive, controlling and illogical, and begs many questions, not least; why would a God of Love condemn the whole of humanity, endless times, for disobeying this command? Why

---

[69] From *The Gospel in the Advaitic Culture of India: The Case of Neo-Vedantic Christologies*. The Rev. K.P Aleaz, Professor of Religions at Bishop's College, Kolkata, India. www.biblicalstudies.org.uk

would the creator of such an awe-inspiring, constantly evolving universe have such a petty attitude to its creation? No doubt the story is full of symbolism, but nonetheless it is a vile teaching that has penetrated our collective consciousness for millennia. I write with considerable anger as I have met and heard the stories of many survivors who have struggled greatly with this religious teaching, and who were abused by their religious leaders. It breeds further fear and hopelessness as they try to heal from their trauma, whereas karma offers a law of universal fairness and justice; it empowers us to take responsibility for our actions, and to my mind offers a much more positive, optimistic view of life, unless one has committed dreadful crimes, of course.

I find so much strength in the knowledge that I am, and I believe we all are inherently divine right now. And what's more, there is a path for us to realise it, which has been walked by others before us. The Christ consciousness, the spiritual consciousness that Jesus realised is, I believe, the spiritual destiny all human beings are able to realise. The prophets and spiritual teachers walked the same journey to recognise the same absolute reality; we just call it different names, and adopt different practices

The first stage of realisation is, as Jesus said, 'I am the servant of God', so we have an awareness of a power greater than ourselves, or at least an awareness of a higher level of consciousness within us that we can turn to for love and guidance. The next stage of realisation is: 'I am son of God'. We have a loving relationship with this inner consciousness and seek to develop it through service, prayer and meditation, which is my interpretation of Step 11 of the AA 12 Step programme. This states, 'Sought through prayer and meditation to improve our conscious contact with God, as we understood him, praying only for knowledge of his will for us and the power to carry it out'. The last stage: 'I and my father are one' is reached. We realise the highest truth that we are this inner consciousness; we realise our innate divinity, Karma is negated, and all notions of identifying ourselves as being the body, thoughts and feelings are thereafter recognised as being a play of consciousness. Our true reality is that we are pure consciousness.

Sai Baba described these three stages of self-realisation as; 'I am in the light, the light is in me, I am the light'. He also emphasised the importance of silence as one of the principle constituents of self-realisation. He pointed out that it is not silence if the mouth is closed but the mind switch is still 'on'.

The real state of silence is when the wandering mind has stopped. This allows one to cultivate the habit of concentration. From concentration one graduates to the stage of contemplation and finally to the stage of meditation.

> *We are so engrossed with the objects,*
> *or appearances revealed by the light,*
> *that we pay no attention to the light.* [70]
> Sri Ramana Maharshi

Eckert Tolle also reminds us of the importance of silence. The following two quotes are taken from his bestselling book *Stillness Speaks*,

> *When you become aware of silence, immediately there is that state of inner still alertness. You are present. You have stepped out of thousands of years of collective human conditioning.* [71]
> Eckert Tolle

It has helped me to see Jesus' life as a way to realising our inner divinity, and that his realisation was similar to that of other spiritual masters (from other religions and none), who have become self-realised or 'enlightened'.

I rationalised that perhaps Jesus attained the highest level of consciousness whilst in the body, the Christ consciousness, such has been his unprecedented influence upon the history of mankind.

In light of Advaita Vedanta, the life and teachings of Jesus now makes sense to me.

> *I am not*
> *my thoughts*
> *my emotions*
> *my experience.*

---

[70] A. Devaraja Mudaliar, *Day by Day With Bhagavan* (Sri Ramanasramam, 2002)

[71] Eckert Tolle, *Stillness Speaks* (New World Library, 2003)

A Small Boy Smiling

I am not the content of my life.

I am life
I am the...
space in which all things happen.

I am
Consciousness.

I am the now..
I Am.
Eckert Tolle

One evening during the Spring of 2016, several weeks into my therapy with Sarah, I was sitting in my lounge watching television, and in the corner of my eye I could see the notes, on the dinner table, which I had written of the abuse. It was the first time I'd had the courage to write down everything I could remember. I felt as if the document was screaming at me, and I knew instinctively that I needed to place the trauma of the abuse into a broader, healthier perspective. That evening I started writing a document which has quite naturally evolved into the book you are now holding in your hands.

Writing this book has been an enormous challenge. It has been very painful and depressing at times, (a friend recently reminded me I sometimes described the emotional process of writing the most difficult times as trying to wade through treacle) yet also deeply rewarding as I have released so much emotion and found a much greater acceptance and peace with my past.

I now see my life, in its entirety, from a much healthier perspective. I have been uplifted by the things that have been positive, and for which I am so grateful: family, friends, the fellowship of Alcoholics Anonymous, SoSAA, my love of travel, and my spiritual journey.

I hope you will also find peace on your journey.

ACKNOWLEDGMENTS

I would like to express my gratitude to the many people who supported me every step of the way in the writing of this book, and without whom it would not have been possible.

Above all I want to thank my family. Mum and Dad, my brother, my sister, and Liz, who have supported and encouraged me throughout this whole process. I do not for one minute underestimate the long and difficult emotional journey it must have also been for them. I love them, and thank them for everything they have done, and continue to do, for me.

My editor, Tom Bartlett, who was always available to provide support and to offer invaluable guidance as he read my somewhat faltering first, second and third drafts of each chapter. Tom has been a significant contributor to this book; I will remain forever in his debt. If you need an editor, he's the man!

I am very grateful to Sarah Paton Briggs, my psychotherapist. She created a sacred space for me to be honest about the most horrific memories of the abuse, and then she gently guided me on my healing journey which has culminated with the writing of this book. I was so pleased when she agreed to write *Soulful Space: Reflections On My Therapy Work With Matt*. Our collaboration has been profoundly rewarding in so many ways.

My much loved friend in Alcoholics Anonymous, Jennie, who has inspired, encouraged, and guided me with unconditional love and kindness. For over twenty years, Jennie has been my 'go to' friend in AA - her wisdom has never ever let me down.

My sincere thanks to my good friend, Clarinda Cuppage for her tremendous support throughout the year it took me to write this book. As a counsellor and communications consultant, her work supporting adults with a history of trauma and childhood sexual abuse, and substance dependency has been especially helpful with development of the chapter entitled *The Last First*.

A very special thanks to Martin Duffy who has so given generously of his time, enthusiasm and expertise to design and build my website, as well as being such a valued friend to me for so many years.

Natalie Esther, the Founder and Chief Executive of Survivors of Sexual Abuse Anon (SoSAA) for offering constructive feedback with the *London Calling* and *The Last First* chapters. For more information about SoSAA please see the Appendix: Information, Resources and Support.

I would like to thank the following very special friends; Carl Kirk, Roy Falloon, Maddie Kitchen, Kevin Lillie, Mark Campbell, Matthew Roberts, Andy Sharratt, Oliver Mason, Dr. Steve Moody, Martin Keane, Michael Feeley and Belinda Nnoka for their unstinting support throughout the psychologically and emotionally challenging times I encountered along the way.

ABOUT THE AUTHOR

Matt has enjoyed working in the world of entertainment for over twenty years, as a theatre manager, organiser of several prestigious international festivals, and of large-scale community-based cultural projects supporting children and young people.

His hobbies include spiritual philosophy, travelling abroad, exploring the countryside, disappearing into secondhand bookshops, Earl Grey tea, meditation, dogs, cricket, rugby, and theatre. As often as possible he visits India.

He is 45 years old and lives in London. This is his first book.

APPENDIX

SARAH PATON BRIGGS

Sarah has worked with many survivors of childhood sexual abuse and other trauma including military veterans. She has undertaken regular Continuous Professional Development training, particularly in trauma-focused therapy approaches.

Professional memberships:
Accredited member of the British Association for Counselling and Psychotherapy (BACP): 541524
Supervisor of individuals accredited by BACP, 2015: 541524
Accredited member of the College of Sexual and Relationship Therapy (COSRT), July 2013: 2404
Supervisor of psychosexual therapy accredited by COSRT, August 2015.
Accredited member of the National Council of Psychotherapists (NCP), 2009: 202502.
Accredited member of the Federation of Drug and Alcohol Professionals, 2009 (FDAP): 1364.
Equine-facilitated therapy/learning practitioner certified by LEAP, 2015.
Member of UK Psychological Trauma Society (UKPTS): 245.
Executive Coach, Member of the Association for Coaching (ACUK).

Qualifications:
Ofqual-regulated Level 5 Certificate in Equine-Facilitated Human Development, IFEAL, 2016.
Equine-Facilitated Psychotherapy/Learning Practitioner, LEAP, 2015.
Accreditation in Margerison-McCann Team Management System® 2012.
Diploma in Psychosexual and Relationship Counselling, 2010-2011.
Diploma in Supervision, 2009.
Certificate in Cognitive Behavioural Therapy, 2009.
Certified NLP Practitioner, UKCPD, 2008.
Diploma in Life Coaching, UKCPD, 2008.
Diploma in Hypnotherapy, UKCPD, 2008.
Diploma in Organisational Development and Executive Coaching, CAP

2006.
Certificate in Working with Survivors of Sexual Abuse, CPPD 2006.
Advanced Diploma in Humanistic Integrative Counselling, CPPD 2003.
Diploma in Humanistic Integrative Counselling, CPPD 2002.
Certificate in Humanistic Integrative Counselling, CPPD 2003.
Chartered Institute of Marketing Diploma, 1992.
MA in Social and Political Science, University of Cambridge 1993.
BA (Hons) in Social and Political Science, University of Cambridge 1989.

INFORMATION, RESOURCES AND SUPPORT

The information listed below is provided for general information purposes only. Whilst every effort has been taken to ensure the information is accurate and up to date (at time of publication), we cannot guarantee it and you should not rely on the contents of this publication. References and links to other websites, organizations, products, services, or publications do not constitute endorsement or approval by Matt Carey Books. Matt Carey Books is not responsible and assumes no liability for the content of any linked websites.

Alcoholics Anonymous (Great Britain) www.alcoholics-anonymous.org.uk
Alcoholics Anonymous is a fellowship of men and women who share their experience, strength and hope with each other that they may solve their common problem and help others to recover from alcoholism. The only requirement for membership is a desire to stop drinking. There are no dues or fees for AA membership; we are self-supporting through our own contributions. AA is not allied with any sect, denomination, politics, organisation or institution; does not wish to engage in any controversy; neither endorses nor opposes any causes. Our primary purpose is to stay sober and help other alcoholics to achieve sobriety.
National Helpline 0800 9177 650 or via email: help@aamail.org

One In Four www.oneinfour.org.uk
Supporting people who are survivors of childhood sexual abuse or trauma. Telephone 020 8697 2112/8022 or 07580 733271 or email admin@oneinfour.org.uk

Rape Crisis www.rapecrisis.org.uk
Rape Crisis in England and Wales provides the following information: how to get help if you've experienced rape, child sexual abuse and/or any kind of sexual violence and details of your nearest Rape Crisis services; information for friends, partners, family and other people supporting a sexual violence survivor; information about sexual violence for survivors, students, journalists and others; more about our work, our members and how you can

support us. There are specialist Rape Crisis centres in London and around the country.

Survivors of Sexual Abuse Anonymous (SoSAA) www.sosaa.org.uk
SoSAA exists to empower adult survivors of sexual abuse to make positive changes for life. The focus is on running peer-to-peer groups for men and women survivors who are 18+, using an adapted version of the Alcoholics Anonymous 12-step framework. SoSAA welcomes people from any and all cultural, social and ethnic backgrounds, from all faiths and none. There are online Skype groups for people who are unable to attend face-to-face groups.

Sex and Love Addicts Anonymous UK www.slaauk.org.uk
Sex and Love Addicts Anonymous (SLAA) is open to anyone who knows or thinks they have a problem with sex addiction, love addiction, romantic obsession, co-dependent relationships, fantasy addiction and/or sexual, social and emotional anorexia. The telephone service is staffed by volunteers from SLAA who will endeavour to return your call within 24 hours. SLAA does not operate a counselling or advisory service, merely information-sharing on the fellowship itself to those seeking recovery through our programme. National UK Telephone voicemail: 07984 977 884 or via email: contact@slaauk.org

SARCs
A Sexual Assault Referral Centre (sometimes referred to as a "SARC") provides services to victims/survivors of rape or sexual assault regardless of whether the survivor/victim chooses to reports the offence to the police or not. Each police force will usually have a SARC locally.
Sexual Assault Referral Centres are designed to be comfortable and multi-functional, providing private space for interviews and examinations, and some may also offer counselling services. "SARC"s have specialist staff that are trained to help you make informed decisions about what you want to do next.

The Havens - London www.thehavens.org.uk
Specialist centres in London for people who have been raped or sexually assaulted, including the provision of counselling.

The Survivors Trust www.thesurvivorstrust.org
The Survivors Trust has over 135 member agencies which provide support for women, men and children who are survivors of rape, sexual violence or childhood sexual abuse. Our Trustee Board is exclusively made up of Managers and Directors of rape and sexual abuse support services. Our core aim is to empower survivors or rape, sexual violence or childhood sexual abuse through supporting and improving effective responses to survivors. Member organisations provide a range of direct services to survivors including counselling, support, helplines and advocacy services for women, men and children. We provide support and networking for member agencies; deliver accredited training; raise awareness about rape and sexual abuse and its effect on survivors, their supporters and society at large; promote effective responses to rape and sexual abuse on a local, regional and national level.
Support, Advice and Info - 0808 801 0818

NATIONAL HELPLINES

Childline www.childline.org.uk
A private and confidential service for children and young people up to the age of 19 years.
Call us free on 0800 1111

CISters (Surviving Rape and/or Sexual Abuse) 02380 338080
Answerphone 023 80 338080 is usually monitored daily during the week and callers can choose to leave their name and phone number, and we will call them back and will take care when doing so. Or can email admin@cisters.org.uk
The helpline is available to female adult survivors of childhood rape/sexual abuse, and others can call if they have a concern about such issues. In the case of the latter we will seek to signpost them to appropriate services.

Frank www.talktofrank.com
Confidential information and advice for anyone concerned about their own or someone else's drug or solvent misuse. Freephone 0800 77 66 00 (24

hour service, free if call from a landline and won't show up on the phone bill, provides translation for non-English speakers)

Get Connected www.getconnected.org.uk
Free, confidential telephone and email helpline finding young people the best help whatever the problem. Provides free connections to local or national services, and can text information to callers' mobile phones. Freephone 0808 808 4994 (7 days a week 1pm-11pm)

MOSAC (Mothers of Sexually Abused Children) 0800 980 1958.
Supporting all non-abusing parents and carers whose children have been sexually abused. We provide various types of support services and information for parents, carers and professionals dealing with child sexual abuse. www.mosac.org.uk
SupportLine 01708 765200
Confidential emotional support to children, young adults and adults by telephone, email and post. www.supportline.org.uk

PODS: Positive Outcomes for Dissociative Survivors www.pods-online.org.uk
A project of Survivors Trauma and Abuse Recovery Trust (START) PODS works to make recovery from dissociative disorders a reality through training, informing and supporting. Helpline: 0800 181 4420 – Tuesdays 6-8pm or appointments at other times by contacting the office.
Email: mail@start-online.org.uk (for START) or info@pods-online.org.uk (for PODS). Alternative website www.start-online.org.uk

National Association for People Abused in Childhood (NAPAC)
www.napac.org.uk
NAPAC provides a national freephone support line for adults who have suffered any type of abuse in childhood. Telephone support line opening hours: Monday – Thursday 10:00am-9.00pm and Friday 10.00am-6.00pm. Call 0808 801 0331 free from all landlines and mobiles

National Society For the Prevention Of Cruelty To Children (NSPCC)
www.nspcc.org.uk
The NSPCC is the UK's leading children's charity, preventing abuse and

helping those affected to recover. For adults concerned about a child please call 0808 800 5000; help fr children and young people is available via Childline 0800 1111.

Samaritans www.samaritans.org
Samaritans volunteers listen in confidence to anyone in any type of emotional distress, without judging or telling people what to do. Tel: 08457 90 90 90 (24 hrs 7 days a week)

SurvivorsUK Helpline Web Chat www.survivorsuk.org
National Helpline Web Chat for adult male survivors of rape or sexual assault (Monday – Friday 10.30 – 21:00; Saturday – Sunday 10:00 – 18:00)

YoungMinds www.youngminds.org.uk
YoungMinds is the UK's leading charity committed to improving the emotional wellbeing and mental health of children and young people. Driven by their experiences we campaign, research and influence policy and practice.

The charity also provide expert knowledge to professionals, parents and young people through our Parents' Helpline, online resources, training and development, outreach work and publications.

YoungMinds does not offer advice to young people – the helpline service is for parents or carers worried about a child or young person. For general enquiries: 020 7089 5050 or email ymenquiries@youngminds.org.uk

WEBSITES

Bristol Crisis Service for Women www.selfinjurysupport.org.uk
Bristol Crisis Service for Women is a national organisation that supports girls and women in emotional distress. They particularly help women who harm themselves (often called self-injury).

First Person Plural www.firstpersonplural.org.uk
UK-wide membership charity led by volunteers who have lived-experience of dissociative identity disorder (previously known as 'multiple personality disorder') or other childhood-trauma-related complex dissociative condition with a similar presentation (e.g. type 1 dissociative disorder not otherwise specified).

Headmeds www.headmeds.org.uk
Straight talk on mental health medication. Look up your medication to find out about side effects and things you might not feel comfortable asking your GP about, and listen to other people's experiences.

National Society For the Prevention Of Cruelty To Children www.nspcc.org.uk
The NSPCC is the UK's leading children's charity, preventing abuse and helping those affected to recover.

Rape Crisis England & Wales www.rapecrisis.org.uk
Rape Crisis England & Wales is a national feminist organisation that exists to promote the needs and rights of women and girls who have experienced sexual violence, to improve services to them and to work towards the elimination of sexual violence. They are a national umbrella body for their network of autonomous member Rape Crisis organisations across England and Wales and was set up to support their specialist work.

Respond www.respond.org.uk
Respond exists in order to lessen the effect of trauma and abuse on people with learning disabilities their families and supporters. Provides psychotherapy for people with learning disabilities, advice and support for

staff and families, training for carers and professionals, and education for people with learning disabilities.

Stop It Now! www.stopitnow.org.uk
Supports adults worried about child abuse, including survivors, professionals, those with a concern about their own thoughts or behaviour towards children, friends and relatives of people arrested for sexual offending.

Survivors Manchester www.survivorsmanchester.org.uk
A useful website with various resource information for adult male survivors of rape or sexual abuse.

SurvivorScotland www.survivorscotland.org.uk
SurvivorScotland oversees the National Strategy for Survivors of Childhood Abuse Through the National Strategy, Strategy Funding and the National Confidential Forum, they aim to:

- Raise awareness of childhood abuse
- Increase awareness of its long term consequences
- Improve support services
- Enhance the health and wellbeing of survivors
- Understand and acknowledge the experiences of people who were in care as children, whether those experiences were positive or negative
- Develop training and skills for frontline workers

BIBLIOGRAPHY

1. Adams, Robert. Silence of the Heart: Dialogues with Robert Adams. Yogi Impressions, 2012. ISBN 978-81-88479-95-5

2. Alcoholics Anonymous. Alcoholics Anonymous Worldwide Services, INC. 2001. ISBN 1-893007-17-0

3. Balsekar, Ramesh S. Pointers from Nisargadatta Maharaj. Chetana (P) Ltd, Mumbai, 2013. ISBN 81-85300-19-4

4. Brunton, Paul. A Search in Secret India. Samuel Weiser, INC, 1985. ISBN 0-87728-602-7

5. Connolly, John. The Book of Lost Things. Simon & Schuster, 2011. ISBN-10: 1442429348

6. de Mello, Anthony. The Way to Love: Meditations for Life.Image, 2012. ISBN 9780307951908

7. Dunn, Jean, ed., Consciousness and the Absolute: The final talks of Sri Nisargadatta Maharaj. The Acorn Press, 2003. ISBN 81-85300-034-8

8. Dyer, Dr. Wayne W, The Power of Intention. Hay House, Inc., Carlsbad, CA, 2004. ISBN-13: 978-1401902162

9. Dyer, Dr. Wayne W, Getting In The Gap.Hay House, Inc., Carlsbad, CA, 2014. ISBN-13: 978-1401947545

10. Easwaran, Eaknath, trans., The Upanishads. Nilgiri Press, 2007. ISBN-10: 1586380214

11. Fredrickson, Renee. Repressed Memories: A Journey to Recovery from Sexual Abuse. Touchstone, 1992. ISBN 9780671767167 |

12. Frydman, Maurice, trans., I Am That: Talks with Sri Nisargadatta Maharaj. The Acorn Press, 2015. ISBN 0-89386-022-0

13. Godman, David, ed., Be As You Are: The Teachings of Bhagavan Sri Ramana Maharshi. Penguin, 1988. ISBN-13: 978-0140190625

14. Godman, David. No Mind, I Am The Self, The lives and teachings of Sri Lakshmana Swamy and Mathru Sri Sarada. Sri Lakshmana Ashram, India, 2007. No ISBN.

15. Hafiz, auth., Daniel Ladinsky, trans., The Gift: Poems of Hafiz. Penguin Compass, 1999. ISBN-10: 0140195815

16. Isherwood, Christopher, trans., and Swami Prabhavananda, trans., Bhagavad Gita – The Song of God. Signet Book, 2002. ISBN-13: 978-0451528445

17. Ladinsky, Daniel, auth., Henry S. Mindlin, ed., I Heard God Laughing: Renderings of Hafiz. Sufism Reoriented, 1996. ISBN-10: 0915828189

18. Laszlo, Ervin. What is Reality? The New Map of Cosmos and Consciousness. SelectBooks, Inc, 2016. ISBN 978-1-56079-391-6

19. MacLaine, Shirley. The Camino. Pocket Books, 2001. ISBN 0-7434-0921-3

20. Mason, Peggy, and Ron Laing. Sathya Sai Baba, The Embodiment of Love. Pilgrim Books, 1987. ISBN 0-19-946259-20-8

21. Mazzoleni, Don Mario. A Catholic Priest Meets Sai Baba. Leela Press, 1994. ISBN-10: 0962983519

22. Merton, Thomas. New Seeds of Contemplation. New Directions, 2007. ISBN-13: 978-0811217248

23. Mother's Agenda 1951-1960. Institut de Recherches Evolutives, 1979. ISBN 978-2902776047

24. Mudaliar, A. Devaraja. Day by Day With Bhagavan. Sri Ramanasramam, 2002. ISBN 8188018821

25. Paramahansa Yogananda. Autobiography of a Yogi. Rider, UK ed. Edition, 1955. ISBN-10: 8120725247

26. Pellegrino-Estrich, Robert. The Miracle Man, The Life Story of John of God. Publisher not specified; 1st Edition, 1997. ISBN-10: 064633767X

27. Pelzer, Dave. A Child Called "It". Health Communications,

Incorporated, 1995. ISBN-13: 9781558743663

28. Powell Ph.D, Robert, ed.,The Experience of Nothingness. The Blue Dove Foundation, 2001. ISBN 1-884997-14-7

29. Redfield, James. The Celestine Prophecy. Bantam, First Printing edition, 1994. ISBN-10: 0553409026

30. Rovelli, Carlo. Seven Brief Lessons on Physics. Allen Lane, 2015. ISBN-13: 978-0241235966

31. Rūmī, Jalāl ad-Dīn Muhammad, auth., Coleman Barks, trans., John Moyne, trans., The Essential Rūmī. HarperOne, 2004. ISBN-13: 978-0062509598

32. Sandweiss, Dr Samuel H. Sai Baba: The Holy Man... and the Psychiatrist. Sai Bhavan, 1975. ISBN-10: 0907704204

33. Scott Peck, M. The Road Less Traveled: A New Psychology of Love, Traditional Values and Spiritual Growth. Simon & Schuster, 2002. ISBN 9780743238250

34. Scott Peck, M. Further Along the Road Less Traveled: The Unending Journey Towards Spiritual Growth. Touchstone, 1998. ISBN 9780684847238

35. Sogyal Rinpoche. The Tibetan Book of Living and Dying. Rider, Reprint edition, 1996. ISBN-10: 0712657525

36. Sri Ramana Maharshi. The Spiritual Teaching of Ramana Maharshi. Shambhala Publications Inc, 2004. ISBN-13: 978-1590301395

37. Survivors' Voices: Breaking the silence on living with the impact of child sexual abuse in the family environment. Published by One in Four, 2015. No ISBN. www.oneinfour.org.uk

38. Survivors' Voices: Supplementary narratives document to complement the main report. Published by One in Four, 2015. No ISBN. www.oneinfour.org.uk

39. Swami Krishnananda. The Chhandogya Upanishad. Divine Life Society, 2004. No ISBN. www.swami-krishnananda.org

40. Tolle, Eckert. Stillness Speaks. New World Library, 2003. ISBN-13: 978-1577314004

41. Waite, Dennis. Back to The Truth, 5000 years of ADVAITA. O Books, an imprint of John Hunt Publishing Ltd, 2007. ISBN 1-905047-61-4

42. Ware, Bronnie. The Top Five Regrets of the Dying. Hay House, Inc., Carlsbad, CA, 2012. ISBN 978-1-84850-999-3

43. Woititz, Janet G. The Intimacy Struggle. Health Communications, Inc. Florida, 1985. ISBN 1-55874-277-8

Printed in Poland
by Amazon Fulfillment
Poland Sp. z o.o., Wrocław